Jackson College Library
WITHDRAWN

LIBRARY LIT. 11-
The Best of 1980

edited by

BILL KATZ

The Scarecrow Press, Inc.
Metuchen, N.J., & London
1981

ISBN 0-8108-1431-5
Library of Congress Catalog Card No. 78-154842

Copyright © 1981 by The Scarecrow Press, Inc.
Manufactured in the United States of America

CONTENTS

Introduction   v

Part I: LIBRARIES AND LIBRARIANS

Research Libraries in the Network Environment:
  The Case for Cooperation (Patricia Battin)   3
The Test of Reference (Thomas Childers)   15
The Implications of Some Recent Studies of Library Use
  (Casimir Borkowski & Murdo J. Macleod)   24
The Chimera of Professionalism (Bonnie R. Nelson)   43
Philosophy or Practice: Can the Real World Be Found?
  (Judith K. Mowery)   52
Documentary Art and the Role of the Archivist
  (Hugh A. Taylor)   56
Aftermath of a Crusade: World War I and the
  Enlarged Program of the American Library
  Association (Arthur P. Young)   70
Finding the Library's Role in an
  Information Society (Bettina H. Wolff)   85

Part II: TECHNICAL SERVICES/READERS' SERVICES

DDC 19: An Indictment (Sanford Berman)   99
Publishers vs. Wholesalers:
  The Ordering Dilemma (Ruth Fraley)   108
Opening a Library Catalog (Maurice J. Freedman)   116
International Indirection (S. Michael Malinconico)   124
AACR 2--A Review Article (Phyllis A. Richmond)   131
Word Processing and the Book Printer (Frank Romano)   148
Precis--A Better Way to Index Films
  (Mary Robinson Sive)   163

Part III: COMMUNICATION AND EDUCATION

Information Fever (Andrée Conrad)   175
Gresham's Law: Knowledge or Information?
  (Daniel J. Boorstin)   188

Telereference: The New TV Information Systems
(Susan S. Cherry) ... 193
Wanted: More Professionalism in Reference
Book Reviewing (Ken Kister) ... 210
A Comparative Analysis of Juvenile
Book Review Media (Virginia Witucke) ... 217
Fifty Years of "Books for the Teen Age"
(Lillian Morrison) ... 227
Rites of Passage (Lois Ruby) ... 241
How We Can Win: A Plan to Reach and Teach
Twenty-Five Million Illiterate Adults
(Jonathan Kozol) ... 253

Part IV: THE SOCIAL PREROGATIVE

Whitewashing White Racists:
Junior Scholastic and the KKK ... 261
Censorship vs. Selection--A Round Table
Discussion (Deirdre Boyle) ... 271
Freedom of Information Act (Robert V. Cuddihy) ... 282
After Five Years: An Assessment of the
Amended U.S. Freedom of Information Act
(Trudy H. Peterson) ... 290
A Progress Report on Information Privacy
and Data Security (Gerald Salton) ... 299
Libraries and Alternatives: An Essay
(Patricia Glass Schuman) ... 317
The Man Who Was Convicted of Reading a Book
(Nat Hentoff) ... 322

Notes on Contributors ... 327

INTRODUCTION

Herewith is the eleventh volume in a continuing series. Once again it represents what the judges and the editor believe to be the best contributions to library literature over the past year or more specifically, material published between November, 1979 and November, 1980. The articles are drawn from a number of periodicals, including several which are not part of the traditional professional library group. It is our goal to present the best material, no matter where it is published, although, understandably most of it comes from library-oriented periodicals.

This past year there has been an unusual number of candidates. Close to 100 articles were considered. Part of the reason for the welcome volume of entries is the cooperation of readers who have sent in suggestions. Also 1980 opens a decade which promises rapid change. Authors and their editors seem to sense this in that the pace of really worthwhile, new material increased substantially. I'm happy to report that most of the articles examined, whether accepted or rejected, took a somewhat optimistic view of the years ahead, possibly, as one wag put it, because the 1980's can't be more difficult than the 1970's.

The usual evaluation was applied to the candidates, i.e. the style of writing and the originality of ideas was the first consideration. After that, the judges examined the topical interest of the material, its potential value to help students and librarians better understand and appreciate their profession, and its significance in the main stream of library literature.

Again, readers are urged to send the editor suggestions for next year's judges to evaluate. And do not hesitate to send me your own material. All is welcome.

          Bill Katz
          School of Information Sciences
          State University of New York, Albany

ACKNOWLEDGMENTS

The 1980 Jury

The jurors were: Ms. Deirdre Boyle, Library Media Consultant; Ms. Pat Rom, Graduate School of Library and Information Studies, Rutgers; Ms. Pat Schuman, President, Neal-Schuman Publishers; Ms. Kathy Weibel, New York State Library; William Eshelman, President, Scarecrow Press; and Bill Katz.

Once more: particular thanks to Ms. Anne Clifford, my graduate assistant who made all of this possible by handling the necessary correspondence and making innumerable wise and useful suggestions. Lucky the library that has her on the staff!

Part I

LIBRARIES AND LIBRARIANS

RESEARCH LIBRARIES IN THE NETWORK ENVIRONMENT:

THE CASE FOR COOPERATION*

Patricia Battin

The library profession today faces the challenge and the opportunity of harnessing the ever-increasing production and flow of information in a variety of formats for the service of scholarship. For our predecessors this format was a physical one, embodied in library architecture and the massive, comprehensive collection of printed materials, as patterns of library construction throughout the past century confirm. Our efforts to contain, despite the massive sizes of the buildings we erected and the collections we assembled, were constantly being thwarted by the sheer unmanageability of the information process.

For example, in 1894 the firm of McKim, Meade, and White was commissioned to plan the new Morningside Campus for Columbia University. The building designed to dominate the campus both architecturally and intellectually was Low Library. The beauty of the large rotunda and its awe-inspiring dome conveys an overwhelming sense of the power of knowledge and its central significance to the academic enterprise. The building was designed to house approximately 750,000 volumes. At the time of construction, the Columbia Libraries contained only 75,000 volumes. It is apparent that the builders believed the magnificent structure would serve forever, since the words, The Library of Columbia University, are carved in mammoth letters on the marble facade. Forty years later, in 1934, Low Library contained almost one million volumes, and a new behemoth, Butler Library, with a capacity of almost three million volumes, was constructed across the quadrangle. The planners in 1934 did not repeat the former folly--the Butler facade bears the names of Plato, Aristotle, Vergil, and other luminaries in the history of scholarship.

The change is significant. For, as early as 1934, the principle of a single, self-sufficient, unified research library collection had proved unworkable at Columbia. The new Butler Library held

---

*Reprinted by permission of the author and publisher from The Journal of Academic Librarianship, 6:2 (May 1980) 68-73; copyright ©1980 by JAL.

only a portion of the Columbia collections, and the transformation of the library from a single, visible force in the center of the university community into a sprawling, decentralized, unmanageable, and mysterious life force flowing into and merging with the unpredictable processes of scholarly communication and research was underway.

We are in the midst of a revolution in research libraries, a revolution reminiscent of that favorite literary metaphor used by scholars of American Studies to describe the industrial revolution in America: the machine in the garden. If we view the recent past decades as a pastoral idyll for higher education, then surely we must view the library's predicament in the 70s and overwhelmingly so in the 80s as the dinosaur in the garden. We grew fat and complacent and blind during the 60s. The siren song of institutional autonomy and self-sufficient collection standards obscured those earlier recognitions that the process of scholarship and its demand for information cannot be confined to one building, to one institution, to one region, or even to one political jurisdiction. As research librarians, we serve a community of scholars dedicated to the untrammeled quest for knowledge. Our responsibility to facilitate that quest by assuring the continuing availability of scholarly information obliges us to search for alternative solutions when our traditional practices are no longer effective or productive.

The Dilemma and the Challenge

We are all familiar with the details of the dreary economic litany which signifies the end of an era for research libraries. During the past decade our professional literature has recorded the devastating impact of inflation, the publication explosion, and the growth and development of computing and communications technology on our traditional concepts of research library services.

The dilemma and the challenge have been succinctly stated by John McCredie, Vice-Provost for Computing, Libraries, and Planning at Carnegie-Mellon University:

> The primary intellectual activities within universities may be described as the creation, storage, transformation, and dissemination of information. Both computers and libraries support all of these activities in areas as diverse as data acquisition, complex processing, text preparation, information retrieval, instruction and administration.... During the past twenty-five years, price/performance ratios for computing hardware decreased at an average compound rate of 20-30 percent per year.... Economic trends are in the opposite direction in traditional libraries. For a number of years, books and journals ... increased in price faster than cost of living indices. The percentage of a university budget dedicated to library services must increase at about the same rate as the cost of living. As utility and space expenses rise, costs of storing hard-copy

materials inflate faster than the cost of living. Even the weakened condition of the U.S. dollar in foreign money markets has an adverse effect on collections dependent on publications from abroad.[1]

If both the library and the computer center budgets of a university each currently consume 3 percent of total university expenditures, and if we continue our present modes of operations, the projected rates of cost increase or decrease indicate that in 40 years, the library will require 27 percent and the computer center 1 percent of total university expenditures to maintain existing levels of service.[2]

The message is clear: we must change to survive. Even though the costs of automating bibliographic services appear overwhelming in the short run, the long-term costs of maintaining traditional library services and collections are beyond the ability of individual institutions to support. Because of the extraordinary developments in communications and computing technology, which have transformed both the products and our environment, our challenge is to provide the unifying concept through the architecture of technology. We must reinvent the research library in the network environment.

The revolution is in process, and the dinosaur has been described from every possible vantage point. But the paradox of this particular revolution is that the social and technological forces which have destroyed the viability of the traditional research library have created an even greater demand for our services and have provided us with the technical capacities to preserve and enrich the intellectual heritage bequeathed to us by our predecessors. However, we will have to depart from our traditional notions of librarianship, developed and nurtured in an era of institutional pride and autonomy, if we are to support successfully our obligations to scholarship and the academic enterprise.

Research libraries have traditionally perceived it their responsibility to acquire, store, preserve, and make accessible the human record. Because in large part we were able to discharge these obligations by building comprehensive, self-sufficient collections, our substantial involvement in influencing the direction, health, and vitality of national scholarly activity has been largely unrecognized. David Stam, in his discussion of scholarly and research services of research libraries, has said,

> in a general way, large research libraries often play an active role in shaping the direction of scholarship itself through their decisions about what is important to preserve for posterity and what is chaff to be discarded. By determining what is retained and made accessible from the human record, research librarians often have the power to determine new directions in scholarship, or at least, to affect the extent of those directions.[3]

It has become increasingly clear, in an era of scarce resources and heightened demand, that national, regional, and local scholarly activities require the existence of comprehensive research library collections. This point was articulated in Research Universities and the National Interest, a report from 15 university presidents:

> Much of the scholarly research carried on in the United States depends heavily on the bibliographic services, publications, and archival resources provided by a relatively small number of large research libraries.... Scholarship in all fields, the scientific and industrial vitality of the country, the national capacity to address public problems at all levels of the organization, and perhaps most important, the ability of individuals to pursue their own intellectual concerns depend to a significant degree on the availability of published information, which is the substance of research libraries.[4]

The Need for a National Cooperative Strategy

The technology which has transformed our use and demand for information has also provided us with the technical tools to meet the heightened demand; but, technology alone will not do the job for us. We must provide the intellectual and conceptual framework for a coordinated information process and create the interinstitutional capacities to assure the continuing, unobstructed flow of information across local, regional, and national boundaries. Since all our traditional concepts and notions of research library services have been developed within the context of a containable activity within an autonomous institutional structure, we lack both the internal and the external organizational capacities for effective cooperative action. The field is littered with networking and consortium casualties. As two writers have indicated in their article on telecommunication in library networks, "some of the networks have been highly successful, and others have failed. Failure has been primarily due to organizational difficulties rather than to technical problems."[5]

The recently published report of the National Enquiry on Scholarly Communication strongly emphasizes the need for research libraries to move away from the concept of self-containment to the model of a "service center, capable of linking users to national bibliographic files and distant collections.... Forging a national bibliographic system from the many elements already in existence plus the creation of new components will be a multiyear job, replete with tedious and time-consuming technical and operating details that must be worked out in a cooperative manner."[6] If we are to acknowledge openly our heretofore implicit acceptance of the responsibility for the health of national scholarship, we must channel our energies into the design and development of effective cooperative activities at the national level, which will then enable us to discharge our obligations to our regional and local colleagues.

Libraries and Librarians 7

Many of our consortium and cooperative activities of the past have made the fundamental mistake of attempting to share resources without giving up our basic notion of the autonomous organization of libraries. We have tried to solve a problem of resource scarcity within a framework premised on affluence and the lack of communications capability among the separate organizations. When resources are not equal to the demand, dependencies replace resources in the sharing equation. We have discovered that we can no longer meet the increased demand by simple exploitation of the existing sharing mechanisms. We must consider today, not the sharing of resources, but the sharing of dependencies. If we are to design and build effective and mutually beneficial networking capabilities for research universities, we must change our underlying assumptions of resource sharing and speak instead in terms of "resource dependency" and "shared dependencies."

The Council on Library Resources has launched a five-year effort, the Bibliographic Service Development Program, to facilitate the transformation of research library services. In the council's analysis,

> Librarians must learn to define their obligations and requirements within a much different environment. One in which each library is not a self-contained entity, but a component of an undefined whole. It is not--it will not be --an easy transition.... The key is access.... Products and services, rather than the production of records, become the principal concern in this environment; those that will best serve librarians and their users have yet to be defined. [7]

The process of change is never easy--or readily welcomed-- and it is particularly difficult for research libraries because of our intrinsic relationship to the academic enterprise.

Since research libraries have traditionally been a support service to the academic program of the university as well as to the national scholarly community, any radical changes in library services can cause serious dislocations to those programs. Changes in the traditional mission and objectives of research libraries will seriously affect the individual scholar's capacity to pursue his or her livelihood. It is equally true that our inaction, our maintenance of the status quo, will have the same effect. We must make changes, but these changes must be thoughtfully designed and judiciously implemented. Since we will continue to serve a vast array of scholarly needs, it is unlikely that research librarians can expect a diminution of traditional activities as we assume the new capabilities afforded by networking. We will undoubtedly run parallel systems for a period of time. We will have books and computer-output microforms. As one library director put it in his recent annual report,

> The map, the manuscript, the special archive, and indeed the book are not about to become obsolete. Long-range

evolution will undoubtedly revamp the ways in which we store and use information, but these will co-exist for years to come with those now available. Thus the problem for libraries will be to continually widen access to information wherever located and in whatever form it will take. Knowledge in its multiplicity of packages and approaches is a complementary matrix; there is no single, final answer in the search for information.[8]

A good example of the kinds of careful decisions required to develop a coordinated network environment is found in the concept of information broker and the current indecision over the primary objectives of the research library. One author has criticized libraries for their propensity to store documents to the detriment of access to information. In his words, "libraries currently conduct their operations as if their strategy were to store and provide access to books, periodicals, papers, and other materials. The current strategy should be to supply information."[9]

But in order to achieve our access goals, we must first create internal and external institutional capacities to allow universities to determine academic priorities and to share collection responsibilities through network capabilities. Then research libraries can shift their emphasis to the provision of information rather than the storing of materials. But until the warehousing function has been outlined and assigned and assured, we have no choice but to continue our traditional activities, upon which the whole concept of networking and information brokering depends. If research libraries suddenly dropped their current storehouse functions without cooperative planning and shifted to information brokerage through the network capability, they would throw the system out of balance.

New Realities

The transition from a system of comprehensive and autonomous activities into an effective network environment will require a carefully coordinated balance of traditional library services with new capabilities. We are projecting potentials based on existing realities, but we must recognize that changes in the existing realities imply radical changes in the projected potential capabilities and activities.

A brief summary of the changes in our existing realities will illustrate the seriousness of our dilemma:

1. The inability of individual institutions to continue to acquire and house comprehensive book collections at traditional levels is beyond dispute. We are not now collecting with the same depth or breadth as our predecessors. It is possibly too early to predict the severity of the impact this deterioration in research library support will have on the level and nature of our national scholarly activities, since we know very little about the relationship of scholarly research and productivity to the proximity and availability of the resources.

Libraries and Librarians   9

2. The Library of Congress, which has long served as our
unofficial national library, and upon which we have depended heavily
for complementary support, particularly in the more exotic languages and obscure disciplines, has been forced, for economic reasons, to curtail sharply a variety of significant services to the research community. These services include the following:

   a. A change in collection policy which will assign a higher
   priority to serving the requirements of the Congress with a
   corresponding deemphasis on the acquisition of foreign materials.
   b. A revision of processing priorities which will favor
   heavily used materials in the English language and will
   provide only minimal cataloging for less intensively used
   foreign language research materials.
   c. The proposed romanization of all nonroman alphabets,
   which will create serious problems of access for scholars
   in these areas. The outcry from the research library
   community achieved a temporal reversal of this decision
   for Hebrew and East Asian scripts.
   d. The phasing out, due to expiration of federal funds, of
   PL-480 programs for materials from Yugoslavia, Poland,
   Israel, and Egypt. The India program is slated for extinction within the next five to seven years.
   e. The proposed shift from the Wade-Giles romanization
   system to Pinyin for Chinese vernacular materials, a shift
   which, if implemented, would create considerable havoc
   and significant added costs for individual research libraries
   which use LC cataloging for Chinese materials.

3. We face a staggering preservation problem. In 1965,
Gordon Williams conducted a study for the Association of Research
Libraries which described the dimensions of the problem and recommended solutions based on a national approach to avoid costly duplication and to ease the burden on individual institutions. Fifteen
years later, the preservation crisis is more severe, but we are
finally beginning to respond. Again, the deterrents to individual action have been the magnitude of the costs faced by individual institutions and the lack of qualified personnel. At Columbia, for example,
we estimate that 30 percent of our collections require some kind of
preservation treatment, at a total cost of $34 million. The New
York Public Library has estimated that 50 percent of its collections
are endangered. As one preservation expert wrote recently, "The
profession as a whole is responding to the needs long recognized by
a few, and the responsibility is passing from the lonely prophets to
the many builders and salvagers and dogged workers. There is real
hope for our imperilled collections."[10] But our inability, for 15
years, to agree on and implement a cooperative national strategy
has resulted in irreparable losses of valuable research materials.

4. There is increasing evidence that, even if the above services were still intact, we would not be able to meet the changing
needs of our clientele. Recommendation Twelve of Scholarly Communication: A National Inquiry urged that a standing committee be

established by the American Council on Learned Societies, the American Association of University Presses, and the Association for Research Libraries to act as a continuing forum "to bring together scholars, librarians, publishers, and technologists for the purpose of discussing the potentials of new communications technologies, the methods and procedures required for their implementation, and their effect on the working arrangements of scholars and other users of recorded knowledge."[11] The American Council of Learned Societies has recently required support from the Carnegie Corporation of New York for a period of three years to establish a committee on changes in the system of scholarly communication.

These changes reflect radical transformations in the publishing world, and it is essential that research libraries understand their symbiotic relationship with the publishing community. The process of scholarly communication in a free society requires the health and well-being of both sectors to ensure the free flow of information. The recent announcement of the purchase of Data Resources by McGraw-Hill indicates the direction of the future. As the New York Times reported,

> The old marketing line in the Harvard Business School is that the problem with the railroads is they always thought they were in the railroad business, instead of transportation.... McGraw-Hill isn't about to make that mistake--they realize they are in information and communications, not just publishing. They have the data in-house, and nobody knows whether it will be more efficient in the future to deliver it in books made of paper or through other methods.[12]

We too must remember we are in the business of information and communications rather than the maintenance of the identity of a single entity, "the library."

How Will Research Libraries Adapt?

The basic question is not "whether," but "how." Where do we begin to reinvent, to build? The old unities have been fragmented and destroyed by the new technology. First, we lost the architectural unification of the all-inclusive building. Next went the idea of a single, comprehensive, self-contained collection. Then, true to form, we turned to the concept of a single, all-embracing computerized network to which we would all belong and which would replace the vanished security of our old unities. But as Richard DeGennaro wrote recently in Library Journal, "A single monolithic national network embracing all libraries and providing all types of services is neither a realistic expectation nor a desirable goal for this country with its tradition of diversity and free enterprise...."[13]

The single underlying message which emerges with stunning clarity from the foregoing summary of our quiet revolution is that

Libraries and Librarians

the magnitude of the costs required to maintain research library services necessary for the continued vitality of higher education in this country is beyond the capabilities of our individual universities and independent research libraries. We must join together to find cooperative solutions in our collective best interests.

We must openly confront the issues of excellence and elitism, which always seem to lurk beneath the surface of any discussion of "difference" in our society. Research libraries must avow their special differences and special responsibilities to the process of higher education and scholarly research. Our society expects from us and depends upon our differences to support esoteric scholarly activities. We are not populist organizations and have never been so. We serve the popular interest by our commitment to the highest standards of scholarly research and investigation which in turn contribute heavily to the cultural and social comforts of our society. It is only by committing ourselves to high standards of excellence that we truly discharge our obligation to present and future generations. We must accept that obligation and solve first the problems of cooperation, networking, and resource sharing on the national level in order to meet effectively our local and regional commitments and obligations.

For a lot of good reasons, among them the lack of effective communications capabilities and the political and financial implications of state and local jurisdictions, research universities and their libraries in the past have tended to ignore the significance and importance of our national responsibilities. We accepted those responsibilities as a by-product of our comprehensive collecting policies. If we are to continue to provide effective service to our local and regional institutions and citizens, we must first assure our own well-being, and that can only be done on a national scale.

Assuring the Availability of Information

Twelve years ago New York State pioneered the development of a statewide interlibrary loan system, designed to provide for all citizens access to the library resources in the state. At that time, New York contained seven ARL libraries; there are now ten. The system, designed to exploit computer technology currently available at that time, is based on a set of hierarchical protocols which route a request from any library in the state through a regional reference center, for purposes of citation verification, to the State Library. If the State Library does not own the material, the request is then referred to one of the large "referral libraries" based on a computer profile of subject strengths. Each referral library contracts with the state to provide materials within certain subject areas. This system has worked well for a number of years, but its effectiveness has now declined for two major reasons. One, we now have the technical capacity to inquire online into data bases of actual holdings, and two, during the past decade, the major research libraries have suffered a dramatic decline in their ability to acquire materials. We can no longer automatically assume that a book or journal in a given subject specialty will be at New York Public, Columbia, or Cornell. The research libraries can no longer serve the people of New York State as effectively as in 1969 until they regain their own collection health by rationalizing and managing collection priorities with research library peers across the country.

The new OCLC interlibrary loan program has been installed with well-deserved fanfare and approbation. But it will not solve the problems facing research libraries. It is a masterful piece of technical accomplishment, affording us with unprecedented communications capability. In the same way that the New York State Interlibrary Loan system, 12 years ago, exploited the current state of the art to locate materials, the new OCLC will locate what exists. The OCLC capability will not serve the major responsibility of the research library, which is to assure the availability of the required information.

Technology alone is not enough. As we move from a storehouse concept to a service center providing access to information, it is essential that we create the kind of program-based consortia which will enable us to solve the problems of collection development, preservation, shared resources, and facilitated access so that we will assure the availability of scholarly information to future generations.

Five years ago, Harvard, Yale, and Columbia Universities and the New York Public Library formed the Research Libraries Group. At the time, the institutions were concerned with developing a regional consortium to share resources and preservation costs. It soon became apparent that the first priority in achieving the objectives of shared resources, cooperative collection development, shared cataloging, and an effective preservation program was the development of a sophisticated bibliographic system responsive to and meeting the requirements of research libraries. The enormous effort to identify, select, and finance the appropriate system consumed the better part of three years, during which the individual members underwent significant internal transformations as they moved toward unprecedented agreement on bibliographic standards, access policies, and assignment of collection responsibilities. As the members' perceptions and activities matured and developed, it became clear that an organization on a national scale was now both technologically possible and programmatically desirable. During the long, hot summer of 1978, RLG members spent innumerable hours with their university counsels in the arduous and pioneering effort to create a corporation owned by the member institutions. As the legal counsels were to discover to their dismay, there were no precedents. The legal effort was followed by the equally arduous task of raising the necessary working capital to launch the organization and support its activities during the period of initial development until income exceeds expense, and RLG becomes a self-supporting research library activity, using pooled income generated by member institutions to meet their own requirements, rather than purchase services from commercial vendors.

In January 1979, membership was extended to all members of ARL; to date, members and affiliates include Yale, Columbia, New York Public, Princeton, Rutgers, Pennsylvania, Dartmouth, Michigan, Iowa, Brigham Young, Colorado State, Stanford, Berkeley, and Davis. In addition to the Research Libraries Information Network, the current programs include expedited (via TWX and UPS) interlibrary loan and photocopy services, on-site privileges, a collection management and development program, and specialized programs in the subject areas of East Asian, art, and law.

To succeed, cooperative activities require one major ingredient--cooperation. A cooperative venture for research libraries will not succeed if research universities and their libraries adopt the wait-and-see attitude reminiscent of the good old days of autonomy. The success of the venture depends upon the participation of all of us.

Research libraries, in the past, sought to control their destinies and discharge their responsibilities through the concept of a self-sufficient comprehensive collection policy and services. If we continue to cling to that concept, in the face of monumental changes in our socioeconomic environment, we will lose our essential viability and control. It is imperative that we recognize the urgency of joining together to develop a collective capacity to regain the mastery of our responsibilities and our activities. If we, by virtue of our inability to achieve broad consensus and recognition of our essential similarities, permit and facilitate the development of a bibliographic monopoly unsympathetic to the mission of research universities and their libraries, the future of higher education in this society will be seriously imperiled. The availability of bibliographic products and services based on need and specialized requirements will be replaced by an availability determined by the economics of monopoly.

Those of us responsible for the operation and management of research libraries find ourselves, by sheer historical accident, facing unprecedented challenges. We have the opportunity for enormous success--or enormous failure. The assurance of the unobstructed flow and availability of scholarly information to future generations requires decisive and creative collective action on our part. The enormity of our professional responsibility is succinctly described in the remark attributed to Stephen McCarthy, that whether a great library makes or brings into being a great university is debatable, but experience shows that the two are always found together.

This article is adapted from the author's presentation at a symposium on "Information, Research Libraries, and the Scholar," held at Louisiana State University on October 25, 1979, on the occasion of the naming of the Troy H. Middleton Library.

References

1. John W. McCredie, "Computer Acquisitions: The Carnegie-Mellon Strategy," EDUCOM Bulletin, Fall 1979, p. 10.
2. Ibid. p. 10.
3. David Stam, "Scholarly and Research Services of Research Libraries," paper submitted for publication in American Libraries Association Encyclopedia.
4. Research Universities and the National Interest: A Report From Fifteen University Presidents (New York: The Ford Foundation, 1978), pp. 89-90.
5. Julius S. Aronfsky and Robert K. Korfhage, "Telecommunication in Library Networks: A Five-Year Projection," Journal of Library Automation 10, (March 1977): 11.
6. Scholarly Communication: The Report of the National Enquiry (Baltimore: Johns Hopkins University Press, 1979), pp. 159, 152.
7. Warren J. Haas, Nancy E. Gwinn, and C. Lee Jones, "Managing the Information Revolution: CLR's Bibliographic Service Development Program," Library Journal, September 15, 1979, p. 1870.
8. Warren B. Kuhn, Annual report: 1977-78 (Ames, Iowa: Iowa State University Library, 1978), p. 1.
9. Charles B. Weinberg, "The University Library: Analysis and Proposals," Management Science 21, (October 1974): 131.
10. Pamela W. Darling, "Preservation Epilogue: Signs of Hope." Library Journal, September 1, 1979, p. 1627.
11. Scholarly Communication, p. 29.
12. Edwin McDowell, "A Data Conglomerate," New York Times, September 9, 1979, Section 3, p. 1.
13. Richard DeGennaro, "From Monopoly to Competition: the Changing Library Network Scene," Library Journal, June 1, 1979, p. 1217.

THE TEST OF REFERENCE*

Thomas Childers

Public Library services had been subjected to hidden testing before the late sixties, no doubt. But if it did occur, it was not widely reported, and the idea of testing services from the client's point of view was surely not on the mind of the average librarian. In 1967 Terry Crowley, at Rutgers University Graduate School of Library Service, applied the technique of hidden testing to reference service: he judged the quality of library responses to questions that had been asked by people who posed as bona fide clients. His dissertation and my own later one--both hidden, or unobtrusive, tests of public library information service--were published in one volume in 1971.[1] General professional awareness of the unobtrusive technique probably dates from that time.

Since then there have been many efforts along the same lines. Published and unpublished reports indicate that over the years hidden testing has been applied to academic, public, and special libraries. Most of the studies have been small ones in which a few questions were applied to a single library. A few studies have included a large number of questions applied to several library outlets. The studies have been undertaken by students in library schools and by reference librarians and managers; and they have been motivated sometimes by pure curiosity about performance and sometimes by the desire to improve services.

There have been mixed responses to the news of the unobtrusive method and its findings. In some libraries management has instituted training programs to improve the question-handling skills of the reference staff; in other libraries staff members have revamped the goals and guidelines of their service; at least one library has established a program of self-evaluation by the individual staff member, by way of videotape recordings of actual reference transactions. Some librarians bristle at the technique or the findings; others fall asleep over the whole idea. Even the _style_ of management's response to the technique and its findings has varied greatly. In one

---
*Reprinted by permission of the author and publisher from Library Journal, April 15, 1980, p. 924-28. Published by R.R. Bowker Co. (a Xerox company). Copyright © 1980 by Xerox Corporation.

library, management might let the staff initiate the request to be "tested" and then use the results to kick off a long series of discussions about reference skills, training, policy, goals, etc. In another, management might impose the method on the staff regardless of staff feelings and use the evidence of the study to justify new operating procedures.

After the dissertations, my work in hidden testing continued. There were a couple of small studies in New Jersey and Ohio, and several reference workshops that used the method to make practicing librarians more conscious of the plight of clients. These all taught me more about the limits and assets of hidden testing and about applying its results in a workaday situation. However, none of these ventures, nor the scattered reports during that period, seemed to harbor much of a message for the profession at large, after the dissertations of the late '60s. This could have been due to the size of the studies themselves: the number of libraries tested and the number of questions asked were small. I was more than happy, then, to be invited by the Suffolk Cooperative Library System to perform a massive study of reference performance in 1977-78.[2]

The site

Suffolk County, New York consists of the major part of Long Island. To reach it from Manhattan, one travels east through heavily populated Queens Borough and Nassau County. Suffolk County is growing rapidly. Within a few years it should be as populated as its neighbor, Nassau County.

The county has 52 independent public libraries and seven branches. They serve anywhere from 450 to 112,000 people, in areas ranging from four to 100 square miles. Their annual operating budgets in 1976 were as low as $12,000 and as high as $1,300,000. All of the libraries are members of the Suffolk Cooperative Library System (SCLS), an organization supported through state and local funds and designed to provide services for the member libraries. The services include materials ordering, a materials back-up collection, consultation in various areas, printing and publicity, and reference and information back-up. SCLS has gone well beyond mere passive response to the member libraries' demands and has taken on a major leadership role among the libraries. It was in this role of leader that the director of SCLS, Robert Sheridan, and the coordinator of its reference services, Evelyn Greenberg, convinced the members that they needed to take a systematic look at the quality of the reference and information services.

The study

With financial support from an LSCA grant, we undertook an unobtrusive study of reference/information performance in almost all the public library outlets in the county. After eliminating a few libraries that were too isolated (one is on a tiny island much closer to Connecticut than Long Island) or too small (where we would expect the library staff to know personally most members of the community), the number of library outlets totalled 57.

In April 1977 the proxies were hired. They were to telephone or visit the libraries, ask the assigned questions, and record the responses. Their prime tasks were to appear to be a bona fide client with a real question, to apply a given question in the same way in each library, and to record the response completely, without judging it. The questioning began in May. Each library was asked the same 20 questions, over a period of six months.

Most of the queries called for simple information (What is the altitude of Cheyenne, Wyoming? What was the 1975 year-end closing price of a share of North American Coal). A few queries asked for bibliographic information (Where can I get a federal publication called "Final Report: President's Task Force on Communications Policy," published in 1967?). Several asked for information about local social services or facts of local government (Is there a county agency that deals with child abuse? What constitutes the first judicial district in the county?). One query was a request for a book.

Three questions were, to my knowledge, unique in hidden testing. We were interested in finding out more about the library staff's readiness to "negotiate" a question. As a simple and admittedly crude test of this, three questions called "escalators" were designed. An "escalator" was a query composed of subqueries and which progressed in steps from broad to specific. For example:

Step 1: Where can I find your books on poetry?
Step 2: I'm looking for something that describes different kinds of poetry.
Step 3: Could you give me a definition of concrete poetry?

The proxy, upon visiting a library with this question, would ask Step 1. If the respondent showed even a slight interest in identifying a more specific need, the proxy progressed to the next level. Through the same process the respondent could get to the third level. The libraries were scored not on the correctness of the answer they gave, but on their success in arriving at the ultimate step on the "escalator."

Another new departure in the Suffolk County study was the testing of nonlibrary resources to which proxies had been steered. In many cases libraries mentioned, or steered the proxies to, some kind of resource agency outside the library that was thought to hold the answer--another library, a government office, a person, etc. For seven queries, we tested the response by any resource agency mentioned by a library. Across the 57 libraries, proxies were "steered" a total of 179 times for those seven queries.

Since it was vital to the hidden nature of the study that the proxies and the questions appear bona fide, most questions were cloaked in a brief rationale--such as "a friend of mine is thinking of moving to Cheyenne," or "I suspect my neighbor's child is being abused."

In order not to bias the study against a particular library, precautions were taken: the first contacts with the libraries were spread across the hours of the day and days of the week in a random way, so that libraries would be tested during moments of both weak staffing and strong staffing.[3] Second, the responses to questions were judged without knowledge of the libraries' names. Third, before a given question was asked, a criterion was devised by which the correctness or incorrectness of the responses could be weighed with consistency. These precautions were meant to minimize the chance of bias against any given library--which is not to say that the study method was without flaws.[4]

The findings, in brief

In all, 1110 queries were applied to the county libraries. Here are the major findings:

● About 56 percent of the time an actual answer was given to the proxy. That is, the respondent delivered a document, a fact, or a citation in answer to the query. In some cases a respondent indicated that he was unable to get an answer after making an attempt; or that he did not expect to find an answer and therefore would not try; or that there was some other reason not to answer the question. This happened about one-third of the time.

● Of the nonanswers, about half contained an attempt to steer the proxy to an out-of-library resource for the answer. Putting it another way, about 17 percent of the time respondents provided neither an answer to the query nor an idea of where the proxy could find it.

● Two-thirds of the steering was to nonlibrary agencies.

● The answers given by the libraries were scored on a scale of Correct, Mostly Correct, Mostly Wrong, and Wrong. It was found that, when an actual answer was forthcoming, 84 percent of the time it was Correct or Mostly Correct. Only 16 percent of the actual answers were Wrong or Mostly Wrong. The range of performance was substantial--one library providing correct answers to all the queries it attempted, and another answering correctly only about half.

● If we were to count "steering" and "non answers" as Wrong, the complexion of performance changes a great deal: about half the time the libraries delivered the correct answer to the query, and about half the time they did not. The low-performing library

Libraries and Librarians

delivered correct answers to 15 percent of all queries; the high-performing library answered 75 percent of all queries correctly.

● The "escalator" queries were designed to show how inclined the respondents were to negotiate the client's initial inquiry. In 67 percent of these cases, the respondents made no effort to probe for the proxy's underlying need. Yet about 20 percent of the respondents did negotiate the query to its ultimate level.

● Seven queries were selected for follow-up. For these queries, when a library mentioned or steered the proxy to an out-of-library resource, the response of that resource was tested. Two-thirds of the responses of the out-of-library resources were either Correct or Mostly Correct. The others consisted mainly of further steering; very few responses were Wrong or Mostly Wrong.

● The respondents were rated on their interest in the proxy's query and the extent to which the proxy felt comfortable with the respondent. Overall, the respondents scored high, well above "neutral, " on both dimensions.

In the course of the study, every library provided a correct answer to at least one question and, inversely, every question was answered correctly by at least one library. There was some pattern, however. Certain libraries were more likely than others to produce the correct answer to a question. While these were most often the larger libraries, the small and very small libraries generated correct answers often enough to cloud the pattern. Clients might have a higher success rate at a larger library, but they would also find some success at a smaller unit.

From the client's point of view, there are two very striking conclusions to be reached. First, the chance of getting the correct answer to these questions is about fifty-fifty. Seeing the library as a black box--one to which the client applies a question and from which the client receives a response that is either correct or not-- the likelihood of receiving a correct response to questions like those in the test is not overwhelming.

Just as striking is the fact that it may be difficult for the client to predict the quality of response that he will receive from a given library on a given question. No library could be relied on to deliver the correct answer all the time, and every library could be expected to provide the correct answer some of the time. Nor could the client depend on the respondents to "negotiate" his or her question--about one-third did, and two-thirds didn't--nor to steer him or her to an outside source when the answer was not located within the library--about half did and half didn't. Again, while larger libraries tended to perform better at these jobs, they did not do so consistently. Just like information-giving successes, information-giving "accidents" occurred in libraries of virtually every size. For example:

"Can you tell me who makes X?"
"I'm sorry, this is a library. I don't know. "

"Can you tell me which American presidents were Quakers?"
"My responsibilities are to tell you where to find it in black and white and not to give you the answers. I know there's a book on the presidents in the children's department, but you would have to come in yourself. I can't do research."

"Could you tell me where I could obtain a federal publication called X?"
"... did you try the Y Library?"
"No. Do you think they would have it?"
"Well I'm not sure--I'm not really familiar with government publications."

Transactions like these and the findings in general conjure up questions of library management. The questions can be posed for all libraries, across all time and space as I have done below. However they can only be resolved in the time and space of a given library. Each library or library outlet must consider such things for itself, and must reconsider them from time to time as the library, its resources or the community around it changes.

What are we doing?

In any number of his writings Peter Drucker warns us to establish a clear statement of purpose, lest we spread our resources too thin and perhaps undertake contradictory activities. Can we answer the question, "What business am I in?" Although librarians have claimed for decades to be in the "information business," the behaviors of librarians refute the claim, as witness some data of this study. More subtly, librarians have not wrestled the two ideas of information-out-of-published-documents and information-regardless-of-source into a state of conscious policy. Are we in the "traditional library reference business," with its reliance on what can be located in published materials--usually those held in-house; are we in the "information business," with the huge range of information sources (published, semipublished, manuscript, electronic, mental) and locations (local, regional, national) that the phrase implies? Is our business defined by information sources that are published? Or by the needs of the client group? Or does it fall somewhere in between?

How much is enough?

What level of achievement signals good or bad performance? Correct answers to every question that's asked? To 75 percent? 50 percent? Is there no objective for the quality of our service? If that is so, does it imply that we don't know what business we're in, that we don't know what to expect of "professional" performance? Probably.

What is the turn-around time of the information service? Commercial information brokers have sometimes adopted quantitative guidelines, such as "Answer 60 percent of a day's queries within the day received; answer another 20 percent within 24 hours; and another seven percent within 48 hours." A library can arrive at similar objectives. Answering the big questions of "What are we doing?" and "How much is enough?" paves the way for a string of smaller but no less critical ones, such as "How does an information professional behave?"

Policy for professionals

The policies that dictate how a client's inquiry is handled seem to be of three kinds: <u>Formal policy,</u> usually written and widely honored by the staff (such as "Answer an in-person inquiry before a telephone inquiry"); <u>informal group policy,</u> established through daily interaction and sometimes adhered to by all the staff (such as "If an inquiry requires a telephone call outside the building, we usually refer it to the department head"); and <u>personal</u> policy, set by the individual and probably followed only by the individual ("I never read out more than 50 words over the phone"). Not all the "policies" for handling inquiries could or should be formalized. Still, hidden testing over the years shows that librarians--sometimes even librarians within the same reference departments--often operate under conflicting sets of policy. If we wish to present a more even level of performance to the public, the policies must be attended to. In some cases it will be necessary to formalize informal group policy in order to gain general compliance. In other cases it may be sufficient to discuss at length the personal policies that each staff member follows and transform them into informal group policies.

Questions questioned

The varied handling of test questions raises many questions about the general handling of inquiries. Among them:

- When is it appropriate to "negotiate" a question or probe for an underlying need?

- What channels are to be used in responding to a question? When is it appropriate to use local or long distance phones, telex, online searching, photocopying?

- When does one drop a query or direct the client elsewhere? When does one simply provide directions to another resource (steer) or actually try to make the contact for the client (refer)?

- How responsible is the library for the answers provided by a resource to which it has steered or referred a client? Should the library systematically determine if the client has gotten the answer to his question? When? How?

• Is the library responsible for the correctness (accuracy, completeness, currency, etc.) of the information it dispenses?

• What constitutes a "correct" answer? A "wrong" answer? How current is current? And even, what is "truth"?

More broadly, it may be that while we have been learning how to be more agile with reference tools we have overlooked a prior question: <u>What kind of question does the library choose (aspire, want, assent, condescend, feel obliged) to answer, and what quality of answer should it give?</u>

Deploying resources

Additional policy questions are raised either directly or indirectly as a result of the testing--questions about how to deploy the information-handling resources in a library or library system. If the members or branches within a system are providing wildly divergent levels of service, is it really a "system"? There is indication that stronger libraries perform better on reference tests than smaller libraries. Why? Perhaps because they have more resources; perhaps because they have more professional time to devote to question-answering; perhaps--and I think this is the key--because they receive a higher volume of inquiries and thus are more practiced in answering questions. If these are truly some of the factors that influence performance, it may be worthwhile to consider consolidating information-giving strengths and providing reference and information services only through a library system's strongest outlets. Should Suffolk County answer questions only from the systems headquarters, through rapid telecommunications to the local outlets or homes?

What can the client expect?

The heart of these policy questions and others yet to be raised is: "What can the client expect?" Should the client be able to expect the same level of performance on every question he/she asks? Should a client be able to expect the same level of performance on his/her question as on any other client's? Should every client have an equal chance of getting an answer from his or her local library, regardless of the size or wealth of the library or the formal training of its staff? Should the client be led to expect libraries to provide information-as-found-in-published-places, or information-regardless-of-source?

Of course, once the decision is made as to what the client will be led to expect, there is the job of making certain that the client gets it a significant part of the time. That is, once the policy matters have been hammered out, the job is to bring practice into line with policy. Suffolk County has taken the first substantive step in addressing policy. It must still write that policy and then honor it in practice. Watch this spot for further developments.

References

1. Crowley, Terence and Thomas Childers. <u>Information Service in Public Libraries: Two Studies.</u> Scarecrow, 1971.
2. The full report of this study has been produced in very limited quantities. The citation is: Thomas Childers, <u>The Effectiveness of Information Service in Public Libraries: Suffolk County: Final Report.</u> Philadelphia: School of Library & Information Science, Drexel University, July 1978.
3. If respondents wished, proxies made two, three, or more contacts in order to get a "final" response.
4. For more detail and commentary on the method of this kind of unobtrusive method, refer to Crowley and Childers, above.

THE IMPLICATIONS OF SOME RECENT
STUDIES OF LIBRARY USE*

Casimir Borkowski & Murdo J. MacLeod

Scholarly publishing in the 1970s has been faced with a gradual chilling of the climate. To be sure, some of the crisis atmosphere of the early years of the decade has passed. University presses and other scholarly publishers have proved--often somewhat to their own surprise--to be both hardy and capable of healthy adaptation to the changed circumstances, while both the general public and university administrations have proved to be supportive with funds and other forms of help.

But the changed conditions of the 1970s are still upon us, and almost all forecasts see these unfavourable circumstances as continuing far into the future. University budgets are shrinking, and as a result the acquisition budgets of many research libraries, which are the purchasers of a large share of the output of scholarly presses, are also shrinking. This comes at a time of inflation in book and journal prices and of explosion in the quantity of scholarly books and journals: fewer dollars are chasing an ever-increasing quantity of ever more expensive materials. Demographic projections are equally bleak. The North American population is aging, and the young population of university age is declining (relatively and absolutely). This may have serious repercussions upon future university enrolments and tax support from the public. Cuts in these two areas would, in turn, affect the sales of university presses.

To all this, and to several other difficulties, scholarly publishers have responded well. The fat added in the 1960s has gone, and, for the most part, efficiency has increased. Thoughtful examination of operations, policies, and marketing continues, and some of it produces sensible suggestions for further efficiencies and improvements.[1]

Nevertheless, many of the measures taken by scholarly presses have been reactive, introspective, and restricted to the

*Reprinted by permission of the authors and publisher from Scholarly Publishing, October 1979, p. 3-24; copyright © 1979 by University of Toronto Press.

field of scholarly publishing. To be sure, there has been a greater attempt to 'sell' the message and purpose of scholarly publishing to university administrations, research institutions, and foundations. But, by and large, scholarly presses have accepted the weather forecasts as given to them, and their energies have been directed largely to putting their own houses in efficient order. It may well be that this was a logical first step, but this essay will suggest that it is time to advance beyond this stage and to play a more aggressive, or at least a more participatory, role in the larger world that works to make knowledge available.

One way to accomplish this is to identify friends and to work with them for common goals. Scholars--that is, book, journal, and library users--are by and large well satisfied with the performance of scholarly presses and research libraries. There are chronic complaints about prices, delays, and here and there sloppy editing, but recent surveys indicate that scholars consider scholarly presses to be important and believe that they are doing their job well.[2] The same is true of research libraries and librarians. At times their interests are not those of publishers. (The whole vexing question of photocopying should be sufficient illustration.) But librarians are generally supportive of scholarly presses and realize the need for them. Common interests are 'ultimately stronger.'[3]

Thus, in spite of squabbles and a few competing interests, scholars, research librarians, and scholarly publishers should work together in an organized manner, not only as a defensive measure, but also as a way of making sensible developmental choices in the next few years. In this context recommendation twelve of the recent report of the National Enquiry is illustrative:

> We recommend that the American Council of Learned Societies join with the Association of American University Presses and the Association of Research Libraries to establish a standing committee composed of scholars, publishers, and librarians for continuing discussion of the nature and direction of technological change in the system of scholarly communication.
> The next decade will present the scholarly community with numerous choices regarding new technologies that can be adopted in libraries and in scholarly book and journal publishing. From the vantage of scholarly communication, the potential for making unwise choices among these technologies is great, particularly if scholars are not active participants in the decision-making discussions. A continuing forum is needed to bring together scholars, librarians, publishers, and technologists for the purpose of discussing the potentials of new communication technologies, the methods and procedures required for their implementation, and their effects on the working arrangements of scholars and other users of recorded knowledge.... The potential changes sketched speculatively in the Epilogue to

this chapter need to be guided by the intelligence and wisdom that resides in the affected communities, not by technological and economic forces alone.[4]

This long quotation from an impressive, unequivocal study points out the direction. Scholarly publishers must join with their natural allies to map the future positively. For too long they have reacted defensively to outside impositions.

Offensive and defensive alliances and a reordering of one's own house are not enough. An excellent recent article (already cited) by Edward Tripp in this journal recommended that storm clouds receive proper attention and that arks be built strongly and effectively to withstand the difficult years to come. Certainly this has been done and will have to continue to be done. But some of these apparent storm clouds, perhaps just a few of them, are smoke screens thrown up by interest groups which do not share the concerns of the world of scholarship. Scholarly publishers must not accept these empty clouds as reality. They must examine each one to find out how much threat it carries--if any at all.

The rest of this essay, then, is in large part an examination of one bank of these apparent storm clouds, various recent studies of the use of the collections in university and research libraries. One study in particular, a study which has received considerable publicity and has caused some controversy, will be discussed. It will then be compared with some other relevant studies.

II

The importance of library use to scholarly publishers is evident. In times of financial difficulties, harried administrators and research librarians will tend to purchase books and journals which will be used, and will cut back on others.

The study to be examined in greatest detail, <u>A Cost-Benefit Model of Some Critical Library Operations in Terms of Use of Materials</u>, by Allen Kent et al. (commonly known at the University of Pittsburgh as the Kent Study, hereinafter KS) states that 'The hard facts are that research libraries invest very substantial funds to purchase books and journals that are rarely, or never, called for.' More specifically, 'when book use in the University of Pittsburgh's central research library was studied over a seven-year-and-two-month period, it was found that any given book purchased had only slightly better than one chance in two of ever being borrowed.' Of the books acquired in 1969 only about 60 per cent are said to have been used in more than seven years. Similarly the use of journals in the Pittsburgh libraries studied is asserted to be 'low.'[5]

Considerable debate and controversy followed the advance announcements of some of these findings and the dissemination of the final version. Some librarians found KS to be useful, and in fact

Libraries and Librarians

In fact, at the University of Pittsburgh's Hillman Library the size of each departmental budget, for example, in the Faculty of Arts and Sciences, is decided by the co-ordinator of library resources, given the total budget made available to her by the director of the Hillman Library. There is no input from faculty members at this stage. The faculty representative of each department or school is then told what his or her departmental budget will be for the financial year. Faculty members commonly do not know the size of the library budget in departments other than their own. It has been agreed by faculty-representative groups over the years that the library resources unit is better placed than any group of faculty members to 'divide the pie.' This is common knowledge among bibliographers and faculty representatives at the Hillman Library.

Acquisition and selection at Hillman Library is an integrated system, including discussion and co-operation between librarians and faculty members. None of this is secret or difficult to discover. Both faculty library committees--such as the Senate library committee and the executive committee for libraries--and librarians at Hillman, however 'reluctantly,' have accepted the financial problems facing the library for many years, and much of their discussion, as minutes would show, has been devoted to ways of coping with these exigencies.

In fact, what KS has done is to construct a model of library acquisition and selection policies in vague and general ways, ways which often do not apply at all to Hillman Library, the 'locus' of this case study. In logic this is sometimes called the fallacy of division or 'the leap from the general to the particular.'

We also find ourselves in serious disagreement with KS over its use and manipulation of data on the use of books. We will not list and examine all the issues but rather offer some typical examples.

Let us begin by taking KS data on books acquired in 1969, that year being perhaps more 'complete' in its data. KS states (on page 11) that through 1975 '22,172 of the 36,869 items acquired in 1969 had been used at least once [see __Final Report__, table 1 for numbers]. This total represents about 60% of acquisitions.'

Let us list first minor additions to this total use. KS dismisses these additions as 'an acceptably small error,' but let us add them on for the moment. Forty-seven items acquired in 1969 for the Hillman Library were used by Hillman inter-library loan but did not circulate externally at Pittsburgh during the period under study by KS (see table 16, page 28). In a similar way, 329 items acquired in 1969 were used in the reserve book room at the Hillman Library but did not circulate externally. These minor additions total 376. Now the 22,172 items used have increased to 22,548, or 61.2%, an increase of just over 1% above the KS figure. (The failure to count __all__ uses in the reserve book room--each item there was counted as one use--also skews downwards the total-use statistics in KS.)

Of more importance is the analysis of 'in-house' circulation or use. We disagree with the KS definition of in-house use and consequently with the KS method of selecting the data on in-house use and with the data themselves. These disagreements will be explained below. But for the moment let us accept the KS definition, methods, and data, and see where they lead.

KS discussion of in-house use is based on a 30-day sample of books collected from return shelves and tables, an analysis of this sample, and an extrapolation of the sample to a 365-day, or one-year, period, including a summer slowdown. (This is very different from the analysis of external use, which is based on some 95% of external circulation.) During the 30-day sample period, 193 items required in 1969 were used in-house, according to the KS definition of in-house use, but had not previously circulated externally, that is, between acquisition in 1969 and early 1976. This group of 193 items was studied for a year after the sample period, that is, until April 1977, and during this time 12 more of them circulated externally (tables 11 and 12, pages 24-5). Thus, by April 1977, 181 items from the sample, acquired in 1969, had been used in-house and had not circulated externally in all that time. Let us now use the KS method of extrapolation to a yearly base (see pages 25-6). Using the 181 items from the 30-day KS sample as the base, this yields a total of 1963 items acquired in 1969 which were used in-house during one year, but which were not used externally (that is, circulated) from 1969 through the year 1976.

By now the 22,172 items from 1969, using KS's own statistics and extrapolations, have changed to 22,548 items, then to 24,511 items. The percentage of items used has shifted from 60.1% to 66.5%. Note that we still disagree with the KS definition of in-house use; and at this point we have simply reordered the KS data using its own criteria and figures. Note also that the KS underestimation of its own 'items used' figures for 1969 acquisitions, more than 6% so far, is repeated in the other years studied, 1969-75, as computation can confirm.

(This may be the appropriate place to demonstrate the dangers of extrapolation from a 30-day sample to a one-year total in a seven-year study of use. Let us perform an experiment. We have seen in KS that 181 items acquired in 1969 were used in-house but did not circulate. By the method of extrapolation used in KS we found that in the last year of the study some 1963 items were used in-house but had never circulated to that time. But KS is a seven-year study, and if we take the 1963 items as typical for a year we find that in a period of seven years at least 13,741 items acquired in 1969 were used in-house but did not circulate. It could even be argued that this figure is too low. First, according to KS and generally accepted belief, books and monographs are used most heavily in the first two or three years after acquisition. Moreover, as KS states, the percentage of books and monographs circulating in-house that also circulate externally increases over time (page 25). Thus, in the early use years of the 1969 acquisitions, say 1969, 1970, and 1971, we should be able to state that much larger numbers of 1969 acquisitions were used in-house but did not circulate externally. But for the purpose of this exercise let us use the figure of 13,741 items. We now find that 36,289 items (22,548 + 13,741) acquired in 1969 have been used during the study period. This would mean that some 98% of the 36,869 items acquired in 1969 had been used at least once by the end of the study. Obviously this percentage is too high, but it illustrates the dangers of extended extrapolation from a small sample. We also believe that it is closer to the real situation of use in Hillman Library than the 60%--now 66.5%--put forward by KS.)

So far we have considered the KS nominators for items used among the books and monographs acquired in 1969. Now let us devote some attention to the use of the 1969 denominator, which we have accepted hitherto. There were 36,869 items acquired in 1969. KS claims (page 10) that it has included a loss rate of 5% per year in its calculations. This is not so (see tables 1, 2, and 3 of Final Report).

It is difficult to place lost, destroyed, misplaced, or stolen items in our calculations. It is tempting and amusing, for example, to consider the theft of a book or monograph as one use, and thus add it to the nominator. But we decided that it makes more sense to deduct lost, destroyed, misplaced, or stolen books from the denominator; these books are not available for use and thus should be excluded from the total available. It is also difficult to decide on the rate of this loss. It is cumulative and may reach as high as 10% to 15% of a given year's acquisitions after seven years have passed (see KS, page 45). To be conservative, we decided simply to deduct 5% from the denominator and disregard the cumulative growth in the number of unavailable 1969 books and monographs. The loss of books acquired in that year is then 1843. This lowers the number of 1969 books and monographs available for use from 36,869 to 35,026 items. Given our total number of items used, 24,511, the percentage of use has risen to 70% (69.979% to be exact).

Another category of books which was not considered in KS was the reference collection. Much of this collection does not circulate, and what circulation there is is usually restricted and, until very recently, manually charged out. In the academic year 1968/9, 572 additional reference items entered the collections. In 1969/70, the total was 698 items. (It is worth noting that this number increased greatly in the last years of the KS study. The 1974/5 total of reference books added, for example, was 1104.) The average of these two academic years is 635 reference additions, and so we have assigned this total to the calendar year 1969. As Hillman patrons are aware, although these reference books are seldom checked out, and although such external circulation as there is would appear rarely on computerized circulation records, the reference collection is very heavily used. Surely some awareness of such use should be part of an account of use such as KS claims to be.

Because these 635 books and monographs added to the Hillman reference collections in 1969 are not normally available for circulation or circulation records, we have deducted them from the denominator for 1969, that is, the number of items available for computer-recorded use. The number of 1969 items available now becomes 34,391 (36,869--1843--635). The adjusted KS nominator (items used) is 24,511. The percentage of 1969 items used now moves to 71.3%, an increase of more than 11% over the original KS percentage. Nineteen sixty-nine is, of course, merely representative. The same holds true with slight variations for every year of the KS study and for the accumulated statistics of KS as a whole.

This exercise in data accumulation so far has not questioned any of the basic premises in KS. It has been carried out simply to demonstrate that KS data as given can yield much higher numbers of items used and percentages of use than those put forward in the report. We shall now move to more substantial concerns and examine the KS study of in-house use and other matters.

We have already questioned the wisdom of using a thirty-day sample and its extrapolations as the basis for a seven-year study, especially when the 'other half' of the study, external circulation, is based on a long and fairly complete record. We also believe that the sampling method is intrinsically flawed and leads to underestimation of use--as is so consistently and so disturbingly the case in KS (see above).

Here is the basis of the KS method for sampling internal or in-house use of books and monographs.

> The policy of the Hillman Library is to request that patrons not reshelve material but instead place it in special areas in the stacks or leave it on the table where it was used. Signs are placed prominently throughout the stack area to indicate this policy. We have assumed that patrons obey this rule. Given the long standing of this policy, the special stack area, a systematic collection method, and our more formal notion of 'use,' we think that we have faced most of the objections raised by Fussler and Simon to the collection method for studying internal use.
> On each of the 30 sample days materials left on tables and designed areas were collected. [Final Report, pages 20-1]

This is a crucial statement. If it is not correct then the part of KS devoted to in-house use becomes invalid. We were troubled by its vagueness. More important, we believed that such a method of data collection would not catch even a majority of in-house uses.

Do patrons obey the Hillman request to place materials on tables or designated areas? Several days of observation showed us

Libraries and Librarians

that many patrons do not. We decided to find out what some patrons perceive themselves as doing as far as this request is concerned. We spoke to members of the faculty, the graduate student body, and the Hillman Library professional staff.

We spoke to fifty-seven people from these three groups. Seven people answered in ways we found somewhat difficult to categorize. Their answers were of little help: three said that they did not use Hillman; one said that he seldom uses Hillman and could not remember what he did with his books when he finished with them; three said that they had not noticed such signs in Hillman!

The question asked of the fifty-seven was:

> There are signs in the Hillman Library asking you not to reshelve materials you have used, but instead to leave them on tables or on designated shelves in the stacks. Do you do as requested: Always: Often: Sometimes: Seldom: Never: ?

The fifty answers were as follows: always, two; often, two; sometimes, fifteen; seldom, twenty-seven; never, four. The worst 'offenders' are senior faculty members and, especially, librarians (the latter identified by KS as relatively heavy users). Senior faculty members believe that they are more careful in reshelving than the library employees charged with this task. Librarians have the same feeling and in addition say it would be selfish to impose the extra work on fellow library workers when they, librarians, are perfectly able to reshelve. A typical pattern of use seems to be to go through several books while facing the shelf, reshelving the ones not needed at that moment, or needed only briefly, and to take one, two, or three books or monographs to a table or to the circulation desk -- for note taking, more comfortable reading because of the availability of chairs, or checking out. Some of the books taken to the tables are left there; others are reshelved when the patron goes to the stacks for a fresh 'browse' or fresh supply of books.

As a result of our observations and the above questioning of some library users, we conclude that most faculty members, graduate students, and librarians do not obey the signs, and that collecting the books deposited on tables or designated shelves will not give an accurate view of in-house use. Notably, such a method will fail to capture the browsing function.

It might be said that KS's failure to take into account the browsing function of a library such as Hillman constitutes a failure to recognize a distinction between lending and research libraries. Research libraries are specifically designed to facilitate the in-house, consultative, and browsing aspects of research--thus the 'open stack' design and the placing of faculty and graduate studies, tables, and chairs within Hillman Library.

To conclude, we find that the KS study of in-house use is invalid both in the size of the sample and, even more important, in the way the sample was gathered. It was based on a use pattern which does not exist among significantly large groups of patrons of the Hillman Library, and it drastically underrepresents in-house use of books and monographs there. This leads to two observations. Throughout, KS equates circulation with use. Because of the invalidity of the in-house sample, this repeated assumption/assertion cannot be defended and is, in fact, simplistic and inaccurate. Moreover, taking the 71.3% of 1969 items used, from our previous calculations based on KS, we are confident that an accurate in-house count would bring the percentage of 1969 acquisitions used to well over 80%. We expect that similar figures and percentages would obtain for the use of terms acquired in other years under KS study and for the collections as a whole.

Since KS consistently underestimates book use, KS statistics on costs per use, per item, per LC class, and so on are invalid. These costs must be lower--probably considerably lower--than KS reports them to be.

To sum up, the number of books reported to be <u>available for use</u> at Hillman is uniformly <u>over</u>estimated and the number of books <u>used</u> is uniformly <u>under</u>estimated.

Professor Kent and his associates set out to investigate certain root hypotheses:

> a study was designed to develop measures for determining the extent to which library materials are used and the full cost of such use. It was our expectation that much of the material purchased for a research library was little or never used, and that the costs entailed are beyond ordinary expectations.

Since all biases in KS statistics are consistent with its root hypotheses, we feel that the defects in the methodology and execution of the study of book use at the University of Pittsburgh justify concern about its objectivity.

III

We shall summarize quickly our concerns about the KS study of the use of journals at Pitt.

Our first objection is that it switches backwards and forwards between several sets of baseline data with respect to the number of journals available for use in the libraries examined. In other words base data are inconsistent. Furthermore, it plumps for the highest and most suspect base data. [9]

We feel that the matter of correct data baselines is a serious one and that Professor Kent has not disposed of it by stating in the preface to the <u>Final Report</u> (page iii):

But as the results of the journal study emerged, it became clear that quarrels about baseline data would be un-ending, so we retained our original figures and merely noted the disagreements in footnotes.

This statement does not describe accurately what actually occurred. <u>It is not true that the original data baseline was retained.</u> The original data baseline was 'the list of current subscriptions.' This baseline was changed in the later part of the investigation, and a new data baseline, the list of periodicals/serials holdings, was substituted for it. The new data baseline was available in two versions: the so-called official version and the so-called librarians' version. While both lists are inadequate as data baselines, the first or 'official' one portrays the use of journals at Pitt, and the cost of such use, even more pejoratively and inaccurately than the second (especially in the case of the Bevier or Engineering Library, where the alleged 'official' figure is twice the size of the 'librarians'' figure). Yet to our regret and surprise the 'official' figure is the base utilized in the <u>Final Report</u> (page 59).

Let us now move on to the sampling technique KS employed to measure journal use. We found through observation that its method, using single observers in the engineering and science libraries, could not possibly record the simultaneous use of journals in several stacks and in other library locations (for example, at the duplicating machines), particularly during the heavier hours of attendance. We also assert that the hours of heavier journal usage were not properly determined. KS assumes that the hours of 'heavier journal use' correspond to the hours of heavier library attendance. This is not the case. Moreover, the estimate of the hours of heavier library attendance is based on a sample of seven consecutive days. There is no way in which a pre-sample of seven consecutive days could possibly provide a valid specimen of usage during an academic term, to say nothing of an academic year.

In the case of the chemistry, computer science, and physics libraries, the KS sample fails to capture the behaviour of the faculty members and graduate students. In all three departments the faculty members and graduate students are issued library keys and frequently visit the library during the hours when it is closed to the general public. A faculty member has written us: 'I, myself, use the journals almost exclusively off hours, and I suspect the same is true for many of my colleagues.'

Furthermore, the study of journal use commits several gross logical fallacies. KS uses the term 'sample' in two different senses. In several places it is used in the sense of 'specimen,' that is, 'a part of anything shown as evidence of the number and quality characteristic of the whole.' Thus the figures obtained in various samplings are presented as characteristic of general use and nonuse of journals at Pitt. This customary, but in this case erroneous, interpretation of the term 'sample' provides a basis for dramatic and well publicized statements such as:

> We have been surprised by the extent of non-use of most journals in science and engineering.[10]
>
> Of 298 current journals subscribed to by the Physics Library, only 37 percent (110 titles) accounted for all journal use in the sample.[11]
>
> In Life Sciences ... of a total of 507 journals subscribed to, only 21.5 percent (109 titles) were used during the sample period. Fifty-one journals, 10 percent of the total current collection, provided for 70 percent of all use.[12]
>
> Engineering students use only nine percent of journals bought for them; physics students, only 37 percent; and students of life sciences and psychology, 22 percent.[13]
>
> The most striking observations relate to engineering journals, where 8.4 percent of the total current collection, 58 of 687 titles accounted for all observed journal use.[14]

On the other hand, the Final Report backtracks from these assertions without retracting them (page 63):

> Projecting Yearly Percentage of Usage: By graphing the data (method described in the Appendix), we can project the sample usage into yearly usage. The results show that most of the titles in a collection will eventually be used, but only very few titles will be used a great number of times.
>
> The fact that nearly all titles eventually get used can be seen by considering the percent of the collection having at least two uses of a given title:
>
> | Library | % of Collection Used 2 or more times per year |
> |---|---|
> | Physics | 95.5 |
> | Life Sciences | 97.3 |
> | Engineering | 84.0 |
> | Chemistry | 97.0 |
> | Computer Science | >98.0 |
> | Mathematics | >98.0 |

This is a striking departure from the widely publicized earlier statements about non-use of journals and from the previous definition of the term 'sample.' This procedure of shifting the definition is well known in logic as 'the fallacy of equivocal definition.' It has no place in serious scientific discourse.

The next paragraph changes 'non-use' to 'small usage,' seemingly en passant (Final Report, page 63):

Note, however, that this is based on 'titles used,' not on volumes. A given title will have anywhere from a few to several hundred individual volumes, depending on frequency of publication and the number of years the library has subscribed to it. Seen in this light, a usage of 'at least two times' per title is small usage indeed.

This procedure is well known in logic as 'the fallacy of changing the subject.' Again, it has no place in scientific discourse.

KS is replete with very precise figures about 'the average costs per journal use' (for example, $1.32 in mathematics, $1.83 in physics) (Final Report, page 67) and 'the percentage of the general collection which is used zero times' (for example, 91.7% in mathematics, 88.1% in life sciences) (Final Report, table 34, page 62). The very high level of precision of these figures constitutes a suggestion of their very high level of correctness, a suggestion which is hardly warranted by KS methodology and data. Some statisticians refer to this device as 'the fallacy of spurious precision' or 'the fallacy of unwarranted precision.'

Let us sum up the whole business of journal use and costs in KS:

1/ Since the statistics on the use of journals are inaccurate, the statistics relating the reported total costs of journals to their reported use are also inaccurate.

2/ KS wholly misrepresents the use of science journals at Pitt, and its conclusions and recommendations based on statistics of their use are simply invalid. Some of the recommendations are also based on the assumption that the costs of resource sharing are less than those of local ownership--an admittedly unproven assumption.

3/ There is a strong correlation between KS's root hypotheses concerning the use of journals on the one hand and the biases in its baseline data and sample data on the other. The root hypotheses formulated and tested by KS were, once more:

> And so a study was designed to develop measures for determining the extent to which library materials are used and the full cost of such use. It was our expectation that much of the material purchased for a research library was little or never used, and that the costs entailed are beyond ordinary expectations. [Final Report, page ii; see also Final Report, page 176 and Progress Report (Abstract).]

Again, all biases in KS statistics are consistent with its root hypotheses. As shown above, the statistics on the number of journals available for use are uniformly overestimated, while the statistics on the use of journals are uniformly underestimated. We feel that the defects in the methodology and execution of the study of journal use at Pitt cause legitimate concern about its objectivity.

IV

As shown above, KS's results simply do not support the validity of its root hypotheses, that much of the material purchased for research libraries is little or never used, and that when costs are assigned to uses, the costs of book use are unexpectedly high. Even tailored as they are to a uniform bias, KS's own voluminous statistics do not validate these hypotheses.

Moreover, KS confuses the functions of lending and research libraries. We disagree with the study's assumption that frequency of 'use' is a 'good,' and that measurement of frequency of 'use' leads to a better assessment of how to provide more 'good.' University and research libraries are only partly structured to please the customer. They are also, and very fundamentally, didactic and pedagogical institutions. In spite of failures and discouragements, teachers are devoted to changing or improving the store of knowledge of their students. To use an example, it is verifiable that the most recent novel by Harold Robbins is 'used' many more times than the most popular edition of Kant's Critique of Pure Reason. Public lending libraries should act accordingly, but university libraries should not buy multiple copies of Robbins and relegate Kant to storage.

Similarly we reject KS's definition of the 'benefit' of a journal title as its frequency of use. This assumption is phrased as follows:

> In assessing cost/benefit, this study has defined 'benefit' in terms of actual use of materials, relegating museum (or archive) value to an unaffordable category. [Progress Report, page 3]

This view is simplistic; indeed, it constitutes a claim that the relatively infrequent use of a journal such as Nuclear Physics makes it less beneficial to the user community than very frequently used journals such as Nature and Science. This may be the proper place to point out that it is not a fact that all journal uses are commensurable. There are many significantly different types of journal uses, and each type should have been investigated by appropriate, possibly separate, methods and counted separately. Members of different sets, the proverbial 'apples and oranges,' are not additive. KS counts them together, and this constitutes a serious methodological flaw.

What are the implications for publishers of this study which we have found so wanting? KS states:

The results of the current study also have implications for publishers. Decisions which may be made to reduce the number of publications purchased will lead to reduction of print runs and further price increases for the smaller number of copies which must then carry the burden of the basic publication costs. This, of course, could lead to a price increase spiral. Recommendations have been made that publishers take on the business of 'leasing' their publications, instead of outright sale. The few publishers that have been checked believe this to be an unprofitable approach. Should this turn out to be the case, the implication, other than ceasing publication of some materials, would be to package information products in different, less costly, forms, or changing the nature of the products substantially. [Final Report, page 179]

We maintain that no decisions to reduce the number of publications purchased can be made by libraries on the basis of KS. Moreover, it is important that scholarly publishers examine studies such as KS for themselves. Some clouds are smoke screens.

Let us now move to other studies. The first of these is a replication of KS, with one important difference. KS has been taken and tried out in a small, academic lending library catering mostly to undergraduate students, and there the study has yielded much the same results as the original KS.[15] As stated above, one of our objections to KS is that it confuses the purposes and practices of lending and research libraries. From this comes its total misunderstanding of what goes on during the research process in a research library, in spite of the fact that it was carried out in a research library. (See, for example, our comments on in-house use and browsing). So it is not surprising that when used in a small lending library, where it may well be more appropriate, the KS approach should yield the same result, especially as little attempt was made to correct its methodology or approach to the data.

The replication of one biased study by one or more similarly biased studies does not constitute a validation of the first biased study; nor will such secondary studies close the credibility gap opened by the first.

Moving away from KS and its offspring, we find that two other recent studies present a much more cheerful set of statistics of library use. The implications are happier for both research libraries and scholarly publishers.

A recent study at the library of the University of California, Berkeley, found that in some parts of the collection book use was as high as 94%. Other parts of the collections had reported uses of as high as 80% and 70%. In general, use of materials was over 72%. (Note that this is approximately the circulation figure for books that we found after we had recomputed KS's own data for

1969 book acquisitions. Compare it with KS's 60%.) All this was based on the number of times 'a title was charged out for home use by a patron.' Browsing and other forms of in-house uses apparently were not counted. 16

Even more promising is a most imaginative but little-known study carried out in Newcastle, England. This study, which emphasized in-house use and how to discover it, did not assume or claim, as KS, did, that in-house use was approximately the same as circulation. It attempted to find out more about what really went on in the stacks. A detection slip was placed in a sample of books in the library so that unrecorded in-house use could be spotted. The study agrees with KS that the number of <u>recorded</u> in-house uses seems 'to be very closely associated with <u>circulation</u> figures.' The study, however, concludes as follows:

> It became clear ... that the method of counting in-library uses greatly underestimated the total amount of in-library use, although the extent of the underestimate varied by subject. Although the actual numbers of uses were not counted, it is clear that the number of books being consulted is approximately twenty times as high as those receiving recorded in-library use. Clearly then, any relegation or withdrawal on the basis of recorded in-library uses (combined with issues [circulation]) would result in many books being removed that would otherwise have been consulted.... This does not take account of the nature or seriousness of the consultations, however, and clearly, further elucidation is necessary to discover, in particular, whether the high level of consultation represented use of interesting and relevant stock, or a search for interesting and relevant stock. 17

Here we seem to be in the presence of a genuine attempt to find out what is going on in research libraries. How do users really go about their business? The result is encouraging as far as the relationships between research libraries, their acquisitions, and scholarly publishers are concerned.

To sum up. It is obvious that hard times will continue, and scholarly presses have been doing, and must continue to do, a thorough job of internal reform. Ark building is a wise precaution. But scholarly presses should work more with like-minded associations such as the American Council of Learned Societies and the Association of Research Libraries to defend themselves and to assert their interests. In a similar way, the world of scholarly publishing must scrutinize every apparent cloud to find out if it really holds the threat of a storm. The so-called Pittsburgh Study (KS) of library use is a case in point. There is no need to accept the findings of such a study and to conclude as a result that research libraries will buy fewer books and journals because they are so infrequently used. After scruting the so-called Pittsburgh Study (KS) presents so many biases and flaws that it is highly suspect, to say the least. And, in fact, upon further search, we find that other studies show us that the books so painstakingly produced by presses, and so carefully selected and purchased by research libraries, are used. It is time to go on the offensive.

References

1. For a discussion of the problems and suggestions for the future, see Edward Tripp, 'Small craft warnings,' Scholarly Publishing, vol. 10, no. 2, January 1979, pp. 99-111.
2. Scholarly Communication: The Report of the National Enquiry (Baltimore: The Johns Hopkins University Press, 1979), pp. 3, 4, 5, 128.
3. Ibid., p. 5.
4. Ibid., pp. 29-30.
5. A Cost-Benefit Model of Some Critical Library Operations in Terms of Use of Materials: Final Report by Allen Kent et al. (University of Pittsburgh, 15 April 1978). This report is available from NTIS (microfiche $3.00, printed $10.75) or from Marcel Dekker, New York ($25.00).
6. See the various comments in 'Pittsburgh University Studies of Collection Usage: A symposium,' Journal of Academic Librarianship, May 1979, pp. 60-70. The unchallenging, 'guildist' view which urges the rapid retraining of librarians can be seen in the editorial by John Berry, 'Pitt and the pendulum,' Library Journal, 15 November 1977, p. 2316.
7. See, for example, Tripp's unquestioning acceptance of KS in an otherwise excellent article.
8. Thomas J. Galvin and Allen Kent, 'Use of a university library collection: A progress report on a Pittsburgh study,' Library Journal, 15 November 1977, p. 2317. See also p. 2320, which repeats this assertion, '...purchase decisions are often made in response to campus political pressures.'
9. For more detailed information on this aspect of KS, see Homer I. Bernhardt, 'Pitfalls of the Pitt study,' presented at the American Society for Engineering Education's 37th annual conference, Louisiana State University, Baton Rouge, La., 25-8 June 1979. Available from the American Society for Engineering Education.
10. The KS 'Progress Report' used the same title as A Cost-Benefit Model above and was dated 1 April 1977 (revised 29 April 1977). The quotation is from p. 2.
11. Galvin and Kent, 'Use of a university library collection,' p. 2319.
12. Ibid., pp. 2319-20.
13. 'Pitt study pegs faulty acquisition patterns' (an editorial), Library Journal, July 1977, p. 1438.
14. Galvin and Kent, 'Use of a university library collection,' p. 2320.
15. Harold J. Ettelt, 'Book use at a small (very) community college library,' Library Journal, 15 November 1978, pp. 2314-15.

16. This research was reported by Neal K. Kaske in 'Library utilization studies: Time for comparison, ' Library Journal, 15 March 1979, p. 685.
17. This intriguing and unpretentious study may be found in C. Harris, 'A comparison of issues and in-library use of books, ' Aslib Proceedings, March 1977, pp. 118-26. See especially p. 126.

THE CHIMERA OF PROFESSIONALISM*

Bonnie R. Nelson

The topic I had the least patience for in library school was the debate over whether or not librarianship was a "profession." What does it matter, I argued, whether we are "professionals" or not? Isn't what's important the work we do? It seemed to me that by calling ourselves "professionals" we were saying we were better than the average working person and revealing the elitist, undemocratic side of our natures. My professor was amused, and, I thought, sympathetic. My fellow students were not.

Now, six years later, I find that I am paid considerably less than acquaintances who have fewer academic degrees, that few of my friends have a clear conception of the work I do, and that my colleagues and I endlessly discuss "professional" activities and the proper work for "paraprofessionals." Suddenly, the whole argument no longer seems insignificant. My pride and all my hard work seem to insist that even if my monetary compensation is inadequate, I can at least reward myself with the grand title of "Professional." But what is a profession? When I grapple with the question I am forced back to my original position: professionalism is a false goal.

Defining "profession"

Any good librarian interested in the meaning of a word must at some point turn to the Oxford English Dictionary. Here we find that before 1500 A.D. the verb "profess" was used only in the religious sense. The noun profession has five separate definitions listed before we get to those relating to occupations, which state simply:

> The occupation which one professes to be skilled in and to follow. a) A vocation in which a professed knowledge of some department of learning or science is used in its application to the affairs of others or in the practice of an

---

*Reprinted by permission of the author and publisher from Library Journal, October 1, 1980, p. 2029-33. Published by R.R. Bowker Co. (a Xerox company). Copyright © 1980 by Xerox Corporation.

art founded upon it. Applied spec. to the three learned professions of divinity, law, and medicine.... b) In wider sense: Any calling or occupation by which a person habitually earns his living. Now usually applied to an occupation considered to be socially superior to a trade or handicraft; but formerly, and still in vulgar (or humorous) use, including these.[1]

These definitions point to: the association of professions with learning, their distinction from trades or handicrafts, and the common use of profession in a wider sense for "occupation." However, it is not the dictionaries that define the word "profession" today, but the sociologists. Actually, A. M. Carr-Saunders and P. A. Wilson, in their pioneering work, The Professions (1933), explicitly state that their concern is not to define "profession" (for that they refer their readers to the O. E. D.) but to study the occupations acknowledged to be professions and examine their attributes. They feel that it is probably impossible to draw a dividing line between professions and nonprofessions, but that it is possible to list a "complex of characteristics" that the acknowledged professions seem to have. These include: a prolonged and specialized intellectual training to develop a technique, the use of this technique to perform a service to the community for a fee, a sense of responsibility for the technique, and the development of associations for testing competence and enforcing standards of conduct. They emphasize that some occupations commonly considered professions may lack one or more of these characteristics.[2]

But by the 1950's, sociologists were preoccupied with definitions and limits. Ernest Greenwood, in a 1957 article in Social Work, lists five attributes that he says a profession must possess: 1) a systematic body of knowledge, i.e., "a system of abstract propositions that describe in general terms the classes of phenomena comprising the profession's focus of interest"; 2) professional authority, i.e., the professional dictates what is good for the client; 3) sanction of the community, i.e., the community gives the profession powers and privileges including control over training, licensing, confidentiality, and immunity from community judgment on technical matters; 4) a regulative code of ethics to restrict abuses that might arise from powers of monopoly; 5) a professional culture consisting of the values, norms, and symbols of the profession.[3]

By this time, sociologists like Greenwood were drawing up many such lists of attributes, each one slightly different from the previous, and using them not just to examine the nature of professions, but to test whether or not a particular occupation was a profession. Specifically, Greenwood applied his criteria to social work and concluded that it had already arrived as a profession, and was now merely seeking to rise in the professional hierarchy.

Librarianship: no theory?

William J. Goode applied a similar test in 1961 to the occupation of librarianship--and gave it a failing grade. To be precise, he said it failed the section on "knowledge base"--he could identify no broad theoretical "science" of librarianship, and argued that its absence would prevent the occupation from ever becoming fully professionalized.[4]

Recently, in the late 1960's and early 1970's, other sociologists have criticized this method of studying professions via the "attribute approach." They criticize Greenwood's list of attributes for showing "no relationship to empirical data. For example, many occupations commonly accepted as professions have no systematic theory; ethical codes are frequently breached or even completely ignored.... Sociologists who focus on lists of attributes do not study [the process of professionalization], but participate in it" by inspiring upwardly mobile occupations to measure themselves against the sociologists' criteria and to deliberately create those items necessary to pass all the tests.[5]

Librarianship, for one, has certainly taken these attributes seriously. When the Code of Ethics passed by the American Library Association in 1938 was found wanting, a new code, sounding more professional, was drafted and passed in 1975. A group in the Reference and Adult Services Division of ALA is currently working to draft a code of ethics for reference work. Identifying a theoretical knowledge base for librarianship has been a larger stumbling block. Thomas Shaughnessy recently made a valiant effort to suggest several approaches to developing such an underlying body of knowledge, making the attempt, like others before him, because "the development of underlying theory is absolutely essential if librarianship is to attain full professional status."[6] The goal seems to be not to develop theory for the sake of advancing library work, but for the sake of passing the attribute test for professionalism. (How absurd the picture of Pasteur and Koch developing the germ theory of disease so that sociologists might acknowledge doctors as professionals.) There seems to be no concern for the relevance of these attributes to librarianship.

The ultimate problem with all this, of course, is that sociologists do not really decide which occupations are professions; the public does. What librarians are aiming for is not to have librarianship added to some mythical list of "Occupations Accepted as Professions by the American Sociological Association," but to be accorded the rewards commonly given to those the public considers professionals.

Professionalism and class

The central reward is increased status, or an improved position in the social hierarchy. As we saw in the O.E.D., professions are considered to be different from, and socially superior to, occupations dealing in trade or handicraft. If money were the primary objective of the quest for professionalism, then we would have expected organizations like unions, the major aim of which is improving the earnings of their members, to have had a greater impact on relatively low-paying occupations like librarianship. Yet unions have been resisted--branded as "unprofessional." The underlying objection is that unions are organizations of the wrong class of society. Unions belong to the working class, while professions belong to the upper and middle classes.

A look at the history of professionalization shows very clearly how professionalization has been used by the middle classes to align themselves with the upper classes. In England, for many years the two great professions of medicine and law were split (and, in the law, still are split) between the upper-class groups of physicians and barristers and the middle-class groups of surgeons/apothecaries and solicitors/attorneys. The physicians and barristers were gentlemen and had been to Oxford or Cambridge. There they received a "liberal education"--a good grounding in classical culture, i.e., an education fit for a gentleman and required for professionals. In 19th Century England the lower orders of doctors and lawyers did not have such an education, although in the technical schools they attended they were often better trained than their professional, gentlemen brethren. The surgeons and solicitors took the lead in improving training and standards and, in the case of doctors, finally united with physicians to assume equal status. [7]

In the United States, although class structures were less rigid, a formal "liberal" education was also a basic requirement for entry into the ranks of the professional elites. Universities and their professional schools helped stratify the ranks of society--the longer educated the higher one's social status. Furthermore, by controlling esoteric knowledge which the layman needed, professionals increased their prestige, power, and monetary compensation. Professions were occupational groups trying to rise in the restratification of society produced by the industrial revolution and the triumph of capitalism. Their means of rising was to control the market for their services. [8] As Magali Sarfatti Larson, a sociologist of the history of professionalization, explains:

> The dominant, and almost the unique, meaning of these professional movements was the conquest and assertion of social status.... Adopting--and adapting--the strategies of professionalization fruitfully used by medicine and the law, occupations in structurally different situations sought the rewards of professional status: prestige, as public recognition of collective worth; income, to be translated into respectable middle-class styles of life; and, to defend these rewards, monopolistic closure of access. [9]

There is considerable irony here in the desire of today's aspiring professionals to raise their status by working towards

Libraries and Librarians

professionalism and rejecting unionization. In the United States, perhaps more than in other countries, as Larson says, "income remained the one truly national and unifying criterion of status."[10] To the extent that others judge us by our style of living, we librarians cannot hope to raise our status without higher salaries. Yet we reject agitation primarily for higher salaries as unprofessional. What we seem to be aiming for is a king of genteel poverty.

Low pay & women

A conspicuous reason for the low pay of librarians is that a majority of librarians are women. In the United States, full-time working women earn on the average 58.8 percent of men's full-time salaries[11]--clearly reflecting the low status of women in American society. In the hierarchy of occupations, the ones that sociologists have labelled "semi-professions" are social work, education, and nursing, in which the majority of the practitioners are women.

How can librarianship hope to raise its status when most of its members hold such a low status in the society at large; when, in fact, women were recruited into librarianship precisely because of their low status? Dee Garrison, in the Journal of Social History, admirably examines how librarianship became a female occupation. One of the chief reasons, probably the chief reason, why women were recruited into librarianship in the last quarter of the 19th Century was that they could be employed for lower wages than men. Garrison quotes Justin Winsor, one of the early leaders of librarianship, as stating in 1877:

> In American libraries we set a high value on women's work. They soften our atmosphere, they lighten our labor, they are equal to our work, and for the money they cost--if we must gauge such labor by such rules--they are infinitely better than equivalent salaries will produce of the other sex.[12]

Librarianship was said to be a natural occupation for women. They could use their innate skills to make libraries more homelike, and were temperamentally better suited for tedious, painstaking jobs like cataloging. Furthermore, librarianship emphasized feminine qualities of serving, self-sacrifice, and high-mindedness.

Garrison then goes on to attack women for imbuing librarianship with these same feminine qualities. How can librarianship hope to become a profession when its practitioners are weak, nonassertive, and believe in helping the client get what he wants rather than what is good for him--when they lack a proper professional service ethic?[13] Goode, too, attacks librarians for being too willing to give the client what he wants, rather than what he needs, for not imposing the librarian's "professional categories, conceptions, and authority on the client."[14]

The professional ethic

We should not accept this conception of the professional service ethic without question, since it is not necessarily one that librarians should seek to emulate. The idea that the professional knows what is best for the client is intended to establish the dominance of the professional over the layman, to maintain the mystery of the profession and to keep the layman in ignorance. Burton Bledstein, in The Culture of Professionalism, notes:

> The jurisdictional claim of [professional authority] derived from a special power over worldly experience, a command over the profundities of a discipline. Such masterful command was designed to establish confidence in the mind of the helpless client. The professional person possessed esoteric knowledge about the universe which if withheld from society could cause positive harm.... Laymen were neither prepared to comprehend the mystery of the tasks which professionals performed, nor--more ominously-- were they equipped to pass judgment upon special skills and technical competence. Hence, the culture of professionalism required amateurs to "trust" in the integrity of trained persons, to respect the moral authority of those whose claim to power lay in the sphere of the sacred and the charismatic. Professionals controlled the magic circle of scientific knowledge which only the few, specialized by training and indoctrination, were privileged to enter, but which all in the name of nature's universality were obliged to appreciate.[15]

The image of the professional is decidedly masculine. The professional is in authority, he commands respect, and he has control over a world of knowledge which the layman cannot enter. The librarian's image is feminine: willing to serve and anxious to give the client what he wants. In fact, the librarian is dedicated to making available to the lay public that knowledge which the professional is anxious to control. The professional keeps his client in a subservient position. The librarian respects his client by collecting information, making it available, and instructing the client in how to locate it; the client is assumed to have the intelligence to know what to do with it. The best illustration of the difference in these two attitudes is the recent effort by many different librarians to make medical and legal information more generally available to the public, often inviting the displeasure of those professions.

The concept of the professional as the powerful monopolizer of knowledge is clearly antithetical to librarianship. However, to advance their struggle for professionalism, librarians are urged to be more aggressive, less "nurturant"--in short, more masculine. Jody Newmyer, in the Journal of Library History, describes many studies and reports urging the use of masculinity-feminity personality tests in the admission of library school students and in the hiring of librarians.[16] Carried one step further, this has led to the recruitment of men into librarianship and especially into administrative positions. Library Journal in the 1940's and 1950's is full of advertisements of opportunities for bright young men in various well-paying positions. John Berry, in a 1972 editorial in LJ, described the death of this movement, noting that "many of us fell prey to the notion that the infusion of maleness into the profession would, somehow, bring a new vigor, and more aggressive library administrators."[17]

The most extreme expression of this idea was voiced by Peter Rossi in Library Quarterly, in 1961:

> Women depress the status of an occupation because theirs is a depressed status in the society as a whole, and those occupations in which women are found in large numbers are not seen as seriously competing with other professions for personnel and resources. It is for this reason that professions such as education, social work, and librarianship develop within themselves a division of labor and accompanying status along sex lines. There are few women school superintendents, and I would venture that there are few women heading large academic libraries. Much could be done to raise the status of the entire field by making the division of labor as radical as that accomplished in medicine where nursing is the female occupation and doctoring the male.[18]

To Rossi, the price for making librarianship a profession is to disenfranchise most librarians. Fortunately, this is not a position that librarians support, yet we have been willing to make equally ill-considered jumps through foolish hoops, all in the name of professionalism. We have not been sufficiently critical of the goal itself, even while the public has recently mounted an attack on the ideal of professionalism as exemplified by doctors and lawyers.

A defense of the medical profession by the president of the Westchester County Medical Society in The New York Times of July 23, 1978 listed the various attacks on doctors: malpractice suits, jealousy of doctors' high incomes, complaints about the cost of medical care, and the ideas of national health insurance and health maintenance organizations.[19]

In December 1978, a New York Times editorial applauded the Federal Trade Commission's ruling that parts of the American Medical Association's code of ethics violate the antitrust laws, noting: "The Federal Trade Commission may be threatening 'the very nature of professionalism' but only that portion of it that has clothed lucrative restrictions in the garb of high ethical standards. It is the sort [of professionalism] the nation can no longer afford."[20]

Librarianship can no longer afford to pursue that kind of professionalism, either. It is an elitist conception that doesn't fit with the concepts, once embodied in the Library Bill of Rights, that used to speak of the library as "an institution of education for democratic living." Furthermore, many of the attributes of professionalism are simply not relevant to librarianship.

Stop chasing the chimera

Professionalism, then, is a false goal, and trying to meet the attributes of a profession as laid down by sociologists is a waste of time and energy. But what should our goals be? Should we resign ourselves to low pay and low esteem, and console ourselves with the label "democratic"? Should we cease trying to improve our occupation? The obvious answer, the only answer is "no." The real question is not whether librarianship is a "profession," but rather do we as librarians value our work, do we believe it can be done even better than at present, and do we want to improve it? If our answer to this is "yes," then these are our goals, and the methods to achieve them must be suitable to them. If library education is not perfect then we must improve it to turn out better librarians, not to make it conform to an ideal of "professional" education. If we are not providing the best service we can to our clients, then let's examine what we can do to improve the service, not the "professional" image. If our pay is too low (and it is), then we must consider the most effective way to achieve pay increases, and if we find this to be unionization, then let's unionize.

Finally, if we feel that our services are not valued by society, we must try to improve our services so they will be valued. However, we must recognize that the fault may not lie all within ourselves, but may be inherent in the nature of our society. Knowledge and learning, to which we are so closely allied, are not really respected for their own sake in American society. Even university professors, who by most sociologists' definitions should rank very high in status, are paid only lip service--their income, compared to businessmen or workers in some trades, is poor. And we are a "woman's profession," and as women are not valued, so librarians are not valued. We must continue working to improve the status of women in society and in librarianship. Most of all, we must stop chasing the chimera of professionalism; it is keeping us from the important work at hand.

References

1. A New English Dictionary on Historical Principles, s.v. "profession."
2. Carr-Saunders, A. M. & P. A. Wilson. The Professions (Oxford: Clarendon Pr., 1933), p. 284-287.
3. Greenwood, Earnest, "Attributes of a Profession," Social Work, 2(1957):44-55.
4. Goode, William J., "The Librarian: From Occupation to Profession?," Library Quarterly, 31(1961):306-320.
5. Roth, Julius A., Sheryl K. Ruzek, & Arlene K. Daniels, "Cur-

rent State of the Sociology of Occupations," Sociological Quarterly, 14(1973):310.
6. Shaughnessy, Thomas W., "Theory Building in Librarianship," Journal of Library History, 11(1976):172.
7. For a description of this process see W. J. Reader, Professional Men: The Rise of the Professional Classes in Nineteenth-Century England (Basic Bks, 1966).
8. Larson, Magali Sarfatti. The Rise of Professionalism: A Sociological Analysis (Berkeley: Univ. of California Pr., 1977).
9. Ibid., p. 155.
10. Ibid.
11. U.S. Department of Labor, Bureau of Labor Statistics, U.S. Working Women: A Databook, Bulletin 1977 (GPO, 1977), p. 35.
12. Garrison, Dee, "The Tender Technicians: The Feminization of Public Librarianship, 1876-1905." Journal of Social History, 6(1972-73):133.
13. Ibid., p. 145-146.
14. Goode, "The Librarian," p. 316.
15. Bledstein, Burton J. The Culture of Professionalism: The Middle Class and the Development of Higher Education in America (Norton, 1976), p. 90.
16. Newmeyer, Jody. "The Image of the Librarian: Femininity and Social Control," Journal of Library History, 11(1976): 44-67.
17. Berry, John, "Death of a Movement," Library Journal, 97(1972):3663.
18. Rossi, Peter H., 'Discussion," Library Quarterly, 31(1961): 381.
19. Oppenheimer, Bertram J., "For Doctors, a Call to the Ramparts," The New York Times, July 23, 1978 (Section 22, Westchester Weekly), p. 16.
20. The New York Times, December 6, 1978, p. 24.

PHILOSOPHY OR PRACTICE:

CAN THE REAL WORLD BE FOUND?*

Judith K. Mowery

As I sat staring out my office door, trying to think of some gambit for this column, a book truck squeaked past steered by a student assistant in a red and white t-shirt with "INDIANA" on the chest. "A sign," I thought, since this text concerns itself with a continuing battle for supremacy between a jaded old veteran librarian and her alter ego, a wide-eyed innocent in an Indiana t-shirt. We're both sitting here at our desk, shivering a little and wondering whether the sought-after synthesis, or even symbiosis, will ever occur.

There's nothing really new in this story. As the song goes, it seems we've stood and talked like this before. Or, to paraphrase the Indianapolis weather woman, you've got your academy and you've got your field. Your theory and your applications, your researchers and your practitioners. Your dream and your reality. Sure, OK. So what else can you learn from a library science doctoral program that you haven't already OD'd on during thirteen years on the front lines?

And why, in the first place, should you abandon the security of home, loved ones, and a fixed salary to expose yourself once again to the ravages of student life, replete with cold coffee, cold chicken, cold feet, and the cold discipline of an A- on your pet seminar paper (oh, the deadly minus!)? The best authorities offer three possible excuses for this reckless behavior.

1. You want to teach the future librarians of the world, and they won't let you until you go doctoral (probably).

2. You want an express ticket to a director's office (maybe).

3. You want to DO RESEARCH (hardly likely, but still an option).

---

*Reprinted by permission of the author and publisher from <u>Ohio Library Association Bulletin</u>, 50:3 (July 1980) 23-25.

Worthy ambitions all, who could gainsay it? And yet they only address the end of the ordeal, the ultimate goals that propel otherwise sensible librarians onto the rocky path that leads to a Ph. D.

My purpose here is to praise the path itself, the "process," to use a more trendy noun, by which all that you know and all that you don't know merge with each other, bringing you a few steps closer to perfect wisdom. And although for me the way did lead into a doctoral program, the principle isn't really that narrowly confined.

"Why did you go back to school?" yet another person, one of my students, asked last week.

Well.

I felt obsolete. Dragged, after thirteen years in my profession, into a strange universe of bits and bytes and baud rates, deceptively precious little concepts that were by all indications revolutionizing librarianship, and not, it began to be clear, with much knowledgeable contribution from the great middle mass of practicing librarians (read Me). Changes were undergoing changes, and I, like many colleagues in the public services, was left out. Unable to interpret the technology to my clients and, still worse, unable to interpret my clients to the programmers. Not effecting change, not affecting change. Ignorant, therefore powerless.

True, it wasn't with complete humility that I first walked the halls of Indiana University's Graduate Library School. The thirteen years had to count for something, after all. I was senior by experience to most of the other doctorals in the program, and while they were 1970's graduates, closer in touch with the new librarianship, I wore with some arrogance the scars of wrecked budgets, cramped facilities, failed programs, and stacks flashers. Atlantic City 1969 was an historical note to my new friends, and telling the tale of that long-ago adventure I began to feel a secret kinship to The Ancient Mariner.

But that was the beginning. As the year wore on, I learned to use the lessons of experience gently, as a tempering influence on the ardor with which I came to embrace the new knowledge, the new insights, the old and new theories. And even more important, those long years in the field provided a testing ground for what I was learning; vague problems and issues from the real world back home suddenly were nameable, suddenly dropped like round pegs into the more-or-less round holes of textbook theory.

Thus in the middle of a lecture on organizational behavior I realized, not only why certain personnel problems arise in libraries, but why they must arise, given all we know (or somebody knows) about the way people and organizations interact. Why, I wondered, did I have to come so far to encounter the literature of management, of public administration, of sociology, of psychology?

And more. I learned to attack my own patterns of thinking about the best ways for libraries to do what they do, and even to question why they do it. Not because it would become a director to indulge in such self-analysis, but because no professional can survive without it.

I learned to worry about education for librarianship, not because I hoped to become involved in it one day, but because the library schools are the source of my future colleagues, and on the quality of these colleagues will hinge the ongoing effectiveness of my profession.

I learned to care about (gasp!) statistical techniques and other research methodology, not because I had a dissertation to write and longed to be published sometime, but because critical and intelligent attention paid to existing research could tell me fascinating, useful things about _my_ library, _my_ services, _my_ clientele, yesterday, today, and tomorrow. And, except for the day in statistics class when too much contemplation of probability theory had me poised on the brink of a one-way plunge into infinity, I discovered that chi-square and Pearson's r and ANOVA were not irrelevant mumbo-jumbo but basic tools of the librarian's trade. I learned to use such tools, and to recognize when others used them well or badly.

I was introduced to decision theory, and innovations theory, and systems analysis, and operations research, and for the first time could put the old devil technological revolution in its place, both in the huge context of information science as a field and in the narrow context of one day's work in my office at Bierce Library.

Sitting in that office, I can feel the insistent tendrils of obsolescence sneaking up on me once again. But I have a defense, now, that I gained with the biggest lesson I learned during my year of retreat.

There _is_ a bridge between the real and ideal, and it consists of the willingness, however latent, of working librarians to jettison their cliches, their habits, their assumptions, their complacency, their weariness, or whatever other blinders keep their attention focused on the narrow trail of daily routine. As Auntie Mame was fond of repeating, "Knowledge is Power," and the power to shape our own future can only grow from a probing, questioning, but ultimately receptive exploration of the world outside a single library. Thirteen years, or twenty, or fifty, behind the same desk can render us, not wise, but moribund. Too, the theories and models and research results will languish in useless obscurity unless they are put to the test by canny practitioners.

The field and the academy need each other. No, correct that. They are each other.

Fiat lux.

DOCUMENTARY ART AND THE ROLE OF THE ARCHIVIST*

Hugh A. Taylor

Not long ago I borrowed a book for our youngest daughter from the local university library. She was preparing an essay on the causes of the First World War, and I thought it might be helpful to allow some images to speak for themselves before we became lost among the great armies of words which tramp across the pages of histories. The work I had chosen was an unusually well-illustrated account with captions which not only described but also explained the photographs. Unfortunately I soon discovered that several pages had been cut up, presumably to adorn someone else's project. When I pointed this out to the librarian on duty, her reply was: "We often have this problem, but as long as the text is still there it isn't so bad, is it?"

    This librarian should have been with us last year when President Rundell triumphantly broke with tradition and treated us to an absorbing presentation on photographs as records making their statements, supported by, and not in support of, the historian's text.[1] This year I will try to make a case for treating another form of visual creation as a document worthy of full membership in an archival family that now embraces not only records and manuscripts but also maps, photographs, film, sound, and that formidable nonrecord until recently, machine-readable archives. I wish to bring before you the watercolor and the oil painting, and I would plead for their legitimacy at a time when I believe many of you have grave doubts about these media, for are they not works of art altogether too wayward in conversation for their more staid companions, the record and the manuscript? Most of us have examples of these charming pieces in our repositories, but are not too certain how they fit into our scheme of values. If they are "good," should they go to an art gallery; and if they are not "good," what kind of rating can we give them? I think there is a small voice in all of us which says: "You can't really trust those painter chaps!"

---

*Reprinted by permission of the author and publisher from The American Archivist, 42:4 (October 1979) 417-28; copyright © 1979 by The Society of American Archivists.

Let us try to go back to the beginning of communication between adults in its simplest form. It seems fairly clear that if a message was to be conveyed in a form other than sound and gesture, its form would have been in some way representational of familiar shapes--humans, animals, birds, and the like--which could be scratched in sand or mud and later painted on rock. In recent times, Indian braves recounted their exploits and counted their coups by recording them on teepees and buffalo hides in just this manner.[2] In short, the first statements to survive the sound of a voice were pictures, not words. Out of these simple shapes emerged the pictogram, the ideogram, and the hieroglyph conveying complex information and ideas in brush strokes still carrying the subtle suggestion of a pictorial origin and influencing the thought processes in a most distinctive way. The loss of this image base before the onset of the phonetic alphabet seems to have had a profound effect on literate society in the West, and the consequent linear stress was further intensified from the fifteenth century onwards by Gutenberg's invention of printing from movable type.[3] What became of the picture?

The craftsmen of ancient Greece, for want of a more flexible medium, executed some of their finest pictorial work on their black and red figure vases, and painted miniatures on glass worked with gold leaf. We can trace a continuous line from this tradition to the illuminated manuscript[4] and the transcendent historiated initials in the psalters of the Middle Ages. These works were designed to be explored through touch, as the vase is raised or the page turned. They were used in elaborate ceremonies which engaged all the senses. Above all, they were not just to be looked at. Such images retained their central place in communication sacred and profane, from which text and voice were never far away. From earliest times the artists had accepted the challenge of building narrative into a basically static form of expression. Few secular examples remain, but the eleventh-century Bayeux Tapestry, protected by the authority of a great abbey church, has survived as one of the finest pictorial documents of the early Middle Ages, essential for an understanding of the Norman Conquest of England. Incidents are elided with great skill, as the narrative is developed in the manner of a strip cartoon.[5] Again, one cannot omit the mosaics of Byzantium glowing and flickering in their vaults, to be matched later by the stained glass of Chartres and York, enveloping the court and the church in total environments of color, design, and record.

Without this wealth of iconography we would know little of the appearance of things during those centuries. The biblical narratives and the lives of the saints were communicated in a mythic way, in "modern dress," and an all-at-onceness which can still be experienced in medieval churches to this day. This has been termed acoustic space, which we are now re-experiencing through the instantaneous communication of electronic media and the reaffirmation of all the human senses through both sides of the brain. This acoustic experience was to be totally at variance with Renaissance tradition in which text and image parted company and developed quite literally along their own lines. Paintings became "works of art" and have remained so. As such they were not regarded as documents in any sense, for documentation as we know it became the prerogative of such textual records as the printed book, the enrolment, the deposition, the letter, and the diary. Even seals, those wonderful, visual, tactile expressions of status which were appended to all medieval conveyances of land, lost their significance with the increasing use of signatures by the literate. In England, the symbol of the sovereign's authority through image and seal, rather than sign manual, was retained only for royal letters patent, a reminder of an ancient usage in a world of print and literacy.

In this harsh, geometric world of continuous space bound by the laws of Euclid and the philosophy of Descartes, which limited the spectator to a fixed point of view, the great machine of passing time slowly revolved. Historians prowled happily amongst the gears and levers, showing us more or less how it all worked, and used as their blueprints those textual records which by the end of the nineteenth century abounded in the archives of Europe and America. The more they found, the better the past could apparently be explained; but the cumulative effect was asymptotic. They never quite got there; scientific history proved to be a delusion, and we now turn to the more human disciplines of archeology, anthropology, folklore studies, and the "new" history, seeking pattern and process within a field rather than cause and effect along a continuum. Textual records have been supplemented and at times even replaced by the whole range of oral and visual media, with which we have now become familiar. In an almost tactile approach to data, the electronic scanner of the cathode ray tube and the selective process of the computer become an extension of ourselves in our search strategy and have helped us to appreciate visual configuration in a new way, not just as illustration in support of text but as a pattern of record in its own right capable of making statements far beyond the power of speech and writing. We must now examine more closely these visual media of record.

First, we should recognise that archival principles, as we know them, were formulated and developed by scholarly bureaucrats from a careful study of textual public records based on the registry and the filing cabinet, and this is reflected in our stewardship over the past century. Non-textual material showed little evidence of a time series and obstinately resisted an original order between inclusive dates. Repositories are filled with map collections, for instance, arranged by size and geographic area with little attention to provenance; the map record group is still comparatively rare. Likewise, photographs were long ignored as records in the archival sense, and collections were plundered for unusual illustrations or, more mercifully, allowed to gather dust pending more enlightened treatment. We now preserve the sanctity of the photographic collection and maintain the photographer's order based on his records, if this is possible. Photographs have joined the family. Film, on the other hand, preserves its original order at twenty-four frames a second. Although film archives tend to operate more like special libraries, the fundamentally documentary nature of a wide range of film, including some feature films, is now clearly recognized, and copyright laws enforce a meticulous record of provenance.

There remains one group of media for which no crisp generic term exists, which include paintings, drawings, prints and occasionally posters, seals, and medals. The term iconography is sometimes used, and I might have included it in my title rather than art, which can be a rather loaded word. For the most part, we do not harbor works of art in our archives in the sense that an art curator or historian would use the term, i.e., as works important primarily as paintings in their own right rather than as documents. We give house room to documentary art or iconography, and we control it after a fashion, so that it can be retrieved, but do we really believe it to be archival? With archivists, like latter-day Noahs, welcoming documents of every kind, nature, and description into their arks, it is time that we gave some thought to the matter. I am limiting my paper to drawings and paintings in oil and watercolor, but much of what is said applies to the other pictorial categories.

Perhaps we can first agree that a picture is a statement in the same way as is an entry in a diary or a paragraph in a letter.

> No other kind of relic or text from the past can offer such a direct testimony about the world which surrounded other people at other times. In this respect, images are more precise and richer than literature. 6

But this is also art, and at once we become nervous.

> If the painter does nothing but render exactly, by means of line and color, the external aspect of an object, he yet always adds to this purely formal reproduction something inexpressible. 7

To those brought up on history written entirely from textual records, the written word has a certain respectability, a deceptive precision, a convincing plausibility that masks its limitations. In a similar way, "most of us regard print as the familiar, comfortable, rumpled dressing gown of communications. We take print for granted."8 We still communicate with words, not pictures (unless we are nonsmokers looking for a washroom), so naturally we feel more at home with them. We believe we can depend on them, and our very literacy blinds us to other modes of expression, even speech itself. But historians and archivists are also very well aware that textual sources can be biased, inaccurate, selective, and downright misleading, but they have one great merit: their content is presented serially, within time, through grammatical statements and logical arguments. Likewise, our literary training has often caused us to "read" pictures "literally" without being aware of certain rules and conventions that are in sharp contrast to the rules of alphabet, grammar, and syntax. How then, should we as archivists approach pictorial art?

In early classical antiquity the Latin ars meant a craft or skill; the modern concept of art was a product of the Renaissance.[9] Non-literate cultures have no art, they simply do their best. Ars in mediaeval Latin became book learning, the liberal arts. Fine arts emerged in the eighteenth century as les beaux arts, which in English became simply art, a century later. In short, art, as we know it, is of relatively recent origin, and as archivists we may do well to consider painting not as art in the nineteenth-century sense, since we will rarely deal in masterpieces, but as the product of a craftsman who has learnt the business as professional or amateur painter, much as fine writing was learnt from the writing master. For Malraux, these are "non-artists" who produce at best "a memory, a sigh or a story; never a work of art. Obviously, a memory of love is not a poem, a deposition given in court is not a novel, a family miniature is not a picture."[10] But all of these can provide reliable records.

Writing, with its origin in the pictogram, may be regarded as a highly stylized form of painting and the word style is derived from the stylus of the scribe. Let me again be clear that I am not denying creative excellence as expressed by the term work of art or the creativity of the great artists who quite transcended their teachers. If we have to consider any of these works from a documentary point of view, we will need all the help we can get from gallery curators and art historians. However, that such a work is a masterpiece should in no way affect its status as a record; it may reveal insights on a level which a lesser artist could not convey, and so increase its value for us. (As an aside, I cannot resist reminding you that every M.A. thesis submitted is a "masterpiece" in its ancient but scarcely in its modern sense.)

Let us now see whether drawings and paintings meet the criteria we apply as tests of archival material. First, we must try to establish authenticity. As with public records, a continuous period of unbroken custody is valuable (but not conclusive) evidence, and over-painting is a real possibility. However, no one forges the second rate or tampers with laundry lists. We can take comfort in the relative obscurity of much that we hold.

A picture may be authentic, but how do we assess its evidential or informational value? If works of art are to be considered as documents, then we have to grapple with the concept of representation which lies at the heart of the problem. Many artists in our collection will imitate styles, especially those of their teachers, but there is no way they can imitate or provide a mirror image of their subjects.[11] We are dealing with an order of truth somewhat different from the compilation of an inventory. We can, however, usually reckon that the artist is not out to deceive by adding significant elements which do not exist in the subject. This does not mean that a painting will look exactly like its subject, but that it will convey and suggest truthful comment as perceived by the artist as observer, which is as much as we can expect from any observer. The caption may, however, be misleading, but this may not be the fault of the artist. We have to recognize that in all representational painting, as in correspondence or report writing, there is selection and omission. This is also how archivists appraise and select records for permanent retention. Even the camera is highly selective, especially in tonal range, and may omit color altogether.

To communicate in a representational manner, the artist must also use techniques acceptable to the viewer if an accurate report is to be conveyed. The language must be understood.

> Up to a point this is done by representing the object literally; but beyond that point it is done by skilful departure from literal representation ... and thus ... produces in one's audience the kind of effect one wants to produce.[12]

We have recently been reminded that the aesthetic of the picturesque, so popular with the early Victorians, was in origin more practical and realistic than we now tend to think, and was closely bound up with the making of an accurate record. The Reverend William Gilpin, champion of the picturesque in England, once wrote: "Your intention in taking views from nature may either be to fix them in your own memory or to convey in some degree your idea to others,"[13] which is precisely the visual aid provided by the modern snapshot.

We must now ask ourselves whether, in the case of a streetscape, for instance, we can isolate topographical fact from the formal conventions of composition with which the artist unifies his work and communicates with the viewer. There are those who would still argue that art and fact are in conflict, but this is true only if one restricts fact to a mirror image of reality, a goal as unattainable as that of "what actually happened" in historical research. Many of the early views of Halifax, Nova Scotia, in the eighteenth century show Citadel Hill more pronounced than it really is, but that may be a way of emphasizing the importance of the hill for the inhabitants and for the military garrison stationed there.

If we are to admit the archival legitimacy of documentary art, we should make a study of those artists who left a record of the territory within our jurisdictions and become familiar with their artistic language and form. Nova Scotia, along with other parts of Canada, is indebted to the work of army and navy officers from Britain for much of the visual record before photography. For purposes of military intelligence they were taught to draw and paint in watercolors as part of their training. Their drawing masters at the military academies included David Cox (1783-1849) and Paul Sandby (1725-1809), who "created the norm for half of the watercolor painting of his time";[14] both were outstanding artists of the English watercolor school. A certain military precision was emphasized and, to aid the neophyte, definite drill sequences for making a watercolor were devised.[15]

The artists painted the world of colonial peace, order, and good government, which they knew best. A fair number of their neat sketches were subsequently published for the comfort and enjoyment of the upper classes. Trade, commerce, factories, and poverty were not fit subjects for art. By contrast, the tradition in the United States was much more down to earth, and commercial enterprise was often recorded by local craftsmen. Travellers, writing in their journals or in letters home, gave the lie to this over-tidy vision of Canada, as did one artist himself when he exchanged the brush for the pen.[16] In general their work was not intended to deceive; it was simply selective in theme and content, and we must be aware of these limitations. An outstanding artist in this group was James Pattison Cockburn, whose record in watercolors of early nineteenth-century Quebec, is unrivalled. To enhance their accuracy he used a camera lucida and placed his buildings in their correct relationships.[17]

Whereas prose is created serially, artists put together their information organically as they build up their compositions. If one substitutes for brush strokes pieces of information on paper, this is also how the documents of an organization accumulate in their groups, series, and subseries, like the secretions of an organism growing more complex and richer in information with the passage of time. We are trained to recognize this pattern of growth, and we should perhaps look at paintings in this manner, as we identify the various elements and their interrelationships to achieve certain effects, in much the same way as our institutions are, or should be, designed to perform a function and leave their paperwork in a configuration which reflects this function.

Artists develop their carefully learned schema, such as the shape of various trees or stock attitudes for figures, modifying them and integrating them into their work or, if they are exceptional, transcend these schema altogether.[18] In this sense they are using figures of paint rather than figures of speech to describe a scene, and this is particularly true of those topographical artists who are thoroughly competent but do not attain the first rank. In this regard Etienne Gilson distinguishes helpfully between painting and what he calls "picturing" or the art of "doing pictures" and goes on to say:

> We do not intend to minimize the importance of pictures or images. On the contrary, if one succeeded in introducing a distinction between pictures and paintings that looks so well founded, pictures would benefit by it as much as paintings. We need a history and an aesthetics of the art of picturing conceived in a spirit of sympathetic objectivity suitable to the importance of the subject.[19]

Rudolf Arnheim suggests that artistic activity and visual thinking can be thoroughly rational.[20] We conceptualize and organize our thoughts around categories, stereotypes, and well-established concepts, which act as comfortable pigeon holes for the initial rough sort of our ideas. This is much the same process as form-filling, and we use the same term, form, in art to denote the deployment of the various elements in a picture. Similarly, the term form is used with legal records in such phrases as "common form," which are in fact groups of standardized legal schema which help tell us (at great length) what the document is about. Likewise formularies were whole books of schema for those drawing up title deeds and similar documents. Forms management may reduce a multiplicity of schema to a common form; form letters are built up from common form statements to give the appearance of uniqueness and spontaneity. The study of diplomatic is the study of forms as a clue to the nature, purpose, and date of early documents.

Although the "life of forms" is a familiar concept in art, this comparison may appear somewhat forced, but I believe it helps us to recognize the documentary nature of works of art. So much of our seeing is a matter of habit and the expectation of the familiar: "The visual arts are a compromise between what we see and what we know."[21] We read the first letters only of a scribbled word and conceptualize the rest, a practice which is most useful in paleography or deciphering poor handwriting, as we all know.

Winston Churchill, a very competent painter who was as familiar as any man with public records and communication, spoke of the artist turning light into paint via the post office of the mind which directs encoded pigment onto the canvas in the form of a cryptogram; the pattern only becomes clear when all the paint is in place.[22] He uses code here as a metaphor, yet the halftone block, the "wire" photograph, and the television screen rely on the code of a pattern of dots from which to build up the image. Seurat did much the same, and so do many of the magic realists of today. If we are to use pictures as record, we must recognize the pattern and read the code correctly as we do in other media.

If, then, art is conceptual, documentary art cannot be true or false, but only more or less useful and reliable for the formation of descriptions. Information reaching the eye is so dense and complex that our awareness must in self-defense select in order to conceptualize, and the history of art is the painful development of conventions through schema and modification. "If we shed any instinctively or throw them out deliberately, either they are replaced before too long or we fall back into private universes, self-immured, incommunicado."[23] Without communication there can be no record.

Finally, we should consider whether the output or collected work of an artist has an organically related quality we can recognize as archival. Let us take some examples: sketches within or attached to correspondence or a report present no problem, largely because textual records are classically archival and lend their archival quality to their attachments, like the label on Jenkinson's elephant. Sketches in a notebook with captions by the artist are probably the closest parallel to a diary, and these too would be accepted in most instances as archival, especially if they are dated. With

loose and perhaps unfinished drawings or sketches of a work to be
completed in the studio, we leave familiar ground but they are statements just the same. And so we come to the easel painting itself,
and I hope that what I have been saying will help us to see this too
as a record whereby the finished works of an artist may be considered as documents. The fact that they have been sold and are
scattered half around the world is irrelevant, provided they have
been authenticated. Some public documents and many manuscript
collections have been dispersed in this way, to be reconstituted on
paper and by the exchange of microforms.

For those archivists who have patiently borne with me up to
now, this last paragraph may well break the back of their patience!

Are all paintings, then, to be regarded as documentary record? At this point common sense must prevail, but let it be the
sensum communis which engages all our senses and faculties.
Clearly we must try to distinguish between an artist's personal record expressed through the painting in non-representational terms, or
a work of art which has no point of reference with the world of appearances, and the kind of documentary art which seeks primarily
to record, using this expression in its widest sense to encompass
paintings which may only remotely look like their subjects but express other qualities, in particular the creation of profound generalized statements about their subjects.

For Malraux the final liberation of painting came when the
artist was able to express his work and his subjects solely in paint,
and not with paint subservient to a recognizable image or story.[24]
Perhaps this is the point where art ceases to be a document that
may be used for documentary content in the archival sense. In any
case, documentary content may be quite irrelevant to the painting as
a work of art. As with many administrative documents, it is to be
used by the archivist for a purpose for which it was not created,
but for which it is perfectly valid. We must, however, still be
cautious, because the development of an artist as expressed in all
of his work is obviously an autobiographical record, of a kind.
Must we then take over all the art galleries; and anyway, why stop
at painting? Why not sculpture and ceramics? The line is by no
means clear-cut and points up the dilemma of a culture that distinguishes art from record in an uneasy dichotomy.

Sometime ago the Public Archives of Canada presented the
retrospective of an artist who had emigrated from Europe to Canada
many years ago. Here was the record by an artist of what it
meant to be an immigrant in Canada, and so it was presented jointly
by the National Ethnic Archives and the Picture Division, both of
the Public Archives. There was not much explicit Canadian content
in the pictorial sense, yet it seemed to me a valid record of an
artist's experience in an entirely non-textual form. Not everyone
agreed, but I believe the point was worth making, if only once.[25]
The retrospective exhibit is, of course, a commonplace in art galleries; but it may also be seen as an archival occasion.

In practical terms we must take a more arbitrary, pragmatic approach to the problem. We accept thankfully that there are art galleries staffed by curators and historians whose concern is with art and excellence, but we, and they, must realize that galleries are rich in visual documentary material such as we have been discussing, and that, because content is not the primary concern of the curator, information retrieval of a documentary nature may be difficult. It is significant that the rediscovery by both curators and archivists involved with the military artists, whose record of early Canada is so remarkable, has resulted in much closer relations between the two professions. Perhaps each will take on some of the characteristics of the other, with the archivist identifying the documentary record wherever it may be and ensuring that this aspect of works of art is fully appreciated.

I have said nothing of genre painting, which is analagous to anecdote, narrative, and literature[26] and may also be designed as illustration. Despite the apparently accurate observation of place and period which may be displayed, the archivist should be very cautious in regarding these documents in the same sense as topographical drawings. They are probably best regarded as the pictorial counterpart of literary manuscripts.[27]

There is one category of documentary art which would seem to have all the attributes of public record, yet scarcely ever finds its way into an archives. Governments in two World Wars have commissioned war artists to prepare records in their own fashion of this most intense of national experiences. There is ample evidence that, despite vast photographic coverage, the artists' contributions were appreciated, if only, at worst, as an arm of propaganda. In general, these artists were permitted a free hand and the total output was quite naturally somewhat uneven. Yet once the wars were over, most of this material found little response anywhere and was bundled into the vaults of reluctant galleries and museums, there to be neglected for years; because, good or bad, it was identified as art before it could be processed as document. Was it because archives laid no claim? This example is cited not to point the finger, but to point up the problem.

It may have struck you as rather strange that I should have spent so much time discussing iconography in classical archival terms, based on textual record. The reverse procedure might provide some interesting observations on manuscripts, which must wait for another time. Sufficient that our increasingly multi-media view of archives is already modifying principles, especially those based on the serial nature of archives. Machine-readable records cannot be viewed in this serial way, and the storage of this information in the computer, when it periodically leaves the tape, is chaotic by human standards.

We must look to future technology, such as the videodisc, for the simultaneous retrieval of multi-media information in the televisual mode with a wide range of "hold" and "browse" capabilities. Picture

as record will then be available with text and sound to provide us
with a balanced media fare. Meanwhile, I believe closer attention
should be given to the reproduction of documentary art through increasing use of slides and microfiche. In this way the fonds of an
artist's output can be assembled through adequate reproduction.
This is what André Malraux is saying in his concept of the "museum
without walls, " by which we may study the entire work of an artist
and make comparisons with all styles and all ages, in a manner once
totally impossible, with some surprising results. The colored
microfiche series, published by the Public Archives of Canada, of
the works of the artists in its collections are a means to this end
and are the direct counterpart of a microfilm edition of a manuscript
collection.

We can catch a glimpse of how records, both textual and pictorial, may be used as evidence and woven into a non-linear presentation, by studying the precepts of Jacob Burckhardt who writes
that only "long and intensive exercises in viewing, the constant par-
allelizing of facts, the laborious steeping in best sources can develop the all important sense of style and awareness of the typical. "[28]
Because he sought to make general statements, he refused to use
concrete images merely as illustration, and yet his command of
words was such that "he could teach art history and lecture on painting and architecture, when projectors and other 'visual aids' were
still largely unavailable. "[29] Like Burckhardt, many of the so-
called new historians are now presenting their history without heroes
in a similar way, and increasingly they need the records of pattern
rather than of achievement for their findings. We archivists should
spend more time looking at pictures if we are to become what we
behold and grasp the true nature of record in all its richness of
form, substance, and texture.

In this brief survey, I have only touched on the problem. We
need to explore the nature of documentary information in the context
of all media of record and to realize that in iconography we have a
great deal to learn from our colleagues, the art curators. At the
same time I would suggest that the present methods of identification
and cataloging of works of art by curators are curiously literary and
oriented toward externals. Entries tell us a great deal about the
physical nature of the painting as artifact, the exhibits in which it
has featured, and (if possible) its impeccable record of provenance,
yet there is often little about the work itself beyond its title or caption, which may be less than helpful. Of course, it can be argued
that the researcher should then view the original or a good copy.
But what if the line of enquiry is, for instance, concerned with form
or detail not related to the information on the catalog card? We
must all learn to describe pictorial content in words if we are to
retrieve it.

Estelle Jussim, a library school teacher by profession, in an
invaluable article on the subject,[30] uses the term "visual information" to describe the visual content of documents and, following
Bernard Karpel, argues for descriptions taken from the language of

art theory and from those who are accustomed to describe art in words. This whole subject is, of course, even more urgent in the context of automated systems of retrieval.

Again, we must try to define more clearly the roles of the archives and the art gallery as repositories, for it makes little sense if galleries are to retain, by implication, the privilege of creaming off all that is excellent and leave archives to deal with the second rate. In fact, and to our credit, archivists have assiduously cultivated the acquisition of the second rate on the correct assumption that in documentary art Oscar Wilde's aphorism that "if a thing is worth doing, it is worth doing badly" holds true; their subsequent discovery by galleries has sometimes left near masterpieces on our hands as the bad turns out to be primitive or folk art. I offer no solutions, but hope you will see that we have a problem here.

I would like to end on a more general note. Barrington Nevitt, a management consultant with a background in communications and a colleague of Marshall McLuhan, challenged the Association of Canadian Archivists last year by asking a number of searching questions which he believed we should face, including the following:

> Has the archivist as communicator yet learned to anticipate the effects of media on his publics?

and in reference to McLuhan's comment that "ever since Burckhardt saw that the meaning of Machiavelli's method was to turn the state into a work of art by the rational manipulation of power, it has been an open possibility to apply the method of art analysis to the critical evaluation of society":[31]

> Has the archivist as art critic yet learned to recognize the 'text' which evokes the context of their times--what to keep and what to destroy?[32]

The study of documentary iconography will not only help us extend our range, it may also enable us to develop the faculty of the artist to program effects and recognize new patterns within an information environment, where process and change have eroded old rules and verities. Only then will we assume once more the role of shaman which the ancient keepers of records knew so well. To perceive, by projection, the future patterns of our documentary galaxy, and to act in the light of this knowledge, must be our awesome task.[33]

This article is the presidential address delivered on 27 September 1979, in Chicago, Illinois, at the Palmer House, to the Society of American Archivists at their forty-third annual meeting.

References

1. Walter Rundell, Jr., "Photographs as Historical Evidence: Early Texas Oil," American Archivist 41 (October 1978): 373-91.
2. Barry Lord, The History of Painting in Canada (Toronto: New Canada Publications, NC Press, 1974), pp. 12-13.
3. Marshall McLuhan, The Gutenberg Galaxy (Toronto: University of Toronto Press, 1968), passim.
4. McLuhan, Gutenberg Galaxy, p. 78.
5. Otto Pächt, The Rise of Pictorial Narrative in Twelfth-Century England (Oxford, England: Clarendon Press, 1962), p. 10.
6. John Berger, Ways of Seeing (Harmondsworth, England: Penguin Books, 1976), p. 10.
7. J. Huizinga, The Waning of the Middle Ages (London: Edward Arnold, 1970), p. 253.
8. Donald R. Gordon, "Print as a Visual Medium," in Lester Asheim and Sara I. Fenwick, eds., Differentiating the Media (Chicago: University of Chicago Press, 1974), p. 34.
9. R. G. Collingwood, The Principles of Art (Oxford: Oxford University Press, 1938), p. 5.
10. André Malraux, The Psychology of Art, Vol. 2, The Creative Act (New York: Pantheon Books, 1949), p. 73.
11. Collingwood, Principles of Art, p. 42.
12. Ibid., p. 53.
13. As quoted in Michael Bell and W. Martha E. Cooke, The Last "Lion" ... Rambles in Quebec with James Pattison Cockburn (Kingston, Ontario: Agnes Etherington Art Centre, 1978), p. 12.
14. Graham Reynolds, A Concise History of Watercolours (London: Thames & Hudson, Ltd., 1971), p. 55.
15. Paul Duval, Canadian Watercolour Painting (Toronto: Burns & MacEachern, Ltd., 1954), text unpaginated. Duval quotes one of these systems.
16. See Mary Sparling, "The British Vision in Nova Scotia, 1749-1848" (unpublished M.A. thesis, Dalhousie University, Halifax, N.S.) for an excellent study of this theme. For a well-illustrated survey of early Canadian topographical art, matched with contemporary textual description, see Michael Bell, Painters in a New Land (Toronto: McClelland & Stewart, Ltd., 1973).
17. Christina Cameron and Jean Trudel, The Drawings of James Cockburn: A Visit Through Quebec's Past (Agincourt, Ontario: Gage Educational Publishing, Ltd., 1976), Introduction.
18. E. H. Gombrich, Art and Illusion (Princeton, N.J.: Princeton University Press, 1972), chapter 5, "Formula and Experience," pp. 146-78.
19. Etienne Gilson, Painting and Reality (London: Routledge & Kegan Paul, Ltd., 1958), p. 261.
20. Rudolph Arnheim, Visual Thinking (Berkeley: University of California Press, 1969), p. v.
21. Bernard Berenson, Seeing and Knowing (London: Chapman & Hall, Ltd., 1953), p. 14.

Libraries and Librarians

22. Gombrich, Art and Illusion, p. 38.
23. Berenson, Seeing and Knowing, p. 11.
24. Malraux, The Psychology of Art, Vol. 1, Museum Without Walls, p. 73.
25. Public Archives of Canada, Karl May Retrospective, 1948-1975 (Ottawa: Public Archives of Canada, 1976), 62 pp.
26. Sacheverell Sitwell, Narrative Pictures: A Survey of English Genre and Its Painters (New York: Benjamin Blom, Inc., 1972), p. 1.
27. What appears to be the only paper ever published by the Canadian Historical Review (CHR) on historical iconography is "The Visual Reconstruction of History," by Jefferys (CHR 17, no. 3 [1936]: 249-65), who discusses the whole question of accuracy in Canadian historical painting and illustration. As a competent artist and illustrator himself, his observations are particularly valuable.
28. Karl J. Weintraub, Visions of Culture (Chicago: University of Chicago Press, 1966), p. 153.
29. Ibid., p. 155.
30. Estelle Jussim, "The Research Uses of Visual Information," Library Trends 25, no. 4 (April 1977): 763-78.
31. Marshall McLuhan, The Mechanical Bride (New York: Vanguard Press, 1951), p. vi.
32. H. J. Barrington Nevitt, "Archivist and Comprehensivist," unpublished paper, 1978, pp. 3, 6.
33. Since most of the examples of documentary art which have been discussed above are Canadian, I would not like to close without special mention of Robert V. Hine whose Bartlett's West: Drawing the Mexican Boundary (New Haven: Yale University Press, 1968) and The American West: An Interpretive History (Boston: Little, Brown and Co., 1973) strongly emphasize the pictorial record.

AFTERMATH OF A CRUSADE: WORLD WAR I
AND THE ENLARGED PROGRAM OF
THE AMERICAN LIBRARY ASSOCIATION*

Arthur P. Young

Prelude

When, in the summer of 1914, an assassin's bullet ended the life of Archduke Francis Ferdinand in Sarajevo, Bosnia, few Americans believed that the incident would trigger the catastrophic conflict familiarly known as World War I or, simply, the Great War. For almost three years, President Wilson pursued a progressively difficult policy of neutrality toward the warring parties, but the continuing threat of Germany's submarine warfare and the very real possibility that western Europe might fall persuaded Wilson and his advisers in April 1917 that America must declare war and join the Allies. That decision had momentous implications for the nation, including the American Library Association (ALA).

    For most Americans, the war became a morally charged, even spiritualized, struggle against the tyranny of German autocracy. Librarians, too, readily embraced the patriotic emotionalism and were eager to contribute their services to the war effort. A significant contribution by ALA was not foreordained by its history. Between 1876 and 1917, the association had made modest gains in defining the field of librarianship and convincing the public of the library's educational value. To accept responsibility for a program of library service to an American army of several million men did not seem probable for an organization of 3,300 members which operated on an annual budget of $24,000. But when the opportunity arose, the association boldly accepted the challenge--and succeeded beyond expectation.

    Shortly after the American declaration of war, ALA established a War Service Committee to explore the type and extent of

---

*Reprinted by permission of the author and publisher from Library Quarterly, 50:2 (April 1980) 191-207; copyright © 1980 by The University of Chicago.

assistance which it might be able to provide. This committee, in June 1917, accepted an invitation from the War Department's Commission on Training Camp Activities to furnish library materials and services to U.S. soldiers throughout the world. The association was one of the seven welfare groups affiliated with the commission. ALA's wartime program, designated the Library War Service, was directed by Herbert Putnam, Librarian of Congress, and later by Carl H. Milam, the future secretary of the association. Between 1917 and 1920, ALA mounted two financial campaigns and raised $5 million from public donations, erected thirty-six camp library buildings from Carnegie Corporation funds, and distributed 10 million books and magazines to over 5,000 locations. Nearly 1,200 persons worked in military libraries administered by ALA.

Librarians, by their zealous promotion of libraries as educational centers and agencies of social reformation, were engaged in what may be considered a global book crusade. For a brief time the crusade transformed ALA from a relatively unknown professional society into a public service organization with national aspirations for leadership and service. The episode of the Library War Service proved to many librarians and civilan leaders that the association could mobilize the resources of the nation's libraries and perform a difficult task with distinction. The results were gratifying. The military departments assimilated the library programs and continued them after the war, the association's headquarters library in France continued as the American Library in Paris, and the war influenced subsequent directions of ALA in the areas of adult education and international cooperation. Above all, the association savored the public recognition that it had sought for so long. That exhilarating experience, in turn, led prominent leaders of the association to sponsor a project known as the Enlarged Program. The story begins several months after the Armistice [1, passim].*

Postwar Aspirations

Apathy, despair, and a "return to normalcy" would follow soon enough after the Armistice; but the mood did not change precipitously. During the immediate postwar months, the nation experienced a period of buoyant expectation. America's future seemed to be on everyone's agenda. Optimism abounded, especially among religious, social, and professional organizations. Now was the propitious moment, many reformers believed, to capitalize on the moral enthusiasm and cooperative spirit unleashed by war. Under the rubric of reconstruction, many ideas and proposals were advanced relating to social justice, economic security, and political reformation [2, pp. 31-45].

Talk was plentiful, but it was not easy to discern a coherent direction. Some viewed reconstruction as a vehicle for spiritual

---

*For an extended treatment of ALA during World War I, consult Young [1].

regeneration, others saw it as an opportunity to revamp the economic system, and still others interpreted it to mean the redistribution of political power. Beneath the cascade of activist rhetoric, however, was a common set of postulates. History was an exploitive process, a continuing tyranny of the few over the many. America was at the threshold of an egalitarian age, and all citizens should enjoy the benefits of modern technology. Certain political, social, and economic imbalances needed correction, and there was a consensus that the transition could be accomplished peaceably. The unfinished agenda would be realized through increased voluntary cooperation and, preferably, through expanded regulatory actions of the government [3, pp. 352-53].

Birth of the Enlarged Program

The reconstruction program of the American Library Association, designated the Enlarged Program, began as a modest proposal for a library survey. In a few months, this project was transformed into a major commitment to organizational change and expanded library services. In many respects, the Enlarged Program was a microcosm of postwar reconstructionism. Leaders of the Enlarged Program emphasized the role of books and libraries as instrumentalities for social betterment. Enhanced organizational prestige and greater regulatory authority within the profession were implicit, if not explicit, goals. And the best way to achieve these ends was to harness the collective strength of the nation's libraries and library supporters.

On January 11, 1919, the executive board authorized William Warner Bishop, president of ALA, to appoint a Committee of Five to survey the entire field of American library services. The survey, Bishop said, would be analogous to the celebrated Committee of Ten report on secondary education in 1893, and Abraham Flexner's influential report on medical education in 1910. A library survey would enable librarians to evaluate the success or failure of their services and internal operations. Bishop wanted specific facts, not "hortatory or theoretical" information. The resultant data would provide the library profession, for the first time, with the information needed to establish standards for buildings, equipment, services, and salaries. Appointed to serve on the Committee of Five were Arthur E. Bostwick, St. Louis Public Library, chairman; Linda A. Eastman, Cleveland Public Library; Azariah S. Root, Oberlin College Library; Charles C. Williamson, New York Public Library; and Carl H. Milam, acting director of the Library War Service. The committee was requested to prepare a report for the Asbury Park (New Jersey) conference in June [4].

Milam was among those who envisioned a much broader program than a general survey of library conditions. Three weeks before the annual conference, he wrote to Walter L. Brown, former ALA president, that the association should continue to support war-related programs, principally the services to the merchant marine, hospitals, and the blind. As for the American Library Association, Milam favored a vigorous new role: "The A. L. A. should undertake the responsibility of making itself the big force behind all library development, issuing propaganda, arousing interest, conducting campaigns in the field for establishment of library commissions, public libraries, libraries in industrial concerns, libraries in state penal, correctional and charitable institutions, etc. No matter what results may come from the discussion of these subjects at Asbury Park, I feel that we have already accomplished somethings [sic] and assume as a matter of course that we can get the money somewhere if we decided that we really ought to do the work" [5].

As instructed by President Bishop, the committee presented its report to the members at Asbury Park. In presenting the report, the committee indicated that the survey was justified on the grounds that present library work was carried on without accurate comparative data. The task of gathering and sifting the data would be largely accomplished by a volunteer staff. Expenses for travel, clerical assistance, and publication of the final report were estimated at $88,000. Four survey areas were defined and assigned to committee members. Root was given responsibility for the acquisition, technical processing, and storage of books. Circulation, reference, and library extension were the topics assigned to Eastman. Library education, staff training, and salaries would be analyzed by Williamson. Milam would investigate library-government relations, finances, and publicity [6, pp. 326-28].

Meanwhile, the council was considering whether the association should raise a $1 million dollar endowment for peace work. Pride in the wartime library service and the reconstructionist mood in the country were conducive to favorable consideration. James Wyer, chairman of the War Service Committee, endorsed the idea, noting that the patriotic motivation behind the Library War Service would sustain a postwar program and fund-raising campaign. Theresa Hitchler of the Brooklyn Public Library worried about the consequences of not supporting an endowment: "If the A. L. A. is not going to sink back and become a reactionary institution it ought to go right on and continue where it left off with the library war service" [6, p. 362]. Charles E. Rush, chairman of the Publicity Committee, delivered a stirring speech on behalf of an expanded program: "We must create prestige and build good will for the entire organization, arouse public confidence in the library as an educational enterprise, interpret the service of libraries to the public and furnish humanized, dramatized reviews of library activities. A publicity service bureau designed to inaugurate a nationwide educational program is the ... most advantageous method to accomplish such results" [6, pp. 364-65].

Not all of the comments on the proposed endowment were favorable. Frank P. Hill, chairman of the Library War Finance Committee and director of the Brooklyn Public Library, cautioned the members that a large sum of money, at least $50,000, would be required to underwrite a drive for an endowment fund. He also feared that the public was tired of money campaigns and that library trustees would not release their staffs to work on another campaign. Further study of an endowment was desirable, Hill conceded, but a good plan would take at least one year [6, p. 368]. Most trenchant of the critics, predictably, was John Cotton Dana of the Newark Public Library. The association, asserted Dana, should consider not what libraries were but what they ought to be; what needed to be studied then was not library activities but rather "the place of the library phenomenon in a print-using society" [6, p. 369]. Any survey should also examine the association's staff and mission. Dana singled out ALA's seventeen-year-old constitution as a major deterrent to progress. He proposed instead a single-page document which would entrust leadership of the association to no more than five persons [6, p. 370].

Deferring to the council's sentiment for expanded postwar services, the executive board, on June 27, 1919, at the Asbury Park conference, appointed a Committee on Enlarged Program. Accompanying the appointment was a declaration by the executive board that it was "the responsibility of the American Library Association to encourage and promote the development of library service for every man, woman and child in America" [6, p. 359]. Members of the Enlarged Program Committee were Frank P. Hill, chairman; Caroline F. Webster, New York State Library; Carl H. Milam; John Cotton Dana; and Walter L. Brown. On September 9, 1919, Milam was appointed director of the Enlarged Program. Milam's new position consolidated his administrative control over virtually all ALA activities. He was now acting general director of the Library War Service, director of the Enlarged Program, and a member of the executive board. Six months later he was to become executive secretary of ALA upon George Utley's resignation.

The Agenda

Taking the executive board's charge seriously, the Committee on Enlarged Program met twelve times during the summer of 1919. A tentative document was approved by the executive board at Richfield Springs, New York, in early September and was published in Library Journal the following month. Recommendations were divided into three categories: continuation of war-related activities, new programs, and constitutional revision. A one-year budget of $1.2 million was proposed. Of this figure, $700,000 was needed to support programs growing out of the war. Library service would be continued for hospitals, lighthouses, the merchant marine, industrial plants, and blind soldiers. It was anticipated that this portion of the program would not extend much beyond one year [7, pp. 645-50].

Another substantial allocation, nearly $600,000, was set aside for new programs. In order to promote library extension in the states, it was recommended that ALA function as a national library commission. States would be helped by the association to secure favorable library legislation and to initiate library service in

unserved areas. A national examining board, empowered to grant
certificates and to set standards for library schools, was to be established. The library survey was also to be a part of the Enlarged
Program. Heeding Dana's earlier admonition, the survey would
evaluate the role of libraries in the social and educational life of the
nation [7, pp. 651-52].

A national program of education and information was highlighted. The association would be responsible for a "nationwide
promulgation of the library idea, designed to stimulate the extension
and development of libraries and to increase the use of print" [7, p.
652]. These goals would be accomplished through exhibits, publicity,
and the promotion of higher librarians' salaries. Provision was made
for a study of ALA's publishing activities. Another objective, unfunded, was to establish closer relations with the National Education
Association. If teachers more fully appreciated the value of libraries, perhaps they might lend their prestigious support to the Enlarged Program. Other features of the plan encompassed service to
institutional libraries and immigrants. Finally, a financial campaign to raise $2 million was recommended [7, pp. 652-59].

Constitutional revision was considered to be within the mandate of the Committee on Enlarged Program. Actually, two committees were writing a new constitution. Frank Hill's group, apparently unaware of the special committee on constitutional reform
appointed at Asbury Park, issued its version in October 1919. The
special committee, consisting of William W. Bishop, George B. Utley, and Chalmers Hadley, ALA president, released its version the
following month. Differences between the two documents were relatively minor. New powers were conferred on the executive board
at the expense of the council. The executive board was vested with
the authority to appoint all committees. Questions of policy must be
submitted to the executive board before any action by the membership. Divested of its former powers, the council was reduced to
discussing professional issues and adopting resolutions. Entanglement of constitutional reform with the Enlarged Program was unfortunate. Those members opposed to organizational change tended to
transfer their distrust to the Enlarged Program itself [8].

Deliberation and Doubt

Almost as soon as details concerning the proposed Enlarged Program were disclosed, rumors began to circulate about the removal
of the ALA headquarters from Chicago to New York. Resentment
was particularly strong in the Midwest. In November 1919, the
Library Journal attempted to defuse the issue, saying that "there is
no foundation for this impression" [9]. There had been several informal exchanges among members, but no formal discussion or proposals had been introduced at the Richfield Springs meeting. However, a month later President Hadley admitted that a proposal to
transfer the headquarters to New York had been introduced at Richfield Springs. At his insistence, Hadley said, the recommendation

was deleted from the committee's report. Any suspicion that such action would be taken without the members' consent, Hadley declared, was entirely unwarranted [10]. Announcement that a "temporary financial headquarters" would be set up in New York City, however, only seemed to confirm apprehensions [11]. No concerted attempt to move the headquarters was ever uncovered, but the rumors served to heighten suspicions.

The first special session to discuss the Enlarged Program was held in Chicago, January 1-3, 1920. Three hundred and twenty-eight delegates braved Chicago's bone-numbing weather to attend [12, p. 251]. Constitutional revision dominated the first day's debate. President Hadley presided, while Bishop explained the new constitution and solicited questions. Constituting themselves as a committee of the whole, the members challenged Bishop on every point down to the punctuation. Disapproval was pervasive concerning the procedures for electing honorary members, the new policy prerogatives of the executive board, the role of affiliated organizations, and the divestiture of the council's traditional powers [13, 14]. With such a reception, there was no choice but to recommit the constitution for further revision. Bishop had withstood the assault with commendable forbearance; nonetheless, he left Chicago disconsolate over the rejection of his work [12, pp. 251-52].

Criticism of the Enlarged Program was more restrained, yet there was disaffection over some actions of the program's leaders and plans for the financial campaign. Phineas L. Windsor, University of Illinois Library, was irritated by the hiring of a publicity consultant, J. Ray Johnson, before the Chicago meeting, and by Milam's forwarding of a letter to journalism schools asking for their assistance. Milam "manfully took the responsibility," making his apologies for any premature commitment [13, p. 56]. Hill and Richard R. Bowker, the library publisher, deflected the charge of a premature use of funds by informing members that a $52,000 loan to the Enlarged Program, from the 1917 Library War Service account, had been approved by the executive board. Later, the Enlarged Program received another loan of $150,000 from Library War Service funds [15, pp. 6-7].

There were differing viewpoints over how funds for the Enlarged Program should be raised. Realizing that some members were against a fund drive of the type conducted during the war, Hill cautiously referred to "raising money" instead of an "intensive drive" [15, p. 5]. The $2 million, to be used over a three-year period, would be obtained from foundations and general subscriptions. To many members, Hill's statement that no intensive campaign would be conducted was unsatisfactory. Finally, a resolution was passed which gave approval for an "appeal for funds," but it specifically prohibited any quota system [15, pp. 7-8]. The committee's inability to fend off this restriction and the members' lukewarm commitment to the financial campaign were harbingers of difficulties ahead. Charles H. Compton, Seattle Public Library, correctly perceived the limiting effect of these strictures: they were "like giving

a general orders to win a battle but instructing him that his army
should go slow" [16, p. 80].

Until the Chicago meeting, there was no way of measuring
the degree of concern over the alleged proposals to move the ALA
headquarters to New York. To air the subject, Arthur E. Bostwick
moved that the Enlarged Program be operated from the Chicago offices. President Hadley, who had earlier denied that a New York
move was contemplated, ruled that the resolution was a matter of
policy and must come before the council. Bostwick appealed the
chair's ruling and was sustained by the members. Although he was
not opposed to a complete move, Bostwick explained, the idea of
two headquarters was a needless duplication. The motion carried.
This motion had no practical effect; the Enlarged Program conducted
its ill-fated campaign from the New York office which it shared with
the Library War Service [15, pp. 8-9].

Unlike the proposed constitutional revision, the Enlarged Program survived the scrutiny at Chicago. During the next few months,
the campaign organization was assembled, regional directors were
appointed, and numerous publicity items were released. Just as the
financial campaign was gaining some momentum, opponents of the
Enlarged Program publicly called for substantial modifications.
Perhaps aware that even more criticism was imminent, the Committee on Enlarged Program issued "An Explanation" on March 16,
1920. In a 3-page pamphlet, the Enlarged Program was defended
as a project authorized by the association and essentially quite modest in conception. Not more than a dozen letters of protest had
been received by the executive board or the committee. Other organizations, such as the Salvation Army and the National Tuberculosis Association, had already run successful appeals. It was time,
declared the committee, to close ranks and stand by the "Committee
and the Association itself and its good repute" [17].

Two weeks later, a circular letter signed by thirteen prominent librarians was sent to every member of the association. A
considerable proportion of the membership, it was asserted, opposed
the Enlarged Program as currently defined, while a still greater
percentage of members favored the imposition of "more definite
limits." Signers of this letter, representing every section of the
country, included Mary F. Isom, Portland (Oregon) Public Library;
John H. Leete, Carnegie Library of Pittsburgh; Henry N. Sanborn,
Bridgeport (Connecticut) Public Library; and Thomas L. Montgomery, former ALA president, Pennsylvania State Library. Three
conspicuous members of the War Service Committee also signed the
letter: Edwin H. Anderson, New York Public Library; Arthur E.
Bostwick; and Gratia Countryman, Minneapolis Public Library [18].

The dissenters enumerated four resolutions which they hoped
the association would adopt: (1) to keep the Enlarged Program
within limits of accomplishment, (2) to discontinue free service by
ALA to government departments as soon as the present funds were
exhausted, (3) to limit the campaign to securing funds for profes-

sional objects which are assured of permanent maintenance, and (4) to require officials of the association to provide adequate information about the Enlarged Program. A postcard was enclosed with the letter, enabling recipients to register their views. Differing somewhat from the resolution, the postcard asked for a decision on whether the funds collected should be used for a permanent endowment [18]. Slightly more than 1,000 postcards in support of the resolutions were turned over to the executive board. With approximately 25 percent of the 4,400 members critical of certain aspects of the Enlarged Program, it would be very difficult to conduct a successful financial campaign [19].

Even if the association could have closed ranks behind the Enlarged Program, public support was not assured. Many citizens, saturated by the wartime fund drives, would turn a deaf ear to appeals after the war. A satiric leaflet, captioned "Some Reasons Why the People Are Opposed to the Financial Campaign of the A.L.A.," conveyed one citizen's frustration over governmental intrusions and the endless charitable appeals. The story related the response of a wealthy San Antonio man to his bank's letter calling in his collateral loan:

> For the following reasons I am unable to send you the check asked for:
> I have been held up, held down, and sandbagged, walked on, sat on, flattened out and squeezed. First by the United States Government, for federal war tax, the excess profit tax, and the liberty loan bonds, thrift, capital stock tax, merchants license and auto tax, and by every society and organization that the inventive mind can invent to extract what I may or may not possess.
> The government has so governed my business that I don't know who owns it. I am inspected, suspected, examined, re-examined, informed, required and commanded, so I don't know who I am, where I am, or why I am here. All I know is I am supposed to be an inexhaustible supply of money for every known need, desire or hope of the human race; and because I will not sell all I have and go out and beg, borrow or steal money to give away, I have been cussed, discussed, boycotted, talked to, talked about, lied to, lied about, held up, hung up, robbed and nearly ruined; and the only reason I am clinging to life is to see what in the Hell is coming next. [20]

Dissent had reached a dangerous level and some form of accommodation was necessary. Supporters and detractors of the Enlarged Program then met in order to work out their differences during a combined meeting of the New Jersey and Pennsylvania Library Associations in Atlantic City, April 30-May 1, 1920. It was agreed to set aside 50 percent of the funds collected toward an endowment, although donations for specific activities would still be permitted. The wisdom of emphasizing the endowment feature was questionable; some potential donors would be reluctant to contribute money for unspecified, long-range programs [19].

Chairman Hill and John Cotton Dana resigned from the committee shortly before the Atlantic City meeting. Hill cited the pressures of his job as the reason for resigning, but Dana was more candid: the circular letter had undermined the credibility of the Enlarged Program [16, p. 82]. To reconcile the various points of view, a Joint Committee on the Enlarged Program was appointed at Atlantic City. Chairman of the new, thirteen-member committee was William N. C. Carlton of the Newberry Library. The wounds were apparently healed and the fund drive would proceed without interruption. A "re-statement" of the Enlarged Program was issued by the joint committee on May 17, 1920 [21]. This report, incorporating the endowment provision, differed little from the original document except for a new section on adult education and a revised statement on special libraries. On June 7, the report was unanimously adopted by the membership at the annual conference in Colorado Springs [22].

Denouement

Even before the Chicago meeting, planning was under way to develop a national campaign organization. Following the precedent of the two wartime fund drives, a national advisory council was created, and regional and state directors were appointed. Hill tried to persuade Frank Vanderlip, president of the National City Bank of New York and wartime head of the Library War Council, to chair another advisory council, but this time Vanderlip declined because of business commitments [23]. J. Randolph Coolidge, trustee of the Boston Athenaeum and an articulate spokesman for the cause of libraries, accepted the post of chairman of the national advisory council. Other influential citizens agreeing to serve on the council were Raymond B. Fosdick, former director of the Commission on Training Camp Activities; John R. Mott of the Young Men's Christian Association; and Mrs. Josephine C. Preston, president of the National Education Association. Most of the ten regional directors were former stalwarts of the Library War Service; among these were Charles F. D. Belden, Boston Public Library; Mary Titcomb, Washington County (Maryland) Free Library; and Milton J. Ferguson, California State Library.

During the war, the American Library Association remained aloof from the Special Libraries Association (SLA). When SLA learned that special libraries were mentioned in the various Enlarged Program documents, it lodged repeated protests with ALA regarding its exclusion from a voice in policy formulation. Finally, in February 1920, the association sanctioned the formation of a joint ALA-SLA committee on the Enlarged Program. After this recognition, the SLA covered Enlarged Program activities in its journal, Special Libraries, and urged members to support the program and the financial campaign [24, 25].

Experienced fund raisers and publicity experts were engaged to run the campaign from New York. Overseeing the campaign organization was Elmore Leffingwell, longtime head of publicity for the Salvation Army. Speaking at the first conference of regional directors on February 9, 1920, Frank Hill was cautiously optimistic: "It is really a momentous occasion. It is a serious time for you, for me and for the association. We are starting out on something new, and yet a continuation of the work which we have been doing for the past three years. It is a perilous venture that we are undertaking, but one which I am sure is bound to end in success. Even if we do not get a dollar we are going to put the libraries on the map..." [26]. By March 1920 there were between twenty and thirty persons on the Enlarged Program payroll [16, p. 77]. As in the wartime campaigns, a newsletter, the A. L. A. Blue Letter, was published to keep members and local libraries abreast of progress. Fourteen issues of the newsletter appeared between January 17 and June 15, 1920 [27]. The term Enlarged Program seemed a bit austere, and in February the slogan "Books for Everybody" was introduced. None of the newsletters carried information about the debilitating quarrel within the association.

At least half a dozen publicity pamphlets were printed, some of which were slanted toward particular audiences. Some of the more ambitious pamphlets were entitled How Books for Everybody of the A. L. A. Will Help Solve Local Library Problems, Universal Education Through Books for Everybody, and Talking Points about Books for Everybody. The most attractive pamphlet, Books for Everybody, was designed for mass appeal. On the cover of this 16-page color leaflet was a picture of three immigrants looking up at a tower of books. The captain read, "Good Books Make Good Citizens" [27].

The newsletter and the pamphlets were supplemented by a publicity blitz in the general press. Near the end of April, it was reported that more than 2,000 newspapers and almost 100 magazines had run stories, often illustrated ones, about the Enlarged Program. Coverage in the general circulation magazines was extensive, including Good Housekeeping, Outlook, and the Saturday Evening Post. Farm and trade journals were also receptive to the publicity releases. Accounts of the Enlarged Program appeared in such diverse publications as the American Lumberman, the Drovers' Telegram, the Nautical Gazette, the Orange Judd Farmer, and the Underwear & Hosiery Review [28]. Circulation of these specialized journals frequently exceeded the readership of local newspapers. By fall 1920, the number of magazine articles and newspaper items about the Enlarged Program was estimated at 300 and 10,000, respectively [29, p. 777].

Although war-related programs were scheduled to receive the largest amount of funds, these activities were not stressed in the publicity. General adult education, library extension to unserved areas, and Americanization were accented as the major services and benefits to be expected from a successful Enlarged Program. Millions of adults, especially women and young persons, would benefit from the self-study courses which would be prepared. The fact that over 60 million American residents were without adequate library service was incorporated into nearly every magazine story and newspaper account.

Publicists for the Enlarged Program were not above pandering to the public's anxieties. Except for German-Americans, immigrants were not generally mistreated during the war. Afterward, the hyphenated nationalities became a "menace" as the Red Scare of 1919-20 swept the country. Frederic W. Keator, Episcopal bishop of Tacoma, Washington, and a member of ALA's national advisory council on the Enlarged Program, believed that libraries should play a vital role in combating the pernicious influence of bolshevism on immigrants [30]. As the following quotation from a press release demonstrates, leaders of the Enlarged Program viewed public libraries as bastions of social control and civil purity: "In these days of social and industrial unrest we are beginning to open alarmed eyes at what we term the 'menace of the unassimilated foreigner,' and to voice growing concern over a problem which the public libraries of America have long been working quietly to solve. Out of the present welter is emerging a tardy appreciation of the value of the public library as the bridge by which the immigrant may pass from old world traditions and prejudices to American ideals" [31].

This vast outpouring of publicity had little chance to succeed without the unified support of ALA members and a receptive public. Neither of these prerequisites was sufficiently present. Scheduled to terminate on June 30, 1920, the campaign lingered on for months. As of July 12, the Enlarged Program had netted only $58,000 in cash and pledges [32]. Three days later, the Committee on Enlarged Program was discharged and the program was transferred to the executive board. Already responsible for the residual war work, the executive board reacted to the inheritance of the Enlarged Program as a "peculiarly perplexing" situation [33]. The executive board decided to terminate the fund drive on November 30, and by December the dimension of the failure was painfully clear. Only $50,702 had actually been collected [34, 35]. Disappointed, but scrupulous to the end, Milam honored his pledge of $200 by making a final payment of $100 on May 3, 1922 [36].

Anatomy of a Failure

Fresh from the intoxicating experience of two successful financial campaigns and widely praised service to several million soldiers, the association appeared ready to believe that an expanded postwar program was not only desirable but achievable. Since the wartime programs would be continued pending their transfer to the government, the temptation to create a parallel program of civilian library services proved irresistible. After all, even the temperate Putnam had told the members at Asbury Park that ALA had emerged from the war as a "public service corporation" [37, p. 263]. And so without adequate planning, an Enlarged Program was formulated during the summer of 1919 and approved by the executive board in September.

Early criticism of the Enlarged Program was sporadic; most of the carping was directed at such peripheral issues as the rumors of a relocation of ALA headquarters to New York and constitutional revision. By the time of the special session at Chicago in January 1920, the opposition was powerful enough to impose severe limitations on the program. There would not be an intensive campaign, and no quota system would be permitted. Substantial disenchantment was evident in the circular letter of March 31, 1920. As a result of this complaint, the executive board decided to allocate one-half of the money raised for a permanent endowment.

The executive board and the Committee on Enlarged Program overestimated the membership's readiness to support an independent program. Although approved by the executive board, the Enlarged Program was not discussed by the membership until June 1920. Because of the patriotic focus of the war, criticism of the powerful Library War Service bureaucracy in Washington was muted. After the war, the association reverted to its tradition of endless debate on every issue. Many members were not receptive to the idea of an assertive executive board or to the prospect of another bureaucracy in New York. This fear of centralized authority was very much on the mind of William F. Yust, Rochester Public Library, a signer of the circular letter: "A committee of 5 tells a board of 7 to decide that an Association of 4,000 members shall go after $2 million from 100 million people" [38].

If the situation is likened to the Senate fight over the League of Nations, it may be said that the Enlarged Program had its supporters, reservationists, and irreconcilables. The supporters, many of whom served in the Library War Service, constituted at most a simple majority of the association. Probably one-quarter to one-half of the members were reservationists, alarmed over certain features of the program. Continuation of the war-related activities, for example, appeared to some members as a responsibility of the federal government. Despite the apparent harmony after the restatement of the program in May 1920 and the unanimous approval at Colorado Springs, about 300 irreconcilables abstained from the fund drive, and their lack of participation was fatal to the campaign [29, p. 776].

Aside from the individual viewpoints of the members, other factors militated against a favorable income. From 1917 to 1920, 1,710 librarians had reportedly left their jobs for more lucrative careers [39]. Active support of the Enlarged Program was surely difficult for those libraries suffering from acute staff shortages. The economy was slipping into a postwar slump, and the public was weary of the numerous charitable fund drives. Many of these campaigns, especially the nonfederated ones, failed to reach their quotas.

There is no disguising the fact that the Enlarged Program met a humiliating defeat, but not everyone was disillusioned. Charles Compton, in New York throughout the campaign, referred to the episode as a "reckless adventure," one which "shall always remain in my mind a noble adventure and it is good at times ... for librarians to attempt the impossible" [16, pp. 73, 83]. For Milam, the Enlarged Program pinpointed new "targets" to follow in subsequent years [40, pp. 122-23]. Out of the debacle emerged a period of salutary reappraisal, with emphasis on the structural reform of the association, the recruitment of new members, and the development of less ambitious programs. The dream would be deferred.

References

1. Young, Arthur P. "The American Library Association and World War I." Ph.D. dissertation, University of Illinois at Urbana-Champaign, 1976.
2. Noggle, Burl. Into the Twenties: The United States from Armistice to Normalcy. Urbana: University of Illinois Press, 1974.
3. Shapiro, Stanley. "The Twilight of Reform: Advanced Progressives after the Armistice." Historian 33 (May 1971): 349-64.
4. "Committee of Five: On a Library Survey." Bulletin of the American Library Association 13 (March 1919): 32-33.
5. Milam to Brown, June 2, 1919, War Service Committee, Record Group (hereafter WSC, RG) 89/1/5 (vol. 40), ALA Archives, University of Illinois Library, Urbana (hereafter ALAA).
6. American Library Association. Papers and Proceedings of the Forty-first Annual Meeting of the American Library Association Held at Asbury Park, N.J., June 23-27, 1919. Chicago: American Library Association, 1919.
7. "Preliminary Report of Committee on Enlarged Program for American Library Service." Library Journal 44 (October 1919): 645-63.
8. "Constitution of the American Library Association." Library Journal 44 (November 1919): 721-24.
9. [Editorial.] Library Journal 44 (November 1919): 688.
10. Hadley, Chalmers. "The Proposed Enlarged Program of the A.L.A." Library Journal 44 (December 1919): 753-54.
11. "Publicity for the A.L.A. Enlarged Program." Library Journal 44 (December 1919): 788.
12. Sparks, Claud G. "William Warner Bishop: A Biography." Ph.D. dissertation, University of Michigan, 1967.
13. "At Chicago." Library Journal 45 (January 1920): 55-56.
14. "Revision of the Constitution." Library Journal 45 (January 1920): 76-77.
15. "The Enlarged Program Proceedings." Bulletin of the American Library Association 14 (January 1920): 2-9.
16. Compton, Charles H. Memories of a Librarian. St. Louis: St. Louis Public Library, 1954.
17. "An Explanation." March 16, 1920. WSC, RG 89/1/5 (vol. 40), ALAA.
18. [Circular Letter.] March 31, 1920. WSC, RG 89/1/5 (vol. 40), ALAA. Also published in Library Journal 45 (April 1920): 363-64.

19. [Editorial.] Library Journal 45 (May 1920): 453.
20. "Some Reasons Why the People Are Opposed to the Financial Campaign of the A. L. A." [1919 or 1920]. WSC, RG 89/1/5 (vol. 40), ALAA.
21. "A Restatement of the A. L. A. Enlarged Program and Budget submitted by the Joint Committee." May 17, 1920, WSC, RG 89/1/5 (vol. 40), ALAA.
22. [Editorial.] Library Journal 45 (June 1920): 560.
23. Hill to Vanderlip. December 17, 1920. Frank Vanderlip Papers, Columbia University.
24. Friedel, J. H. "Special Libraries in the Enlarged Program." Special Libraries 11 (January 1920): 1-6.
25. Friedel, J. H. "A. L. A. and S. L. A. Reach Agreement." Special Libraries 11 (March 1920): 90.
26. Minutes, Committee on A. L. A. Enlarged Program, Conference of Regional Directors, February 9, 1920. WSC, RG 89/1/21, box 2, ALAA.
27. WSC, RG 89/1/5 (vol. 40), and Enlarged Program Committee, RG 92/10/10, ALAA.
28. [Milam, Carl H.] "Report of the Secretary of the Committee on Enlarged Program on the Appeal for Funds." April 27, 1920. WSC, RG 89/1/5 (vol. 40), ALAA.
29. Carr, John F. "A Greater American Library Association." Library Journal 45 (October 1920): 775-78.
30. "Librarians Name Campaign Chiefs." New York Times (February 13, 1920).
31. [Enlarged Program Press Release.] February 29, 1920. WSC, unprocessed item, ALAA.
32. "Final Report of the Committee on Enlarged Program as It Was Presented to the Executive Board July 15, 1920." WSC, RG 89/1/5 (vol. 40), ALAA.
33. "An Open Letter from the Executive Board to Members of the American Library Association." September 25, 1920. WSC, RG 89/1/5 (vol. 40), ALAA.
34. "American Library Association." Library Journal 45 (December 1920): 987-90.
35. "Books for Everybody Fund 1919-1920." WSC, RG 89/1/72, box 1, ALAA.
36. [Books for Everybody Fund Ledger, 1919-22.] WSC, RG 89/1/72, box 1, ALAA.
37. Putnam, Herbert. "Statement of the General Director, A. L. A. War Service." Bulletin of the American Library Association 13 (July 1919): 261-63.
38. Yust, William F. "Shall the Executive Board Rule the American Library Association." [n. d.] WSC, RG 89/1/5 (vol. 40), ALAA.
39. "Library Workers Quitting." New York Times (March 18, 1920).
40. Sullivan, Peggy. "Carl H. Milam and the American Library Association." Ph. D. dissertation, University of Chicago, 1972.

FINDING THE LIBRARY'S ROLE IN AN INFORMATION SOCIETY*

Bettina H. Wolff

We are entering (or have already arrived at) an auspicious era for the library profession. In our post-industrial society, dating from about the end of World War II, information workers have become predominant in the labor force, information industries account for close to half of the Gross National Product (GNP), and success and failure are defined as "functions of one's ability to acquire, organize and use information." (11:40) As librarians we perceive clearly that libraries as institutions which provide access to information, and we, as professionals trained and skilled in the retrieval of that information, can expect to play an increasingly vital role.

Society however seems to be somewhat less clear about the value of libraries. Libraries seem to be suffering setbacks: a limiting of public library hours and services as a result of urban fiscal crisis, burgeoning costs and frozen budgets for libraries in government settings, elimination of libraries in elementary schools. At a time when information appears to be more important than ever why do library budgets suffer defeat, and libraries lack the universal strong, public, administrative, and governmental support we librarians think they deserve?

I see three major components of the problem. The first is a wide-spread public unwillingness to carry the cost in taxes for present levels of government (public) services. Libraries are not a particular target of this dissatisfaction but they are inevitably affected by it. The unity of this movement comes from the objection to levels of taxation; there is no evidence of agreement on services to be cut. Its resolution will come either in terms of acceptance that people are not willing to pay the cost of continuously expanding government activity and services, with ensuing decisions about services to be shifted from the public to the private sector, and services to be eliminated; or it will come in terms of public acceptance of increasing tax levels (many countries have higher taxes than the U.S.) and continued government growth.

---

*Reprinted by permission of the author and publisher from Public Library Quarterly, 1:2 (Summer 1979) 169-82; copyright © 1980 by The Haworth Press.

The second component lies in the shifting basis of societal values accompanying our transition from an industrial to a post-industrial or information economy. Libraries developed and were defined in the industrial society just passed; in this context their role and desirability was secure. Virtually everyone thought the library was a good thing, worthy of being supported whether or not one personally used it. Thus, data from the Public Library Inquiry indicated that while 18% of the population were library users, 75% of the population were willing to support libraries. In the emerging post-industrial society, where the market economy is shifting from product domination to service domination, the library is moving out of benign obscurity into apparent competition with private sector interests in the storage, communication, and provision of information, and in its interest in the development and regulation of information channels and information technology. The lack of clarity about public vs. private responsibilities for the provision of information in an information based economy, the lack of public policy results in ambiguity about libraries. Libraries are one of those industries "in the vanguard of technological upheaval (which) will experience the greatest and most severe policy problems" in the emerging economy. (11:27)

A third component relates to the many meanings inherent in the word "information," which is applied indirectly to "a wide range of forms, manifestations, and processes even though they are significantly different" (2, Otten:95). The three components are interrelated; they are highly complex and they are just beginning to be addressed. A great many decisions of critical importance to the library profession are going to be emerging from the political/economic/public arena in the next decade. Most may be beyond the ability of librarians to influence significantly. If we are to say anything important to public policy issues of equal interest to the corporate giants of the communication and computer technologies, it would behoove us to start thinking very carefully about what we deal with, what we do, and our role in society. Jesse Shera has cited as the "greatest failure" of the library profession during its first 100 years, that librarians have denied the importance of a philosophical frame of reference and therefore have never developed a cohesive synthesis for their activities. (12:282) This he says has manifested itself "in subtle and obscure ways." I would suggest that unless we address carefully "librarianship qua librarianship" and what that comprises in an information based society, the results may be neither subtle nor obscure.

As librarians have joined other information professionals in the interdisciplinary exchange referred to as information science, it has become increasingly obvious that information is a rich and complex concept without adequate definition or a common basis of understanding. At a 1972 NATO Institute on "Information Science: Search for Identity" a major speaker warned that use of the phrase "information science" suggests there is a science whereas we are only working on the basic elements from which a science can be developed. (2, Otten:91)

A great deal of attention has been given to defining information, but for a word that all of us use with confidence and frequently, there seems to be a remarkable lack of conformity in the way it is used. The same conference speaks of "meaningless discussions which result from calling too many little understood non-physical properties and actions simply 'information'." (2, Otten:97)

In defining information most authorities seem to make a two-fold distinction between static or stored information, and active or dynamic information. That is, information is both a source and a process of acquisition. Information acquired by an individual need not come from recorded or coded information. Static information is sometimes referred to as coded fact, in economic terms as a commodity, in scientific terms as a basic component of reality as pervasive as energy and matter. As a commodity, information has properties like matter and energy, it is bound to a location, it can be transported, and it can be altered. It cannot, however, be measured either directly or indirectly. (2, Further:21, Otten:76, 6:48)

Dynamic information, sometimes called operative information, encompasses the action of knowing how to act in or on a situation. It is a process. It deals with information acquired by the individual. The distinction is sometimes made between academic information and practical information, information received from a coded source and information derived (or capable of being derived) directly from experience. Static information is sometimes cited as source oriented; active information as receiver oriented. While authorities tend to identify two general classes of information (occasionally three), it is misleading to group them as I have done since the different terms grouped together are not necessarily equivalent.

In seeking to understand the meaning of information, participants deal with more than definitions. They consider models of information utilization, manifestations of information, operations performed on information, relational components of information, and formulations of information. (All of these for some mysterious reason seem to come in groups of three). Without going into more detail, each classification represents a different way of perceiving and therefore of clarifying information. It is hard to tell whether they represent basic insights which will contribute to a unified information science or whether they derive from and describe different ways of currently looking at and dealing with information. They do demonstrate that information encompasses more than libraries can or should hold themselves responsible for, and represent a useful source for sharpening our concepts of our own role.

When we speak of information as librarians we tend to speak of coded or recorded information. "Information is a symbol or a set of symbols which has the potential for meaning." (10:147) The National Commission on Libraries and Information Science (NCLIS) in its Goals for Action defines information as including "facts and other recorded knowledge found in books, periodicals, newspapers, reports, audiovisual formats, magnetic tapes, data banks (bases), and other recording media. " (8)

It seems fairly clear that the central function of libraries is to acquire, organize, and make available recorded information. Again NCLIS defines a library as "an institution where diverse information is stored, systematically organized, and where services are provided to facilitate its use. It may contain books, films, magazines, maps, manuscripts, microfilms, audiovisual materials, tape recordings, computer tapes, etc. It also provides information services to requesters from its own and from outside sources." A librarian is "a specialist in the organization, management, and utilization of recorded information." (8:81) Or, "The librarian is not a specialist in information in general, but in information about records. The librarian's job is a job of management of information-bearing objects, and the continually improved performance of that necessary job is a natural and reasonable goal for the future. " (13:121)

Obviously all information is not recorded, or coded in any way. Recorded information makes up the composite knowledge of all people, which constitutes one major universe of information from which the individual acquires information or knowledge. There are two other sources of information for all individuals: The natural universe and the social universe. We all acquire information directly from our environment. For almost all people in the past, and probably for most people in the world today, these two aspects of the environment represent the major source of information. This information is acquired by direct action or interaction and falls into the second type of information cited earlier.

Areas of research and study include the process by which information is assimilated and made useful by the individual; the value of information to the individual; the utilization of information in decision-making. One school defines information as that which modifies uncertainty and enables the recipient to make decisions (solve problems), and proposes a measure of information relative to its decision-making value. (2, Furth:40ff)

Information is very closely tied to communication. Otter suggests the hypothesis that information exists by virtue of the communication process, and that all information processes reveal transfer of a physical information carrier as a fundamental element. This factor influences libraries in two ways: the first is technologically, libraries have a very large stake in the way communication technology develops, is regulated, and functions; the second is service-wise. Recognizing that information must be communicated to be useful brings the receiver into the picture and highlights the fact that information must be taken in and assimilated to be used.

A wide range of literature focusses on this. "Being informed is not the same thing as having information. We have focussed on the 'information' and not the 'informing'. " (4:328) There is a literature developing on how people acquire information, how and under what circumstances information is taken in and assimilated. This study is of interest to computer scientists because it has the possibility of providing a basis for improving the processing ability of computers. It is of interest to librarians and others who deal with the public in light of the relatively small percentage of people who use the library effectively.

Here the question is raised, how useful are documents (recorded information) to most people's information acquiring process? In Public Information, Private Ignorance, Patrick Wilson suggests "It is safe to predict flatly that even the instant availability of every document in the world to everyone would not significantly alter the quality of decisions in a notable fraction of instances. Universal physical access to documents is a librarian's ideal, but not an ideal with much attraction for anyone else." (13:122) "It is not the difficulty of access, but the time, effort, and difficulty of using documents that are the major deterrants [sic] to library use." Or as Brenda Dervin puts it "The purposive seeking of information is a time consuming and troublesome detour. Most people rely on the advice of others." (3:32) "The collection of information and its mastery and application in decision-making are simply means to the end of a satisfactory life situation; if we can attain the end without effort, we will do so." (13:122)

This assertion that people may want informing and instruction rather than data, that information and data are irrelevant to many people's needs has been developed by Dervin in studying the information needs of the poor. But it has wide application at all levels of society. Only a limited number of highly educated and highly motivated professionals want to seek out and process their own information. Many professions, including our most distinguished, exist to master, analyze, and provide necessary information to individuals in need; the legal and medical professions for example. Dervin calls them "information keepers." Very probably in an information society, as all information (as data) increases, every profession will develop its information keepers who provide this service to clients.

As stated, we are in an era when the groundrules for libraries appear to be shifting. In an information economy, there is a shift from selling products to selling services, and the services being sold are largely informational. This imposes a new and different requirement on libraries to define the information service provided in terms that recognize the widespread interest by other professions and commercial enterprises in the provision of information. Not a new requirement perhaps, but a new impetus to rethinking what we do and positioning ourselves in the economy.

It has become commonplace to refer to current American society as an information society. This description derives from Fritz Machlup's (7) pioneer study in the economics of information: The Promotion and Distribution of Knowledge in the United States; Marc

Porat has extended the work. This study documented that the manufacture of goods no longer dominates the American economy but that information industries account for 46% of the American gross national product; and that the nation's information workers account for about 46% of the work force and about 53% of total employee compensation. The original work was done with data from the late 1960s and those figures are still cited, however, succeeding scholars agree we are in a new era.

Actually, divorced from context, some of these ideas may be misleading. Machlup divides the knowledge industries into two major categories: primary with 25% GNP and secondary with 21%. He includes in information industries all government, the administrative/management component of all companies in so far as they can be segregated or estimated, education, public relations, and training both as separate industries and as components of non-information industries, as well as the mass communications industry and publishing. (This is a partial listing meant only to indicate the breadth of inclusion.)

Libraries represent two to three tenths of one percent of the GNP, not quite one per cent of that portion of GNP attributable to the information sector broadly defined by Machlup. (5, Buchman: 50) In speaking then of society as information dependent, an important portion of that information is internally generated and communicated information which typically does not fall within the scope of public information or the function of libraries, but resides in the locus of the management information system. Office supplies, equipment and expenditures, secretaries and other office staff, management and administrative staff salaries, and expenditures are all part of the information economy as defined. Library information is a very small part of management system information.

Information has certain characteristics that present difficulties in an economic sense. Unlike other economic goods, it can be simultaneously owned by two or more people without denying the benefits of ownership; it can be reproduced with very low resource costs, it does not depreciate with use, in fact use may increase its value; it does not vanish when utilization or service ends, it can be stored in inventory. It therefore lends itself poorly to classical economic and legal concepts of property rights. (11:32) This means we are in a transition without clear concepts, without precise precedents, without established guidelines for establishing those policies, economic and public, which are going to affect libraries. The history of the development of television shows that public policy and regulation were determined and applied before the consequences could be ascertained. This will inevitably happen in the regulation of information services and communications channels.

We need our best minds studying as carefully as possible what we are about, and how and where we should put our effort in trying to affect developing policy.

Porat (11) identifies three contexts in which information policy needs to be worked out: the right to privacy, disclosure of public information and production, and dissemination of government information. These are highlighted by NCLIS in its goals for a national program. From the library's point of view, the more significant areas for consideration are economic: what information services shall be free and what shall be paid for? Obviously in an economy which is information based and a society which is service based, information services will be provided for a price. The question is how and where do public libraries fit into this environment? In the predictable future the "provision of information thru other channels, many of them fee-based, may preempt some of our functions. We need to reexamine what we're doing and do what we can do better than anyone else." (5, Buckman:50) Porat notes that the banker, newspaper publisher, and postmaster general are all information "brokers" specializing in retail packaging and distribution of (unlike) information services. Governmental and social agencies are experimenting with Referral and Information Services to enable more people to seek and find needed services. The Federal Government is providing federal information services. "Should society invest in libraries as the 'information utility' of the future, or should that function be left to the private sector?" (11:28) The information field is now understood as the turf for interindustry conflicts with a bottom line of profits and jobs. According to Porat the less practical criteria--social welfare and the legacy we leave to future generations-- have hardly been addressed. (11:28)

From an economic point of view recorded information is not a pure public good. It is possible to pay for what is consumed in terms of the market conditions prevailing. If society feels that the availability of information will significantly promote universal education, will provide cultural enrichment and vision, will enlighten the electorate and/or promote the general welfare, it becomes a mixed good, something politically acceptable to be paid for out of public funds. (5, Buckman:49)

Public authorities may take the view that free and universal access to all recorded information is unrealistic and social goals can be achieved without it. The rapidly developing information technologies and profit service industries will certainly take this position in the public policy struggle.

Government is a strange entity in our society. On one hand it is the manifestation of our deepest and most cherished value: a free and democratic process; on the other it is everyone's enemy. While government action brings about public control, government is not synonymous with public. One author speaks of our need to take action "before industry and the government take complete control of networks and services on an exclusively profit and regulatory control basis." He also refers to competition between public and private services in the control of information channels and the establishment of information policy, and he advocates elevating public services "over private and government privileges because of the profound benefits to all society thru participatory-democracy possibilities via on-line voting and the possibility of enhancing human intelligence via lifelong education and participatory social planning." (2:416)

Government publication is a source of concern in the emerging information economy. Government produces and retains vast amounts of economically useful information. It is therefore besieged by two kinds of complaints: those who demand access to the information because it has private economic value and those who would enjoin the government from releasing information on the grounds that its publication is in conflict with private enterprise. (11:40)

Libraries are concerned that as much knowledge as possible be as easily available as possible. We ought therefore to promote the concept of government as public and work to keep it that way.

One of the major concerns of the library profession at this time then is to identify what aspects of information provision fit the various ideological, economic, and political criteria that will justify its continued existence and increased support. Although there is a commonality in the profession and activity of librarians, in the organization, management and retrieval of information there are distinct differences how and why different types of libraries are financed and therefore in how they are justified in the society.

Academic and school libraries are parts of educational institutions and therefore justify their existence in terms of their contribution to the institution's educational goals. Dervin says the "education system is geared primarily for the transmission of information rather than instruction and practice on how to become 'informed.'" (4:329) When education emphasizes how to find information and solve problems, the importance of libraries increases.

Special libraries are justified on their value to the institution or profession served and are typically supported by designated or private funds representing someone's willingness to pay for information. They do not seem to be affected by the emergence of an information economy. Perhaps their development before the end of the "industrial era" was an early manifestation of the increasing importance of information to industry and the professions, a precursor of the information era.

It is in the area where public funds are sought, in public libraries and in public system and networking activities, that it is essential to differentiate between the private information services domain and identify those areas or bases on which the provision of public funds can be justified.

Our society accepts that culture is a public good; that it is something from which everyone benefits, but which cannot be paid for by the limited audience of those who choose to partake of it. Libraries which retain the past and current record of human thought and expression represent society's most important cultural object. (12:126)

We accept the necessity for government providing essential services to those who cannot pay for them and for whom the lack of those services would result in greater cost or serious deficiency to society. This is another plank on which libraries can politically justify public support. With the coming of the information society, there seems to be evidence of an emerging "information underclass." There is evidence that people are becoming increasingly functionally illiterate in an increasingly information intensive society. (11:40) Clerical functions in an information intensive organization utilizing computers and modern telecommunications, are not so simple and routine that they can be performed by semi-skilled personnel with a little training. Our schools need to shift their emphasis to promoting skill in selecting relevant information from a multitude of sources and in analyzing information to solve problems and make decisions. For those who haven't developed the skill in school, there needs to be some continuing education mechanism for developing that skill.

When our librarians complain that electronic innovations in the library: bibliographic and information data bases just increase the barriers between many people and information, they are right. But this is a manifestation of a larger phenomenon which is having an even more critical effect on their lives. Banks, offices, warehouses, every area of the work environment is utilizing computerized technologies which require increased levels of skill from employees. Rather than advocating that libraries avoid technological applications in public service, librarians should be seeking ways to assist those who lack the skill to meet their own information needs and who lack the ability to perform adequately at clerical levels in information processing environments, to develop these skills. Since recorded knowledge probably plays a limited part in meeting the information and development needs of most people, librarians need to work with the involved public, educators, social workers, and media specialists to seek possible solutions. Information technologies, like television and cable, have a great potential in mitigating the problems of an unskilled public. To promote public policy which will assure public access to communication channels and information technology requires widespread awareness of developing communication policy and an informed voice in behalf of the public interest. Meeting the information needs of people seems to require innovative cross agency efforts. Working as facilitators and central components of citizen-based local, state, and national teams, librarians can promote both the public interest and their own welfare. "All citizens are potentially 'information literates'"; (9:25) libraries will flourish as this potential is realized.

It is essential to preserve the notion of public knowledge and the mechanism to insure public access. Concerning public knowledge the problem is not only "how can we provide equal access, but how can we insure equal use? Equal access is a necessary but not sufficient condition for equal use. " (6:58) People may want informing and instruction rather than data. This applies to highly skilled and literate professionals as well as the information poor. With the rate of information production now experienced, even the well educated are inevitably ignorant, and overwhelmed by the quantity of information available. The ideal information system must "adjust the document supply to the information appetite. " (13:127)

The distribution of data through networks implies a deceased emphasis on the collection and storage of information and an increase on analysis and interpretation. The information society sees a progression toward selection and arrangement of materials for use, and the assistance and instruction of users. It is inevitable that in this area of selection and arrangement of materials, and the assistance and instruction of users, private sector information services will arise. This has several advantages for libraries. First it will put a dollar value on what we do. A major handicap in dealing with the budgeting, justification, and cost effective evaluation of library services has been the difficulty of assessing for those who support libraries the value of information to those who use them. A vigorous fee based information service industry will do this. Second, in an information dependent environment the demands for information are so pervasive that libraries could not meet the almost universal demand for this service. Selection and arrangement, assistance and instruction are time-consuming and expensive. It is unlikely that public authorities would be willing to support these services for all institutional and individual users. Finally, a broad spectrum of individuals, agencies and institutions functioning as information brokers with some dependence on library collections will provide impetus and support for the development and maintenance of strong information resources and networks.

What then emerges as a role for the library in an information economy? First, the concept of public knowledge must be retained and strengthened. Information recorded to increase the scientific, social, and cultural awareness of others, in any form, should continue to be stored and made available through libraries and networks to which the public has free access. "That the stock of public knowledge is and should be treated as a common possession, the use and benefits of which should be available not to a restricted few but to mankind generally, is a plausible axiom for information policy. " (13:121) It is not clear that the demand for light, popular reading should be subsidized by public funds.

Second, the analysis and selection for use of information from library and information networks will be an operation carried on more extensively by non-librarians than by librarians, who will however contribute significantly. This is appropriate as it is a very expensive activity for which society would probably not be willing to pay to meet the demand.

Third, a major function of libraries will be to provide the document resource (print and media) from which other information brokers, private and institutional, will search and retrieve relevant information. Librarians as experts in processing recorded information will team with these various subject specialized information brokers to conduct comprehensive, difficult information searches in ever expanding print and electronic data banks.

Fourth, by making information available to, and cooperating with the broad range of public and private institutions and individuals in processing document information, libraries will secure broader understanding and support for continued and increasing levels of public support.

Fifth, collections developed to meet the broadened possible information needs of a wide range of information brokers will be available directly to those who cannot or prefer not to utilize the various brokers.

Sixth, it will be the particular responsibility of public libraries to be aware of and seek to meet the information needs of all those who cannot, will not, or are not eligible to, utilize available information brokers. Recognizing that meeting the information needs of much of the population is a process in which recorded knowledge plays a limited role, public librarians will be alert to initiate, promote, and/or participate in innovative community controlled, self-improvement programs which involve educational, social work, and library trained professionals. The aim is to increase the information literate population and to support, not compete with, other agencies.

Seventh, public libraries will continue to be sensitive to critical societal and community information needs which are not being met, such as is done by the current job information centers.

Eighth, librarians will increasingly be dealing with experts who know as much or more than the librarian about the content of subject matter being searched. This may require a change of attitude on the part of some librarians and will result in a form of ongoing two way inservice training for both librarian and information broker.

References

1. Conant, Ralph W., ed. The Public Library and the City. The MIT Press, Cambridge, Mass., 1965.
2. Debons, Anthony, ed. Information Science: Search for Identity. Proceedings, 1972, NATO Advanced Study Institute in the U.S., Marcel Dekker Inc., N.Y., 1974. (The following are cited: Furth, Hans "The Operative and figurative aspect of knowledge and information," pp. 21-28 and Otten, Klaus, "Basis for a science of information," pp. 91-106).
3. Dervin, Brenda. "The Every Day Information Needs of the Average Citizen: a Taxonomy for Analysis," Information for the Community, ALA, 1976:19-38.

4. Dervin, Brenda. "Strategies for Dealing with Human Information Needs," Journal of Broadcasting, 20:3 (Summer 1976):324-333.
5. Josey, E. J., ed. The Information Society: Issues and Answers. American Library Association's Presidential Commission for the 1977 Detroit Annual Conference, Oryx Press, Phoenix, 1978 (Cited is: Buckman, Thomas R. "The Impact of economic change on libraries," pp. 47-62).
6. Katzman, Nathan. "The Impact of Communication Technology: Promises and Prospects," Journal of Communication, 24:4 (Autumn, 1974):47-58.
7. Machlup, Fritz. The Production and Distribution of Knowledge in the United States, Princeton University Press, Princeton, N.J., 1962.
8. National Commission on Libraries and Information Science. Toward a National Program for Library and Information Service: Goals for Action, Washington, D.C., 1975.
9. Owens, Major. "The Information Function: A Theoretical Basis for the Development of Information Networks and Centers," Drexel Library Quarterly 12 (Jan.-Apr., 1976): 7-26.
10. Owens, Major. "The State Government and Libraries," Library Journal 101 (Jan. 1, 1976):147-56.
11. Porat, Marc U. "Communication Policy in an Information Society," Communications for Tomorrow, Glen O. Robinson, ed., N.Y. Praeger Publishers 1978.
12. Shera, Jesse H. "Failure and Success: Assessing a Century," Library Journal 101 (Jan. 1, 1976):281-7.
13. Wilson, Patrick. Public Knowledge, Private Ignorance: Toward a Library and Information Policy. Greenwood Press, 1977:156pp.

Part II

TECHNICAL SERVICES/READERS' SERVICES

DDC 19: AN INDICTMENT *

Sanford Berman

In open-stack libraries--public, school, or college--classification performs <u>one</u> primary function: it allows patrons (and staff) to successfully "retrieve" material in particular genres and subject-areas by browsing, without first making a catalog search. It does this through the assignment of notations--call-numbers--derived from a standard scheme. The scheme, ideally, is so organized that all major disciplines and topics--old and new--are fully represented, with related or congenial fields and forms appearing near one another.[1] The scheme, in short, should be logical, comprehensive, and contemporary.

To permit "successful" browsing, the notations or call-numbers themselves--the shorthand surrogates for topics and genres--must be:

1) reliably constant in meaning or value (What "301.412" signifies today, it should also signify tomorrow);[2] and
2) moderate in length. A notation longer than seven or eight digits--that is, four or five digits beyond the decimal point--not only becomes nearly impossible to remember, but also invites labeling, shelving, and keyboarding errors.[3]

A classification scheme like Dewey should be "managed" by its stewards, its producers and designers, in a way that promptly reflects new scholarship, research, and publishing developments, while simultaneously respecting the needs and limitations of its consumers in the "real" library world.

In mid-1979, Forest Press issued a three-volume 19th edition of the <u>Dewey Decimal Classification</u> (DDC), which the Decimal Classification Division (DCD) at the Library of Congress began to implement in January 1980.[4] According to Benjamin A. Custer, DDC 19 editor and DCD chief, writing before publication, completely remodeled provisions will appear for the following:[5]

---

*Reprinted by permission of the author and publisher from <u>Library Journal</u>, March 1, 1980, p. 585-89. Published by R. R. Bowker Co. (a Xerox company). Copyright © 1980 by Xerox Corporation.

301-307 Sociology will be expanded from the former 301, making use in addition of 302-307, numbers that have not been used for nearly 20 years, when they were the standard subdivisions of the social sciences.

324 The political process will be revised from the former 324 and 329, and will supply detailed numbers for political parties of the United States and many other countries.

In addition to the relocations in the phoenix schedules [301-307 and 324], there will be about 340 other relocations.... Not surprisingly, nearly half of these are in the social sciences and technology classes, 300 and 600. 5.

Forest Press should immediately recall the 19th edition and DCD refuse to further implement it for these reasons:

"Phoenix schedules, " however satisfying to ivory tower scheme-makers, create absolute havoc on library shelves and effectively undermine both "successful" browsing and the library's own credibility. [6] The common "management" nostrums--to either reclassify all the affected materials or insert wooden "dummies" that refer from "old" to "new" numbers and vice-versa--are laughably unrealistic, particularly in a time of budgetary retrenchment, staff shortages, and continuing backlogs. [7] If a new "Phoenix" in fact replaced a hopelessly outdated, confused, and constricted schedule with something indisputably more thorough and modern, a substitute also highlighted by consistently shorter basic notations than the original, an understandable--if still tenuous--argument might be made for it. That is not, however, the case with DDC 19's 301-307 substitution for the earlier 301/309 ranges. For example: "Social control and socialization, " 301. 15 in DDC 18, becomes 303. 3 in Edition 19, the chief "advantage" being a one-digit-shorter notation, but nevertheless a notation completely alien and unknown to regular, live browsers and library staff.

DDC 18, in its 301. 43-. 435 sequence, provided discrete numbers for "Children, " "Adolescents, " "Mature and middle-aged persons, " and "Aged persons. " Edition 19, by contrast, retrogressively specifies places for only "Young people" (up to age 20), "Adults, " and "Adults aged 65 and over" (305. 2-. 26). "Teenagers" have thus been eliminated as a separate, shelve-together category, and the "new" edition entirely fails to introduce a useful notation for "Young adults" (ages 18-25). [8]

Edition 18 allotted one number each to "The sexes and their relations" (301. 41), "Men" (301. 411), and "Women" (301. 412). DDC 19 allocates no number to "The sexes and their relations, " instead declaring that "comprehensive works on specific sexes" should be classed in the single slot for "Men" (305. 3). A whole, vital category of comparative "sexual relations" materials, which previously enjoyed a distinct location, is now illogically and unreasonably subsumed under the number for one of the two sexes. Further, while

Technical Services/Readers' Services 101

the "Women"-sequence has been rightly expanded (from one number to four), "Men" underwent no comparable refinement. And it may be strongly claimed that both topics deserve even more than four numbers apiece.[9]

Although Edition 18 can hardly be credited with a wholly up-to-date and accurate breakdown for "Sexuality" themes, at least it recognized individual subjects or subject clusters like "Courtship," "Dating," "Premarital relations," and "Incest/Bestiality/Sadism/Masochism," investing each with a special number. DDC 19 lumps all those previously separated topics into one number, 306.7 ("Institutions pertaining to relations of the sexes"). Further, it continues the unpardonable neglect of Gays by again assigning only one five-digit spot to "Homosexuality," making no provision for the independent collocation of materials dealing uniquely with Gay men, with Lesbians, and with the Gay Liberation Movement.[10] Moreover, "Bisexuality" has been ineptly subsumed under "Homosexuality," while "Transvestism," "Transsexuality," and "Heterosexuality," all ignored in Edition 18, similarly appear nowhere in DDC 19--not in the schedules nor the index.[11]

Like the "Phoenixes," numerous single-number "relocations" destroy the integrity, the trustworthiness, of old and/or new numbers without compensating benefits.

"Subject cataloging," for example, has been switched from 025.33 to the new 025.47, now following--rather than preceding--"Classification." And "Abstracting" and "Indexing" alike have been transferred from the now-abolished 029s to the revamped 025.4s. What was the compelling need to move them at all? And if it were agreed that, yes, indexing should inhabit the same shelf-space as "subject cataloging," why not inflict minimal devastation by simply expanding 025.33 to accommodate the indexing topics (which even in DDC 19 run to six digits, anyway)?

"Safety" is wantonly transferred from 614.8 to 363.1, and "Product hazards" from 614.3 to 363.19, distances of nearly 300-digits! And "Family planning" is forcibly and illogically moved from the 300s to the 600s. The four places traditionally and appropriately specified for North American Indians--970.1 (History and civilization), 970.3 (Specific peoples), 970.4 (Specific places), and 970.5 (Government relations)--have been rendered "optional," meaning--from a purely practical standpoint--that DCD won't apply them and consumers therefore won't find them on LC cards and other "outside copy." What will DCD apply instead? The newly "preferred" 970.00497 as a catch-all for the first three notations, and 323.1197 in place of 970.5. There's an adjective that nicely describes such changes. It's "irresponsible."

Expansions of many fields and subjects that should have been effected years ago by means of semi-annual Dewey Decimal Classification additions, notes, and decisions (DC&), have not yet been instituted. The overriding example is "Popular music." Edition 18 accorded this genre--of tremendous import to public and school collections--a single finite number: 780.42. DDC 19 practically repeats that woeful treatment, merely inserting a four-number "Popular song" sequence at 784.5 (encompassing Country, Blues, Rock, and Soul vocal music), which prompted this comment from a public library cataloger:

> Public libraries, in particular, have for years been ill-served by Dewey music schedules that allocate a single notation for "Popular music." That sole number, presumably, is sufficient to accommodate thousands of records and tapes in genres as diverse as Blues, Rock, Country, and Soul. Well, it doesn't accommodate them. And while the Dewey-directors had long ago promised a 780-phoenix for Edition 19, it won't be there. The explanation: "serious reservations" among members (whoever they are) of the Decimal Classification Editorial Policy Committee. But a whole phoenix isn't necessarily required. What is needed--and could have been supplied already--is a sensible, usable breakdown for pop music. Forest Press, et al. not only haven't met this demonstrated need, but probably won't do so--at least until Edition 20 (i.e., about 1986). Which is inexcusable.[12]

What could have been done to bring overdue relief and consistency to "pop music" classifying without wrecking the integrity of existing 780 numbers? Perhaps something akin to the sequence developed over several years at Hennepin County Library (HCL):

780.4	General special
.42	Popular music
	Class jazz in 785.42, ragtime in 785.422 Further divide .42 schedule like numbers following "78" in 784.1-.3 (Vocals) and 785-789 (Instrumentals); e.g., blues vocal, 780.42643
.421	General popular
	Examples: Mancini, Welk, Streisand, Sinatra, Martin, Andrews Sisters
.422	Country-Western
.423	Bluegrass
.424	Rock
	Class Rock opera in 782.2
.42499	Disco
.425	Soul
	Including Rhythm-and-blues
.426	Blues
.427	Reggae

Scores of "new" topics for which ample "literary warrant" exists, and often has existed for years, remain unrepresented in either the schedules or index, with the result that increasing holdings in these areas are likely to be scattered or buried under imprecise

Technical Services/Readers' Services

or too-broad numbers rather than collocated in specified and expectable places. As examples, indicating how and when the Hennepin County Library validated each subject:

Topic	HCL No.	Date
Alternative medicine[13]	610.42	Nov. 1978
Appropriate technology	604.3	Sept. 1977
Backpacking [DDC subsumes under "Walking," 796.51]	796.53	July 1977
Ballooning	797.57	July 1977
Barbershop quartets	784.72	Sept. 1978
Battered women	362.882	July 1977
Belly dancing	793.325	Apr. 1974
Bermuda Triangle	001.946	Nov. 1977
Biorhythm theory	133.34	Nov. 1978
Cinematic poetry	791.4354	Sept. 1974
Computer art	744	Sept. 1978
Copy art	778.1	Nov. 1979
Dance drill teams, chorus lines	793.326	Sept. 1977
Ethnic publishers	070.596	Mar. 1975
Frisbee	796.23	July 1977
GI Movement ("Including coffeehouses, underground press, American Servicemen's Union, anti-war activities")	355.227	Aug. 1975
Genetic engineering ("Including cloning and sex-selection")	575.3	July 1977
Governesses/wet-nurses/nannies	649.2	Jan. 1974
Government grants	336.395	May 1978
Greenhouses [DDC subsumes under "Farm buildings," 728.92]	728.93	May 1978
Hang gliding	797.553	June 1975
High-fiber cooking	641.5637	Sept. 1977
Holistic health	610.42	Nov. 1978
Homesteading	630.43	Aug. 1975
Hospices	362.19604	July 1978
Ice skate dancing	793.336	Apr. 1977
Jury reform	347.0753	Oct. 1975
Kirlian photography	778.38	Sept. 1976
Mainstreaming (Education)	371.9046	Sept. 1978
"New Age"	132	May 1979
Oral history	907.204	Mar. 1978
Orienteering	796.55	Apr. 1977
Packhorse camping	796.546	Sept. 1977
Paddle tennis [DDC subsumes under "Racket games," 796.34]	796.344	Mar. 1979
Paddleball	796.348	Mar. 1979
Parent education	649.107	July 1977
Planned unit development	333.382	Nov. 1977
Police malpractice	363.25	Jan. 1974
Popular culture	301.17	Jan. 1978
Protest songs	784.67	May 1976

Topic	HCL No.	Date
Psychic archaeology	133.87	Sept. 1978
Pyramid energy	118.2	Apr. 1977
Race walking	796.427	Mar. 1975
Rape victims	362.883	Sept. 1977
Rock opera	782.2	Apr. 1974
Roller skate dancing	793.336	Apr. 1977
Rope skipping	796.45	Dec. 1976
Runaway services [DDC subsumes under "Maladjusted young people," 362.74]	362.75	Apr. 1977
Senior Power	301.43532	Oct. 1975
Singing commercials	784.69	July 1977
Skateboarding [DDC subsumes under "Roller skating," 796.21]	796.22	Sept. 1976
Small presses	070.598	June 1975
Space colonies	629.447	Sept. 1977
Sports betting	796.04	Oct. 1975
Style manuals (Journalism/publishing)	070.0202	July 1978
Volunteer workers/volunteerism	331.53	Sept. 1976
War games [DDC subsumes under "Indoor diversions," 793.9]	794.4	Apr. 1974
Women and labor unions	331.882	Mar. 1975
Women's music	780.46	Sept. 1976
Women's publishers	070.596	Mar. 1975
Women's songs	784.65	May 1976
Wood heating	697.041	Aug. 1975

In sum, it is time to totally reform the process of DDC revision, perhaps according to these guidelines:

No more Phoenix schedules;

No more "Relocations" except when approved by two-thirds of an editorial board composed of representatives elected--on a proportional basis--by the public, school, and academic libraries that actually use Dewey (this formula would exclude from voting membership all Library of Congress and Forest Press personnel, as well as library school faculty);[14]

Timely integration of new or expanded topics within existing schedules, which can easily be achieved by adding digits to current numbers, reviving latent notations of redefining the scope of active numbers.

References

1. Berman has posited as one of three "cardinal principles of classification" that "similar materials should be found in the same or nearby Dewey-ranges." See "Deweying the supernatural," HCL cataloging bulletin, No. 36 (Sept./Oct. 1978), p. 38.

2. Maurice Freedman observes that "both users and classifiers ... profit from the non-duplication of numbers with different subject matters. It is a horror in the real world to have totally different categories of materials occupying the same Dewey number. It is bad enough that a given subject is split between two numbers, but when a multiplicity of categories reside at the same address, the user's resultant confusion is the kind of public service problem that libraries can do without." See "Better latent than never--a few short comments on the proposed DDC 19, and the Custer/Comaromi statements in HCLCB No. 35," HCL cataloging bulletin, No. 37 (Nov./Dec. 1978), p. 6.

3. John P. Comaromi, who chairs the Decimal Classification Editorial Policy Committee, recently suggested that "if your library is large or intends to become so, use the Dewey number to its fullest extent. If that is impossible, set your limit on number length at seven-past-the-decimal point...." See "DDC 19: the reclass project," HCL cataloging bulletin, No. 35 (July/Aug. 1978), p. 14. Freedman subsequently responded that to: "extend Dewey numbers at least seven-past-the-decimal-point is one of the most impractical suggestions made, and the one I would recommend that all non-research libraries ignore. The Branch Libraries of the New York Public Library, possibly the largest public library in the country, extends to five-past-the-decimal-point, and even then pages have trouble properly shelving materials. The long Dewey number is error-prone for the classifier, processor, shelver, and reader. Further, the justification for these long numbers can only be sustained--at best--when one considers their use in large research libraries. One omitted the reference librarian, who, even more importantly than the cataloger, must have a working memory of the more common Dewey numbers. Requiring this person to do floor work, "schlepping" around ten-digit numbers, seems unreasonable.... Ten digits are just too many for practical application in a browsing library.... Even in a closed stack situation, the page or shelver is still prone to error....

"The larger issue, and one can only guess this was an unstated motivation of Prof. Comaromi in his advocacy of these long numbers, is the elegance and manipulability of extended numbers for machine retrieval purposes. In Great Britain there is an interest in classification research and the use of computers for retrieval purposes which has no parallel here. In a closed stack collection for which classification is primarily or solely a means of subject analysis and retrieval rather than shelf location, lengthy classification numbers can be quite useful and of significant value. But in the American public library context, one finds them most impractical and confounding for all of the people who must deal with them."--"Better latent than never," p. 9. And Katharine Gaines has similarly argued for more mnemonics and shorter notations. See "Dewey: for--or against--the

public library?," HCL cataloging bulletin, Nos. 23/24 (Sept. 1, 1976), p. 7-8, 10.
4. Benjamin A. Custer, "DDC 19: characteristics," HCL cataloging bulletin, No. 35 (July/Aug. 1978), p. 9.
5. Custer, p. 9-10.
6. Freedman has commented that: "the DDC, or for that matter any classification system which functions primarily as a shelf arrangement device for a browsing ... library, should minimize dislocation and change so as to avoid the attendant hardship on the library's users--both the public and the staff who use the collections in order to help the public. Changes must be based on more than just aesthetic or theoretical considerations.... The basic point is that classification is ... both a physical and conceptual arrangement of library materials, and as such each shift, be it unique or part of a body rising from its own ashes, should be viewed from a principle of necessity and utility: is this change absolutely necessary, and will the benefits far outweigh the ensuing problems?"-- "Better latent than never," p. 7. And Marvin Scilken, editor of the Unabashed librarian and director of the Orange (N.J.) Public Library, adds that "DDC 19, AACR2, etc. will only make us look more foolish in the eyes of our users, that small percentage of the public that's willing to put up with us now." Letter in HCL cataloging bulletin, No. 37 (Nov./Dec. 1978), p. 12.
7. Comaromi recommends reclassification and shelf-dummies in "DDC 19: the reclass project," p. 12-15. Berman replied in HCL cataloging bulletin, no. 36 (Sept./Oct. 1978), p. 37: "Ordinary libraries, already faced with reduced income and inflationary costs, plainly cannot implement the sort of 'reclass project' recommended by Prof. Comaromi. They don't have the staff nor time. And even the 'dummy'-approach may be unfeasible when dealing with literally hundreds of 'relocations' per library in systems composed of ten, twenty, or more agencies." And Scilken (p. 12) characterized the Comaromi-approach as "unworldly," explaining: "It's my impression that most public libraries are lucky if they have one cataloger. And most school libraries have none.
Comaromi assumes that libraries have a reclass platoon on the beach waiting for its eight-year cycle to come up so it can 'get in there' and reclass for the old Dui. This would be great, but we all know what a mess most of our catalogs are in and DDC 19 will only add to the morass of trash.
If we lived in a perfect world, with books and cards reclassifying themselves, change would be wonderful. In the world of Jarvis/Gann, it seems foolish to foist extensive changes that increase both librarians' guilt and libraries' disorganization."
For another "reclass"-critique, from the perspective of clerical and page staff, see Steve Thompson's letter in HCL cataloging bulletin, No. 37, p. 13-14.
8. HCL did so in early 1979 by inserting between 301.4315 (Adolescents) and 301.434 (Mature and middle-aged persons) and

Technical Services/Readers' Services 107

otherwise-unused number: 301.432. See HCL cataloging bulletin, No. 39 (March/April 1979), p. 33.

9. For HCL's 1975 expansion of the 301.41s, including specifications for topics like Androgyny, Men's and Women's Studies, Men's Liberation, the Women's Movement, Sexism, Homemakers, and Consciousness-raising groups, see "New and revised DDC notations," HCL cataloging bulletin, Nos. 11-13 (March 15, 1975), p. 13-16.

10. For HCL's handling, see "New and revised DDC notations," HCL cataloging bulletin, Nos. 11-13 (March 15, 1975), p. 16. Also: S. Berman's "Gay access: new approaches in cataloging," Gay insurgent, Nos. 4/5 (Spring 1979), p. 14-15. Unsurprisingly, the DDC 19 index includes absolutely no "Gay" entries nor cross-references. It does, however, predictably site "Homosexuality" in no less than four separate medical/clinical numbers (e.g., 157.7, "Disorders of character and personality"), in "Social issues" (363.49), and in "Social theology," as well as referring to "Moral issues" and "Sexual deviations" for "other aspects" of the topic.

11. HCL in late 1973 reactivated 301.413 (formerly denoting "Celibacy") to "cover sociologically oriented material on Transvestism and Transvestites" and innovated 301.416 to represent "Transsexuality." See "Classification," HCL cataloging bulletin, No. 4 (Nov. 31, 1973), p. 12. A notation for "Bisexuality" (301.4156) was created about two years later. See "New and revised DDC notations," HCL cataloging bulletin, No. 17 (Oct. 1, 1975), p. 13.

12. S. Berman, HCL cataloging bulletin, No. 36 (Sept./Oct. 1978), p. 37. For another critique, see Freedman, p. 7.

13. Only one "Alternative" entry appears in the DDC 19 index: "Alternative education."

14. Pre-publication input from DDC users seems to have been minimal. And even unwanted. There appears to be no mechanism for Dewey-consumers to directly elect representatives to advisory or policy-making bodies. And there is little or no visible effort to secure advance opinion on proposed changes. Indeed, the whole revision process comes across as marvelously secretive and hush-hush, almost as if "national security" would be threatened by "leaks" or--much worse--public discussion. For further comment on DDC governance, see Freedman, p. 9, and Gaines, p. 7, who sagely noted that "since catalogers have so little clout (and too many have their feet stuck in detail), the designer doesn't hear enough about what's wrong and goes on merrily constructing abstract cobwebs. These designers of revised schedules probably never use them ... in actual public library practice."

PUBLISHERS VS. WHOLESALERS:

THE ORDERING DILEMMA*

Ruth Fraley

In attempting to come to terms with the economic aspects of the library-publisher-wholesaler relationship, two major problems emerge. The first has to do with the scope of the matter. The present situation in acquisitions is such that almost every issue discussed here today creates an economic impact. Each decision in marketing and services generates publisher or wholesaler costs which must either cut into profit, be passed along to the consumer, or both. When these costs are passed along, the library costs go up. The second major problem concerns assimilation of all the data which has been painstakingly gathered over the years.

Initially, the best way to approach these problems of scope and assimilation of data is through statistical analysis. It is important to bear in mind that most of these figures are affected by the fact that I come from a small library; therefore I cannot affect any economy of scale because I deal in small quantities.

Publishers Weekly recently published tables excerpted from Book Industry Trends which compare total net book sales for 1973 and 1977 and include projections, by market segment, for 1982. The PW category, "libraries and institutions," recognizes a tendency for libraries to rely more heavily on the wholesaler as opposed to dealing directly with publishers. It is interesting to note that projected library purchases are seen as declining in total overall amount by 1982. Purchases direct to retail outlets are projected at a constant 1.6% of total; direct from publishers purchases show a decline of a little over 1% of the total. Purchases from wholesalers by libraries naturally also show a decline. The most revealing estimate is that by 1982, wholesalers will account for about 63% of total library sales; this figure is up from 56% in 1973 and 61% in 1977. My perspective indicates that these projects may be low. Libraries may be purchasing more than 63% of their total volume from wholesalers by 1982. It is strange that two groups with the

---

*Reprinted by permission of the author and publisher from Library Acquisitions: Practice and Theory, 3 (1979) 9-13; copyright © 1979 Pergamon Press Ltd.

symbiotic relationship of libraries and publishers are becoming increasingly more reliant on the "middle man" and his services and discounts.

Obviously, libraries are not immune to inflation. Those in the public sector, even on the smallest scale, are being forced into a more accurate and detailed cost justification of their very existence, as well as having to justify each line item in their budget. Although I am not as familiar with private as I am with public institutions, I know that even private institutions are not immune to inflation. The book line is no longer sacred; it is no longer untouchable. Some libraries are even being forced to choose between staff and books. Attempts to retain both must be documented so that a non-librarian, such as the administrator of the county board who really works for the local power company, can understand the needs of the library. We do not have enough industry-wide standardization so that a librarian can approach the county board or the public library trustees or the school principal and present a viable budget. Librarians are forced to generate their own statistics in order to justify their requests. Effectiveness and credibility are impaired by this type of situation.

Our institution, for example, bases the book budget for the next year on a calculation which I submit to my Director. She submits it to the Dean, the Dean submits it to the President, the President submits it to the College Board, and they in turn submit it to the County Board. The calculations generally begin the month before when we determine our actual cost per volume for the previous academic year. I determine the actual cost of processing which is then added to this average per volume cost. The inflation figure of the previous year is added to determine a projected cost per volume. We then request a number of titles based on the actual percentage of total title output as listed in the Bowker Annual. Throughout the subsequent year's budget cuts and reviews, we defend our calculations. Sometimes we rewrite the same rationale ten times. The problems caused by Proposition 13 create difficult monetary situations which are decidedly unpleasant and frustrating. How does this relate to the situation concerning publishers, libraries and wholesalers? When all is said and done, and I compare what I actually purchased this year with what I claimed I could purchase, I have, at best, a poor correlation. In other words, the two do not match up and that makes an impact on my credibility for the next year. If I say that for $5,000 I can buy a certain number of volumes and later I find that I cannot possibly buy that number for $5,000, then I must explain the discrepancy. Very rarely, if ever, have we received the actual discount publishers supposedly offer libraries for dealing direct. When the discount was given, the cost of postage added to the net frequently brought the total over the list price or the list price was changed after the promotional literature was issued. This one factor brings to light many variables affecting the library-publisher-wholesaler triad.

    1. Small institutions usually have small staffs. One individual is frequently assigned responsibility for more

than one area within the library. Thus, time available for acquisitions during a working day becomes a very real problem. I do not think that this occurs only in small libraries either. Answering questions and dealing with the public sometimes requires a great deal of time and may cut in to the time allocated for acquisitions work.

2. The requirement of the institution with regard to the mechanics of purchasing affects academic institutions as well as libraries purchasing through a central office such as the U.S. Government libraries, or public libraries who may purchase through the sponsoring agency. For example, in our institution the business office is the "Bill to" location. Unless a problem on a direct order is perceived by the office staff, or unless the publisher notifies us directly of a problem, there is no routine feedback to the library on individual accounts other than the report that the publisher cannot supply the book. We have requested notification, but staff and time are not available. Our particular business office is very responsive to our needs; however, they are responsible for the entire institutional accounting and we must assume a position on a series of their priorities. Those priorities occasionally differ from ours. When a bill comes in listing the cost of a direct order as $30.00 and we have it encumbered on the basis of $15.00 list, the chance is that we will not discover the difference until we find that our reconciliation, which we attempt monthly, is in error. The inability to check or follow up on each order produced which arrives at a higher cost than list, or which results in overpayment, erodes our budget. This problem actually occurred with a direct order sent by one library. The correct price was finally charged, but not until mutually costly correspondence was sent and invoices were re-issued. Both publisher and library incurred costs almost three times the price of the book before the question was settled.

3. More business office or institutionally created problems exist in the required paperwork area. Wholesalers seem to be able to accept the varied requirements such as not paying without a signed claim form and not paying any partial orders. Many publishers either choose not to read or do not read the claim form; it may be that they are trying to avoid the costs of the additional bookkeeping step required to submit the signed claim form. In any case, the library does not pay. Our next order is simply not shipped because we have become listed as a poor customer. The business office then holds the requisition open, the library has an entire drawer of unfilled orders, and the publisher decides that selling to us is the least desirable item on his agenda for the day. Unrealistic publication dates and incredible delays create the same kind of situation. If I send a direct order to a publisher for fifteen titles and all are shipped except one title, my institutional rules prevent payment. This kind of thing has to

be costly to the publisher; on the other hand, the wholesaler seems to understand and be better equipped to deal with this kind of situation. It becomes non-productive to deal direct.

4. A small library generates a small volume. Therefore, if there is a discount schedule, as I mentioned before, somehow it rarely is applied. I recently attended a program in which a university press representative assured everyone that the close operating margin and implied backlist maintenance are such that discounts are actually available only to those who place standing orders for all university press titles. We have no intention of doing this; personally, I think this borders on blackmail.

5. In a cost-conscious institution, the costs of placing a direct order must be carefully calculated to determine if they are offset by the preferred discount. Here the problem of staffing becomes important. The publishing industry seems to be exceptionally fluid. Staff members may spend months just checking as to ownership, distribution, and location of certain publishers. Often the next step in the process is to actually place the order before someone takes over the publisher or they relocate. Once the material arrives, the staff has to take the time to inspect each item. When the only copy of a much-needed item arrives with two signatures missing, or one in upside down, it creates a real problem for the library. When dealing direct, the staff must spend an inordinate amount of time determining the particular publisher's return policy and attempt to follow through on it. Generally speaking, a wholesaler's return policy is more flexible. The wholesaler charges for this flexibility; however, considering staff time, in the long run, dealing with the wholesaler is less expensive. The time involved in the additional separate requisition must be considered, as well as the supplies consumed and the amounts of superfluous information which must be maintained.

6. Publishers, wholesalers, and libraries are staffed by humans or by computers operated by humans. Humans are not perfect and any error results in expensive, frequently absurd situations. The reprint houses seem to be among the worst offenders in this area. One library recently received a packet of 10 MCOF's with a very nice letter indicating that someone had just found these orders, which had been submitted in 1969. The publisher wanted to know if the library was still interested! The house was considerate enough to list price changes on the orders. Most increased in price over 100%!! Many libraries find that orders sent for heavily promoted materials are returned marked "no longer available"; or if they are sent, a check indicates that the price has increased exorbitantly just since the order was initiated. One begins to wonder if it is really desirable to deal directly, or if it would be possible for the publisher to put

a caveat on the sales material stating his position regarding direct orders, such as "dealing through wholesalers preferred, " or, "list price direct, " the actual cost to libraries.

The community college library has a special problem concerning publishers and wholesalers because of its unique status. It is neither a public nor a strictly academic library. As a result of this status, acquisitions librarians deal with several specialized publishers and associations which have almost as many complicated sets of circumstances as does the library itself. Most of these publishers which are attainable through jobbers will either give no discount at all or less than 13%. The result of this, in our institution at least, is that over 38% of our orders submitted to jobbers during one academic year were discounted between zero and 13%. The fill rate from our two major jobbers was 82% for one and 83% for another. Actual cancellations were 2% and 5% respectively. Obviously, we have an incredible amount of material in limbo. This has a serious impact on my total available funds. Sixteen percent of all orders with Jobber A and 13% of all orders with Jobber B are in suspension. Since we must close out book orders at the end of each fiscal year, then reencumber or issue confirming orders in the next fiscal year, usually at a new price, the library is faced with a vast bank of floating orders which we cannot quantify. We do not request a 90-day cancellation cycle because most of the items in suspension are those we really need for our collection. We do not mass order in any area. Each title is requested to fill a real or perceived need, and some titles are sent to jobbers only after we have accumulated a file of correspondence with the publisher. Any business with 29% of its orders on a suspension basis at the end of the fiscal year would find its management in serious trouble.

As a result of the "mix" and its subsequent problems, we encumber for each jobber on the basis of a formula. For example, last year our actual average book cost for Jobber A was $14.16 per title. Therefore, this year, we encumber our requisitions to Jobber A at the rate of $14.16 multiplied by the number of titles, multiplied by the average actual percent of increase over the previous year. Jobber B is encumbered at $13.88 per title plus the increase, etc. Fortunately, the jobbers send invoices to us so that we release the encumbrances when at least 95% of the requisition is accounted for or when the year ends in our records. Thus, we retrieve some of the funds relegated to limbo. Our direct orders averaged $18.17 per title. The Bowker Annual average cost for all books during the same period was $18.03. As for actual discounts on list price to us during the past year, Jobber A averaged 26% and Jobber B 19%.

The schedule distributed indicates some of the most puzzling aspects of the discounting question. Our discounts for the same publisher vary considerably. Those listed are ten of the largest publishing houses. I kept track of discounts received over the

PERCENTAGE OF ALL TITLES ORDERED AT VARIOUS JOBBER DISCOUNTS FROM 10 MAJOR PUBLISHERS

Discounts

Publisher	Jobber A 0%	Jobber A 10%	Jobber A 13.2%	Jobber A 36%	Jobber B 10.5%	Jobber B 11%	Jobber B 20%	Jobber B 36%
1	—	—	33[a]	66	—	50	50	—
2	—	—	—	100	14	—	—	86
3	—	—	20	80	—	100	—	—
4[b]	2.8	78.7	28.5	—	—	—	—	—
5	—	—	43	57	—	—	—	100
6	—	—	14	86	—	—	5	95
7	—	—	10	90	—	—	—	100
8	—	9	50	41	—	—	86	14
9	—	—	42	58	—	—	100	—
10	—	32	68	—	—	5	95	—

[a] Represents percentage of all titles ordered from the numbered publisher at the varying discounts.
[b] No titles ordered through Jobber B.

course of a year and the diversity clearly indicates that libraries cannot assume a certain percentage discount when ordering the output of a particular publisher. When acquisitions are placed in machine readable form, it seems as if there should be a field assigned to the price which would include a reliable discount indicator. Currently the prices are not listed accurately.

Somewhere in the chain of ordering, the list prices become unreliable and the discounts become unreliable. The library is then faced with the problem of justifying its budget with inaccurate data.

The end result of these variables is difficulty in accurately projecting budgets. Once the budget is determined, it is often indefensible. The potential effect is a reduction in the book line and a subsequent reduction in our purchasing. If this condition becomes common, there will indeed be an impact on publishing sales. Even though libraries represent a very small percentage of overall sales, I believe that if we go under there will be an impact.

We recognize the fact that libraries create problems for publishers just as publishers create problems for librarians. Perhaps establishing firmer publishing dates, sending copies of discount schedules to libraries, coding prices in BIP, and firmly defining trade and non-trade books would remedy the situation. Perhaps the general wholesalers could pay attention to associations such as the National Fire Protection Association and the IACP as well as the National Association for Non-destructive Testing.

Just as our procedures cost publishers money, the unreliable list price and secret discount rate cost us money. Although libraries represent a relatively small percentage of total book sales, for some publishers we account for almost all sales; in 1977 we spent approximately 1.2 billion dollars. We have been buying books for hundreds of years. It is time to streamline operations so that we can continue to do so without using our money for clerical paperwork requirements and so that the entire process can be mutually cost beneficial.

References

Baumol, William J. and Matityaku Marcus. "Economics of academic libraries." (Washington, D.C.: American Council on Education; 1973). Includes suggested methods for analysis.
Bowker Annual (New York: Bowker Co.; 1977, 1978).
Dessauer, John P. "Projecting profits at Hypothesis Press." Publishers Weekly (July 24, 1978): 48-52.
Dessauer, John P. "U.S. consumer expenditures on books, 1977." Publishers Weekly (October 23, 1978): 33-34.
Doebler, Paul. "New data reveals industry reorientation." Publishers Weekly (October 9, 1978): 46-48.
Geiser, Elizabeth A. "Book marketing and selection: a publishing/library forum." Library Resources and Technical Services 20 (Winter, 1976): 65-69.

Kim, Ung Chon. *Policies of publishers; a handbook for order librarians* (Metuchen, N.J.: Scarecrow): 1976. Unfortunately, most policies are dated.

Melcher, Daniel and Margaret Saul. *Melcher on acquisitions* (Chicago: ALA): 1971.

Roth, H., ed. "An analysis and survey of commercial library supply houses." *Library Trends* (April, 1976).

OPENING A LIBRARY CATALOG*

Maurice J. Freedman

The library catalog has been the traditional means of access to the library's collection, but it has proven to be a barrier, as well, to reaching the library's information resources. For the last 75 years or more, the card catalog has been the almost exclusive form of catalog in American libraries.

The basic principles governing the catalog in United States libraries were defined by Charles Cutter in 1876, and elucidated upon and amplified by Seymour Lubetzky in the 1950's and 1960's. Fundamentally, these greatest American theoreticians of cataloging posited that the catalog had the following fundamental functions:

> 1. "To enable a person to find a book of which either the author, the title or the subject is known." (Charles A. Cutter, <u>Rules for a Dictionary Catalog</u>, 4th ed., rewritten, GPO, Washington, D.C., 1904, p. 12.)
> 2. "...be an efficient instrument for ascertaining ... which works by a particular author and which editions of a particular work are in the library." (<u>Statement of Principles Adopted by the International Conference on Cataloguing Principles</u>, Paris, October 1961, annotated ed., IFLA, Sevenoaks, England, 1966, page facing p. 3.) One can extend this to include which works under a given subject are in the library. Note that "book" and "work" should be taken as including information in all of its physical manifestations, i.e. all editions, translations, media formats, etc.

A basic problem of the card catalog is its inertness and lack of flexibility. As the library's card catalog grows over time, it becomes harder to use for a variety of reasons:

> 1. <u>Sheer size:</u> As the number of cards increases, there is a larger file to be queried; this becomes even more difficult as large files of cards accumulate under a given author or subject. One

---

*Reprinted by permission of the author and publisher from <u>Library Journal</u>, November 1, 1979, p. 2277-80. Published by R. R. Bowker Co. (a Xerox company). Copyright © 1979 by Xerox Corporation.

Technical Services/Readers' Services   117

must examine each card, in many cases, to conclude a search, and there is no way to obviate the need to handle each card.

2. <u>Resistance to change:</u> Because so many cards accumulate under a given heading, it can become too costly to change that heading, even if the manner of referring to it is different, has changed, or the area covered by a topic has been redefined. For example, the Library of Congress (LC) would have to shift many drawers of cards if it wanted to change the anachronistic name "Motor trucks" to "Trucks." Consequently, LC is retaining the antiquated form. As a result of this inflexibility many anachronistic, insensitive, and otherwise objectionable terms have been retained in library card catalogs; it is just too costly to change them.

Technological alternatives

Present technology has eliminated or ameliorated some of these problems of the card catalog and facilitates a more open view of the catalog as a medium of access to all forms of information. There are three technological considerations bearing on the role of the catalog at this time:

1. Because of the existence of such huge data bases as OCLC's (presently, over 4,000,000 catalog records), the costs of converting a card catalog to machine-readable form are as little as one-third to one-half as expensive as they were ten years ago. (If one includes a factor for inflation, the costs are even more dramatically reduced.) This means that libraries can now have all of their catalog information in the computer for a far more manageable price than ever before. This cost can be offset by the elimination of the continued maintenance cost of the individual library's card catalog in many instances. It has now become economically viable for many libraries to convert their card catalogs to machine-readable form.

2. Automated authority control, pioneered by the New York Public Library (NYPL), allows the library to make the change described above, "Motor trucks" to "Trucks," simply and quickly, whether there are one, 1000, or 10,000 entries under "Motor trucks." Earlier in the decade, NYPL was virtually alone in the development of automated catalog control facility, but now, apparently, all major library network agencies are in the process of developing this capacity.

3. The development of computer-output-microform (COM) as a catalog medium allows for the complete regeneration, cumulation, and duplication of the catalog (on reel microfilm COM or microfiche COM) quickly and cheaply. This avoids the expensive terminal, telecommunication line, and computer charges associated with the online catalog while still dramatically improving upon the costliness and diminishing the inflexibility of the card catalog.

Opening the catalog

Without belaboring points made elsewhere by many writers on the subject, many of the LC subject headings and name entries are neither timely, relevant, nor sensitive to the constituencies served by vast numbers, if not all, of American libraries, and the overwhelming majority of libraries LC purportedly serves insofar as it claims to be the de facto national library. Whereas in the card-based past a single form of entry, in effect a single standard record, seemed the only economically sound alternative, the machine-based present allows for a master machine record which can contain alternate forms suitable to the needs of different library publics. The National Library of Canada's machine controlled dual entries (i.e., English and French equivalents of a heading) and LC's provision of the National Library of Medicine's MESH headings, as well as juvenile headings, are, in effect, examples showing that a multiplicity of forms are possible with respect to a given bibliographic entry.

The catalog can thus be opened to meeting the needs of disparate publics through the dissemination of machine-readable records which carry alternate forms of headings suited to those publics. Because of the efficacy of machine-based authority control systems, the new forms of headings usually can be integrated into a master authority file, and through the cost efficiency and timeliness of COM, updated reaccumulated versions of the whole catalog can be published. (Whether LC is either capable of or interested in such an alternate service is only partially relevant; what is critical is that the technology now makes such a service possible.)

The abandonment of the card catalog now permits libraries to drop the undesirable forms of entries and headings used in that catalog, and initiate terms which promote rather than hinder access to the library's collection. Of course, many of the LC changes needed will well serve both public and research libraries, but many others will entail dual or alternate forms--a manageable problem with a machine-based authority controlled catalog. Further, some of the entries will not involve one-to-one differences. For example, a book on eight famous black leaders held by an American public library would be much better cataloged by having added subject entries for each of the leaders described, whereas a collective biographical heading has been viewed by LC as meeting the needs of a U.S. research library.

Integrating formats

In both of these cases, a national cataloging distribution center would open up the service range of the nonresearch library's catalog through such an enriched standardized record. Although not specifically tailoring the service to a single library, it would come a lot closer to meeting the needs of the clientele of the nonresearch library than the single heading service which is based solely on LC's own research library needs.

Librarians have tended to discriminate against nonprint media. Public libraries are probably the worst offenders in view of their frequent practice of segregating catalog files by media format. There is usually a separate sound recording catalog and a separate film catalog. When there are media forms other than film and sound recordings, there is limited if any cataloging for them at all. If the Cutter/Lubetzky principles are to be taken seriously: that is, the requirement that all materials by a given author or on a given topic be brought together in a single place, then it is mandatory that an open catalog integrate all of the materials on "pollution" or by Maurice Sendak, irrespective of their format. The library user should not be forced to look in several catalogs to satisfy an information need. Or worse yet, having looked in the catalog for print materials, think that all of the library's holdings on Picasso have been displayed, thus hiding, in effect, a fine documentary film interview or a slide-tape presentation on Picasso's blue period. Of course, machine-readability does allow, as appropriate, for the display of information by medium and does not preclude the generation of a separate film catalog. One cannot deny that the adult education instructor who wants a series of films to supplement a course being taught, will find it far more efficient to select from a catalog containing just films.

It is especially true of research libraries that the catalog has been closed all too long to their users in the area of government documents, technical reports, and journal literature. The technology discussed has less bearing on these areas, but nonetheless these materials must be included in any discussions of opening the catalog and providing access to all of the library's holdings. A major step forward was the production and dissemination of the Monthly Catalog in the MARC format, no small feat. It is particularly important that valuable information contained in documents be brought to the attention of the reader, much in the same collocative way discussed in reference to nonprint materials. An excellent government pamphlet on home repair, child-rearing, farming, or first aid may satisfy the information need of the library user, but because it is not referred to in the catalog, it is not accessible. Commendably, many libraries do catalog especially worthy documents and thus make them available with the library's book materials.

As to technical reports and the journal literature, these are still far away from integration into library machine-readable cataloging files. However, the first and necessary step is being taken with the procurement of data base services by libraries so that access to these materials is greatly enhanced. It is absolutely critical that individuals using these services not be personally charged for that use. One is not talking about "free" access; nothing is free. But people currently do not pay special fees for the printed bibliographies and indexes which libraries provide at great expense, Chemical Abstracts, for example, or for that matter, the card catalog, the most expensive tool in the library. One sees no compelling reason why an individual should be separately charged for the same information in machine-readable form that can be obtained without added charge in print form. The catalog is the instrument through which access is gained to the full variety of materials held by the library. Materials such as technical reports and journal literature should at least be considered in our future thinking regarding organized access to all of the library's holdings.

Local information

Another major area of concern--in effect, another place in which the catalog has been closed--has been the absence of access to local information resources. It is not surprising that network planning and automation development have been focused almost exclusively on bibliographical and material delivery systems which will meet the needs of scholars at Harvard, HEW, the Rand Corporation, and the rare public or academic library user who effectively emulates those researchers. But what of the information needs of the local community? Of the people who want to know which city agency will help them with the landlord who's turned off the heat, or where to get redress when a merchant will not take back defective merchandise, or where to take their children for free inoculations, or where the nearest private tennis club is located. These are all examples of community information needs that are not met through traditional card catalogs, and do not seem to be the concern of those planning America's bibliographical networks or, for that matter, local catalogs. But is it not reasonable that, if someone is looking up "methadone" in a local library catalog, in addition to print and nonprint materials on methadone held by the library a citation be given for the local methadone clinic, certainly a place where a great deal of information is available on the subject? The notion here is to integrate all information resources into the catalog, and indirectly break down the fortress-like setting traditionally provided for it by the library. We can now see the library as being not just a custodian for the materials it houses internally, but a more aggressive referral agent. Getting these local information resources into machine-readable form and disseminated locally is a local information network problem which must be addressed and provided for. The national context of discussions should at least take cognizance of the development requirements involved in the integration of local information resources into the local library's data files. For example, there is no MARC format for community agencies-- that is, no subfield code for phone number, address, eligibility requirements, etc. Recognition of the value of this kind of information, and its standardization and appropriate thesauri and service protocols, must be focused upon and developed. Each library should not have to create its own information and referral format.

How the information resources of one community will relate to those of another requires further thought, but one can see potential uses made both by scholars and nonscholars. The head of a NOW chapter might want to find out the names of all of the women related organizations in nearby counties. On the other hand, a university professor might conceivably want a list of all of the local consumer advocate offices in a given region of the country, or perhaps throughout the country. Thus the inclusion of local information resources opens the catalog to a wider and more integrated variety of information.

Special catalogs

Another major area of enriched access to library collections would be the production of special purpose catalogs. These would not have been practically feasible prior to automated systems. An innovative application was the use of NYPL's automated system, created originally to meet the needs of its Research Libraries, to produce a special book catalog for a media center created in the George Bruce Branch in Harlem. Enough copies of this catalog were printed so that each teacher in the branch's four neighborhood schools had available in each classroom, a wholly integrated catalog of all of the specially acquired media materials and all of the print and nonprint items held by the branch serving the neighborhoods of those schools. It is through the machine manipulability of a data base that such special products or services are possible. Obviously, the catalog, at least in this instance, is a tool which is actively promoting library service by going where the students and the teachers are, as opposed to waiting for them to show up at the library.

This leads back to the more general points about opening the catalog through the use of machine-based products. The COM catalog is readily reproducible and usable in as many places as there are COM readers. The Georgia Institute of Technology put COM copies of its catalog in dormitories, faculty and department offices, libraries, etc. at relatively little cost in the early 1970's. The University of Toronto COM catalog has been widely discussed at meetings and in the literature. This dissemination of the catalog is a major advance in research library bibliographic or catalog service.

ISBD

The International Standard Bibliographic Description (ISBD) is probably of usefulness to national libraries, and conceivably to some of the large research libraries. It performed a valuable service by prescribing a standard sequence of descriptive elements. However, the value of the prescribed punctuation and Latin and other abbreviations required by ISBD, especially for public and school libraries, is totally unconvincing. In addition, the necessary repetition of the author statement when it is identical to the main entry, violates any principle of reason or economy. The 1946 Report of the Advisory Committee on Descriptive Cataloging of the Librarian of Congress (p. 5) stated: "The omission of author statements that are identical with author headings is a clear gain in the catalog entry." One hastens to point out that machine-readability makes it possible for the library to exercise the option of deleting the relatively useless and obligatory ISBD punctuation from its own catalog records through local programming or the programming of their bibliographic utility. For nonresearch libraries, it has been proposed that a format be developed which actively promotes recognition or understanding by the layperson; i.e., those who have not been exposed to the meaning of the religious symbols of revised Chapter 6 of The Anglo American Cataloging Rules. The creation of such a descriptive format would attempt to foster the immediate comprehension of the data elements of the catalog record. Marvin Scilken has offered one alternative, having the words author, title, subject, appear immediately adjacent to the appropriate headings to which they refer. In this light, one study which should be considered is the development of an optimum nonresearch library catalog record display format. Such an alternative standard display could then be made available to libraries and library processors in the commercial and noncommercial area. In the process preceding the adoption of ALA of ISBD, no use studies were conducted. This alternative standard should include empirical investigation.

Lest one think that this notion of opening the catalog is "bluesky" or impractical, a brief description is offered of a place where much of this has been done. Using NYPL's automated authority control system to its fullest potential, the Hennepin County Library (HCL) of Minnesota converted its shelflist to MARC in 1972. HCL produced a computer typeset book catalog widely available in all of its facilities as well as some nonlibrary agencies such as the county government building and a local police station (the branch head wanted her community to have 24-hour bibliographic access). HCL wholly revised antiquated and otherwise deficient LC headings in a simple and relatively painless way from a cost and time standpoint, integrated all of its nonprint media into the catalog, and even lists several community information resources as well as most of the government documents it acquires under appropriate headings in the catalog. In addition, HCL refers the catalog user to the vertical file via a public catalog note under the appropriate subject heading when pamphlet, ephemeral, or other noncataloged material is available on that topic. The HCL also routinely and automatically strips ISBD punctuation from LC/MARC records entering Hennepin's data base. In 1973 it closed all of its card catalogs and eventually removed them from its branches. Some of the work of HCL was described in the author's "Cataloging systems: application status 1973," in Library Automation: State of the Art II, ALA, 1973. It has since been elaborated upon in the writings of Sanford Berman in the Hennepin County Library Cataloging Bulletin, of which he was editor, and in his paper in the forthcoming Closing the Catalog, edited by Kaye Gapen and Bonnie Juergens, to be published by Oryx Press.

Opportunity in closing

Librarians can insure that the closing of the card catalog is an opportunity to truly open the library catalog and promote the satisfaction of all user information needs. To do so they cannot follow, lemming-like, the de facto national library's practices nor countenance a bibliographic utility's practices if neither meet the local library's needs. When LC or OCLC or any other agency does not do the job local library users need, librarians should lobby for change and the services those users deserve. If neither LC nor one's bibliographic utility can meet the information users' information needs, try to satisfy them locally or in concert with similar libraries. Work to make the information resources of your library and your community as accessible to the library users as is within your power.

In that way bibliographic service can be enhanced, greater access to more information will be provided, and, ultimately, the user will be better served.

INTERNATIONAL INDIRECTION*

S. Michael Malinconico

Bernardo: How now, Horatio! you tremble and look pale.
           Is not this something more than fantasy?
           What think you on't?
Horatio: Before my God, I might not this believe.
           Without the sensible and true avouch
           of mine own eyes.
                                        Hamlet, Act I, Scene I

Ten years ago the International Federation of Library Associations (IFLA) met in Copenhagen, Denmark. At that meeting a group of international cataloging experts set in motion machinery that would result in 1974 in the first International Standard Bibliographic Description (ISBD). (ISBD's are prescriptions for the creation of bibliographic entries for various forms of material. Their most characteristic feature is their highly stylized punctuation, which it was thought would be useful in the machine encoding of bibliographic data.) The ISBD program, the first step in a program for Universal Bibliographic Control, was perhaps also the first clear demonstration of the ability of the Library of Congress (LC) to influence international standardization activities, and in an indirect, but nonetheless ineluctable manner bibliographic control in the United States. IFLA celebrated the tenth anniversary of that historic meeting by returning to Copenhagen in 1979. The Library of Congress was also very much in evidence throughout that meeting; its automation juggernaut, though stalled domestically as a consequence of its inability to provide leadership through concrete achievements, was in excellent working order and well lubricated in Copenhagen.

On numerous occasions LC has ably represented United States bibliographic interests in international fora; in particular, in those fora concerned with library automation. LC representatives when participating in international activities are generally assumed by all other participants to speak for the entire United States library com-

---
*Reprinted by permission of the author and publisher from Library Journal, December 15, 1979, p. 2628-31. Published by R. R. Bowker Co. (a Xerox company). Copyright © 1979 by Xerox Corporation.

munity despite the lack of any formal warrant. To Europeans accustomed to the idea of national bibliographic agencies whose authority and responsibility are defined by law, LC is naturally assumed to be the national library of the United States, and hence an agency with authority to speak for the entire nation. However, LC representatives to international gatherings are accountable to the Library of Congress, not to the general American library community. Thus, LC has for the most part represented the United States library community internationally without formal review by, or conscious delegation of authority from, that community.

At its 1976 meeting IFLA promulgated revised procedures intended to insure wider participation in its activities and to prevent the perpetuation of vested interests, which had come to characterize IFLA. The new rules of procedure were gradually put into effect during 1977 and 1978. Most of the IFLA membership greeted the new rules not simply as the dissolution of a decadent order, but rather as the portent of a bright and vital future for the Association. Ironically, it has not been the European delegations, reputedly unversed in the democratic process, that have attempted to resist the new order, but rather some elements of the American delegation. In particular, in 1978 and 1979 LC's automation representatives demonstrated remarkable creativity in devising means of circumventing those newly established procedures that were in conflict with their perceived interests.

It should be noted, however, that the actions of LC's representatives were by no means uniform in this regard. The chair of the Cataloging Section (LC's Director for Cataloging) established a laudable precedent in 1978, which was continued in 1979, by declaring one of the meetings of that section's Standing Committee open. (IFLA is organized into a number of sections, each of which has a standing committee that is responsible for its work.) The record established by other representatives of the Library of Congress, however, was not quite so exemplary. Unfortunately, in any society in which there is an attempt to insure equity by legislative fiat those who would resist have a clear advantage, as a finite set of rules cannot anticipate all possible eventualities. In the end, one must rely on the good will of the participants to insure conformity with the spirit of the law. This simple truth was demonstrated most convincingly in Copenhagen. The Library of Congress, which has come to dominate IFLA's automation activities, continued to do so and perhaps even strengthened its influence despite the new rules of procedure.

International indirection

The issues with which international organizations deal inevitably affect all libraries; there are few, if any, issues which can be thought to be the special province of a select group of libraries or librarians. It might be argued that international agreements affect only institutions with national responsibility such as the Library of Congress, not the average library. However, because of the extent to which most libraries seek to remain consistent with LC bibliographic practices in order to make the most effective use of the products and services it provides, this argument is gainsaid by reality. It is pure illusion for libraries to assume they are insulated from international developments. In fact, it is far easier for an institution such as the Library of Congress to initiate changes domestically by indirect means--e.g., by first having a desired program adopted internationally and then invoking the need for international cooperation to insure its adoption domestically--than it might be to introduce such changes directly! The mere adjective "international" is often sufficient to spare a proposed program the tedious indignity of domestic review.

U.S. endorsement of ISBD

The manner in which endorsement of the ISBD's was obtained in the United States should serve as an excellent illustration. For whatever reasons, the Library of Congress had in the late 1960's become committed to a data creation technique for MARC records known as Automatic Format Recognition (AFR). It became obvious early in its application that AFR was proving unwieldy for English language bibliographic data. After a great deal had been invested in AFR, it became painfully clear that an attempt to use it for cataloging data in foreign languages was impractical. Thus it would either have required that the LC MARC Office acknowledge that it had erred in its choice of AFR as an input technique or that some other means be found to make cataloging data self-identifying to a computer. IFLA's interest in developing a standard bibliographic description in 1969 must thus have seemed a ready-made opportunity for the latter approach, if only that program could be manipulated to serve LC's particular objectives. Henriette Avram, LC's automation representative to IFLA at the time, acknowledges the importance of the ISBD to format recognition in a report on the RECON Pilot Project written in 1972:

> ... the International Standard Bibliographic Description (ISBD) has broad implications for format recognition.... As a result of the International Meeting of Cataloging Experts sponsored by the International Federation of Library Associations and held in Copenhagen in August 1969, a working party was appointed to prepare a draft proposal for an International Standard Bibliographic Description. The objective was to formulate specifications for bibliographic description, including a standard order of data elements, a minimum set of mandatory data elements, and standard punctuation. <u>Use of the ISBD</u> by national bibliographies and cataloging agencies <u>would aid in the interpretation of cataloging data</u> by humans and <u>by format recognition programs.</u> If all cataloging agencies were to prepare their entries according to the ISBD, format recognition algorithms could then be more easily expanded to encompass foreign-language catalog records ... --Henriette D. Avram,

"RECON Pilot Project," Washington, D.C.: Library of Congress, 1972, p. 20 (Emphasis added)

Thus, whatever intrinsic merits the ISBD might have had, it was of particular importance to the Library of Congress to have it adopted in the United States. If it had not been adopted, foreign language MARC would perforce be delayed and a significant investment in data input software would be lost. The result was that ISBD(M) was adopted without much consultation with, or discussion by, the American library community. There was only some confused, unfocused debate which could never find an appropriate forum; indeed, none existed in the U.S. Throughout that debate, those who insisted that the proponents of ISBD should be required to demonstrate its advantage to American librarianship were effortlessly dismissed as opponents of international standardization--if not as neo-isolationists. The result is the highly stylized punctuation which was incorporated into the AACR for monographs in 1974, and for all materials in AACR2.

A decade later we find the Library of Congress actively seeking to manipulate yet another IFLA working group--a working group on an international authority control system. This might seem to be pretty heady stuff and far from the concerns of most librarians. But consider that part of the justification given for AACR2 is that it will foster international exchange of cataloging information. We can understand the importance of an international authority system by realizing that this is largely a spurious argument. All AACR2 will facilitate is the ready exchange of the descriptive portion of cataloging records, and LC has been doing that since 1967 without "AACR2." To go beyond the advantages already being derived from the Shared Cataloging program will require that the parties engaged in exchanging cataloging records adopt a common authority file. Thus the significance of an international authority system becomes apparent, as does the potential effect this will have on cataloging records used by every library in the United States. Likewise, participants in shared cataloging systems will no doubt need access to the international authority file, presumably controlled by LC, if they are to create authoritative cataloging records. Here again is an example of the potentially widespread influence of an international authority system.

It is not at all clear what the effect, if any, on American librarianship of an international authority systems will be, but if we are to find out before it's too late to act, we cannot passively abdicate responsibility for international developments to the Library of Congress or any other agency not accountable to the profession as a whole.

Circumventing IFLA rules

Since actions taken by international organizations such as IFLA potentially have a profound effect on all libraries, it is important that we understand how simple it is for those who would circumvent established rules and have undue influence to do so. A few examples from this year's IFLA meeting should serve to illustrate the point.

In order to insure the greatest diversity of participation in IFLA activities, a rule was adopted which precludes delegates from simultaneously serving on more than one standing committee.

The solution to this irksome constraint lay in the creative use of language. The chair of the mechanization section simply named herself liaison to the cataloguing section and then arranged to have a member of the cataloguing section (who had been working for LC on contract for some time), serve as liaison to the mechanization section.

The result is that a single person is able to influence and take active part in the deliberations of two sections without violating the letter of the law.

Likewise, in order to prevent working groups from becoming the private preserve of a few--as they had all too often in the past-- it was decided that members of standing committees could not serve on working groups established by their section. (Working groups are groups of technical experts in a particular field formed to address a specific issue, e.g., a working group to consider an international authority control system. Working groups play a very important role in IFLA's activities, as the product of their deliberations often become de facto or de jure standards, e.g., the ISBD's.)

The solution to this equally nettlesome hindrance is effected by naming oneself, as did the chair of the Mechanization section, "liaison" to a working group.

In this manner, quite contrary to the spirit of the IFLA constitution, members of a standing committee can influence the deliberations of a working group. Through the use of this ploy, the chair of the Mechanization section was able to assume such an active part in the deliberations of the working group on an international authority control system that she reported on the activities of that working group in the first person plural.

Because of the importance of working groups to the realization of IFLA's objectives, it was decided that criteria for selection to working groups should be openly specified before such groups are formed.

This particular requirement was perhaps one of the most difficult to circumvent--especially so when in 1978 criteria to be met by candidates for membership on a working group on an international authority system were announced at three open meetings. The solution to this dilemma required that a criterion--restricting participation to staff of national bibliographic agencies--be hastily added, at a closed meeting, to those announced publicly.

This permitted the chair of the Mechanization section to add a staff member from her office to the working group despite the fact that the person might have had some difficulty satisfying the criteria originally announced.

IFLA regulations permit each member of a section to nominate only one candidate to serve on the standing committee of that section.

Here again the enormous richness of the English language provides the solution to petty constraint that would limit the influence of a single institution. Without formal definition of its significance, the status of "observer" to the Mechanization section was established. In this manner a member of the LC Automated Systems Office, who was not formally named to the standing committee, was permitted to take part in its deliberations and have entree to its closed meetings.

The Cataloguing Section established a laudable precedent by declaring one of its standing committee meetings open in 1978. The section on Mechanization chose belatedly to follow this precedent in 1979. (Oddly, the printed program did not betray the existence of an open meeting.)

In order to circumvent the annoyance of having to conduct business before the "uninitiated" required some sacrifice on the part of the standing committee. Trivia were discussed in painful detail, and sensitive topics avoided by making language ambiguous, for the scheduled duration of the meeting.

At the appointed ending time for the meeting, the chair very politely excused the observers with assurances that "nothing of importance" would be discussed. However, the meeting was continued behind closed doors for an additional half hour.

As we can clearly see it is impossible to prevent abuses by rules alone.

It is distressing to find that, despite the many successful attempts by American delegates to reform IFLA's procedures, some members of the American delegation would nonetheless engage in overt, undisguised attempts to subvert these reforms. A Scandinavian colleague likened LC's tactics to Blitzkrieg; surely many of the other non-U.S. delegates must have viewed LC's actions in like manner.

For international accountability

Actions taken by international organizations such as IFLA have important consequences for all libraries in the U.S. It is, therefore, irresponsible of us to abdicate passively our responsibilities in this potentially critical area to the Library of Congress or any other single institution. It is essential that U.S. librarians assume direct involvement in international activities, or at least demand accountability from those who would speak for them in such fora. This can be done by working through those library associations which are members of IFLA. One can also take advantage of his or her institution's membership in IFLA. A surprisingly large number of libraries hold institutional membership. Institutional membership grants the holder a vote in elections, and the right to nominate candidates for election to various standing committees. Organizational and procedural information can be found in the IFLA Journal, which many libraries probably receive and shelve unread.

ALA's RTSD and LITA have already taken the initiative by forming committees to study means of enhancing ALA's influence in international activities. Other divisions and associations can perhaps profitably do the same. But the simplest action one can take is to attempt to remain informed of international activities, to determine in each case who is representing the United States, and how that representative might be influenced and held accountable for decisions made on behalf of the United States.

AACR 2--A REVIEW ARTICLE*

Phyllis A. Richmond

The task of writing a critique of the second edition of the <u>Anglo-American Cataloguing Rules</u> is a formidable one. No doubt details of the code will be dissected and discussed at great length during the next few years so that in time a thorough analysis will emerge. This essay will concentrate on fundamentals underlying construction of the code, leaving details for other and later reviews. Even with this limitation, there is much to consider.

Study of the <u>Anglo-American Cataloguing Rules</u>, second edition, hereafter referred to as AACR 2, should begin with a careful reading of its glossary and a comparison with glossaries of earlier rules for the terms: entry, entry word, main entry, added entry, headings, and unit entry (or equivalent).[1] This is in itself an education (see Appendix).

Principles of Cataloging in AACR 2

In looking for the principles underlying AACR 2, rather than treating what is past as prologue, this review article proposes that principles be extracted from the text. Further into this essay particulars are discussed in terms of these principles.

The first and most striking feature of AACR 2 is its operational aspect. The book is laid out according to formula. Every chapter in the first half follows the pattern set down in Chapter 1. The formula is a highly pragmatic one; it treats materials to be cataloged as objects. It describes these objects as a scientist describes a natural phenomenon, using a special methodology called the International Standard Bibliographic Description (ISBD). A very elaborate set of guidelines and rules has been devised to indicate what should be looked for, what to use or what not to use, what types of data must be used, may be used and may not be used, and how it is to be used.

---

*Reprinted by permission of the author and publisher from <u>The Journal of Academic Librarianship</u>, 6:1 (March 1980) 30-37; copyright © 1980 by the JAL.

Since the objects to be described usually have some kind of identification or labeling, this is the chief source of information. Failing this, other sources may be used, but must be indicated by brackets. In a book, for instance, the label is the title page itself. ISBD itself is actually a very carefully designed faceted classification, complete with facet indicators and a definite facet order, for purposes of descriptive cataloging. The facets and their indicators are shown in Figure 1.

Nucleus of Guidelines

The first principle used with ISBD is that each type of bibliographic material to be published as a physical entity should be identified. The ISBD for 11 such forms may be found in Chapters 2 through 12 in AACR 2. Space has been left for the addition of seven more as, or if, they are developed.

The second principle used with ISBD is that there must be a general framework of parts applicable to all forms (plus individualized sections where the form is unique).[2] Classifying the parts of the description and putting them in a definite facet order produces, uniformity in description, which was the overall goal of ISBD. The generalized elaboration of this description appears in Chapter 1 of AACR 2. It is used for routine identification of parts and their order in an entry.

These two principles may be named the Principle of Suitable Description for Different Kinds of Bibliographic Entities and the Principle of Uniform Description for All Kinds of Bibliographic Entities. The principles complement each other and form the nucleus of guidelines for the cataloger so that description may be made more or less consistently in spite of variant physical forms of a single work. In other words, the media shall not alter the format of their description, except where absolutely necessary by reason of their peculiar physical nature.

Why We Catalog This Way

After the material object has been described according to ISBD, then and only then may the cataloger start to think about access points: describe first and then consider how to prepare the object for use. Is this putting the cart before the horse? To answer this question, a number of other questions beginning with the word "why" arise.

Why does the library catalog exist? Why does anyone use it? Why does it matter how it is arranged? Why worry about basic order or uniform description if the computer can find anything wanted? Why do users approach the catalog with notes or citations arranged in a traditional order? Why is the main entry (unit record) defined as "the form by which the entity is to be uniformly identified <u>and cited</u>? [emphasis added.]<u></u>[3]

Before we begin to answer these questions, several comments are in order. ISBD was designed to serve the needs of national bibliographies, publishers, and acquisitions librarians as well as the library catalog. Apparently it was not designed with the standard citation form in mind, since citations begin with the author's name if possible because of reasons relating to the social organization of scholarship.

If one looks at AACR 2 as a reversion to one of the premises underlying the ALA Rules, whereby things were cataloged according to physical appearance (or so the argument for a new code went in the early 1960s), then some things fall into place. Thus a serial, which is defined as a publication issued in parts and without a foreseeable end, also may be defined as something incomplete and therefore treated differently from completed works. In Rules for Descriptive Cataloging (1949), serial catalog copy was to supply "an entry that will stand the longest time and will permit the making of necessary changes with the minimum of modification."[4] This view is not found in AACR 2. Furthermore, one may say that many media are incomplete without special machines to make them usable. In addition, although an ISBD format is included for manuscripts and a brief description for rare books, in these cases, the catalog would be only a finding device because their nature requires a much more comprehensive description.

Completeness and incompleteness in a bibliographic object are physical characteristics. One thing that is lacking in AACR 2 is the notion of a "work" as an intellectual effort, its nature transcending the medium in which it is contained. Strange to say, the term "work" was introduced into the ALA Rules, although perhaps not with the special meaning given to it by Seymour Lubetzky. It is a most convenient concept and unifying device, as opposed to physical description based on form and not content.[5]

The Purpose of the Catalog

The notion of a work, whether issued as a solo venture or by collaboration, packaged as a single physical object or as a variety of physical objects, complete in itself or forever incomplete, ephemeral or enduring, was a most convenient intellectual device for recognizing the bibliographic unity of what is the same thing in different clothing. This brings us to the purpose of the catalog: Is it an inventory of physical objects? Or is it an inventory of recorded intellectual activity? Descriptive cataloging may suggest the first, but it also applies to the second.

Sociology of science and other disciplines take the position that a person who shares knowledge with society is entitled to a reward and that reward consists of recognition. The recognition, besides providing prizes, promotion, etc. also consists of the right to expect tribute, in the form of citations from those who use this knowledge ... another reason for use of author main entry wherever possible.[6] The catalog is a base not usually considered for a cita-

Figure 1
The International Standard for Bibliographic Description Treated as a Faceted Classification*

Facet	Indicator	Name of Facet	Sub-Facet Indicators	Names of Sub-Facets
1	Indention	Title Proper and Statement of Responsibility	[ ] = : / ;	Supplement or section General medium designation Parallel title Subtitle Author or equivalent Statement relating to authorship
2	. —	Edition	/ , / ;	Name of editor Subsequent edition Editor of it Statements relating to later edition
3	. —	Publication, Distribution, etc. (i.e., Imprint)	; : , ( )	Further places of publication and/or publishers Publisher's name: distributor Date Printing imprint: (place: printer, date)

4	Indention	Physical Description (i.e., Collation)	
		:	Illustrations
		;	Size
		+	Accompanying materials
		( )	Physical description of accompanying materials
5	. —	Series	
		( )	(around each series statement)
		=	Parallel title in series
		:	Other title information
		/	Statement of responsibility
		,	ISSN
		;	Numbering in series
		.	Title in sub-series
6	Indention	Notes	Normal punctuation
7	Indention or . —	International Standard Book or Serial Number	
		( )	Qualification
		=	Key-title
		:	Price (option)
		. —	Second standard number

*The remaining facets (if any) relate to supplementary items, reprints, and special types of material, such as special data areas needed in certain forms—maps, serials, etc.

tion index, but with the monograph still the fundamental form in which new knowledge is presented in the humanities, it could become the source of such an index.

Paris Principles

According to the Paris Principles, which underlie AACR 2, the catalog is supposed to be used to ascertain the following:

2.1 whether the library contains a particular book specified by
   (a) its author and title, or
   (b) if the author is not named in the book, its title alone, or
   (c) if author and title are inappropriate or insufficient for identification, a suitable substitute for the title; and
2.2 (a) which works by a particular author and
   (b) which editions of a particular work are in the library. [7]
3 The rules [for choice of access points and form of heading] apply to works and not generally to physical manifestations of these works, though the characteristics of an individual item are taken into account in some instances. [8]

It appears that the Paris Principles have been followed only partially. A corporate body is defined[9] in such a way as to ignore the dictionary definition: "authorized by law to act as a single person" (Webster) or "as an individual" (Oxford), and its extension to bibliographic usage by Cutter. [10] The notion of a "corporate person" is perfectly legal. It seems unnecessarily restrictive to limit its authorship functions to "those of an administrative nature" and "those which record the collective thought of the body (e.g., reports of commissions, committees, etc.; official statement of position on external policies)."[11] This is especially illogical because some works of corporate bodies are arbitrarily excluded from these definitions. The problem here is a basic one: Is a corporate body to be considered the author of its works? In AACR 2, the answer appears to be "not unless the works are reports and other housekeeping details, and except when the corporate body is a conference, workshop, symposium, seminar, etc., etc." This is probably in part the influence of Eva Verona's work on corporate headings. She rejected the definition of a corporate body as a legal person, and then doubted whether what was left was capable of authorship. [12]

This is a change in principle, similar to that involved in the abandonment of the notion of a single intellectual work as overriding its multiple physical forms. Here the notion of the legal individual (human person and collective person) as author is fragmented into a new Principle of Limited Authorship: all works of a person (or two or three such persons) are included, but only selected works of a collective person (or two or three such persons) and the works of selective kinds of collective persons.

Actually the old Principle of Authorship is replaced by a vague notion of responsibility, and further restricted to exclude editors and compilers (except those who compile bibliographies!). Responsibility is not necessarily authorship, but in AACR 2 it is only defined in terms of specific kinds: shared and mixed. Authorship includes personal authors, such as writers of books, composers of music, cartographers, artists, photographers, and some performers in sound recordings, films, and videorecordings. A joint author is one collaborating with one or more other authors. All of these authors are considered equal in that all are considered to perform the same function. This is in contrast to shared responsibility, where collaborators perform mixed functions. AACR 2 does not have a definition for "corporate author," but "corporate body" is identified as a named group acting as an entity. In the ALA Rules, a corporate body was defined as the author of its works. "Editor," in AACR 2, is narrowly defined as "one who prepares for publication an item not his own." While the rule does say editing may include "the addition of an introduction, notes and other critical matter," there is no recognition of the type of expertise called for in creating a definitive edition. "Translator" similarly gets short shrift: "One who renders from one language into another, or from one older form into the modern form, more or less closely following the original."[13] The authors of AACR 2 were aware of how much work went into the making of a bibliography, but apparently had little grasp of the tremendous amount of effort required to create a definitive edition. Some translators add significantly to the work translated, as in the case of Nathaniel Bowditch's contributions to his translation of the Système du Monde of Pierre Simon de Laplace; others produce a literary work, such as Shakespeare in Russian at the hand of Boris Pasternak.

The statement of responsibility following the title proper in AACR 2 has some interesting variations, such as: authorized by, collected by, created by, developed by, drawings by, educational collaborator, foreword by, presented by, prepared by, principal investigator, produced by, selected by, selected and edited by, sponsored by, written by (film), written and narrated by, and written in the italic hand by.[14] Obviously these are not all authors or equivalent in other media. One wonders how they will be cited in the literature. Cutter defined editor as "him who is the cause of the book's existence."[15]

In AACR 2, dramatists, poets, novelists, and other writers who change one literary form into another, composers who create variations on the theme of another composer, and so on, following AACR 1, are treated as authors. It is not clear whether this practice extends to creative translators or not. ISBD format itself calls for a statement of authorship, without the notion of main entry heading for the author.[16] Since "responsibility" is not defined in AACR 2, a connotation both broad and narrow has been utilized in the text.[17]

Some of the Paris Principles are still highly controversial, especially those dealing with entry of serials published by corporate bodies. AACR 1 rejected a number of the Principles out of hand.[18] In Verona's work, on Corporate Headings, there is a long discussion of "corporate" as related to corporate authorship, apparently rejecting the notion of the corporate person.[19] The question as to whether a legal person is capable of authorship seems to have led to the adoption of the verb "to emanate" in AACR 2. This is variously defined as "issue, originate (as from a source)" (Oxford) and "issue forth from a source as fragrance emanates from flowers" (Webster) --an interesting cultural difference in connotation. (American readers may wish mentally to substitute "issue" as they now replace "full stop" with "period.")

From Principles to Particulars

Access Points

What further principles may be deduced from examining AACR 2? For the first time, the term "access points" has been used for headings which earlier would have been called "entries." This new addition probably reflects the influence of the computer. To the basic ISBD record, AACR 2 adds access points defined as "a name, term, code, etc. under which [emphasis added] a bibliographic record may be searched and identified."[20] If this definition had said, "by means of which," these access points could have been anywhere in the unit record, as in fact they are. As it stands, access points are limited to headings for the record, or, by default, the title with which the ISBD begins. Theoretically, if a library, bibliography, or whatever so desires, the ISBD title may be the primary entry point and all headings, including author, may be added entries.

Main Entry Heading

In actuality, the concept of "main entry heading" has been retained in AACR 2. This main entry heading is the name of the author where the rules permit, or where the rules do not permit, the title. It is not clear whether the title main entry heading is to have a hanging indention as heretofore or not, but in any case this entry will continue to be identified in boldface type. In fact, boldface is the only way to identify a uniform title used as main entry.[21] Furthermore, "main entry heading" comes from the text of AACR 2[22] and not from the glossary. It is a welcome neologism. The term "author" has been replaced by "statement of responsibility" which is both broader and narrower than previous concepts of authorship.[23]

Statement of Responsibility

AACR 2, then, is based on definitions only partly continued from AACR 1. "Main entry" is now defined solely as the unit record,

Technical Services/Readers' Services 139

which in turn, by definition, includes the "main entry heading" for authors as well as the tracing for all other access points used. These are added to the basic ISBD format, which itself, as indicated earlier, begins with the title, and includes only such parts of authorship as may appear in specified ("prescribed") sources, such as the title page for books. Careful examination of the AACR 2 rules for the statement of responsibility (a broader concept than plain authorship), taken with the sets of examples used to indicate choice of main entry (heading) in Chapter 21, strongly suggests that the ISBD record taken by itself and without a main entry will not be adequate in some cases for identification of that main entry heading. That is to say, one cannot always construct a main entry heading from the statement of responsibility. The cataloger may have to use sources other than the prescribed sources and/or the legitimate statement of responsibility to construct the main entry heading. The reader can verify this statement by taking the statement of responsibility following the slash and trying to create a main entry heading from it alone. In cases where an initialism or part of the name of an author or issuing body appear in the title, there is no name for the responsible agent in the statement. By a most unfortunate choice, when an author or issuing agency's name is included in the title, even as initials only, it is not repeated in the statement of responsibility.[24] So we see, for example, no explanation for an initialism such as "ARC." For ease in making headings, either main or added, the rule should have been the other way around: "If the name is separable from the title proper, omit it under title and give it in reasonable fullness in the statement of responsibility with initialisms or incomplete names expanded."[25] In other cases, what appeared in the prescribed sources may not have included something vital like the name of a jurisdiction or the place of origin for an issuing body of indeterminate name:[26] Bureau of Statistics.

Elusive Entry Headings

It will not be possible to generate main entry headings automatically by computer unless the statement of responsibility is augmented to include information not contained in the prescribed sources. Augmentation, on the other hand, would violate the traditional practice of transcribing data from the title page exactly as given on the title page. It will take the same amount of effort to generate a main entry heading as to generate an added entry for author(s) where title main entry heading is used. One suggested solution to this dilemma consists of adding information in the notes area.[27] This practice would be necessary to justify the use of an added entry in traditional cataloging, though it is not emphasized in AACR 2. It is very easy, with the item in hand, to neglect inclusion of this information because the detail in AACR 2 tends to emphasize form over content.

The verb "to enter," in the imperative mood, is used to indicate the selected access point (what is to be the main entry heading). It is unclear in places in AACR 2 as to which added entry headings are to be added to a unit record that does not have a main entry heading. This undoubtedly will be cleared up in practice. In theory, every tagged point in the MARC format can be used as a point of access. Some of these things are unclear because AACR 2 does not follow AACR 1 in showing sample entries as they would appear in the record.

Throughout AACR 2, it is obvious that there was a struggle between the desire to work exactly from the data in the item at hand and the desire to provide authoritative data about the item even if it meant using alternative sources. This appears in the matter of using birth and death dates for authors, for providing hierarchy in some kinds of corporate authors, for distinguishing among types of documents issued by corporate bodies, for designations of pseudonyms and various kinds of names, for use in a variety of notes, and so on. An even more fundamental point of conflict comes at the very beginning with the statement which replaces the notion of a work with that of form: "It is the cardinal principle of the use of Part I that the description of a physical item should be based in the first instance on the Chapter dealing with the class of materials to which that time belongs.... In short, the starting point for description is the physical form of the item in hand."28 Resolution of such conflicts requires a general agreement on principles of cataloging.

Other Changes

Other points where there are changes of one kind or another also may be mentioned. Arrangement in AACR 2 is predicated on the assumption that the cataloger first identifies the physical form of the material. Then the description is written and, after that, the decision is made on what to use as access points. The text of the rule book is laid out accordingly. Earlier rule books began with the decision on entry.

In Chapter 21, on choice of entry, and the following three on form of entry, understanding would have been aided if some simulated entry formats had been inserted, in this case main entry (unit record) plus main entry heading. In AACR 2, examples are scattered throughout the text and not necessarily attached to the point they best illustrate. The user must constantly go from chapter to chapter because of the large number of references from one rule to another. Perhaps this was inevitable, but one wonders whether, after the initial chapter on ISBD in general, it might not have been easier for the user if each ISBD facet in turn had been applied to all kinds of media. This would have made it possible to go through the book from title/statement of responsibility to edition to imprint to collation and so on. Surely this would have been closer to the spirit of Lubetzky, in terms of using general principles which logically could be applied to all media, rather than in terms of special treatment for each medium.

In spite of all the unkind comments about the <u>ALA Rules</u> during the late 1950s, it is interesting to note that the uniformity im-

Technical Services/Readers' Services 141

posed by ISBD is only on the surface. When it actually comes to applying rules for descriptive cataloging, the form of the material still matters. Entry of the majority of serials probably will be under title. This will result in catalogs and lists arranged like the World List of Scientific Periodicals. Readers who want a glimpse of things to come should examine this book carefully, preferably with a citation like "Comp. rend. " or "Ber. " in hand. The most unsatisfactory parts of AACR 2 are those for: serials, where there is not enough allowance made for constant change in all descriptive parts; law, where jurisdiction is not an entirely satisfactory basis for initial decisions relating to entry; and music, which is still very hard to handle because of so much cross-media involvement.

Quo Vadis?

After the heady years of Lubetzky's logic, is this the pragmatists' revenge? Like the 1949 ALA code, this one is highly pragmatic. In terms of fullness of data, we have cycled back in part to the logic of the 1908 rules. [29] Was Lubetzky on the wrong track in trying to develop a code based on reason? Can any code be based on reason when there is so little reason in the architecture and content of title pages or equivalent? Yet if one goes by the title page (or equivalent), is the result a true description?

The treatment of rare books is the ultimate descriptive approach in cataloging. Catalog codes are a pale copy of this, though perhaps less pale now than in the era of short form cataloging. The MARC formats designed for machine-readable cataloging permit even greater fullness on ordinary works than AACR 2. One can, after all, vary the amount of data received at output to suit the needs of users by means of selective programming. This is one approach, since even MARC can be further augmented if need arises.

Another, perhaps more interesting, approach is almost completely different. It depends on looking at knowledge content, as found in sources normally cataloged, in terms of transferability rather than as a package to be described physically. With such a system one would depend on something closer to the way scholars acknowledge their intellectual debts. The citation system, for example, is to some extent based on the same type of data produced by the process of cataloging: identification of authors and titles. As every librarian knows, users do not necessarily identify a document or source in exactly the same format as that developed through catalog codes. This is not to say that the user is right and the cataloger is wrong; quite the opposite. The user is interested in tracing the transfer of information and in enabling other users to gain access to the sources upon which research was based. These interests call upon the descriptive power of the cataloger. But the purpose of the citation is more than just this; the citation is to the labor of human beings, singly or in groups. A work may have multiple authors but no work has ever appeared without an author of some kind. The citing author is not citing a mere title; the citing author is pointing to human effort--specifically those humans who contributed some kind of information in the physical object serving as its medium of interchange. The source document itself is secondary; the human who wrote it is primary. And it is the work and not its format that matters.

This has been recognized in AACR 2 by the singling out of conferences, symposia, seminars, and other kinds of meetings for special treatment by permitting corporate entry. At the same time, recognition has been withdrawn from editors, translators, compilers, and others, except in dealing with some kinds of media. Although probably alien to most catalogers, a methodology called co-citation is available as a bias-reducing, unobtrusive device for tracking ideas through the publications of authors. The method is sufficiently accurate to identify future Nobel Prize winners in science.[30] In the long run, it may prove helpful in evaluating library collections, measuring actual use of circulating materials for research, and even for devising collection development policy. We have come full circle on systems of descriptive cataloging based on the whims of those who make title pages. Is it not now time to build on a surer foundation?

The late Paul Dunkin, in his Cataloging USA, covered all of the problems discussed here and many more. Since his personal preference was for simplicity and brevity, one wonders what he would have said about a catalog code book of 620 pages. Nonetheless, he recognized the changing nature of cataloging over time and ended his book with a comment appropriate for ending this review: "Change is a fact in cataloging. But is it the substance of cataloging--or only the surface?"[31]

References

1. ALA Cataloging Rules for Author and Title Entries, 2d ed. Edited by Clara Beetle (Chicago: ALA, 1949), pp. 229-235; Library of Congress, Descriptive Cataloging Division, Rules for Descriptive Cataloging in the Library of Congress (Washington, D.C.: GPO, 1949), pp. 109-110. Definitions limited to terms not in ALA glossary; Anglo-American Cataloguing Rules, 2nd ed. Edited by Michael Gorman and Paul W. Winkler (Chicago: ALA, 1978), pp. 536-572.
2. AACR 2, Rules 0.21, 0.23, 20.1, pp. 7, 277.
3. AACR 2, p. 567.
4. Rules for Descriptive Cataloging in the Library of Congress, p. 51.
5. "Work" is undefined in the glossary to the ALA Rules, but is present in the Introduction and probably was taken from Wyllis E. Wright, "Some Fundamental Principles in Cataloging," Catalogers' and Classifiers' Yearbook, no. 7 (1938), pp. 26-39.
6. Cf. Norman W. Storer, The Social System of Science (New York: Holt, Rinehart & Winston, 1966); Robert K. Merton,

Technical Services/Readers' Services 143

"The Reward System of Science," "Recognition and Excellence...," "The Matthew Effect in Science," The Sociology of Science: Theoretical and Empirical Investigations (Chicago: Univ. of Chicago Press, 1973), pp. 281-459. When a sociologist says "science," the term is broad enough to include sociology.

7. For some unknown reason, Paris Principle 2.1 refers only to books, giving a specific order for their access. Paris 2.2 is a restatement of Seymour Lubetzky's objectives, which, in turn, are a modification of those of Charles A. Cutter. [Cf. Statement of Principles Adopted at the International Conference on Cataloging Principles, Paris, October 1961. Annotated ed. by Eva Verona (London: IFLA Committee on Cataloguing, 1971)]; Seymour Lubetzky, Code of Cataloging Rules: Author and Title Entry: An Unfinished Draft ... (s.l.: ALA, 1960); Charles A. Cutter, Rules for a Printed Dictionary Catalogue, 4th ed. (Washington, D.C.: GPO, 1904), p. 12.
8. Verona, Statement of Principles.
9. See also AACR 2, p. 565. "Entity" is used rather than the legal individual.
10. Cutter, Rules, p. 40: "As a matter of fact these bodies are authors."
11. AACR 2, p. 285 (Rule 21.1B2 a, c).
12. AACR 2, p. 285 (Rule 21.1B2 b, d, e); Eva Verona, Corporate Headings: Their Use in Library Catalogues and National Bibliographies: A Comparative and Critical Study (London: IFLA Committee on Cataloguing, 1975).
13. AACR 2, personal authors, p. 568; Rule 21.1A1, p. 284; joint author, p. 567; corporate body, editor, p. 565; translator, p. 572; ALA Rules, p. 230.
14. AACR 2, pp. 23, 25, 221, 206, 58, 25, 132, 57, 58, 205, 150, 58, 59, 24, 169, 115 respectively.
15. Cutter, Rules, p. 14.
16. ISBD(M) International Standard Bibliographic Description for Monographic Publications, first standard ed. (London: IFLA Committee on Cataloguing, 1974), p. x, 36p.
17. AACR 2, Rule 21.1A1, p. 284 (broad); Rule 21.1B2, p. 285 (narrow).
18. These were Paris Principles 9.4, 9.5, 9.12 (footnote), 10.3, 11.14, and 12, (AACR 1, pp. 3-4).
19. Verona, Corporate Headings, pp. 8-31.
20. AACR 2, p. 563.
21. See AACR 2, Chapter 25, especially pp. 458-469.
22. AACR 2, p. 283.
23. See Rule 21.1 (AACR 2, p. 284) for the narrower concept and descriptions of this "statement"; for broader concepts, see Rule 1.1F (p. 23-26), especially the examples in 1.1F1, 1.1F4-1.1F6, 1.1F8, 1.1F11-1.1F12, 1.1F14-1.1F15, and also 2.1F1, 2.1F3 (pp. 57-58).
24. See Rules 1.1B2, 1.1F13, 12.1F2 (AACR-2, pp. 18, 26, 253).
25. Rule 1.1F3 (AACR 2, p. 23). This rule does what is suggested, but it does not appear to have been used in any of the examples in AACR 2.

26. See, for example, the author statements in LC cards: 74-231062, 74-189068, 74-189769, 74-188607, 74-600686, 74-189829, 74-194368, 73-89555, 74-622225, 74-189250, 74-602643, 74-189788. All except the first are on MARC tapes. The first is entered under "South Africa. Bureau of Statistics."
27. Rule 1.1F2 (AACR-2, p. 23) and similar rules in other chapters support this practice.
28. Rule 0.23 (AACR 2, p. 7).
29. ALA. Catalog Rules: Author and Title Entries, American ed. (Boston: ALA, 1908).
30. Belver Griffith, Susan Crawford, Henry G. Small, Daniel Sullivan, et al. Special Session 3, in Information Choices and Policies: Proceedings of the ASIS Annual Meeting, 42nd, Minneapolis, Minnesota, October 14-18, 1979 (White Plains, NY: Published for American Society for Information Science by Knowledge Industry Publications, 1979) v. 16, pp. 254-285.
31. Paul Dunkin, Cataloging USA (Chicago: ALA, 1969), p. 153.

APPENDIX:

ENTRY

In the glossaries of the ALA Cataloging Rules for Author and Title Entries, 1949; the Anglo-American Cataloging Rules, North American text, 1967 (AACR 1); and the second edition of the Anglo-American Cataloguing Rules, 1978 (AACR 2), "entry" was defined as a "record of the book/bibliographic record/unit in a catalog(ue)/or list." The 1949 and 1967 ALA Rules further defined "entry" as the "heading" chosen for such a record. AACR 2 has a cross-reference from "entry" to "heading" in preference to this second definition. AACR 1 had a third definition of "entry" as a verb, representing the "aspect of cataloging that is concerned with the choice of entries ... particularly the choice of main entries." (ALA Rules, p. 231; AACR 1, pp. 344-345; AACR 2, p. 565).

ENTRY AS HEADING

Where "entry" included "heading" in its definition (i.e., ALA Rules and AACR 1), this "heading" was further defined as "the name, word or phrase used/placed at the head of the entry/catalog record to indicate some special aspect/provide a point of access" (ALA Rules, p. 232; AACR 1, p. 345). AACR 1 added a second definition for a uniform type of heading. In AACR 2's definition, "heading" is "a name, word or phrase placed at the head of a catalogue entry to provide an access point in the catalogue" (AACR 2, p. 566). All three codes have defined "entry word" as the first word of this heading, used to arrange the entry in the catalog (ALA Rules, p. 231; AACR 1, p. 345; AACR 2, p. 566). ALA Rules further referred to

Technical Services/Readers' Services   145

this headword as the "filing word." The use of the term "entry" for both the unit record (including full description and tracings) and for its access point (heading) has been the source of much confusion. This is because in practice both meanings have been used interchangeably. Unfortunately such practice continues in the text of AACR 2, even though only one version appears in the glossary.

MAIN ENTRY

The confusion is compounded with the term "main entry." The first definition in all codes considered the main entry as the fundamental and total catalog record given "in the form by which the entity is to be uniformly identified and cited" (AACR 1 and AACR 2) or "usually the author entry, giving all information necessary to the complete identification of a work" (ALA Rules). The definition of main entry is such that it "may include/includes tracing(s) of all (the) other headings under which it is represented/entered in the catalog(ue)" (ALA Rules, p. 232; AACR 1, p. 345; AACR 2, p. 567).
The second definition of main entry in both the 1949 and 1967 codes identified it as the entry or heading for the main card in the catalog. (The main card being the one without any added entries typed above the main entry heading--the unit record.)

MAIN ENTRY HEADING

As if the confusion was not already enough, in the text (but not in the glossary) of AACR 2, another term, "main entry heading," has been introduced to cover what formerly was the second definition of "main entry" (as heading) in the ALA Rules (p. 232) and AACR 1 (p. 345). The "main entry heading" and the added entry "headings" in AACR 2 are treated as access points to the catalog, although access points is not limited to headings. When examples in AACR 2, especially in Chapter 21, call for "Main (or Added) entry under title, it means that the entry should be made under the title proper or uniform title ... as appropriate." (AACR 2, p. 283).

ADDED ENTRY

To round out the definitions, "added entry" in the ALA Rules and AACR 1 was defined as a secondary record and also as the "heading" for such a record (ALA Rules, p. 229; AACR 1, p. 343). The secondary record was a unit record (or copy of the main entry card) including the main entry heading. AACR 2 defined "added entry" as "additional to the main entry" (i.e., to the "complete catalogue record of an item"--AACR 2, pp. 563, 567). While the definition in AACR 1 specifically differentiated an added entry from a subject heading, the definition in AACR 2 has not distinguished between types of entries additional to the main entry (as unit record). It merely states that they are part of the total record, including "all other headings under which the record is to be represented in the catalogue. " (p. 567). The emphasis is less on kind of heading than on "headings" as access points.

UNIT RECORD

In both ALA Rules and AACR 1, "unit card" was defined as "a basic catalog card, in the form of main entry [definition 1] which, when duplicated, may be used as a unit for all other entries of that work in the catalog by the addition of the appropriate heading(s)" (ALA Rules, p. 235; AACR-1, p. 347). In practice, this unit card included subject headings, class numbers, and series tracing as well as purely descriptive data. Altogether, the added entry as a filing or higher heading (literally) was added to the main entry (as unit record) which already included the main entry (as heading). The unit card and main entry (complete record including main entry heading and tracings) were, for all practical purposes, the identical record.
    In AACR 2, neither unit card nor unit record is used. The ISBD performs the essential descriptive part of a unit record, needing only the heading-type of main entry and the added entry tracing to make it equivalent to the unit card of the earlier codes. However, for a true unit record, so much more has been added to the type of unit card issued by the Library of Congress, that nowadays the MARC record more nearly fills the position held in earlier catalogs by the unit card.

ISBD

Using the International Standard Bibliographic Description (ISBD), the unit card has been replaced by a headingless unit record called the "bibliographic record. " Essentially ISBD is a codified basic description, apart from entry. The Rules for Descriptive Cataloging in the Library of Congress (1949) covered exactly the same area-- description apart from choice and form of entry (as heading). As a rule, the Library of Congress descriptive cataloging was much nearer to the design of AACR 2 than to that of AACR 1. Both the Library of Congress descriptive rules and AACR 1, however, included a section of added entry tracing. ISBD(M)--for monographs --had nothing on tracings and AACR 2 defines the term but does not have a section on usage (AACR 1, pp. 151, 224-225; Rules for Descriptive Cataloging in the Library of Congress, Sect. 3.25, pp. 41- 42; AACR 2, p. 571).
    ISBD begins with a title statement consisting of the title and the name(s) of three or fewer authors or equivalent, and ends with the area for the International Standard Book Number (ISBN), Binding and Price, following the area for Notes. AACR 2 adds a few odds and ends to these areas, such as keytitle, terms of availability (an option), qualifications of ISBNs, and makes price an option. It further adds rules for "supplementary items, " "items made up of several types of material, " and "facsimiles, photocopies and other

Technical Services/Readers' Services

reproductions" (AACR 2, Rules 1.8C, 1.8D, 1.8E, 1.9, 1.10 and 1.11. "Levels" of ISBD(M), pp. 31-32 are described in a different configuration in AACR 2, Rule 10D).

WORD PROCESSING AND THE BOOK PRINTER*

Frank Romano

Once upon a time there was a printer who happened to be visiting one of his customer's offices. While wandering around, trying to find someone to sign the delivery receipts, he came upon the typing pool. Being an observant printer, he noticed that instead of normal, everyday typewriters, the typists were keyboarding on typewriters connected to magnetic media recording units. After recording the particular letter or report, the typist replayed the medium and corrected any errors that were made. A final automatic retyping was then made from the medium and the resulting "clean" typescript was sent out.

Venturing forward, the printer inquired as to the nature of this strange machine. "It's an Input Revision Typewriter," answered the department manager. "It allows us to type at our fastest possible speed, what they call draft speed, because we can correct our errors when we're typing by just backspacing and overstriking the character, or catching the corrections during playback." The printer asked if the messy first copy was used. "No, that's just a draft; our goal is to get all the typing done and then make any changes."

During his visit, the printer learned several things. The IRT made a typist much more productive and allowed office people to make changes without the need for complete retypings because the information was stored on the media. He also discovered that after the report, or whatever was finally typed out by the machine automatically, the media was reused by rerecording them. The typed pages were then copied, or, in some cases, sent to the printer. That's when the light bulb went off.

Calling several large companies in his area, the printer found out that these IRTs were part of a wave of office automation called word processing. He found that most large companies used them. He then checked with several phototypesetting machine

---

*Reprinted by permission of the author and publisher from Book Production Industry & Magazine Production, 55:6 (November/December 1979) 33-46; copyright © 1979 by The Innes Publishing Co.

Technical Services/Readers' Services   149

suppliers and asked them if they could take input from word processing cassettes. One answered, "What's word processing?" another replied, "What's input?" The printer did find a few manufacturers who had interfaced (fancy word for connected) IRT media to their typesetters.

The printer reasoned this way: after the final typing the recorded cassette was more or less discarded, yet it had some value because it contained all of the corrected information that was on the typewritten paper. It was like boiling the vegetables and throwing the water away, wherein one's mother always said the vitamins were found. If the information on the cassette was going to be printed and/or typeset, why not find some way to use the medium?

The printer took two actions. He installed a typesetting system that could read the media (if he already had a typesetter, he might have just purchased the reader and connected it). Next, he organized a selling campaign to companies with these word processors and sold the benefits of typesetting (saves paper, storage, postage) and faster turnaround (no redundant re-keyboarding). All this came from a by-product of the word processing operation. Needless to say, our printer lived happily ever after.

Word processing began as a machine and became a movement. The machine was the IBM MT/ST, or Magnetic Tape Selectric Typewriter. It added a new dimension to the typist's skill: recording and playback, or storage and retrieval. Eventually, these devices made typists more productive and gave rise to a movement aimed at automating the modern business office.

The key device is a reader, one that reads the magnetic tape cassette or floppy disk. It replaces the traditional paper tape reader standard with most phototypesetters (on some typesetters you can use paper and mag media interchangeably). There is no significant change in the typesetter.

Since typesetting consists of both the characters you see and the commands necessary to instruct the typesetter about how to set them, commands will be needed. In most cases, for straight text, the phototypesetter may be set up, either on an external format panel of switches, or internally programmed, with a standard format (typeface, point size, leading and line length). Codes for boldface or italic can be inserted by either the originator or by the printer himself.

The normal type of IRT or word processor is the stand-alone kind. It is essentially a typewriter connected to a magnetic recorder with a small amount of computer logic. There are several extra keys that let the operator control what's going on.

The term _word processing_ (WP) was coined in 1965 by the IBM Office Products Division in Germany. IBM defines word processing as "the transition of a written, verbal or recorded idea to typewritten or printed form." However, it should also be added that word processing has come to encompass all methods for increasing office economy and efficiency through the use of more sophisticated equipment, such as copies, dictating equipment, typewriters, text editing devices and systems, and typesetting equipment.

Essentially, the text editing devices and systems used in word processing allow ideas to be typed at rough draft speeds, without regard to errors. Everything that is typed is captured on some recording medium, the most common form being magnetic, since it is reusable. As an error is sensed, a backspace key is used to cancel incorrect characters, and the correct character is typed over the incorrect one on the typescript, automatically correcting the recording medium. The final error-free typed document is produced from the recording medium at an average of 175 words per minute. One of the principal reasons for the success of these text editing devices and systems is that the user is able to easily make modifications to previously typed text, without having to re-type the information which is not affected.

Word processing and publishing

Every word published is typed or keyboarded at least once by the author and once by the typesetter. Through the use of text editing devices and systems, keystrokes could be captured during the original keying--either the first time information is created by the author or during one of the innumerable retypings common to the publishing industry. The rekeyboarding operation performed by a typesetting service is then eliminated.

A typist can, therefore, produce manuscript copy more rapidly, and in addition to the typescript, maintain a machine readable record of that typing. Thus, the manuscript is only typed once and successive revisions are generated by correcting this machine readable medium.

Capturing keystrokes by the originator results in substantial cost reductions for the following reasons:

1. Typists' skills and salary levels are lower than those of typesetting keyboard operators.

2. Elimination of rekeyboarding removes all opportunity for the introduction of new errors by the typesetting service.

3. The time required from copy submission for typesetting to the receipt of typeset galleys or pages is cut substantially.

However, since the typesetting service is not rekeyboarding the information to be typeset, the burden of input, proofreading and submission of perfect copy is placed on the publisher or other originator. Thus, the concept of printer's errors disappears and all changes of errors are not chargeable to the publisher.

Technical Services/Readers' Services

There are three basic procedures involved in preparing input for typesetting when text editing devices and systems are used. These are: a) original keying, b) proofreading and editing, and c) encoding typesetting commands.

The automatic typing and text editing devices and systems provided for word processing applications can be grouped into five distinct categories.

Automatic repetitive typewriters

These devices are the most basic units used in word processing. They provide for the automatic repetitive printout or typing of pre-recorded information, and are similarly used for generating form letters and standard letter clauses which require minor insertions or modifications. Automatic stops are used to allow the operator to manually type in variable information such as names and addresses for form letters. Since these devices do not allow for editing changes to the recording medium, they are not applicable in the composition function, and will not be discussed further.

Correcting typewriters

Since most of the errors that a typist makes are essentially wrong characters, and most of these are discovered during typing, a correcting typewriter has a special ribbon that "lifts" the impression off the paper. No medium is produced.

Memory typewriters

Up from the Correcting Typewriter is one that has a dynamic memory (dynamic means that the information stays recorded as long as there is power to the machine). Thus, a page or several pages can be typed and then replayed, and during the replaying one can correct errors. Copy cannot be moved around and, again, no medium is produced.

Intelligent typewriters

Introduced by Oyx division of Exxon and later by IBM, these devices use some form of memory that is not dynamic and lets you store more pages and manipulate the information to a greater extent. The mini floppy disk is common here, and it will probably be removable as time goes on (it is fixed inside the unit now). Price tags here will be as low as $5,000 for a typewriter that stores and retrieves and lets one edit. Time and the semiconductor electronics industry may bring this unit down to the $2,000 level in a few years.

Stand-alone mechanical text editing devices

These devices are essentially a typewriter keyboard and some form of digital recording medium to accomplish automatic typing and text editing functions. Text editing is usually performed by typing out the line which is in error and then correcting it and replacing it on the recorded medium with its corrected version. The MT/ST was one.

Stand-alone mechanical devices use a variety of different techniques to accomplish the text editing function. Some of the devices, such as the Savin 900 Word Master, have only one recording station (mag tape cassette) whereas, others such as the Redaction R-5C (mag card) and R-5T (mag tape cassette) have two recording stations. In general, when one recording station is provided, the recording medium is line oriented, where each line is recorded in a fixed amount of space on the medium such as 200 characters on the Savin unit.

In order to edit text, the user must find the line which is to be changed on the recording medium, and then make the necessary modifications. On some units, such as the Savin 900, the lines are prenumbered. These numbers appear on the rough draft, but are suppressed on the final copy. The user must then search for the line number, type out the line up to the point at which modification is necessary, and then make the necessary changes. Since the same cassette is used for the original and all successive versions of the document, insertions are limited to the maximum line length on the tape--200 characters in the case of Savin. Editing on a mag card is somewhat similar, except that the user does not need to search for a line--the mag card is physically arranged by lines, and a mechanical line selector is used, which moves the recording head along the edge of the mag card.

Due to the inherent editing limitations found in most single station devices, the majority of these devices are only applicable in the composition function as simple data capture devices. Dual media units are readily adaptable in the typesetting input function because of their ability to perform high speed search, to duplicate data at high speeds, allow error correction at the time of typing with simple backspace-over-type procedures and the ability to play out data with all function codes suppressed for easier proofreading.

Devices providing two recording stations do not have the editing limitations found with most single station devices. For text editing, a fixed line length on the recording medium is not needed, since a new copy of the recording medium is generated during each stage of editing. Due to this unlimited insertion capability, the dual station devices are found to be very applicable in the composition function. (By their very nature all paper tape oriented devices are of the dual station type.)

A unique advantage of dual station text editing devices is the ability to merge information at high speed. Information on one medium may be merged into existing material on a second one. Thus, the ability to handle catalogs, directories and other forms of material that must be updated on a regular basis becomes possible in-house.

Video-word processors

The major change that has taken place over the last few years is the introduction of video based word processors. The keyboard is similar to that of a typewriter but the screen takes the place of the typewritten paper. Thus, editing is far better than that of typewriter based units. For printout, one has a line printer connected. There is also single or dual recording media.

These devices are very similar to their mechanical counterparts, however, cathode ray tubes (CRTs), which resemble tv tubes are used to let the user see and correct the copy before it is actually committed to the recording medium. The CRT is used to display part of a typed page of text or an entire typed page, making the editing task much easier. An additional difference between the display-oriented devices and the mechanical ones, is that the display-oriented devices use the keyboard and display for input and editing, and a separate device for printing out the final copy.

Thus, the user can be editing a page of text, while the previous page is being printed out. In the mechanical devices, the typewriter is used for all three tasks--input, editing and printout, which means that the user must wait, while a document is being printed out. The major difference between these units and VDTs used primarily in the typesetting process lies in the area of command coding--the word processing units do not allow for typesetting functions such as quad right, etc.

Shared logic text editing systems

These systems consist of a number of input typing or editing stations connected to a central processor, which is usually a mini-computer. The input stations may all be used simultaneously, and are usually typewriter oriented. However, some systems provide CRT display oriented stations, which would be used primarily for the editing of previously inputted text. These systems provide an optional high speed line printer, which would be used for draft or proofreading. The printout quality of the line printer is somewhat lower than that of an electric typewriter when high quality final typed copy printout is needed.

By using the high speed line printer, the input stations are then relieved of the slow printout task. The input stations could then be used primarily for input and editing functions thereby resulting in higher efficiency. Several of the presently available shared logic systems provide typesetting programs, thereby, making these systems even more attractive for uses in the composition function.

The principle behind shared logic systems differs from that of stand-alone devices where there is a one-to-one ratio between the logic console and the typewriter or display-type work station. The shared logic systems allow this ratio to increase. In most shared logic systems, a ratio of up to eight-to-one or higher can be achieved. These systems are applicable in situations where a large number of jobs are typeset. In word processing applications, these systems have proven to be of value primarily in situations where the total volume of text is large and the length of each document is in excess of 20 pages.

The systems are usually justified by prorating the cost of the entire system over the total number of input stations. Each input station can handle specific and separate jobs, with the total volume of all work justifying the cost of the system, although individual work volume may not justify a separate text editing device for each location.

In shared logic systems, each job, such as a report or a book, is given a name. Whenever work is to be done on this job, its name is used in order to tell the computer where the corresponding text is stored. Line numbers are used to identify portions of the text, and editing is then done by referencing these line numbers. Then line numbers are automatically generated by the system and appear on the output of the line printer, or the input station. Because the line numbering may change when text is edited, its use is dependent on "updated" printouts after each successive editing cycle. Otherwise, a great deal of confusion may result.

Time shared editing

This category of text editing capability is a service rather than hardware, where a large central computer located at a service bureau is used to handle many simultaneous users. A typewriter terminal located in the user's office is connected through normal telephone lines to the central computer. The terminal is usually a Selectric typewriter, with the necessary electronics for communicating with the computers. The service bureau also has a high speed line printer for providing printout of long documents. These printouts would then be delivered to the user. For the storage of material, magnetic discs and magnetic tapes are used. Documents requiring immediate access are stored on the disc, and those that are not are stored on tape.

Interfacing word processing and typesetting

The major disadvantage to direct interfacing arises when the originator does not insert the commands for typesetting. The recorded medium must then be played back on the word processor in order to insert the commands. Since most word processors have highly effective search and edit capabilities, this action is not a significant

Technical Services/Readers' Services

disadvantage if the person who is editing in the commands is accurate and efficient. The direct method eliminates the possible problems of dealing with multiple forms of media. In general, magnetic media is less likely to read or record incorrectly than paper media. Indirect interfacing does allow you to perform more than one function--you can edit the information and convert it more or less simultaneously. Many practitioners advocate inserting commands at the video editing terminal. They claim that it is faster and more effective than inserting commands on a typewriter-oriented word processor.

For the typesetting service or other organization that wishes to accept information prepared on a variety of word processors, it is necessary to acquire a separate interface for each type of word processor. Even though a Phillips cassette may be used, the method of encoding the data and the coding system are thoroughly different from one device to another. One of the potential methods for solving this is via a communications system that converts the recorded medium on the end of a telephone line to a standard transmission code and then transmits it to a receiving end where the data is recorded on one common medium.

This would mean that output from any word processor would be converted to a transmission code (such as RS232 systems) and converted again on the receiving end into the typesetter code. In all other cases, the lack of standardization requires separate and distinct interfaces.

Interfacing can also be accomplished on a service basis. For instance, Telesystems Network in Chicago provides a conversion service that takes IBM MT/ST cartridges and converts them to 9-track computer magnetic tape and then, converts that to IBM magnetic cards or to communications transmission. There are other firms that provide a similar service.

The presence of magnetic media is not always indicative of word processing. Many typesetting-related peripherals presently utilize magnetic tape cassettes or floppy disks. This does not mean that they can interface to word processing media. In most cases they can only record and playback information for the device in use. In making the conversion from the word processor to typesetting the interface must take into account characters and commands that exceed the number of typewriter keys.

Thus it is necessary to "double up" by typing multiple keystrokes for typesetting functions and special characters. Review the keystroking method established. As much "intelligence" as possible should be placed in the interface so that the operate does not have to key intricate sequences. A word processing device should not be made to emulate a typesetting keyboard.

The interface between word processing and typesetting is one of the fastest growing areas of the graphic arts. The need for aesthetic output of information in a form that conserves paper by putting more data on a page than typewriting can, also reduces printing and postal costs. There is a natural relationship between word processing and typesetting, a profitable and productive one.

Word processing, in its narrowest definition, refers to equipment specially designed for the input, editing and output of textual information. In most cases the output is either a typewriter or some form of line printer. Another form of output is typesetting. Since all word processors store information in coded form on some type of recorder medium, it is possible to "read" the medium and convert the coding in order to use the date for input to a typesetting system. This report covers the various alternatives for accomplishing this.

An interface is a method or device for facilitating communication between machines and other machines (or even between machines and people). The first step in interfacing involves the physical acceptance of the recorded medium or the transmission of a signal from one device to another. The second step is the "translation" of the coding system of one device into the coding system of another device. The recorded media of word processing include cassette, cartridge, card and other magnetic methods. The standard medium of typesetting is paper tape. Coding for word processing is usually a modified ASCII, although there is no standardization, and the coding for typesetting is usually TTS (TeleTypeSetter) with modifications, although there are no real standards here either.

Most typesetting devices incorporate automatic functions for hyphenating words and justifying margins. Identions for paragraphs and mixing of type styles (regular to italic) are also automatic. However, to instruct the typesetting device in performing any action that affects the output format of the information, it is necessary to insert typesetting commands in the data. These commands, or instructions, tell the typesetter how to typeset the information being input. Commands may be inserted by the originator or later by a typesetting specialist. In any case, any interface must take into consideration the command requirements of the particular typesetting device or system.

The most direct method for interfacing word processing to typesetting is to connect a reader for the recorded medium directly to the typesetter. The medium is then read and the information recoded so that signals enter the typesetter in a manner that emulates a paper tape reader. Most direct interfaces to typesetting table connect to a point just behind the paper tape reader and translate the recorded data to TTS and send it to the typesetter as though it came from paper tape. Most word processing devices use serial data encoding; most typesetting devices use parallel data encoding.

Since paper tape is such a common medium in the typesetting process, some interfaces convert the recorded information from the word processing device to paper tape--which is then input to the

Technical Services/Readers' Services   157

typesetter. Indirect interfaces usually convert from one medium to another more commonly used medium. This type of interface may be as simple as a reader for the recorded medium connected to a paper tape punch or it could be a device or system into which the information is input, operated upon and then output as another form of media. An example of this is an editing terminal that can accept word processing media. It allows the operator to edit the information or insert commands electronically and then produces a paper tape to run the typesetter. This method permits human intervention during the conversion of the data.

Communication oriented text editing devices

Most of the word processors provide a communications capability. This feature enables one unit to transmit text over telephone lines to another stand-alone device, which also has a communications capability. In addition, the unit could also serve as a terminal for either a time shared service or for a shared logic system, with a remote terminal capability. In this latter mode of operation, the unit could be used as a stand-alone device for the keyboarding of text, which would be stored on the recording medium for later transmission to the computer system.

The editing of the text could then be done either by the stand-alone unit prior to transmission, or after transmission, by using the more sophisticated editing capabilities of the computer system.

One application of communicating typewriters in the typesetting process is the use of such devices by trade typesetting services who may receive data for composition from their customers via phones lines.

Time shared services vs. shared logic systems

The principal difference between time shared services and shared logic systems is that the time shared service is a low fixed cost service, with short term cancellation, whereas, shared logic systems entail a high fixed cost commitment and/or a high initial investment. However, as the text editing work load increases, the cost for using the time shared service also increases, and could conceivably exceed the cost of the shared logic system.

In order to provide text editing services to many users simultaneously, the time shared service bureaus use large digital computers, as opposed to the smaller mini-computers used in shared logic systems. This enables the time shared services to provide a more powerful text editing capability to its users than that available with shared logic systems. This capability might include a very sophisticated typesetting program for generating input to the Videocomp phototypesetter for example. An additional advantage of time shared services is that the user does not have to develop the skills needed in running a computer--the only hardware on the users' premises is a terminal. The handling of magnetic disks and tapes is all performed by service bureau personnel.

In word processing, the commodity is words, millions of them, linked together in sentences and paragraphs, and sometimes even thoughts, and packaged an information explosion, words are Molotov Cocktails.

As words wind their way from the mind of an author to the printed page they undergo more than one metamorphosis. The author goes through one or more re-writes; the editors change and modify; the typesetter proofreads and corrects; the author makes alterations, and finally the finished page is ready to be photographed, stripped, plated, printed, cut, collated, bound and shipped.

With each successive revision, copy is either re-typed or written over. As alternatives we seek a mystical something called "clean copy" and forbid changes under penalty of death, or worse. It is amusing to hear that publishers will do their own typesetting when some of them won't even re-type a manuscript to make it easier to typeset.

If we think about all of the words and all of the things that happen to those words from mind to matter, then it is possible to envision a sort of word bank in which those words can be deposited initially. From there they go through an infinite number of editing cycles from the author to the editors to the typesetter to the lawyers or whomever. The technology necessary to make this concept workable is here, now. The keys that will allow it to pass from the blue sky to solid earth are the ability to input or record information for re-use via a device that is essentially typewriter oriented, that the input be correctable and modifiable during the input operation, and that the information be retrievable from the recorded medium for successive editing and then re-stored. To summarize; you must be able to input, store, retrieve, edit and re-store.

Input is the conversion of information from human understandable to machine understandable form. An input device usually performs this function. For instance, when you type on a typewriter you hit a key which converts the character indicated thereon into a series of operations, mostly mechanical, to select the right character for impression on the paper. The IBM Selectric typewriter actually generates a code when a key is hit which internally selects the character for output. If you were to hook up a magnetic recording medium to the device, it would simultaneously record the code on tape and output the character. The important part of the input operation is the "capturing" or recording of the information as early in the evolution of the word bank as possible. Input has always been a redundant operation--after many revisions and re-typings copy is re-keyed to record it for typesetting.

Redundant input introduces the opportunity for the creation of new errors which must be found and corrected. If we were to input once and then edit electronically, we would reduce error generation and speed up the editing and typesetting cycles. Input used to be someone keying on the keyboard of a Linotype; now it is someone typing on a keyboard of a special data entry device; soon it will be you and me--and even them--typing on a typewriter that really isn't a typewriter but that looks and acts like a typewriter.

The methods that we will discuss in the context of the word bank are word processing or input revision typewriters, telecommunications and time sharing, optical character recognition, and video editing systems.

Word processing began as a machine and evolved into a philosophy. The machine was the IBM magnetic tape typewriter, which allowed its operator to re-play type information over and over again for corrections and changes, each time re-recording the new version on a magnetic tape. Today, word processing experts (anyone who can type) claim jurisdiction over all aspects of business communications from dictation equipment to copying machines. They even want to automate the water cooler.

After the IBM MTST came an onslaught of innocent looking typewriters connected to a great variety of magnetic recording media. Sperry Univac, Wang, Olivetti, Savin, Xerox and others have entered the fray. Redactron was also part of this group of companies with ideas on how to bring the business office into the twentieth century.

They applied a broader view, especially in their approach to linking word processing to the typesetting process.

Word processing is to words what data processing is to data. A more apt name for the word processor's tool is input revision typewriter or IRT. It allows the author or typist to type as rapidly as they wish and to make correction of sensed errors as they occur. The recorded medium may be played back on the typewriter and further changes made. With any revision only the information that must be changed is changed, unlike the present re-typing of an entire page for a change in one line. IRTs cover three areas; input, because you type and record, revision, because you change then or later, and typewriter, because that's what most of us are accustomed to.

IRTs are becoming a common communications tool. They are used in business offices, typing services and by authors. The ideal application for the publishing industry would be the author's submission of a magnetic tape or other medium along with the manuscript. A similar IRT in the publisher's office would be used to edit the copy (the editors would mark up the manuscript and a typist would edit the medium accordingly) and produce a new medium and a new manuscript.

From here the manuscript and medium would go to the type-setter who would follow the marked manuscript for typographic format. After typesetting, the galleys and medium could be returned to the originator or publisher and any alterations would be made to the medium. The typesetting service would then re-run the edited medium. Or, the manuscript or galleys could be edited and the typesetting service would do the actual modification of the medium. The entire concept is based on a new element in the published process: a recorded medium.

Even before IRTs have been applied, they are being changed. Newer devices incorporate tv sets that replace the typing mechanism so that editing becomes faster and paper is eliminated until you want a print out of the information. New types of recording media are being applied. The so-called floppy disk looks like a 45 rpm record but can hold a quarter of a million characters of information, or upwards of 50,000 words. Other capability in IRTs allow you to search for a particular word or group of characters so that the device can automatically jump to a section for editing instead of having the operator read through the entire medium. Redactron has a peripheral device called a Quick Writer that prints out the contents of a tape or cassett at many times the speed of a typewriter. They also have typewriters that can communicate over telephone lines.

Telecommunications is a method for bringing distant locations closer together. The concept was born with the telegraph and later the telephone. In 1926 the concept was applied to the Linotype with the introduction of TeleTypeSetter, or TTS, a transmission system for typesetting information. A tape could be input at any location and then transmitted to another location to be run on a specially adapted linecaster. Today we have voice communication as exemplified by the telephone and data communications as exemplified by the Telex, TWX and Dataphone networks.

Almost all of the methods that we described for doing your own input and editing can be made to telecommunicate. Redactron's communicating word processors, Graphic Products' (Bloomfield, Connecticut) OCR transmission, TTS transmission of keyboarded tape, telephone modems for computer to computer communication, and even two tin cans and a string for the economy-minded. McGraw-Hill inputs and edits in New York and transmits to their typesetter/printers in Brookfield, Wisconsin and other locations. Some publishers have their originating source transmit the information to a central computer system where the copy is edited and typeset. Telecommunications from author to publisher to typesetting service can save time, money and the problem of lost manuscript pages.

"Pictorial" telecommunications is called facsimile or FAX. With this technology we can transmit layouts, galley proofs and copies of illustrations over telephone lines in from two to six minutes per document. Newer types of FAX will permit the transmission of camera-ready art, or even page negatives. The creative possibilities are endless.

Another method that links word processing and telecommunications is time sharing. A central computer system is "connected" to literally hundreds of users by telephone lines. In your home or office is a typewriter terminal with a holder (modem) for the telephone receiver. You call up the computer, place the phone in the modem and you are now connected. You can type, correct, edit, move entire sections around and either type out a clean manuscript yourself or have it done at the computer site. The information is stored there for future editing or for typesetting. You pay for the "connection" and for the time you actually use the computer (so sitting there trying to think up a new metaphor does not cost you anything).

You could also have the terminal in the form of a tv set (video terminal). There are a number of time sharing services that offer this text editing program, and although the computer may be hundreds of miles away, you have all and more of the word processing capabilities at your fingertips as if they were your own.

Since most of the material that passes through an office is typed, it can be seen that the common denominator in all our input and editing methods is--or should be--the typewriter. The method that uses the typewriter itself as a device for input and editing and uses the typewritten page as a recorded medium is optical character recognition.

OCR, like word processing, lets the typer (that could be either a typist or an author) input, proofread, and correct copy before it is scanned by a machine that converts the typewritten pages into coded signals. A little bit more care must be exercised but there is minimal difference between typing and OCR typing, especially with the use of newer intelligent OCR devices.

OCR may not offer all of the editing cycles that might be needed since the typed page is only capable of sustaining a certain level of changes or corrections. It is not re-recordable. To overcome this limitation and to provide additional capability OCR and other input methods are combined into total systems. The long name is video based computer and data management systems.

These systems allow you to use any form of input from keyboarded tape to OCR to word processing to telecommunication lines. The information enters the system and is stored on magnetic media capable of retaining as many as 60 million characters. For editing purposes the information is viewed on the screen of a video display terminal (with a typewriter keyboard attached) to permit the editing of copy in view. After editing, the copy may be printed out on a line printer in a format that emulates the typeset lines. This line printer output is essentially a galley proof. After reading, corrections are once again made via the video terminal. The copy can then be printed out again or go right to typesetting. All devices are usually connected together in these systems.

These systems are also device independent so that any input or output machine can be connected with minimal effort. The front end of the system (input and editing and computer processing) could be in an office and the back end of the system (typesetting) could be in service somewhere else. As we have seen, many operations can take place simultaneously even though separated by great distances. The total systems concept is beginning to dominate the typesetting industry.

To say that we cannot have copy originators use these new methods is to lose sight of the past. Ball point pens did replace the quill and typewriters had a rough time converting the handwriting affionados but they succeeded. Some authors can only write while sitting naked in a gazebo under a full moon. The reality of the situation is best summed up when you look at the rising costs that confront all publishers.

None--or even all--of these methods can provide a total solution. Our industry, like our society, appears to abhor pat answers to problems. It is for each publisher to apply new technology with care and with deliberation. As you can see, there are technologies within technologies. As soon as you select one way, a better one rears its head. That is why publishers must work closely with their service bureaus. We may not realize it but the relationship is symbolic.

By working with their services publishers can apply some of these new methods with minimum investment and can also develop techniques that allow them to be used without adversely affecting many of the time honored approaches that we hold so dear. We are somewhat tradition bound when it comes to certain aspects of the business and the test of a "good" technology is its ability to be used without changing many of the ways that we do things. Change without change--such is the paradox of our industry.

The concept of the word bank is down to earth and workable reality. Its only limitations will be the imagination of those who apply it.

PRECIS--A BETTER WAY TO INDEX FILMS*

Mary Robinson Sive

The British take indexing seriously--seriously enough to award an annual prize, the Wheatley Medal, for the best-indexed book from a British publisher. Several years ago, I began hearing about a new indexing system called PRECIS (PREserved Context Indexing System), developed for the British National Bibliography. When an article about PRECIS in the September 1978 issue of Library Journal mentioned in passing that the National Film Board of Canada (NFBC) was planning to use PRECIS for its film collection, I wrote to the author, Professor Mary Dykstra of Dalhousie University, Halifax, Nova Scotia, to learn more. As a result of this correspondence, I found out that the originator of PRECIS, Derek Austin, was to teach a course in it at the University of Toronto. I signed up.

Last August, I spent two intensive weeks studying with Austin and Dykstra. I found PRECIS a highly exact form of subject analysis and indexing methodology that offers retrieval capability superior to conventional indexes.

What exactly is PRECIS, and why do film librarians need to know about it? One reason is pragmatic: The 1981 National Film Board Catalogue will sport an unfamiliar-looking index, somewhat resembling the sample page reproduced below. Note that the index of the 1979 Catalogue of the Atlantic Region of NFBC, from which this page is taken, does not simply list the titles of 14 films about Newfoundland, it pinpoints the exact focus of each film. Thus, the reader need not flip pages 14 times and refer back to the full annotations. (That the text has both English and French in one alphabetical sequence is not a function of PRECIS, but was done to test public acceptance of bilingual catalogs.)

The page reproduced here has the typical appearance of a PRECIS index. The 1981 general catalog of the NFBC will follow the prototype of this regional catalog with some additional features.

---
*Reprinted by permission of the author and publisher from Sightlines Winter 1979/80, p. 14-17; copyright © 1980 by the Educational Film Library Association.

The other reason for learning about PRECIS is also practical. Existing indexes to film collections are quite frustrating to many users. Anyone who is bothered by the fact that blacks are still known as "Negroes" to the National Information Center for Educational Media (NICEM), or the Union of Soviet Socialist Republics as "Russia" to the Library of Congress has reason to be interested. So does anyone who does not like scanning eight-and-a-half columns under "psychology" in the <u>Educational Film Locator</u> to find films on, say, behaviorism.

PRECIS grew out of just such dissatisfaction with existing subject access tools. In the late '60s planning began to convert the <u>British National Bibliography</u> (BNB) to computer production. (BNB is the printed catalog of all monographs published in Great Britain.) The folks in London, unlike their counterparts at the Library of Congress (LC), determined that the process of automated catalog production should consist of more than pouring old wine into new bottles (the old wine in this case being traditional indexing terms and methods). A team under the leadership of Derek Austin, now Head of Subject Systems at the British Library, thoroughly examined the problem, unfettered by time-honored practices and thinking prevalent in the library world.

Austin's team determined, first of all, that using computers to their fullest effect indicated they do the tedious clerical chores associated with indexing. The team set out to devise a system by which a computer would generate all desired index entries from a single set of coded terms. Next, it established that the bibliography avoid arcane or unnatural language and be comprehensible to the ordinary reader. Further, indexing would be as extensive or as brief as the document being indexed warranted. There would be no set number of subject headings, irrespective of the document's length or significance. Because the system had to serve a national bibliography, it had to be adaptable to a broad data base, to all formats, print and nonprint, and to the creation of a permanent record. It had to be designed for application by indexers who were not subject specialists.

The outcome was PRECIS. The BNB began using it on January 1, 1971. A major technical revision of the format took place in 1973, but the general appearance and underlying methodology have not changed appreciably.

As can be seen in the example reproduced here, each entry in a PRECIS index generally consists of two lines. The first defines the exact subject and, on occasion, its location, as in "Marine Farming. Indigenous industries. Cape Breton, Nova Scotia" or "Marine Research. Canada." The subject formulation may consist of more than one word, or of one word, e.g., "Mothers."

The first line by itself permits reader selection or rejection. The second line narrows the matter down to a specific process. The reader searching for a film illustrating marine farming at Cape

Technical Services/Readers' Services

From *Atlantic Region 16mm Films Catalogue 1979*, the National Film Board of Canada

McCulloch, Charles. Managers. Building materials supply industries. Halifax. Nova Scotia Personal success — *Biographies*	The Journeyman
Maillet, Antonine, *1929-* Auteurs acadiens	Antonine Maillet
Managers. Building materials supply industries. Halifax. Nova Scotia McCulloch, Charles. Personal success — *Biographies*	The Journeyman
Margaree Harbour. Cape Breton Island. Nova Scotia. Residents. Life styles	Margaree People
Marine Agronomy *See* Marine Farming	
Marine Farming. Indigenous industries. Cape Breton. Nova Scotia Employment of young persons. Life styles	Scoggie
Marine Farming. Seaweeds. Coasts. Atlantic Provinces	Seaweeds
Marine Research. Canada Technology	Down to the Sea
Mermaid Theater. Wolfville. Nova Scotia. Performances of Micmac Indian legends.	Medoonak the Stormmaker
Messer, Don Musical tours	Don Messer, His Land and His Music
Micmac Indians. Nova Scotia Legends Legends — *Dramatizations*	Glooscap Country Medoonak the Stormmaker
Middle East Oil. Chedabucto Bay. Nova Scotia. Transport by super-tankers Environmental aspects	Still in One Piece, Anyway
Mining *See also* Coal Mining	
Montague. Prince Edward Island Local newspapers: "Eastern Graphic"	Eastern Graphic
Mort Réflexions de la Sagouine	La Sagouine: la mort
Mothers Welfare mothers Working mothers. Accessibility of day care facilities	Would I Ever Like to Work Tiger on a Tight Leash
Mount Carmel. Prince Edward Island Royal visits, *1973*. Preparation by residents.	The Queen, the Chef and the President

Mulching	Tara's Mulch Garden
Mushrooms — Guides	Those Wild, Wild Mushrooms
Music See also Folk Music	
Music. Curriculum subjects. Schools. Halifax. Nova Scotia Teaching methods: Kodaly method	Halifax Music — Part I
Musical Activities See also Ukelele Playing	
Musical Activities. Students. Schools. Halifax. Nova Scotia	Halifax Music — Part II
Musical Tours By Messer, Don	Don Messer, His Land and His Music
National Parks See also Names of Individual Parks	
Naval Reserves. Canada	Citizen Sailors
New Brunswick	New Brunswick Promenade
Crafts	Crafts of My Province
Craftsmen	Crafts of My Province
Economic conditions. Protest, 1972 by Acadians	A Sun Like Nowhere Else
Farmers	Potatoes
Fundy National Park	Atlantic Parks
Independent production. Influence of corporate forest industries	More Than Just the Trees
Potatoes. Farming	Potatoes
Rural regions. Young persons. Alternative life styles	Crazy Quilt
Saint John. Cemeteries: Fernhill — Caretaker's perspectives	Boo Hoo
Université de Moncton. Acadian students. Identity crisis, 1968-1969	Acadia, Acadia
Newfoundland	
Architecture	Come Paint and Photograph Us Architecture of Newfoundland
Baymen. Life styles	The Baymen
Coasts	Ocean Heritage
Etching. Blackwood, David, 1941-	Blackwood
Fishing by Portuguese schooners	The White Ship
Fogo Island. Fishing communities	The Winds of Fogo
Fogo Island. Social change. Use of films	Newfoundland Project A Memo from Fogo The Specialists at Memorial Discuss the Fogo Films
Great Island. Puffins. Extinction by herring gulls — Ecological perspectives	Puffins, Predators and Pirates
Gros Morne National Park — Geological aspects	Gros Morne
Outports. Former residents. Personal success — Biographies	The Brothers Byrne
Politicians: Smallwood, Joseph Roberts	A Little Fellow from Gambo

Technical Services/Readers' Services   167

Sailing
Salmon. Fly-casting
Western Newfoundland

Newfoundland. *Special themes*
Folk music

Newfoundlanders. Brampton. Ontario
Family life. Effects of relocation

Newspapers
See also
    Local Newspapers

Noël
Réflexions de la Sagouine

Norway
Coastal communities. Fish. Farming
Economy
Salmon fishing industries & trout fishing
  industries

Nouveau-Brunswick
Acadiens. Effets des industries forestières
Acadiens. Vie quotidienne — *Perspectives
  sociologiques*
Baie Sainte-Marie. Villages
Acadiennes. Vie quotidienne. *Satires*.
Conditions économiques. Protestations,
  1972, par des Acadiens
Fermiers

Pêcheurs acadiens. Vie quotidienne
Pommes de terre. Agriculture

Sainte-Marie. Acadiens. Effets de la crise
  économique, *1929-1934*
Université de Moncton. Etudiants
  acadiens. Crise d'identité,
  1968-1969

Nouvelle-Ecosse
Régions rurales. Jeunes gens acadiens.
Vie quotidienne.

Sailing in Newfoundland
Leaping Silver
Western Newfoundland

A Rosewood Daydream

When I Go — That's It!

La Sagouine: Nouël

The Farming of Fish
The Farming of Fish
The Farming of Fish

Y'a du bois dans ma cour

Acadie libre
Les Gossipeuses

Un soleil pas comme
  ailleurs
La ferme familial en
  danger
La noce est pas finie
La ferme familial en
  danger

Abandounée

L'Acadie, l'Acadie

La Cabane

Breton Island finds out that this particular film concerns the lifestyles of young persons so employed. The two secondline entries under "Mothers" tell us that neither of these films is about mothers in general; one film is about welfare mothers, the other about the accessibility of day care facilities to working mothers.

In technical parlance, the word or phrase in bold print ("Marine Research") is know as the lead, the one following it on the first line ("Canada") as the qualifier, and the second line as the display. Thus, a PRECIS index entry may always be schematically represented as:

    Lead. Qualifier
    Display.

The example:

    Marine Research (lead). Canada (qualifier)
    Technology (display)

appears on other pages as--

    Canada (lead)
    Marine research. Technology (display)   and

    Technology (lead). Marine research. Canada (qualifier).

Note that the film is accessible to users interested in marine research, technology, or Canada. In each case, the presence of the other two terms helps to establish the context, and aids selection decisions.

The sequence "Canada-Marine research--Technology" is known as the string. The only job the human indexer performs in preparing a PRECIS index is writing the string and coding it appropriately. Shunting its components into their various positions is done by a computer program. In writing the string, the indexer is not restricted to an "approved" list of subject headings but draws the terms from the document itself or--as has to be the case with films and other audiovisual media--from a well written abstract.

Most computer-produced indexes other than PRECIS are designed for computer retrieval as well. A familiar form of such an index is KWIC (keyword-in-context) index, a sample of which is reproduced below. An index of this type is achieved by rotating a title until each significant word comes into display, the rest of the title appearing before and after on the same line. This requires minimal input of human intelligence. The computer does almost everything, including disregarding "stop" words such as "the," "and," "a," and so forth. Retrieval involves scanning entries under each desired term and printing out those with the required combinations. In the example shown here, the computer would match 50 references displaying "student" or "students" against 20 displaying

"Catholic," "Catholics," or "Catholicism" to locate the one dealing with students in Catholic schools. Computers do not tire of such tasks. Human beings, subject to eyestrain, have more limited attention spans.

An index employing title permutation, such as a KWIC index, is suitable only where titles give adequate indication of subject matter, as is generally the case with papers in professional journals. It is no help with many books, other than technical treatises or texts, nor with most films.

The user is less interested in how an index is produced than in how it works. Is it easy and quick to use? Can the user find in it common terms? How much hunting around does it require to determine the exact meaning of the terms it does use? The NICEM Index to 16mm Educational Films, for instance, gives no clue whether a film about social concern with nuclear power might be indexed in "Social Science-Resources-Power," "Industrial and Technical Education-Engineering, Nuclear" or "Science-Physical-Physics-Atomic." It turns out that LOVEJOY'S NUCLEAR WAR is found only under the latter. The difference in emphasis between "Home Economics-Consumer Education" and "Social Science-Consumption (Economics)" in the same publication may seem fairly clear; however, we don't find MORE, a film about consumption gone wild, listed in either category.

PRECIS' built-in hospitality to new words permits the user to enter a PRECIS index under any likely term. The NFBC Atlantic Region Catalogue, from which we have drawn our examples, includes entries for "identity crisis," "insecticide spraying," "urban development," along with other quite current topics.

The user also wants to know how specific an index is. Do
its terms produce lists of entries extending over several columns?
Tests have shown--and most of us know from our own experience--
that readers are turned off by more than 20 or so entries under one
subject and will not follow them through all the way. LOVEJOY'S
NUCLEAR WAR (about a nuclear power plant protest) is but one of
some 500 films on attomic and nuclear energy in the NICEM Index
with no notation to distinguish it from films documenting the fission
process.

Here's an example from the Educational Film Library Association's (EFLA) upcoming Instructional Film Guide: The title, VERONICA, does not tell us that this NFBC film is about a girl of
Polish extraction growing up in a multi-ethnic Toronto neighborhood,
nor does its conventional indexing under "Ethnic studies" and "Social
Studies. " Its PRECIS notation "Ontario-Toronto-Children-Polish-
Canadian children-lifestyles" reveals a good deal more.

Lack of currency and specificity are not problems with comprehensive bibliographies of national scope alone. Selective catalogs
of regional and state film libraries share it, though to a lesser extent. The right film is in there somewhere, but it's a lot of trouble
to track it down. As a result, film programmers depend on other
sources of information--reviews, word-of-mouth, previewing, promotional and advertising circulars, filmographies. This is not necessarily bad. Certainly no index can do justice to a film like THE
SAND CASTLE. But a different indexing system could allow the
catalogs to open up the film collection more readily.

The National Film Board of Canada and PRECIS

In the early '70s, the NFBC found that some of its films were under-utilized. Some highly popular titles were in constant demand:
many newer releases remained unused on the shelves for over a
year. The NFBC commissioned Professor Mary Dykstra to study
the problem. She concluded that it was one of subject access: if
booking clerks could have a clearer way of knowing each film's subject matter and application, they would be in a position to recommend substitute titles more readily and get some of those shelf sitters into circulation. They could get new films out for showings
without the delays inherent in the existing system which depended
almost entirely on printed catalogs.

Dykstra set out to investigate subject access techniques in
order to identify one "designed to be efficient, to satisfy user needs
effectively, to be sophisticated in its utilization of computer technology, and at the same time ... as simple and straightforward as possible. " In her report of August 1975, she recommended the adoption of PRECIS as meeting all these requirements. Other reasons
for this recommendation were that a proportion of NFBC productions
were already PRECIS indexed and stored in a data base, and that
programs already existed for machine translation of PRECIS strings

Technical Services/Readers' Services 171

into French--an important consideration in an officially bilingual country.

The Dykstra proposal was for PRECIS indexing as one aspect of an integrated and automated information/distribution/booking control system accessible on-line or on tape at NFB offices in Canada and branches in Chicago, New York, and overseas.

Implementation of this plan has been gradual and paced to available funding. The Atlantic Region Catalogue was the pilot PRECIS project. It and some subsequent catalogs were produced by hand, i.e., humans, not computers, did the "shunting" of strings. Judy Gardhouse, Senior AV Librarian, reports that the Film Board expects the system to be fully operational by the mid-1980's. Bilingual indexing is routine, and automated booking is in place now in several offices and run through NFB's internal data processing unit. She and Colin Neale, Project Director, welcome inquiries. They are anxious to know film programmers' reactions to the 1981 printed catalog with its PRECIS index and to the proposed system.

The NFB is not the only PRECIS user in Canada. Earlier, Ontario school librarians Audrey Taylor and Irene McCordick became convinced that here was a better tool to serve students in school libraries. The Board of Education of York County (a rural area north of Toronto, rapidly turning suburban) shared their concern for better utilization of media center resources and facilitation of independent inquiry by students. Taylor was commissioned to prepare a PRECIS-based catalog for the print and non-print collections of the new Aurora High School which opened in September 1972. Her staff has since prepared similar catalogs (on microfiche) for newly opened elementary schools. In late 1979, the Ontario Ministry of Education was studying the feasibility of extending this data base to a network serving all the schools in the province.

The Canadian Non-Print Materials Project has compiled an index, prepared by Chris Robinson, to 1,753 filmstrips produced in Canada or on Canadian themes. This project is located at the University of Toronto Faculty of Library Science and was funded by the Film Board and the Ontario Education Ministry. It is another piece of the NFB's eventual total Canadian AV information system. The Ontario Educational Research Information Service (ONTERIS) employs PRECIS for its indexes to educational research reports. Other Canadian agencies are seriously considering adopting PRECIS, among them the Quebec Ministry of Education and the Bibliotheque Nationale du Québec.

In Great Britain, the British Universities Film Council produces the Higher Education Learning Programmes Information Service Catalogue and the British Library publishes the British Education Index, in addition to the already mentioned British National Bibliography. The Australian National Bibliography utilizes PRECIS, as do agencies of the European Economic Community to whom the translingual features are an important asset.

In the United States, adoption of PRECIS will have to come through the private sector. A feasibility study by the Library of Congress in 1978 effectively squelched consideration of PRECIS by the library establishment. As yet, there has been no concerted effort by the various individuals in this country who are trained in or conversant with the new indexing system. It is used in isolated fashion here and there: a career information file in Florida, a bank of instructional programs for computer application in Minnesota, abstracts of psychology articles in Maryland, instruction in a few schools of library and information studies.

Following my return from Toronto last Fall, I prepared a PRECIS index for EFLA's Instructional Film Guide. Scheduled for publication early in 1980, the Guide is a compilation of evaluations of some 300 films released in 1978 for curriculum use. This will, it appears, be the first published PRECIS index to audiovisual materials in the United States.

It is fitting that the pioneer PRECIS project in this country concern itself with an audiovisual medium. Retrieval of data for such materials is ripe for an innovative approach. Traditional library cataloging and classification systems have not proven effective --not surprisingly so since they were designed in another age and for books. The leading reference works do not use them. EFLA Evaluations, the Educational Film Locator, and the NICEM Index to 16mm Educational Films each uses an idiosyncratic scheme for indexing films, none apparently designed for compatibility with any other. The reviews and the annual "Audiovisual Guide" in Previews use still other terminology, as did the 1974 Index to Instructional Media Catalogs. The last two titles are published by R. R. Bowker, which does utilize Sears and LC List of Subject Headings for some of its other products. Individual authors, editors, school districts, film libraries and other educational agencies devise indexing language according to the needs of the moment. Such profusion and confusion do not make the life of the busy AV director or film librarian any easier.

During my two weeks in Canada, I saw evidence of Canadian nationalism everywhere. It seemed to me a healthy kind of national pride and drive for identity. In PRECIS, Canadians are importing an excellent British invention and developing it in imaginative ways to help order data in areas where such order is desperately needed: film selection and booking, and information services to students. We would do well to follow their lead.

Part III

COMMUNICATION AND EDUCATION

INFORMATION FEVER*

Andrée Conrad

Here is the situation. Our culture is now solidly entrenched in the stage of the Advanced Concrete. Knowledge, concretized in the form of facts, data, informational bits, has become the viable commodity. In a growing industry, this commodity is produced on campuses across the country not only by scholars, the former custodians of knowledge, but by a new breed called "knowledge generators." These people produce a commodity which has the virtue of being storable in centralized data banks for retrieval "on demand, " by other knowledge generators, or by anyone willing to master a programming primer.

On the knowledge-commodity exchange, trading is brisk (though hardly broad-based) as data is moved in and out of heavily footnoted papers. Knowledge traders rarely notice when some of their data leaks out into the mass media, just as pork bellies traders don't have a thought for the packages of bacon in supermarket coolers. On the other hand, in concepts, theories, and intellectual constructs which might impose order or significance on this informational chaos, the market is somewhat depressed. Indeed, investing here is distinctly not advised.

What characterizes the advanced-concrete thought culture is accumulation, not discrimination and interpretation. For some time now, the majority of scholars have been hard at work on the fact-specific peripheries of their fields, leaving the central issues to a few foolhardy adventurers. The safest course, as experience proves, is peripheral fact-gathering, which is increasingly validated by the cost and magnitude of the technology being devised to process, store, and retrieve its bits. The gold which a scholar mines from shelves of books or piles of computer print-outs is coin of the realm for buying advancement, tenure and prestige; whereas the kind of intellectual audacity demanded by interpretation or generalization tends to buy nothing but trouble. It is not surprising, therefore, that many academic conversations have become the exalted version

---

*Reprinted by permission of the author and publisher from Book Forum, 5:1 (1979) 34-46; copyright © 1979 by The Hudson River Press.

of baseball-card trading sessions. Not "What do you think?" but "What is your source?" is the gamesmanlike question of the day.

In asking this gamesmanlike question, is a scholar doing anything more than recognizing the handwriting on the wall? Consider this statement from the recently published Scholarly Communication: The Report of the National Enquiry, the fruit of a five-year project sponsored by the American Council of Learned Societies and prepared with the support of the National Endowment for the Humanities and the Ford, Mellon, and Rockefeller Foundations: "...[T]he observation that knowledge is a public good must be qualified by the recognition that, when embodied in the form of books and journals or library services, it is fully capable of being produced in discrete units and sold to private individuals, much like any other commodity." It's important to give some thought to the step that has to be taken to get from the phrase "knowledge as a public good" to the concept that knowledge can be handled and traded "much like any other commodity." At once you will perceive that this is no small step. The Report, excerpted elsewhere in this issue, is in many respects a remarkable document, not least because it considers the step such a natural one. The Report makes several recommendations on how to negotiate this step, through creations such as a National Periodicals Center, accessible to scholars through nationwide computer hookups; synoptic publishing, in which computers will print out "on demand" all those papers and bibliographies which the conscientious scholar will want to cite; and a multitude of other technological miracles designed to make scholarly communication as easy as dialing your telephone. Of course these monuments to our advanced-concrete thought culture are also designed to facilitate computing the cost of each "discrete unit" of public good that's demanded and bill the demander for "user charges that cover partial or full costs."

To give you some idea of what this may mean, the price of a bibliography on a topic in a field that has been plugged in runs between $100 and $200 (perhaps a sound investment, if it really means the difference between tenure and looking for another job). Devotees of the school of hard knocks will at once propound the virtue of pay-as-you-go research, as plastic is certain to make an early appearance and be swiftly followed by delinquency and eventual default.

The fiscal uncertainties of the concretization of knowledge are one thing: its intellectual uncertainties, however, are quite another; especially because they will not be confined to the 793,000 persons comprising the American community of professionals in higher education. Already we have an intellectual system which causes facts to ionize and float away from their core; which causes them to be picked up not just by other scholars but by the media, those painters and interpreters of most people's picture of the world. And here we have the chief uncertainty masked by The Report. In contemplating the new breed of knowledge generators and their new hardware, everyone's glance seems to have been studiously averted from the 99.6 per cent of the population who don't belong to the

Communication and Education 177

academic community--the so-called public. There is no acknowledgment of the public's inconvenient tendency to want information: "thirst for knowledge" and "need to know" are both clichés extracted from reality, and they don't apply merely to hard news. To the scenario of a knowledge-commodity exchange, one really ought to add an image of starving masses pounding at the gate, demanding grain.

The norms of scholarly communication have traditionally created great problems in bringing the work of academics to the public. Now the new system promises to create a fact vacuum into which enterprising blackmarketers will happily allow themselves to be sucked. These blackmarketers are the nonpureminded popularizers, the self-styled communicators whose work makes the chaotic gamut of fact appear to be orderly at any cost, usually through the use of veneers of plausible fantasy. Informational bits, in their work, are arranged in configurations giving the appearance of meaningfulness, and the public devours them owing to an innate taste not for sensationalized distortions, but for coherent bodies of fact. The public likes sequences of cause and effect, explanations of origin and relation, and so forth. The most remote and unrelated phenomena can be connected together by verbs in the conditional tense and labelled "one possible explanation, " and the public will pay respectful attention; it will also eliminate the conditional tense and replace "one possible" with "the. " This is how the public becomes infected with information fever, today's infatuation with fact. And the dangerous characteristic of this fever is that it increases in virulence in direct proportion with the distance between knowledge generator and knowledge consumer.

1. Etiology

We ought to consider the origins of information fever, the environmental hazard of the advanced concrete. This means we must consider how thought became concrete in the peculiar way it is now.

The advanced concrete has almost nothing in common with the primitive concrete, which we know a little about, owing to Bronze Age texts in cuneiform and hieroglyphics, and owing to its vestiges in the poems of Homer and Hesiod. The purposes of writing and thought, and also the kinds of people who do these things, have changed so much that great historical imagination is needed to project ourselves back into the primitive concrete. During the first two millennia of literacy, the cumbersomeness of vast phonetic syllabaries kept writing in the hands of religious and governmental dynasties; now, literacy is not dynastic in such a restricted sense, and the least productive uses of letters are in the service of religion and government. Written thought is no longer a utilitarian phenomenon smothered by an infinitude of overfocused phonetic symbols which tax the memory and tire the mind. In the primitive concrete, there were no tracks headed for the kind of knowledge that comes of speculation. A Kant was unthinkable, a Wittgenstein destined to be called the village idiot. Advances owed to informed guesses were simply not in the picture. Correlative thinking, which serves to associate such things as the cause and locus of disease with its cure, or signs and numbers with important decisions, was the sole process of conceptualization available. The primitive concrete generated between magic and the observation of reality a static, unhealthy compatibility that kept medicine, science, and social progress at a standstill for almost twenty centuries.

When the Greeks adapted the Phoenician alphabet to their own dialects (probably first on the island of Rhodes), a crack appeared in the primitive concrete. By dismantling verbal sound into the handful of visual shapes we call vowels and consonants, an act of abstraction was committed, though its revolutionary impact took almost four hundred years to feel. This is a process described by Eric A. Havelock on several occasions, most recently in his observant and interesting book, The Greek Concept of Justice: From Its Shadow in Homer to Its Substance in Plato (Harvard University Press). Havelock shows that the emergence of the peculiar speculative quality of Western thought is in great part owed to the abstract principle of the Greek alphabet, which gradually insinuated itself into the broader process of thought, stimulating a propensity to think abstractly. (Reading the Homeric poems, which are partly transcriptions of oral tradition passed down by memorization during primitive-concrete times, will show that the opposite is not the case, that the alphabet was not the achievement of a predisposition to abstract thought.) Thinking emerged incarnate in the profession of philosophy, and among many philosophers and their followers, primitive-concrete habits of mind were found severely wanting. But not everybody was transformed into an abstract thinker. That the abstract was even felt as a threat is clear from what happened to Socrates, his predilection for the abstract ridiculed by Aristophanes in Clouds and his distance from the masses ended in execution.

Nearly two millennia after Socrates, the printing press, by changing the technology of written communication, made possible the advanced concrete, in which abstract thought acquired the character of matter, and the mind could treat and process intangibles as if they were physical things. The philosopher and his hostile public were, in certain respects, brought together by the printing press.

The pseudoutilitarian associations of the printed book may have been a factor at work in this. Printed books, concrete in format, were plentiful and cheap enough to be used without qualms for things other than reading. While one might never use the Très Riches Heures du duc de Berry to prop open a door or throw at a cat, one wouldn't hesitate with most printed books, especially nowadays. Also, there is the strange process whereby books come to symbolize the knowledge contained within them ("If you own a book you don't have to read it," I've heard scholars ironize). Then, too, the lines of type in a book may appear to be two-dimensional, but in fact they are (or were until the introduction of photo-offset printing) tactile, a reality exploited for the use of the blind in the inven-

Communication and Education

tion of braille. One hears of any number of non-reading uses that books may be put to (for example, estate libraries being bought at wholesale by interior decorators, Cuban cigars being shipped in hollow volumes to avoid customs, tomes of Shakespeare being used as code books in espionage, and so on). This materialism is surely absorbed by knowledge in its progress toward concretization.

Less crudely palpable but more conceptually influential is the apperceptive process by which material value is conferred upon a text merely by its being set in type. The psychologic impact of a text set in type is indisputably distinct from that of a typewritten or a handwritten text, and consists in an impersonal, godlike arbitration between author and reader. It costs money to set a text in type: that cost is paradigmatic for all other capitalist enterprises, and in a market economy it's only logical that the step into print should universally be considered a step up. The investor looks for eventual repayment in such things as big dollars paid for a reprint sale, or prestige brought by publication of an important writer. The invested-in writer hopes for his share of the profits, tangible or intangible. Yardsticks to measure intangible profits are evolving, too; recently Science magazine published a survey rating scholars according to the number of citations of their work in other people's footnotes, in the process discovering that there was a direct relationship between the number of citations and the probability of nomination for the Nobel Prize. Thus intangible can be converted to tangible; and soon, perhaps, each citation will be treated as an account receivable like book royalties, or, more aptly, like quarterly dividends on stocks and bonds.

Because magnification in value takes place in anything set in type, from timetables to histories, it does not necessarily explain the concreteness, the "thinginess," which knowledge has acquired. In an interesting and comprehensive study called The Printing Press as an Agent of Change: Communications and Cultural Transformations in Early-Modern Europe (Cambridge University Press), Elizabeth L. Eisenstein, a wary professor of history, depicts the modern scholar as looking upon the past as a container of objects to be placed in glass cases and investigated by specialists in diverse scholarly fields. These objects are not just "facts" (names, dates, statistics and other measurements) but less finite intellectual phenomena too, things like ideas, explanations, and interpretations. One can see that Professor Eisenstein's glass cases are the typographical containment forced upon ideas which converts them into finite "objects." This is a concretizing progression on the atomic level; it moves from letter-in-metal to word to fact to idea. In any historical perspective, it is natural for fact and idea to be equally objectified, since both exist in the past tense (fact: Napoleon was defeated at Waterloo on June 18, 1815; idea: the abuses of dictatorship and ruinous wars brought about the restoration of the monarchy in France). Even the most elusive philosophic principles, such as Hegel's Idea, congeal into tersely definable, memorizable bits, objects under glass.

What are we to make of ideas that are not relics of the past, or ideas which, like legal cases, exist vividly in the present but are based on circumstantial evidence from the past? In science, ideas take the form of testable hypotheses: falsification (or verification) of these is seen by philosophers of science as steps in a progression toward an ultimate truth, which some consider to be attainable, others not. In the humanities and "soft sciences," by contrast, hypotheses are neither proposed nor verified. In fact, except as curiosities they are shunned. Even the most current of ideas is objectified and concretized just as if it belonged to the past. This is explained as a side-effect of the norm requiring the scholar to keep his material at a distance; progressions in the humanities look like bar-graphs, rising lines truncated at the top by violent disagreement or pessimistic phrases like "No more can be known."

One effect (if not cause) of this is to domesticate ideas, make them more manageable, less threatening. Ideas in the time of Socrates were threatening not just to the general public, but even to other philosophers and well-informed laymen. The nature of the threat may have changed in 2,400 years; but it remains to be seen whether or not the threateningness has disappeared.

2. Immunology

Many are the threats posed by thought. The virtue of objectified, concretized knowledge in the form of collections of information is that it lends itself to compact storage, encapsulation, packaging, assemblage in endless configurations, and economical dissemination -- which may have some effect in alleviating fears. But of course these things also open the door wide to another threat: that of theft.

The guarding of intellectual property is something that has been thought right and proper from the beginning of print, that is, from the beginning of the advanced concrete. Over the centuries methods of defense evolved, with the law increasingly encouraged to participate. It's only in this century, however, when "intellectual" and "scholar" became two clearly separated professions, that different tactics of defense arose. How the intellectual defends his property, by imposing personality on his work, is a far cry from the scholar's reliance on professional ethics -- unwritten but well-articulated laws -- for the definition of territory that will allow him to carve out an area of specialization. It's the difference between indelibly writing one's name on every object of value in the home, and installing a Holmes Alarm System.

Personality may be said to exist in any work containing ideas inseparable from the author representing them and from the facts inspiring them. Often this cohesion is the result of literary style, but I don't mean merely the identifiability of an excerpted paragraph through a syntax that is characteristically epigrammatic or discursive or whatever. The form-equals-content people have long recognized the esthetic virtue of this unity, but they never expressly stated its proprietary functions.

Communication and Education

In the work of intellectuals, it may even happen that ideas belonging to various thinkers are combined through the force of a single personality in such a way that their originators are eclipsed even when credited. This makes no difference, for those ideas are reaching a much larger audience than would ever have heard of them in their original state. What is important is that the element of personality creates a milieu that makes fact irrelevant outside the larger structure of a thesis, makes fact and idea inseparable and inalienable from that structure. The ideas of a strong intellect, no matter how eclectic, cannot be watered down without making the person attempting to simplify them sound ridiculous.

In the academic world, the imposition of personality is anathema. When personality is found in a scholar's work, the castigation is severe. Most scholars do not even rely on innate gift, a part of personality, in carving out their territories, like the musician who gives up his beloved 'cello because the orchestra only has room for a drummer. The principle of academic selection is simple: find the turn nobody else wants, and once the word is out, defending it won't be much of a problem.

In most scholarly papers, one encounters an unwillingness to generalize that waters down any embryonic theory, as well as a fear of attacking a discipline's ideological foundations (more on this will be found in Erika Duncan's essay on risk-taking as an essential factor in intellectual breakthrough, in this issue). Thus the tacit agreement arises to deny the importance of ideas, and inflate the importance of fact. How this is manifested is in the hundreds of half-baked papers that appear in scholarly journals, full of bits and pieces of information, always said to represent ongoing projects which the pressures of a teaching career prevent a scholar from publishing in coherent, well-organized works. Why not wait for a sabbatical year and produce something worthwhile? As it turns out, scholars are rushing into print not merely to have something on their vitae--to show they are thinking--but also to protect their property, according to many accounts: a problem you might think had been solved by the custom of working on the periphery.

What is happening, it seems, is unique to America, and it must have something to do with the amalgam of educational traditions that is American pedagogy. It is certainly striking to the eye of most visitors. One Finnish scholar, over here for a brief stay, remarked: 'I could never work here. No sooner do you discover a problem than you must rush out an article to keep your position. You Americans scatter and waste yourselves in print: twenty articles by the time you are forty, none of which you like very much, bits and pieces scattered here and there, incredible!' (Quoted by John MacAloon of the University of Chicago's Committee on Social Thought, in an essay commissioned by the Danforth Foundation, a major American academic philanthropic organization which is trying to counter certain trends in today's community of educators by emphasizing the importance of good teaching.)

We really ought to ask where the paranoia about idea theft originates: there is strong evidence that it starts in graduate school. What is most sinister about it is that the rapaciousness or competitiveness of fellow students--from whom one understandably expects perfidy--is not the main cause. There are so many stories --so many verifiable stories--about the unscrupulous senior professor who helps himself to the ideas that are a routine byproduct of those enthusiastic first years of graduate research, that the phenomenon has even acquired a nickname: The Sting, after the Redford-Newman con-game movie.

After decades of taking it for granted that students' ideas were the property of the advising faculty member, it is reassuring to see faculties reprimanding members who don't respect the scholarly confidences of their students. But other than appealing to the faculty, a student has little recourse, since there are almost no precedents in law for dealing with intellectual theft in the absence of a printed text, the prerequisite for protection under existing copyright and plagiarism laws.

Thus in America we continue to exhaust that tired phrase, "publish or perish," reinforcing it with two fears: the fear of losing a job, and the fear of losing an idea. We minimize the importance of ideas, in hopes that no one will notice them or think them important enough to steal. And because we cannot steal them ourselves, we don't read other people's work for the brilliant ideas it may contain, but rather for the factual matter in it, which is in the public domain. When we ask that gamesmanlike question, "What is your source?" we are telling the other person his ideas are dispensable, but his facts are not.

What has happened is quite natural: the matter easiest to generate, facts and informational bits, has gained the ascendancy over what is more difficult to generate, namely theories and interpretations. By acceding to the natural, what we have done--probably unwittingly--is to create a utopia of the severed head, in which knowledge is completely cut off from personality, and the idea of intellectual property unequivocally compromised.

3. Symptomatology

As academics grow increasingly narrow in their intellectual concerns, taking less and less responsibility in the arrangement and dispersal of informational bits, they leave to false popularizers the task of disseminating knowledge, feeding the public's information fever.

McLuhan had predicted that the size of the audience for the printed word would contract as a result of television; the opposite seems to have happened, proving once again that the public is unpredictable. One side effect of an expanded reading public is that popularization in print has blossomed, in part to provide "further reading" to follow television shows. Some forms of popularization have proved complementary to the good custody of knowledge, while others are clearly inimical to it. What is happening now makes it possible to define popularization as almost any kind of informational nonfiction that is not directed toward a special audience or published in a specialized journal.

It's important to view the work of our most prominent intellectuals as a variety of popularization, because their popularity shows that the public is not infatuated merely with fact. Many of today's intellectuals (as opposed to scholars) are masters of the ability to make abstract points tangible, of a vivid imagery that makes texts memorable and intelligible. Not just organic complexity of thought, not even that major intangible good, quality, is what distinguishes intellectuals from the mass market popularizers: it is really their incapacity to trade in facts.

When intellectuals set about handling the chaotic multiplicity of the real world, they initiate a thought process that simplifies and at least partially explains by using example or comparison. In a word, they use metaphor. The heuristic possibilities of metaphor, which have long been known to science, are so immense that the expression of abstract concepts has come to depend almost entirely on it: the concreteness of metaphor is daily transferred to the abstract for the sake of getting important ideas across to the largest possible public.

Metaphor reduces chaos to coherent sequences of information, and it's no secret that a mass of chaotic information can be made manageable through the more memorable kind of simplification allowed by bold example and sharp image. The danger is that a powerful image, whether or not it is valid, will dominate and become an ineradicable cliché. The temptation to make a point quickly, conclude a proposition prematurely, short-circuit a progression in the testimony, facilitates the creation of volumes of false knowledge.

The success of false popularization gives the supercilious the opportunity to sit in judgment on the public and decree that the largest part of literate humanity is still capable of inventing the interior placement of organs and the topography of unmapped regions; will always insist on the reality of imaginary animals and extraterrestrial visitors; will never see the interest of truth. The public mind is explained as a relic of some primitive stage of development (two names for this: the R-complex, after the reptilian hypothalamic-limbic complex governing the basest instincts; and the fabulous mentality, which is not supposed to have outlived the Middle Ages) which we all recapitulate in childhood and which some of us never outgrow. But this is an explanation that ought not to be accepted too hastily. For one thing, the adult "fabulous mentality" is identical to its highly respectable counterpart, the factual mentality, in its demand to know. Any human mind without brain damage demands to know everything it can about its environment, both internal and external, and then explains as best it can, deferring only to the more appealing explanations, the more powerful metaphors, it may encounter on the way.

If the public is not adept in the interpretation of fact, it does not mean that the hunger for fact does not exist. The consumption of information appears to be a human need; it may even be a survival mechanism programmed into the hypertrophied human brain. In any case, as a compulsion it is shared by the public and by the scholar, only one of whom has the possibility to satisfy it continually. This in itself explains the seemingly limitless success of false popularization.

What we may consider more intriguing is why the false popularizers choose some subjects and not others for their predations. As Leslie Savan reports elsewhere in this issue, many institutions of learning maintain press and public relations offices to make certain that important developments in research are not relayed to the public full of misconceptions invented by the popular press. These PR people are chiefly concerned with scientific discoveries; consequently science is least distorted in popularization. We are told that this is not merely because scientific discoveries can affect us all in ways that yet another brilliant essay on Shakespeare or Michelangelo cannot, but because most science is funded by the Government and it's incumbent on the sheltering institution to make it look like something is happening with the taxpayer's money.

This doesn't really explain why there is a problem with popularization in the humanities. For one thing, my citing Shakespeare et al. as potential subjects for popularization is meant to mislead, to point up how one can obscure any comparison between science and the humanities. No popularizer (unless a biographer) would choose to present an artistic personality to the public--it would be just too much work. What they mainly go after is that far end of the humanities called the "soft sciences," on which the public keeps a proprietary eye: the social sciences, anthropology, archaeology, psychology, any field studying the origin or condition of man. Though funding sums don't begin to compare with what the Government gives hard science, federal help in these fields is significantly more than anything allocated to the traditional branches of the liberal arts, such as languages, literature, philosophy, history, art history and the like. But this funding doesn't account for the public's eye on the soft sciences and isn't what inspires the thousands of enthusiastic amateurs. And the wrong people to ask for an explanation are the professionals in those fields. For example, when I asked an Egyptologist what was causing the Tutankhamun craze, which at one point was so wild that Ticketron passes to the Metropolitan Museum exhibit were being counterfeited, he said, "People love to look at gold, that's all." Does that explain the success of Hoving's The Untold Story?

One answer might be that any scrutiny of the human race-- which is, after all, the subject matter of most of the soft sciences --is certain to attract a readership, thanks to what Christopher Lasch sees as the narcissistic worldview of our time. But explanations of this phenomenon by narcissism don't really go to the heart of the matter. If one wants to say that the public, the mass of humanity, is insatiable for information about itself, and one sees that the community of scholars studying humanity is doing nothing to gratify that insatiability, leaving the job to popularizers who inevitably get it all wrong, then one must ask what there is to misinterpret, and why it is being misinterpreted.

The problem with information coming from the soft sciences is that it's capable of fragmentation into matter which is intellectually, if not politically, noxious. Furthermore, those fragments of informational matter are attractive enough in themselves to win over, just as "the truth" can, audiences which believe vehemently in the novel constructs encasing them. These audiences will sometimes go so far as to attack anyone who says it isn't so. And they can be of significant numbers, not just one or two unbalanced unfortunates.

False popularization differs from fiction in one main respect: in fiction, there is a conventional contract between the writer and the reader. You agree, when you begin to read something labelled fiction, that everything in it is an invention, even what is not. You are not going to cite a novel chapter and verse to support forensic points. On the other hand, false popularization does not post any warning signals that it is taking up fact and forming some new kind of reading matter out of it. False popularization can even go so far as to become politically inflammatory literature, sensationalist history, doctrines of racial superiority, and so on. The dominant feature--presumably the purpose--of all of these textual abuses of fact is the emotionalizing of thought, the transformation of a contemplative into an active state, in short the excitement of the reader. In politics this can be lethal, in simple popularization it is merely avaricious.

Occasionally a reprimander will emerge who tells us that the public ought to be more discriminating between fact and fable. But he will fail to be heard, for several reasons: he is addressing other reprimanders, not the public; he does not emphasize--does not even recognize--the factual content of fable; but most importantly, he does not see that because the abuse of soft-science fact doesn't have any immediate drastic consequences such as a home-made plutonium bomb might, the problem is one that will be put off indefinitely. This is why most scholars go on about their business, pretending to ignore the bookstore shelves full of phony soft-science paperbacks, refusing to write a good popularization themselves, ostracizing colleagues who do, all the while secretly trying to figure out how to get more money out of their own work.

4. Prognosis

The temptations of computer technology are hardly likely to be less seductive than the fabulous fruit tree in the garden of Eden. Data banks are the natural resting place for the informational bits which constitute knowledge-as-commodity and as storage places will have the virtue of being endlessly expandable, their capacity limited only by what we as scholars are going to be willing to put into them. Since it's common practice to put everything possible into print, how much more is likely to be available when synoptic or "on demand" publishing turns the computer into publisher! We will stand in awe before this great technological vat of facts, all retrievable at the least motion of our fingertips. Instead of pouring over journals, we will have only to "demand" single-copy print-outs of any paper we want to read; we can worry about what to do with it afterwards, whether to drop it into a shredder for recycling, cheat the author of his "user charge" by lending it to a friend, or invent a novel form of storing it so that our libraries don't become flooded with pleated computer paper.

Clearly the beneficiaries of this system are intended to be the members of the scholarly community; I have never heard anyone pretend otherwise. The party line has it that it's only fair that scholars, as custodians of knowledge, should reap the benefits of a system conceived to amplify the fund of knowledge. That 99.6 per cent of the population is going to be paying for it (through NEH grants and the like) is of course never mentioned in the prospectus.

When scholars have keypunch access to every reference on a single topic, it stands to reason that specialization will increase, because specific completeness is sure to encourage the delusion of apparent immensity. Through the lens of technological myopia, the most trivial topic will seem to merit the intensest scrutiny. I don't see how it can be avoided that fact banks will increase the value of facts, just as money banks increased the value of money. Fact banks are analogously likely to widen the distance between rich and poor, intellectually speaking. The professional scholar will become the investment banker of knowledge, while the public becomes the analogue of a people inexperienced in money economies, savages who think coins are something pretty to sit in the sand and play with.

On the other hand, there is always the possibility of an informational breakdown. What would happen if the majority of scholars were overcome by an expansion of the delusion that says you don't have to read the books in your own library? Imagine the intellectual megalomania that will arise from the belief that one can sit before a computer terminal and research any topic, resolve any informational problem, in a matter of minutes; therefore to sit before the computer need not be done at all? This would cut the human mind adrift from all those informational bits, and the fantasy of the mind machine would expropriate our most serious imaginations....

When ideas are devalued by the very people who are supposed to be having them, by the custodians of knowledge, of course ideas are going to lose cogency as the matrices for facts. The point is, this condition blocks progress in various disciplines at the same time as it cheats the forgotten public of real information. Scholars and false popularizers are alike in that both are doing nothing but trading in facts.

The need to explain is a human trait, a reflection of the challenge to make order out of chaos that comes with the enlarged size of the human brain. Jacob Bronowski once showed how major scientific discoveries came about through the ability to encapsulate related phenomena, and how this scientist's skill is akin to the metaphoric capabilities of the poet. Metaphor is imagination; and the imagination of scrupulous scholars is essential to the ethical custody of knowledge.

This is why the analytic processes of the mind must be reconnected to imagination, and both restored to a place of dignity. Scholars must again become interested in other thinkers' work. Opinions must be expressed in dialogue. Conversations must cease being fact hunts disguised as social amenities; listening must be expanded. The forever advocated return to the general, which is made impossible by a system rewarding nothing but the specific, can begin by sanctioning the re-examination of general themes, and by such acts as introducing broad topics for colloquia at annual meetings. Above all, the free exchange of ideas must be encouraged. It should not be something established members of the scholarly community teach the young to fear and disdain.

GRESHAM'S LAW: KNOWLEDGE OR INFORMATION?*

Daniel J. Boorstin

As the Librarian of Congress I speak for a national fortress of Knowledge. In other words, I speak for a Library, and for Libraries. Our relentless Jeffersonian quest temps us to believe that all technologies (and perhaps, too, all ideas) were created equal. This favored axiom is only slightly clouded by another axiom, equally American. For we have a touching national belief in annual models. In our national lexicon, "newer" is a synonym for "better." The result is illustrated in the title--and I suspect, too, in the preoccupations--of this conference. Libraries--or as you say "Library Services"--are here equated with "Information Services." Which is perilously close to saying that Knowledge can or should be equated with Information.

Knowledge and Information

In the few minutes allotted to me this morning I would like to focus your attention on the distinction between Knowledge and Information, the importance of the distinction, and the dangers of failing to recognize it.

You have a hint of my theme in the melodramatic difference today between the condition of our Knowledge-Institutions and our Information-Institutions. The last two decades have seen the spectacular growth of the Information Industry. We are exhilarated by this example of American ingenuity and enterprise--the frontier spirit in the late 20th Century. A magic computer technology now accomplishes the dreariest tasks in seconds, surpasses the accuracy of the human brain, controls production lines and refineries, arranges inventories, and retrieves records. All this makes us proud of the human imagination.

All this, too, I am glad to say, has produced a widening unpredicted world of profit and employment. The Information Industry,

---

*Reprinted by permission of the author and publisher from Special Libraries, 71:2 (February 1980) 113-16; copyright © 1980 by Special Libraries Association.

we are happy to note, is flourishing. It is a growth-industry. It enjoys the accelerating momentum of technology and the full vitality of the marketplace.

The Information Industries are a whole new world of business celebrity. The jargon of the stock exchange accurately describes theirs as "glamour" stocks. Their leaders hold the national spotlight, and with good reason. The President of the United States appoints the head of one of the greatest of these companies to be perhaps our most important ambassador--to the Soviet Union.

Meanwhile, what has become of our Knowledge-Institutions? These do not deal mainly in the storage and retrieval of information, nor in the instant flow of today's facts and figures which will be displaced by tomorrow's reports or bulletins. Rather they deal in the enduring treasure of our whole human past. They include our colleges and our universities--and of course our libraries. While the Information Industry flourishes and seeks new avenues of growth, while people compete for a chance to buy into them, our Knowledge-Institutions go begging.

Knowledge-Institutions do not pay the kind of dividends that are reflected on the stock market. They are sometimes called "philanthropic"--which means that they profit nobody except everybody, and their dividends go to the whole community. These Knowledge-Institutions--and especially our public libraries--ask charity, the community's small change, just to keep their heat and their lights on, and to keep their unrenovated doors open. We, the Knowledge-Institutions, are the poor relations. We anxiously solicit, and gratefully acknowledge the crumbs. Today I would like to put into historical perspective the distinction between Knowledge and Information. For it is especially appropriate in this White House Conference that we should focus on the distinction.

Publishing and Broadcasting

In my lifetime we have moved from an Age of Publishing into our Age of Broadcasting. In that Age of Publishing launched by Gutenberg, printed materials (bearing the community's memory) wisdom, literary imagination, and knowledge were, of course, widely diffused. The great vehicle was the book. Knowledge was thought to be cumulative. The new books did not displace the old. When today's books arrived people did not throw away yesterday's--as if they were newspapers or out-of-date bulletins of information. On the contrary, the passing years gave a new vitality to the books of past centuries.

We too easily forget that the printed book, too, was a triumph of technology. The dead could now speak, not only to the select few who could afford a manuscript book, but to thousands at home, in schools and in libraries everywhere. The very words of Homer, of Plato, of Machiavelli, of Dickens now could reach everybody. Books became the carriers and the record--also the catalyst and the incentive--for most of the knowledge, the amusement, and the sacred visions of the human race. The printed book has given all humanity its inexpensive, speedy, reliable vehicles across the centuries. Books have conquered time.

But the peculiar, magic vehicles of our Age conquer space. The tube makes us constant eye-witnesses of riots in Iran, airplane wrecks in India, children starving in Cambodia, guerrilla attacks in Rhodesia. Along, of course, with an ever-flowing current of entertainment programs. Yet the special commodity of our electronic Age of Broadcasting is Information--in all its amplitude, in all its formats.

While knowledge is orderly and cumulative, information is random and miscellaneous. We are flooded by messages from the instant--everywhere in excruciating profusion. In our ironic 20th century version of Gresham's Law, information tends to drive knowledge out of circulation. The oldest, the established, the cumulative, is displaced by the most recent, the most problematic. The latest information about anything and everything is collected, diffused, received, stored, and retrieved before anyone can or could discover whether the facts have meaning.

The Mountain-Climbing syndrome rules us. Information is gathered simply because it is there. Electronic devices for diffusion, storage, and retrieval are used, simply because they too are there. Otherwise, the investment would seem wasted! I am not complaining. On the contrary, I am charmed and amazed. For so much of human progress has come from people playing enthusiastically with their new technologic toys--with results that are astonishing, and often productive.

Whatever the motive, we see the Knowledge-Industry being transformed, and even to some extent displaced, by an Information-Industry. In the schoolroom, history tends to be displaced by current events. The resources of science and of literature are overwhelmed and diluted by multiplying journals, by looseleaf services, by preprints, and information stored in computers, quickly and conveniently modified, and instantly retrievable.

To the ancient question, "What is Truth?" we Americans now reply, "Sorry, I haven't yet seen the 7 o'clock news!"

Myopia and Mission

What does all this mean for the world of knowledge which, of course, is the world of libraries? It should be plainer than ever that our libraries are needed to keep civilization in perspective. The more electronic our society becomes, the more urgent it is that we have prosperous Knowledge-Institutions. Yet this urgency is less noted every year. If you consult the authoritative Encyclopedia of the So-

Communication and Education

cial Sciences, published in 1933, and look under "Libraries" you will be referred to "Public Libraries" where you find an extensive article. But if you consult its successor the International Encyclopedia of the Social Sciences, published in 1968, and look for an entry for "Libraries" you will find no article. Instead you find a cross-reference which says, "See under Information Storage and Retrieval."

The fashionable chronologic myopia of our time tempts enthusiasts to forget the main and proper mission of our libraries. "Libraries have been selling the wrong product for years," one such faddist exclaims. "They have been emphasizing reading. The product that we have is information." But these are false messiahs. Of course we must use computer-technology and enlist the whole information industry. At the Library of Congress we have tried to be a leader in these uses and in exploring their applications. We will continue to do so.

In the long run, however, we will not serve the Information Industry, nor our civilization, if we encourage extravagant or misplaced expectations--for the role of information or the devices which serve it up. We must never forget that our libraries are our Fortresses of Knowledge. If we allow these rich and redolent resources --still preserved mainly in books--to be displaced by the latest thing, by today's news and journals and pre-prints and loose-leaf services and telephone conversations and currently revised printouts, we will isolate the world of scholarship from the world of libraries. To avoid such dangers as these we have set up in the Library of Congress a Center for the Book, to use old and find new ways to keep the book flourishing, to keep people reading books, and to enlist other media to promote reading. One such project, "Read More About It" with the enthusiastic collaboration of CBS, the other night after the showing of "All Quiet on the Western Front" brought our suggested reading list to some 31 million viewers. We must and will do more of this.

If Librarians cease to be scholars in order to become computer experts, scholars will cease to feel at home in our libraries. And then our whole citizenry will find that our libraries add little to their view of the world, but only reinforce the pressures of the imperial instant-everywhere. To enlist scholars more actively and more intimately in the activites of the Library of Congress we are now setting up in the Library a Council of Scholars. They will help us discover the needs of the scholarly world and will help us provide an on-going inventory of the state of our knowledge--and of our ignorance.

Finding Order and Meaning

A great civilization needs many and varied resources. In our time our libraries have two paradoxical, sometimes conflicting roles. Of course we must be repositories of information. But we must also somehow remain a place of refuge from the tidal waves of information--and misinformation. Our libraries must be most conspicuously the treasuries of news that stays news.

The era of the Enlightment, the later 18th century, the age of Franklin and Jefferson, the founding epoch of our nation, was an Age of Publishing. That age has left us a happy phrase. They said that people should read for "Amusement and Instruction." This was why they read the poetry of Dryden and Pope, the philosophy of Hume, the history of Gibbon, the novels of Sterne and Fielding. The two delights--"amusement" and "instruction"--were inseparable. The book was the prototypical provider of both. A person who was "a-mused" (from Latin "muser," to idle or pass the time) was engaged in a quite autonomous activity--set off by a catalyst, in the form of a book. In those days book-publishing was an "amusement industry."

Today our Age of Broadcasting tends to displace "amusement" with "entertainment." While we once had to amuse ourselves, we now expect to be entertained. The program is the entertainment. The amusement is in us. But others can and must be our entertainers. Now, of course, there is a flourishing "Entertainment Industry." We generally do not consider book-publishing to be part of it.

This is something to reflect on. It is another clue to our special need for libraries. The more omnipresent is the industry that tries to entertain us, the more we need libraries--where pleasure and amusement are found by the free and active spirit.

It is a cliché of our time that what this nation needs is an "informed citizenry." By which we mean a citizenry that is up on the latest information, that has not failed to read this week's newsmagazine, today's newspapers, or to watch the 7 o'clock news (perhaps also the news at 10 o'clock!)--always for more information, always to be better informed.

I wonder if that is what we need. I suggest, rather, that what we need--what any free country needs--is a knowledgeable citizenry. Information, like entertainment, is something someone else provides us. It really is a "service!" We expect to be entertained, and also to be informed. But we cannot be knowledged! Each of us must acquire knowledge for ourself. Knowledge comes from the free mind foraging in the rich pastures of the whole everywhere-past. It comes from finding order and meaning in the whole human experience. The autonomous reader, amusing and knowledging himself, is the be-all and end-all of our Libraries.

TELEREFERENCE:

THE NEW TV INFORMATION SYSTEMS*

Susan Spaeth Cherry

You stumble on a word as you're plowing through a textbook, but the dictionary has disappeared. You've forgotten to pay the electric bill, due last week. Your mother's birthday is just around the corner, and you haven't started to look for a gift. You need airline reservations for your trip tomorrow, but every time you call the airport you end up on "hold." And the line is busy at the library's information center when you need to know the author of a book.

In such a situation today, your only recourse might be the panic button; but in a few years, you'll be able to solve your problems by simply turning on your television set and pressing a few buttons on a hand-held keypad, similar to a remote-control device. This action will connect you with a central computer system that will enable you to look up the definition you're seeking, transfer funds from your checking account to the electric company's billing department, browse through a catalog of merchandise from the local department store, reserve seats on an airplane of your choice, or tie into the library's bibliographic data base.

The technology that will turn the television into a home information center already exists and is being tested worldwide by postal authorities, telephone companies, and cable TV firms. It promises to change the role of libraries and print material and raises endless questions concerning access to information, privacy, and copyright.

"In 10 years, TV will become integral in distributing information of all types," says Paul Storfer, manager for business development at LINK Resources Corp., a New York consulting firm that monitors the growing and changing field of electronic information.

Two TV-based systems are leading the way in the home information industry--videotext (also known as videotex and viewdata)

―――――――――――
*Reprinted by permission of the author and publisher from American Libraries, February 1980, p. 94-98, 108-10; copyright © 1980 by the American Library Association.

and teletext. Although their services and technology may differ, both are accessible through the adapted television set, distinguishing them from other home information utilities that operate through computer terminals.

Videotext is a two-way, or "interactive," easy-to-operate medium linking computer databases to TVs through telephone or cable television lines. It is considered more sophisticated than teletext, which is a one-way, noninteractive medium transmitting information through regular or cable TV broadcast signals. With their potential to conserve fuel and paper by transmitting information electronically to the home--and with a profit potential--videotext and teletext are attracting interest worldwide. Britain and France, leaders in the home information field, are perfecting systems of their own and selling the technology to other nations. Videotext and teletext are in various stages of development in Germany, Switzerland, the Netherlands, Finland, Spain, Denmark, Sweden, Norway, Austria, Belgium, Italy, Japan, Hong Kong, Singapore, and Australia. In Canada, field tests are planned or underway on TV-based home information systems from Quebec to Manitoba.

Although the U.S. has been slow to enter the videotext/teletext arena, educators, information scientists, and electronics industry executives here are quick to acknowledge the systems' potentials. In September, New York University instituted a first-of-its-kind master's degree program in interactive telecommunications, including teletext and videotext. Manufacturers such as Texas Instruments, RCA, and Zenith are working on transmission and reception equipment for future TV home information systems. Cable companies are showing great interest in videotext and teletext due to CATV's potential for two-way communications. And American Telephone and Telegraph is becoming increasingly involved with videotext experiments nationwide, realizing the medium's potential for profit through the phone lines.

From Washington, D.C., to Salt Lake City, from Miami to St. Louis, television stations and newspapers are field testing videotext and teletext. In two Kentucky counties, the U.S. Department of Agriculture and the National Weather Service are cooperating in an experiment to give farmers access to weather and crop information through their home TV sets. And in Columbus, Ohio, OCLC, Inc., is working on a videotext system that will enable users to browse the catalogs of the Denison University library and the Public Library of Columbus and Franklin County.

How Videotext Works

A variety of videotext systems exist, but all operate basically the same way. To access those transmitted via the telephone network, users must have special decoders built in or attached to their home television sets. To connect themselves to the central database, they first dial a telephone number and put their phone receivers in a

Communication and Education   195

coupler. An index page appears on the screen, and users begin to
search for the information they are seeking by pressing numbered
keys on their hand-held control panels. Instructions continue to appear on the screen, telling users which keys to press for particular
types of data. [Information retrieval is somewhat different for videotext transmitted by CATV. Users access it in a manner similar to
the way they retrieve teletext data (see teletext section of this article).]

The central videotext database may contain an unlimited
amount of information provided by sources ranging from local newspapers to travel agents, the stock exchange, area shops, and the library. The data is stored in "frames," or screenfuls, and can be
updated instantly. Several frames of information on the same topic
comprise a "page" and may be accessed sequentially.

Videotext can display simple graphics in seven colors. It
"provides an impressive degree of convenience for the American consumer," says Alvah H. Chapman, Jr., president and chief executive
officer of Knight-Ridder Newspapers, Inc. The firm plans to test a
videotext system called "Viewtron" in Coral Gables, Fla., this
spring.

"It is possible that some day the consumer might be able to
shop, bank, send messages, do business research, make stock purchases, learn algebra, check on inventory, get business advice, buy
a bicycle, look up the name of a Nobel Prize winner--without ever
leaving the livingroom. The potential is limited only by the imagination," says Chapman.

Because videotext is so individualized and focused, it does
not lend itself to browsing. To find information in the database,
users employ a "tree structure" search method, starting with broad
subject headings and narrowing down their choices until they arrive
at the frame of information they need. This method may seem slow
to sophisticated online researchers, especially those used to Boolean
logic.

Because it can exhibit only a limited number of characters
per frame, videotext is most appropriate for displaying "pieces of
short, sweet information," according to LINK's Beverly Powell,
editor of Viewdata/Videotex Report.

Teletext's Technology

Unlike videotext, teletext is a noninteractive system linking the information provider to the home user through a regular or cable TV
broadcast signal. Only televisions equipped with special decoders
can pick up teletext, so commercial TV viewers do not see it on
their home sets.

Teletext information is sent to the upper, currently unused
horizontal lines on the TV screen, the "vertical blanking interval."

"Pages" of information are broadcast one at a time in recurring cycles. To access them, users consult a contents page, then press buttons on a hand-held keypad corresponding to the numbers of the pages they wish to see. The decoder then "grabs" the selected pages when they cycle by, and the information appears on the visible part of the TV screen.

Like videotext, teletext can display a variety of data, including updated weather forecasts, news and sports headlines, advice on road conditions, local TV and movie listings, stock market reports, and community events schedules. It can transmit information in eight colors and has limited graphics capabilities.

Teletext's chief virtue is its ability to be updated continuously for a large viewing audience. It can provide users with the most current information on a range of subjects and is easily accessible. Because it is a broadcast rather than telephone-based service, teletext also is less expensive than videotext, which requires users to pay for phone service and the individual information frames they access.

Teletext has potential as an educational tool; the largest school district in Utah already has plans to use it. The medium also can serve people who hear a story on radio or TV news and want more details.

Teletext has drawbacks, however, the greatest being its limited database size. To access information, users have to wait until the specific page they are seeking cycles by, giving the decoder the chance to grab it, decode, and display the data. Most experts agree that the wait time is too long if the teletext database exceeds 100 pages. Thus, unlike videotext, teletext has limits on the amount of information it can carry efficiently.

Technology for videotext and teletext is developing at a breakneck pace, finding new applications in scores of experiments and field tests. The following roundup discusses some of the major projects.

Prestel: Videotext Guinea Pig

In the 1960s, Sam Fedida, an engineer at a British Post Office research center, failed in his efforts to develop a videophone. However, his experiments with the telephone network eventually resulted in a prototype videotext system called Prestel, now being marketed in London, Birmingham, and Norwich with plans to go nationwide.

A guinea pig in the telecommunications world, Prestel is operated by the British Post Office (BPO), which also controls the United Kingdom's phone service. The agency developed the videotext software to generate more telephone traffic, according to Bob Quinn, formerly of Insac Viewdata, Inc., a New York firm with

Communication and Education 197

rights to market Prestel in the U.S. The BPO hopes that by the mid 1980s, 60 percent of Britain's phone users will have access to the system.

Because it is a videotext utility, Prestel has no limit on the amount of information it can store in its database. As a result, new information providers join the system every week, adding countless new frames of data ranging from stock market quotations to airline schedules. Several American firms are Prestel suppliers, notably Knight-Ridder Newspapers, which provides data on Miami's weather, transportation, restaurants, hotels, and tourist attractions.

The BPO is not an information provider for Prestel; rather, it serves as a "common carrier," operating the computers, publicizing the services, maintaining the telephone networks, and billing the system's users. It profits from selling "space" to the information providers and from charging users for the telephone and computer time.

The Post Office sees potential for Prestel in speeding up communications between headquarters and branch offices--just as it could speed up interlibrary communications. The BPO's Alex Reid says the system is inexpensive compared with conventional subscription computer information services.

The Ministry of Agriculture, Fisheries, and Food in London sees Prestel as a means of providing farmers with information on crops and weather. It currently is sponsoring a year-long field test with 10 farmers, hoping to determine what kinds of data they seek, how they want it presented, and how often they need updates.

The British Library sees potential in Prestel for changing public attitudes toward information and the ways the library provides it. BL is currently funding a Prestel exploratory project conducted jointly by the Library Association and Aslib, a non-profit research and development association and recognized authority on information acquisition, storage, and retrieval.

The project involves six public libraries serving a diverse clientele in Birmingham, Norwich, and four London boroughs. In each library's reference department, an Aslib research team monitors Prestel patrons independently or with a librarian's help. The object is to assess the effects the videotext system might have on library acquisitions and services. By interviewing patrons and staff, the researchers hope to determine what sorts of demands, constraints, and costs Prestel would impose on the library.

The participating libraries also are collecting community information for Aslib, which puts it into the Prestel database. Through BPO records, Aslib is keeping track of which information is used most. It plans to prepare guidelines for libraries on information input methods, types of data in demand, and updating techniques.

Aslib staffers interviewed 44 librarians about Prestel shortly after the system was installed in their reference departments. The librarians expressed attitudes of what Aslib calls "guarded optimism, a positive but cautious approach to a new information system. " They ranked Prestel's advantages in the following order: it provides up-to-date information to library patrons; it draws more people to the library; it fills gaps in existing information coverage; it provides a quick way to retrieve data; it broadens the means by which information is available, presenting it in a novel manner of interest to those turned off by books; and it has potential to relieve staff workload.

The librarians said Prestel's disadvantages included its potential to take too much time from staffers who must help inexperienced users; its costs; its space needs; and the hubbub it often creates.

Reports on the Prestel library experiments will be available this fall in British Library and Aslib publications.

Although Prestel is now several years old, it is still a child whose potential remains unknown. It is struggling with growing pains that only time and experience can resolve. Snags have occurred in interfacing the telephone network with Prestel-adapted TV sets and in getting information from the providers into the central computer. The system's graphics are still considered poor. In addition, the public has been slow to embrace Prestel because only a small number of adapted television sets now exist. Manufacturers are reluctant to produce more until the system's technology is more stable. A low-key marketing effort on the part of the Post Office has done little to encourage users to try the system.

Prestel's cost may also be inhibiting its popularity. An adapted TV set costs twice as much as a non-adapted one, although costs are expected to fall in the future. To access Prestel, users must pay the information providers from half a penny to 10 cents per frame of data in addition to fees they pay the Post Office for phone and computer time. Such charges definitely discourage browsing. Although some information provided by advertisers and public agencies is free, using Prestel may be more affordable for large companies than individuals at present.

The British Post Office has plans to run a 12-month international market trial on Prestel this year. Open only to some 50 multinational corporations in the U.S., Britain, Germany, Australia, Sweden, the Netherlands, and Switzerland, the trial will offer information such as stock prices in major nations, currency exchange rates, and worldwide airline schedules.

Granted a license by Prestel's American marketer, Insac Viewdata, Inc., General Telephone and Electronics Corp. will begin Prestel tests in the U.S. this year.

Viewtron: A $1.3 Million Test

Several years ago, executives from Knight-Ridder Newspapers, Inc. (KRN) visited England, France, Germany, and Japan to study developing videotext systems. Their findings will take shape this spring when they begin a six-month trial to assess U.S. consumer interest in a videotext system similar to Prestel. Between 150 and 200 families in Coral Gables, Fla., will test the system, called Viewtron, at a cost of some $1.3 million to Knight-Ridder.

KRN has set up a subsidiary called Viewdata Corp. of America, Inc., to administer the test. It will supply participants with adapted TV sets that function as video display terminals. Rather than use Prestel technology, Knight-Ridder commissioned AT&T to build the system's hardware, according to Tom Dozier of KRN. The information available on Viewtron will include local, national, and international news, weather data, sports results, calendars of local events, lists of adult education courses, product ratings, local movie, restaurant, and theater hours, and boating and fishing advice. Information providers will include companies, organizations, and publishers such as the Consumers' Union, Universal Press Syndicate, Congressional Quarterly, Associated Press, Macmillan, and the Miami Herald.

In addition, Viewtron test participants will have access to informational ads from firms such as Eastern Airlines, J.C. Penney, Shell Oil, B. Dalton Booksellers, and local stores.

All information will be stored and updated in the KRN computer center in Miami. Telephone lines will link the center to the adapted TVs in the test homes.

"We're undertaking this project to make an initial assessment of consumer response. If we are encouraged by the continued evaluation and testing results, we will consider a broader market test program before launching full-scale development of the service," says KRN's Chapman.

Although Viewdata Corp. of America has no plans for library tie-ins to its initial videotext experiment, it probably will work closely with libraries if it decides to market Viewtron commercially, according to Dozier.

While Knight-Ridder experiments with Viewtron, AT&T will continue videotext tests it began last year in Albany, N.Y. Through its Electronic Information System, the company is linking users to a database containing residential and business phone numbers within a 10,000-square-mile area, Manhattan Yellow Pages listings, information on products and services, weather reports, and sports scores.

Project Green Thumb

The Prestel experiment with farmers is being duplicated in the U.S. in a slightly different way. Last month the National Weather Service and the U.S. Department of Agriculture were scheduled to begin "Project Green Thumb," a test involving videotext and 200 farmers in two Kentucky counties. Funded by the National Weather Service, USDA, and the University of Kentucky, the $360,000 experiment will continue through the next growing season, according to Howard F. Lehnert, Jr., of USDA's Extension Service.

Project Green Thumb participants will be able to access weather and crop information through home TV sets adapted for two-way communication through a "green thumb box" manufactured by Motorola. The device is unique because it has a "memory" that can store information carried through the phone lines and displayed on the TV screen. Farmers can access up to eight screenfuls of information per call, then view them at their leisure with the memory box's help. Adapted TV sets also are available for general use at USDA extension offices.

Lehnert says the project sponsors are hoping to expand the test eventually to 150 counties in 10 states.

OCLC Involves the Library

In 1977, OCLC, Inc., Columbus, Ohio, began a major project called "Home Delivery of Library Services." Among the 40 research tasks encompassing the project was a plan to develop a videotext system with library applications.

To date, OCLC has built several prototype videotext terminals that differ a bit technologically from the British Prestel sets. It is planning to test its system late this summer by providing free videotext decoders to some 200 households in Columbus. Test participants will include library users and nonusers with differing educational backgrounds and reading levels. The experiment is expected to last a year.

By using the OCLC videotext system, participants will have access to the catalogs of the nearby Denison University library and the Public Library of Columbus and Franklin County. In turn, the libraries will be able to use the system to publicize their services.

OCLC also will provide test participants with access to information from the Arete encyclopedia and from community agencies such as emergency health centers. The database may contain weather, news, and sports information, and the system will allow users to pay their bills and check the status of their accounts.

OCLC is no stranger to interactive video systems. Last year, it cosponsored a successful experiment involving the Public

Communication and Education   201

Library of Columbus and Franklin County and Qube, Warner Communications' commercial two-way television system (AL, Oct. 1979, pp. 511-12). Each month, Qube broadcast Home Book Club, an hour-long show featuring citizen panels which discussed current novels. Home viewers voiced their opinions about the books through their TV consoles during the broadcast and voted on which novel should be discussed next.

At its peak, Home Book Club had 1,000 viewers per broadcast, according to Tom Harnish, OCLC research scientist and manager of the Home Delivery of Library Services project.

The number of orders in the library's books by mail program increased as a result of the show.

Like OCLC, the Lexington (Ky.) Public Library has its eye on videotext as a means of providing library service to the home. It is currently converting its catalog to machine-readable form, hoping to make it available in its service area via cable TV. The library plans to give users the opportunity to conduct transactions with its computer through a touch-tone telephone system.

Canada's Experiments

Canadian telecommunications companies are pioneering multiple distribution channels for videotext. Several experiments are underway or in the planning stages involving videotext delivery through coaxial cable and fiber optics transmission, as well as through the telephone network.

"We're all working toward one goal--universal [videotext] service within Canada," says William E. Buckland, manager of business development for TransCanada Telephone.

Telecommunications experts have their eyes on a sophisticated form of technology being developed for both videotext and teletext applications by the Canadian Department of Communications. Called Telidon, the technology can transmit unusually precise graphics in colors and shapes no other videotext system has been able to duplicate. Telidon videotext can be distributed by coaxial cable, the broadcast network, fiber optics, or phone, making it more versatile than other systems.

Using Telidon technology, Bell Canada and the Department of Communications will begin the largest videotext field test in Canada this year after completing a smaller pilot trial with a system called Vista. The sponsors will place more than 1,000 Telidon terminals in the homes of users in Toronto, Montreal, Quebec, Ottawa, and surrounding cities, as well as in some business offices. Participants will be able to access some 100,000 pages of information ranging from news reports to classified ads. Data suppliers will include newspaper publishers such as Torstar and South Press, the

Ontario Educational Communications Authority, and TeleDirect, a Montreal Yellow Pages publisher.

Although Vista is a phone-based system like Prestel, it has a unique "intelligent" main computer that can locate and retrieve a mosaic of information in an unlimited number of databases nationwide. Bell and the Department of Communications will pour some $9 million into the system's field test over the next two years.

In Headingley, Manitoba Telephone is conducting a year-long test of a videotext system distributed by coaxial cable. The trial, part of an encompassing communications experiment called Project Ida, will allow participants to use their adapted TV sets for obtaining information, recording and retrieving messages, monitoring their homes for smoke and fire, reading their utility meters, sending mail, and shopping. Alberta Government Telephones is working on a similar system that uses the telephone network for delivery of these services.

Teletext: Paris to St. Louis

Although teletext is considered less sophisticated than videotext, it is a medium that telecommunications experts are investigating and testing worldwide. Britain, a pioneer in videotext, also designed the first teletext systems, called Ceefax ("see facts") and Oracle (Optical Reception of Announcements by Coded Line Electronics). The former is a service of the British Broadcasting Corp.; the latter, of the Independent Television Authority, which controls commercial TV and radio in Britain. Both systems are expected to expand service from London into the rest of England this year.

Although the systems use basically the same technology, the content of their databases varies. The BBC-sponsored service features news, sports, and financial information from wire services. By contrast, the ITA service is more entertainment- and consumer-oriented, featuring advertisements for goods and services as well as information.

Shortly after the British developed Ceefax and Oracle, the French began testing Antiope, a more sophisticated teletext system that can be distributed by phone as well as broadcast. First displayed in 1974 and now operating on a limited basis in Paris and Lyons, Antiope is a noncommercial system controlled by the French national postal and telephone authority, PTT. This year, programming for the system will be tested in some 3,000 homes near Paris, and the PTT hopes to provide every telephone user in France with an Antiope decoder by 1981.

In the U.S., several television stations are testing Antiope, Ceefax, and Oracle technology and adapting it for their own uses. The European systems cannot operate in the U.S. in their present form due to differences in foreign and American TV broadcasting standards.

In St. Louis, the CBS station KMOX conducted technical tests last year to determine what type of teletext system will work best in the U.S. Major TV manufacturers such as RCA and Zenith provided the station with special television sets which, housed in a van parked at locations throughout St. Louis, picked up special teletext transmissions at various frequencies. Through the experiment, technicians hoped to learn the fastest and most efficient way to transmit teletext data.

The KMOX test results, along with others, are being analyzed by a committee of the Electronic Industries Association, which is trying to develop technical standards for teletext in the U.S. The committee eventually plans to make recommendations to the Federal Communications Commission (FCC).

Other teletext tests are underway nationwide from Los Angeles, where public TV station KCET is conducting technical experiments, to Philadelphia, where Micro-TV has been sending teletext transmissions to its own employees since 1976.

"We know the technology works, and we're waiting for the standards to be set," says Micro-TV President William Gross.

A nontechnical experiment to test teletext as a public information service is scheduled to begin this year and run until 1983 in the Washington, D.C., area. Conceived by New York University's Alternate Media Center for the Corporation for Public Broadcasting and the National Telecommunications and Information Administration, the test will place teletext decoders in selected Washington homes, libraries, schools, and public buildings. The National Science Foundation will fund the experiment.

WETA-TV, a public television station, will broadcast 100-400 pages of teletext information supplied by libraries, federal and local agencies, and schools. The information will be geared toward small, defined audiences. Test sponsors will study the types of information users access and the amount of time they are willing to wait for particular types of data.

Washington's Martin Luther King Memorial Library plans to participate in the WETA test, according to Lawrence Molumby, assistant director, D.C. Public Library.

"We are very interested in working with any project using new technology to extend the library's information role," he says.

As a result, the King Library will house an adapted TV set that patrons can use to access teletext. The library will also provide information pages for the teletext database.

At KSL-TV, Salt Lake City, a teletext experiment has led to a suggestion for a new type of system that would combine the best features of both teletext and videotext. The Bonneville International

Corp. station has plans to build and demonstrate a "touch-tone" system using a standard telephone as the control device and a teletext-adapted TV set as the receiver. Users would access teletext pages through their keypads; if they wanted additional information, they could press a button on their touch-tone phones to connect with a videotext computer. They then would have access to additional pages of data not available via teletext.

The touch-tone system would be advertiser-sponsored; thus users would pay for nothing except the adapted television set. They would have access to abundant services at teletext's low cost, according to William D. Loveless, director of engineering at Bonneville.

"It's the only way to do it in the U.S.," says Loveless, who has helped produce a 13-minute videotape demonstrating the touch-tone system. "Everyone who sees the tape says, 'Hey, I want it right now.'"

Many telecommunications pioneers have expressed interest in making videotext and teletext systems technologically compatible without merging the two. Some simply would like to see compatibility between all teletext systems themselves; others feel the same way about videotext systems. Five Electronic Industries Association subcommittees currently are studying the advantages and disadvantages of compatibility.

Their conclusions will help determine whether one technical standard for the systems should be adopted worldwide.

Consumer Acceptance

In addition to testing the technical properties of teletext and videotext, many field trials are attempting to determine whether a market exists for the two systems. A number of firms, ranging from the British Consumer Association to New York's LINK, have conducted preliminary research on the subject.

"Most proprietary reports and market studies have shown there's a viable consumer market [for TV-based home information systems]. The problem is to put sets in the home, make the information interesting, and make the technology affordable and understood by the public," says the Library of Congress' Jean Paul Emard, analyst in information sciences for the Congressional Research Service's Science Policy Research Division.

Gus Hauser, co-chair and chief executive officer of Warner Amex Cable Communications, is optimistic about the future of videotext. His firm, a subsidiary of Warner Communications, operates Qube.

Communication and Education

"I think there's a market. The presentation of information in the home is a convenience. There'll be a cultural development. But it won't happen immediately, " he says.

Beverly Powell of LINK speculates videotext will sell but observes, "It won't be an overnight success--it will develop slowly because people are not used to it. "

OCLC's Tom Harnish says "it looks like whether or not people use these systems will depend on their reading levels. " But Knight-Ridder's Tom Dozier thinks the market question boils down to dollars and cents.

"The consumers are excited, but the excitement also has to do with what they'll be charged, " he says, speculating that videotext systems may not be affordable to the average user for a long time to come.

KSL's Loveless agrees. He sees "a tremendous consumer market for teletext" but predicts that "viewdata [videotext] won't make it in the U. S. because of the charge. "

Exactly what the charge is will depend on whether or not the information providers set user fees and on who carries out the billing procedures. Even if user charges are low, the average consumer may not be able to afford an adapted TV set. In Britain, televisions with videotext capability range in price from $1, 200 to $2, 200; similarly, teletext decoders run from $500 to $700.

Information Stamps and Fish Wrap

If teletext and videotext systems do catch on despite their cost, a society could evolve in which only the affluent have access to information. Government officials in the legislative and executive branches already have discussed the idea of "information stamps" for the poor. But many telecommunications experts do not think videotext and teletext systems will create an information elite. They are confident the systems will not supplant other more affordable types of media now in existence.

"Each of these things will have its place, " says Warner's Hauser. "Just as radio and movies weren't wiped out by television, print won't be wiped out by these systems. Everything builds on the next thing and provides one more level of convenience. "

People will continue to read books no matter how popular videotext and teletext become, Hauser adds.

"You're not going to read War and Peace on the television-- you'd go blind, " he says.

Most experts feel that since videotext and teletext rarely provide in-depth information, the public will continue to turn to books and newspapers for details.

"The systems complement print and may actually increase and stimulate readership. They will draw people to their paper to read the whole story leisurely, " says Knight-Ridder's Tom Dozier.

Viewdata Corporation's marketing research director, Philip Meyer, says people looking for a quick item of information, such as a movie listing, will find it easier to pick up a newspaper and flip through the pages than to turn on the television and start pressing buttons on a keypad. OCLC's Tom Harnish adds that people will always turn to print for the tactile stimulation and other uses it provides.

"You can't wrap fish in an electronic system, " he observes.

Recently, Quantum Science Corp., a New York consulting firm, conducted a $400,000 study of home computers and concluded that newspapers have a high "susceptibility to being replaced" by videotext systems. But a $600,000 Arthur D. Little study sponsored by newspaper publishers, newsprint producers, and electronic industry representatives speculated that videotext would not send newspapers the way of the dodo.

LINK's Paul Storfer thinks newspapers eventually may stop printing a physical product, becoming information providers to videotext and teletext databases instead.

"It's becoming too expensive to keep storing information in print form, " he says.

Will the Library Vanish?

Videotext and teletext systems are likely to affect the library of the future. If the systems are too expensive for the poor to afford at home, the library may be obliged to make them available free or for a small charge. If the systems burgeon in popularity, the library may be called upon to be an information provider. (Bell Canada already has asked the National Library of Canada to supply information for the Vista system.) And if teletext and videotext stimulate certain types of reading, the library may have to change the nature of its print collection.

But the systems are unlikely to replace librarians or render the library obsolete, according to many experts.

"Information in the home will not replace the library down the street. In fact, it may augment the library's role by making it the local teletext/videotext 'tavern' or access center, " says LC's Emard.

Communication and Education   207

OCLC's Harnish agrees. After conducting market studies on the subject, his firm concluded electronic home information systems would not supplant libraries.

"My objective is to make these systems available to libraries so they become the information choice of the community, " says Harnish. "Libraries are becoming more and more the focus of information. We want to make it possible for them to compete with commercial information brokers. We want people to make libraries the first place they go for information. "

Libraries shouldn't feel threatened by videotext and teletext, Harnish adds. He urges librarians to find out more about the systems and become involved in determining their future.

Warner's Hauser thinks "the definition of a library may change" when electronic home information systems become more widespread. "Maybe the library will become a data bank people will access from the home, " he speculates.

In a speech presented at the regional White House Conference in Illinois' Cornbelt Library System, Paul B. Snider, professor of journalism at Bradley University, took Hauser's prediction one step further.

"[In the future] the familiar community library may be nothing more than an electronic relay station--a means of sending requests to other collection centers and playing responses to the questioner, " he forecast.

But Kathleen Criner, program manager for home information technology, National Telecommunications and Information Administration, sees a much more human-oriented role for libraries as videotext and teletext gain popularity.

"The library has the role of introducing people to these services, " she says. Criner notes libraries will be able to use the systems to help themselves operate more efficiently. Because they require no paper, the systems can reduce the cost of inhouse and interbranch communications. Libraries will be able to use teletext and videotext to publicize their services, hours, new acquisitions, and programs instead of mailing newsletters and calendars of events. The systems also will aid in answering reference questions and in expediting orders for services such as books by mail.

Librarians will require little training to learn to use videotext and teletext.

"In many respects, these systems are designed to be self-taught. It's not hard to use them, " says the FCC's Gary Rosch, a widely known spokesperson on home information systems.

"This will be another toy in the librarian's hands. It's no different from using a microfiche reader or online terminal," adds Emard of LC.

Unanswered Questions

Because teletext and videotext are in their early stages, information scientists have been more interested in perfecting their technology than in addressing important questions they raise about protection of privacy, database monopolies, and copyright.

The privacy problem hinges on the billing structure for videotext and teletext use. Each time someone accesses a page of information, the computer records the "transaction" for billing purposes. Present regulations concerned with records confidentiality have not yet been studied for videotext/teletext applications. Only the strictest legislation and the severest penalties can prevent users' privacy from being violated.

"It's a seriously confused situation right now," says Jeffrey Krauss, former assistant chief of the FCC's Office of Plans and Policy.

Another question that remains unanswered concerns information providers and their potential to manipulate the market. Will a handful of companies control all the information available via videotext and teletext? Will they withhold data they feel is against their interests?

OCLC's Harnish does not think the public will tolerate information monopolies and censorship.

"It's a two-way street. Information providers will have to meet the public's need. The areas people find useful will be the ones that are developed," he says.

But no regulations now exist to make certain that Harnish's predictions come true.

Copyright also will become an issue as videotext and teletext systems grow in popularity. The FCC's Rosch says copyright violations have not occurred yet in Britain, where the party that puts the information on the electronic system makes an agreement with the information source. But in the U.S., regulations may be needed to prevent database copying. Questions such as, "What pricing policy should be instituted to ensure that royalties go to those who own materials?" remain unanswered.

Some of the thorny issues videotext and teletext raise may be tackled by the FCC, whose role in regulating the systems is undefined as yet. However, the agency is likely to deal mostly with the systems' technical aspects. Questions of privacy, copyright, and monopolies will be left to legislators and judges.

If videotext and teletext systems become household items, will enough energy be available to run them? What will happen if a massive power failure takes place? Who will decide how long information remains in a particular system before being erased? And perhaps most important, in the words of Bradley University's Snider, "Will librarians become clerks adept at organizing information, or will they become the elite custodians of information, dispensing only to those selected persons who meet certain criteria?"

If librarians hope to have a say in their future, they will have to "stay tuned" to the developing home information field.

WANTED: MORE PROFESSIONALISM

IN REFERENCE BOOK REVIEWING*

Ken Kister

Librarianship and reference book criticism are naturally related inasmuch as librarians buy and use a large share of the reference works published each year. Obviously, as heavy consumers of reference materials, librarians are in an advantageous position to assess the strengths, weaknesses, and idiosyncrasies of these materials. It is no accident, for instance, that librarian-reviewers completely dominate the major sources of reference reviews, namely, American Reference Books Annual (ARBA), Booklist (which carries reviews prepared by the ALA Reference and Subscription Books Review Committee), Choice, College & Research Libraries (if Eugene P. Sheehy's semiannual "Selected Reference Books" notes can be construed as reviews), Library Journal, RQ, Reference Services Review, and Wilson Library Bulletin (in Charles A. Bunge's column "Current Reference Books").

With the exception of Bunge and perhaps Sheehy, the librarians and library school faculty who review for these publications do so very much as a sideline. Their real work is elsewhere; occasional reviewing is looked upon as an interesting and doubtless serious but hardly remunerative business. The upshot is that most reference criticism is the work of volunteer reviewers. This fact surely helps account for the noticeably uneven quality of opinion found in most reference review publications. The preponderance of volunteer reviewers also acts to discourage qualified individuals from pursuing reference book reviewing as a full-time career. With so many librarians willing to part with their informed opinions for nothing more than a review copy and a byline (and sometimes not even that), what chance does anyone have of making it professionally at such work?

In point of fact, opportunities for the professional reference book critic† are very limited. As already noted, most of the quan-

───────────
*Reprinted by permission of the author and publisher from RQ, Winter 1979, p. 144-48; copyright © 1979 by Kenneth F. Kister.
†I have used the terms critic/criticism and reviewer/reviewing interchangeably in this article. I am, of course, aware that a dis-
(continued on next page)

titatively significant reference review publications, like ARBA, Library Journal, and the ALA committee in Booklist, use librarian-reviewers who donate their services. General trade book review sources, like the New York Times Book Review and Publishers Weekly, ordinarily give scant notice to reference works, and when they do the results are often lamentable. The New York Times, for instance, had a former food editor review the Random House Encyclopedia! And the many specialized journals that sometimes comment on new reference works in their field--the American Historical Review, Art Journal, Modern Philology, the Quarterly Review of Biology, to name but a few--draw their reviewers from the subject discipline involved, most often from the academic ranks, where publish-or-perish pressures spur no end of willing critics.

Prospects for the would-be professional reference book critic, however, are not hopeless. Jobs do exist that entail making and communicating honest, intelligent judgments about reference materials. For example, ARBA, the largest of the current reference review services, employs several editor-reviewers, all of whom possess library science backgrounds. A position like Charles Bunge's at Wilson Library Bulletin (which, while not full-time, is paid) comes along once in that proverbial blue moon. And there are free-lance situations like mine, though they too are few and far between. The chief qualifications for these and similar positions would appear to be extensive library experience, principally in the reference and/or teaching areas, plus some initiation into the art of reference book reviewing. Add to this the necessity of being the right person in the right place at the right time, which sounds trite but is nevertheless true.

The move from librarian to professional reviewer--one who criticizes for a living--can be accomplished without great difficulty. The commonality of purpose shared by librarianship and book criticism is at least partly responsible for the likelihood of easy transition from one to the other. The two professions, while very different in perspective and method, complement one another in terms of their ultimate mission. Both the librarian and the critic stand between information and potential users of that information. Both act as interpreters and guides, assisting people in the discovery and evaluation of needed information. In an age of proliferating knowledge, these functions are crucial. Nearly half a century ago, the Spanish philosopher José Ortega y Gasset foresaw the librarian of the future "as a filter interposed between man and the torrent of

---

tinction is often made between these terms; e.g., Anatole Broyard once remarked that the critic has "an eternity to express himself in and the reviewer has two hours." This is a fair distinction between literary criticism and book reviewing. In the case of reference book evaluation, however, there really is nothing comparable to literary criticism, or criticism as Broyard was using the term, unless it would be the evaluations found in a quality textbook like Bill Katz' Introduction to Reference Work.

books." To be successful, said Ortega, the librarian must become "master of the raging book."[1] This sentiment applies equally to the critic, who bears a similar responsibility.

Be that as it may, librarianship and book reviewing are not one and the same; nor does training in one automatically render a person adept at the other. The critic generates information, whereas the librarian handles it. Each of these activities requires a distinctive set of aptitudes, skills, and qualifications. Not all professional critics would make good librarians. Likewise, not all librarians have the wherewithal to be successful book critics, even if they wanted to be, which of course most do not. The same could be said of scientists, lawyers, physicians, educators, lexicographers, et al. Subject expertise alone does not ipso facto make an authoritative book reviewer. But because of the natural affinities between librarianship and book criticism, an interested librarian who possesses the right combination of talents has a good chance of making the grade as a full-time reference book reviewer, should the opportunity arise.

Specifically, what is required of the professional reviewer? What capabilities should the librarian considering reference book criticism as a possible career possess? In what way, if any, does the library science qualification contribute to the development of these capabilities?

The initial requirement for any critic is the ability to write clearly, succinctly, and sometimes quickly. It matters little that reviewers know their subject or have a fine critical sense if they cannot construct an intelligible sentence. One of the several recurring faults found in the reviews produced by the ALA Reference and Subscription Books Review Committee, for example, is a cumbersome style that now and again becomes downright abstruse. Only the most dedicated seeker of information will slog through, say, the committee's long, tedious encyclopedia reviews. As Bill Katz rightly observes in his Introduction to Reference Work, "a poor presentation is often indicative of poor thinking or, even worse, a lack of impartiality."[2] Unfortunately, proficiency in writing appears to be a casualty of the times, with television and the decline of educational standards often fingered as the chief culprits. Whatever the reasons for our pervasive literacy problems, the professional reviewer must maintain a clear and concise pen. In this instance, library training and experience are of little, if any, help. No one ever learned syntax at library school. On the other hand, a journalism background is ideal.

The second requirement for the professional reference book critic is a thorough and comparative knowledge of reference materials and their makeup, characteristics, and uses. Without this kind of particularized knowledge, the critic will be hard put to provide a balanced assessment of new reference works and trends. The critic must also be conversant with the various evaluative criteria used to determine the quality of reference materials, as well as how best to

Communication and Education   213

apply those criteria. For instance, the critic will want to find out
if the work under review is reliable or not. How does one arrive
at an honest, objective, informed determination of a reference
work's reliability? Or how does the critic ascertain if the work is
reasonably current? Or if the contents of the work are normally
accessible? Or how good the work's physical format is, including
the binding, paper, and print quality? Or how well the work compares with existing sources of similar size, scope, and purpose?
Or who, if anyone, might find the work useful and, if so, in what
manner and to what degree? The responsible reviewer will cover
these and other pertinent questions as concisely and impartially as
possible within the limits of available space.

All too often, however, amateur reference reviewers ignore
or slight important aspects of the work being evaluated, due either
to ignorance or to bias, witting or unwitting. The critical reception
of the 30-volume New Encyclopaedia Britannica (1974+), a radical
revision of the old Encyclopaedia Britannica (1768-1973), is a case
in point. Many of the reviews, especially those in the popular
press (the Christian Science Monitor, Commonweal, Newsweek, Parents' Magazine, Time, etc.) described the encyclopedia's so-called
arrangement (Propaedia, Micropaedia, Macropaedia) and commented
on the set's long and generally impressive articles in the Macropaedia section. But these reviews lacked any serious discussion of
the encyclopedia's most controversial feature, namely, its indexing
system (which many librarians, including Nat Josel, who reviewed
the set for RQ, have come to view as a terrible flop). In addition,
most reviews of the new Britannica neglected to compare the set
with competing encyclopedias. Any review that fails to cover such
important aspects of a major reference work leaves much to be desired.

Yet such reviews are commonplace in the majority of our
reference review publications. This situation will improve when and
if more reference reviews are prepared by professional critics capable of thorough, comprehensive, and comparative evaluations.
Whether or not more opportunities for full-time reference reviewing
will open up in the future is not known. It can be noted, however,
that a person who possesses a library science master's degree (or
its equivalent) is probably better prepared for reference reviewing
than the individual who lacks the qualification, simply because the
librarian has already been exposed to basic reference materials,
evaluative criteria, and the like as part of the library school curriculum. Knowledge of the reference universe is part of the business of being a librarian. The same is true of the reference book
critic. Here the requirements of the two professions are identical.

The third requirement for the professional reference book
critic is an objective stance toward the material under review.
True, no person is capable of total objectivity; human beings are
not made that way. But blatant or willful bias has no place in reference book reviewing, or any sort of reviewing for that matter.
Such bias includes indulging in ad hominem attacks and public ax-

grinding, being cute or showing off at the expense of the book, and plugging a work in which the reviewer has a vested interest.

It would be prejudicial, for instance, for a member of the Board of Editors of the New Encyclopaedia Britannica to review the set for a leading national magazine, would it not? Apparently Clifton Fadiman doesn't think so, because that is exactly what he did in Saturday Review/World soon after the set appeared in 1974.[3] Small wonder that Fadiman, who did not attempt to conceal his Britannica connection, found the encyclopedia's publication "an event of singular importance" and professed astonishment "at the fact that an encyclopedia with such severe intellectual standards should by and large be so readable." Indeed, Fadiman found absolutely everything right about the new Britannica!

It would be grossly unfair, would it not, for a disgruntled former editor of a dictionary to review the revised edition of that dictionary? Apparently Laurence Urdang doesn't think so, because that is exactly what he did with the revised edition of the Random House College Dictionary (1975) in his little sheet called Verbatim.[4] To his credit, Urdang professed some guilt pangs about his behavior: "Having been the editor in chief of the original of this dictionary, we struggled with our conscience on the subject of whether or not it was proper to write this review. On the grounds that it is unlikely that a better-qualified reviewer could be found who is as familiar with the work as we are, we declared an armistice." Urdang then proceeds to savage the dictionary in a dazzling display of nitpickery, beginning with a "blow to our ego: our name had been removed from the title page" and concluding with the supercilious (not to mention malicious) observation that, although his original edition was a "superior work of lexicography," the book's "reputation had been compromised by the appearance of the Revised Edition." Indeed, Urdang found absolutely everything wrong with the revision of the Random House College Dictionary!

Fadiman and Urdang may be outstanding practitioners in their chosen fields, but neither knows beans about responsible reference book reviewing. From the consumer's standpoint, tainted reviews like those offered by Fadiman and Urdang are worse than no reviews at all. Actually, such reviews are not meant to inform but to serve as political thrusts, either to settle some old score or to participate in that ageless game called logrolling. Reviewers with library training are perhaps less likely than some others to get caught up in the politics of reviewing and more likely to appreciate the need for objectivity in book criticism if for no other reason than the profession's long-standing concern with principles of intellectual freedom and the need for balance of controversial issues in library collections. But librarians are people and people are political and, as might be expected, there have been instances of questionable activity on the part of librarian-reviewers. For an interesting case history, see this author's article "ALA Reference & Subscription Books Review Committee as Censor: Experiences" in Bill Katz' Library Lit. 9--The Best of 1978 (Scarecrow Pr., 1979), p. 398-402.

The fourth and final requirement for the professional reference book critic is an honest and independent spirit. The critic must tell the truth or get out of the business. The critic must, in the words of Gore Vidal, possess "a truth-telling nature."[5] There is always the temptation to tone down or delete strong negative criticism, so that no one--authors, editors, publishers, sales representatives--will be offended. Or the reviewer may simply place being liked above being honest. We live in a society that loves and rewards the sycophant. Conversely, sometimes the price of telling the full truth seems too high. But the professional reference book critic (and this of course applies to all critics, no matter the field) has no choice. The job requires not only a fair and objective assessment of the material under review but also a rendering of that assessment in the clearest and most forthright terms possible. The library qualification hardly prepares one to be honest and independent. On the other hand, the library profession has its share of brave, incorruptible souls.

To recap: There is a need for more professionalism in reference book reviewing, but the opportunities are very limited and the outlook, though not entirely bleak, is not encouraging. Perhaps freelance work offers the best approach at the present time. Certainly, there are enough good library-oriented publishers around today to guarantee that a quality manuscript will not go begging. For instance, a book that professionally reviews the many reference sources that are now available in the area of energy not only would be snapped up by any of a dozen publishers but would earn the author a reasonable return as well. In any event, interested librarians would be well advised to try their hand first at reviewing for such volunteer services as ARBA, the ALA committee in Booklist, Library Journal, and RQ. This experience will eventually reveal whether the librarian-reviewer possesses the basic requirements of the professional reference book critic: (1) the ability to write clearly, succinctly, and sometimes quickly; (2) a thorough and comparative knowledge of reference materials and their makeup, characteristics, and uses; (3) an objective stance toward the material under review; and (4) an honest and independent spirit.

References

1. José Ortega y Gasset, The Mission of the Librarian (Boston: G. K. Hall, 1961), p. 22, 19. Originally an address to the International Congress of Bibliographers and Librarians in Paris in 1934, The Mission of the Librarian was first published in 1935 in Spanish and French. In 1961, G. K. Hall published the first English-language version.
2. William A. Katz, Introduction to Reference Work (3d ed.; New York: McGraw-Hill, 1978), V. 1, Basic Information Sources, p. 22.
3. Clifton Fadiman, "Must Encyclopedia Writing Be Stodgy?" Saturday Review/World (13 July 1974), p. 22, 26-27.

4. Laurence Urdang, Verbatim (Dec. 1975), p. 11-12.
5. Diane Johnson, "Gore Vidal, Scorekeeper," New York Times Book Review (17 April 1977), p. 47.

A COMPARATIVE ANALYSIS

OF JUVENILE

BOOK REVIEW MEDIA*

Virginia Witucke

Even as attitudes toward selection change (e.g., the Hardy Boys are finding their way back into libraries while jobbers provide preselected collections), the review remains an important tool for the selector.

How well served by the major review sources are those libraries for which children's books are purchased? To explore this question, review periodicals consistently found to be used in selecting juvenile books were examined: Booklist, Bulletin of the Center for Children's Books (Bulletin), Horn Book, New York Times Book Review (NYTBR), and School Library Journal (SLJ).

Contents and policies

Sponsorship of the major reviewing tools varies: a professional association (Booklist, American Library Association), a library school (Bulletin of the Center for Children's Books, University of Chicago Graduate Library School), a publisher concerned with the criticism and improvement of children's literature (Horn Book, Horn Book, Inc.) a publisher for the library field (School Library Journal, R. R. Bowker), and a major newspaper (New York Times Book Review).

Booklist reviews appear frequently (twenty-two times a year). NYTBR carries a few reviews of children's books each week, plus one spring and one fall issue that highlight juvenile literature. The Bulletin appears eleven months a year; SLJ, nine. Horn Book is bimonthly.

Only Booklist has a reviewing policy statement of any length, and it is published annually. SLJ's statement also appears annually.

---

*Reprinted by permission of the author and publisher from School Media Quarterly, Spring 1980, p. 153-60; copyright © 1980 by the American Library Association.

The brief policy statements made in Horn Book and Bulletin are repeated in each issue. New York Times Book Review seems to have no policy in print.

Arrangements of reviews are alphabetical by author (Bulletin and Booklist) and by age grouping (School Library Journal); Horn Book uses a combination of age and topic. Retrieval of titles by subject is available through Horn Book's topical listings and NYTBR's topical listings in the two special issues and through its separately published index. Author and title access is possible to all reviews.

Bulletin does nothing but review juvenile books. Booklist, while limited to reviewing, covers a broad range of library materials and clienteles. The other tools carry articles and news as well as reviews. All but the Bulletin carry advertising.

Horn Book and Booklist publish reviews only of titles recommended for library purchase although these recommendations may be qualified. Booklist and SLJ star reviews of highly recommended titles. Bulletin uses a series of symbols indicating its assessment of quality. Horn Book notes recommended paperbacks.

For each title reviewed, all periodicals give author, title, publisher, date, price, illustrator statement, and suggested audience; the number of pages is generally given, as are LC number (Booklist, Bulletin [when furnished by the publisher], School Library Journal), ISBN (Booklist, Bulletin, Horn Book, SLJ), and CIP availability (Booklist, Horn Book). Only Booklist gives cataloging information (Dewey number, subject headings).

Handling of reviews

To study the actual performance of each periodical, a random sample of thirty titles was taken from the lists of Notable Children's Books of 1972, 1973, and 1974. Reviews for the selected titles were identified through Book Review Index, assembled, and analyzed.[1] The titles in the sample are listed in appendix A.

Coverage. Ninety-seven percent (twenty-nine books) of the sample titles had been reviewed by the Bulletin of the Center for Children's Books; Booklist and School Library Journal did 93 percent each (twenty-eight books). Horn Book reviewed twenty-three of the titles (77 percent) and New York Times Book Review, seventeen (57 percent). Thus, at least three-quarters of the selected titles were reviewed by all but NYTBR. Among the five sources studied, 125 reviews of the sample titles were found for a mean coverage of 83 percent.

Eleven of the thirty sample titles were reviewed by all five periodicals, fourteen by four. Four titles got three reviews each, and one book was reviewed by only two sources.

These data suggest that, for the most part the target sources are effective at pinpointing high-quality books. However, the choice of sample method, Notable Books, skews the findings in favor of inclusion. Therefore, a look at total annual coverage was taken (see table 1). The number of juvenile titles published in the United States in the sample years was compared to the number of reviews published in the tools studied. Resulting percentages must be looked at quite warily, since a title is not necessarily reviewed in the year in which it is published. Nevertheless, some light is shed on total coverage by this procedure.

TABLE 1
PERCENTAGE OF U.S. JUVENILE BOOKS PUBLISHED 1972-74
THAT WERE REVIEWED BY MAJOR REVIEWING MEDIA*

Major Reviewing Media	1972 (N = 2,526)†	1973 (N = 2,042)†	1974 (N = 2,592)†	Total (N = 7,160)†
Booklist	31	47	42	40
Bulletin of the Center for Children's Books	30	38	30	32
Horn Book	20	19	14	17
New York Times Book Review	17	7	14	13
School Library Journal	82	119	90	97

Sources: *The Bowker Annual of Library & Book Trade Information*, 19th ed., 1974. New York: R. R. Bowker, 1974; *The Bowker Annual of Library & Book Trade Information*, 20th ed., 1975. New York: R. R. Bowker, 1975.
*Since the titles reviewed in a given year are not always those published that year, these percentages are indicative rather than exact.
†N refers to the number of titles published during that period.

For the three years of the sample, SLJ reviewed 97 percent of the total juvenile output, Booklist covered 40 percent of titles published, and Bulletin, 32 percent. Horn Book (17 percent) and NYTBR (13 percent) reviewed less than a fifth of the available titles. [A check of 1978 data shows that Booklist's 1978 coverage of publishing output increased to 64 percent, with slight rises for all of the others except NYTBR.]

Promptness. How promptly do reviews appear? The number of days before or after publication date that each review appeared was counted to determine the time lag (see table 2). The date of a title's appearance in Weekly Record (WR) was originally chosen as publication date. Not only could some titles not be identified this way, but it was also difficult to know how the WR date actually corresponded to the date of publication. Therefore, the publication date listed in Kirkus Reviews was accepted for all but Where the Sidewalk Ends, where the date on the dust jacket had to be used. For books and periodicals giving no indication of the day of the month when published, the first was arbitrarily chosen as the date of publication. Mean time lag for each periodical was then computed.

TABLE 2

PUBLICATION AND REVIEW DATES OF THIRTY TITLES, SELECTED FROM NOTABLE CHILDREN'S BOOK LISTS, 1972-74

Titles of Books in Order of Publication Date	Booklist	Bulletin	Horn Book	NYTBR	SLJ
Wicked City 3/15/72		12/72 (− 261)	4/72 (− 17)		4/15/72 (− 31)
When Clay Sings 3/15/72	6/15/72 (− 92)	10/72 (− 200)	8/72 (− 139)	11/5/72 (− 235)	5/15/72 (− 61)
Only Names Remain 3/16/72	6/1/72 (− 77)	4/72 (− 16)	6/72 (− 77)	11/5/72 (− 234)	5/15/72 (− 60)
Freaky Friday 4/12/72	6/15/72 (− 64)	9/72 (− 142)	8/72 (− 111)	7/16/72 (− 95)	4/15/72 (− 3)
Count and See 4/17/72	7/1/72 (− 75)	7/72 (− 75)	8/72 (− 106)		5/15/72 (− 28)
William's Doll 5/10/72		7/72 (− 52)	12/72 (− 205)	5/7/72 (+ 3)	9/15/72 (− 128)
Anansi 5/22/72	10/1/72 (− 132)	7/72 (− 40)		5/7/72 (+ 15)	9/15/72 (− 116)
Beethoven Medal 7/21/72	10/1/72 (− 72)	9/72 (− 42)	10/72 (− 72)		10/15/72 (− 86)
Snow-White 12/22/72	2/15/73 (− 55)	3/73 (− 69)	4/73 (− 100)	11/5/72 (+ 47)	3/15/73 (− 83)
Tales of Olga . . . 3/26/73	6/15/73 (− 81)	11/73 (− 220)	6/73 (− 67)		4/15/73 (− 20)
Taste of Blackberries 5/21/73	10/1/73 (− 133)	11/73 (− 164)	12/73 (− 194)		9/15/73 (− 177)
An Old Tale 8/31/73	11/1/73 (− 62)	3/74 (− 182)	12/73 (− 92)		9/15/73 (− 106)
Cathedral 9/73	11/15/73 (− 75)	1/74 (− 122)	10/73 (− 30)	12/16/73 (− 106)	12/15/73 (− 105)
Benjamin & Tulip 9/28/73	12/1/73 (− 64)	2/74 (− 126)	12/73 (− 64)		11/15/73 (− 49)
And Then What Happened . . .? 10/73	1/1/74 (− 92)	3/74 (− 151)	4/74 (− 182)	11/4/73 (− 34)	12/15/73 (− 75)
Pocket Full of Seeds 10/5/73	12/1/73 (− 57)	3/74 (− 147)	10/73 (+ 4)	11/4/73 (− 30)	11/15/73 (− 41)
Court of Stone Children 10/25/73	1/1/74 (− 68)	1/74 (− 68)	4/74 (− 158)	11/4/73 (− 10)	
Foundling 11/12/73	2/1/74 (− 81)	4/74 (− 140)	6/74 (− 201)	11/4/73 (+ 8)	12/15/73 (− 33)
Mushroom in the Rain 2/74	4/15/74 (− 73)	7/74 (− 150)	8/74 (− 181)	5/5/74 (− 93)	5/15/74 (− 103)
My Grandson Lew 3/74	4/1/74 (− 31)	6/74 (− 92)			4/15/74 (− 45)
Firerose 3/12/74	4/1/74 (− 20)	7/74 (− 111)			5/15/74 (− 64)
Why the Sky . . . 3/15/74	4/15/74 (− 31)				9/15/74 (− 184)
Wrapped for Eternity 3/19/74	5/1/74 (− 43)	10/74 (− 196)		5/26/74 (− 68)	5/15/74 (− 57)
My Black Me 4/74	7/1/74 (− 91)	10/74 (− 183)		5/5/74 (− 34)	9/15/74 (− 167)
Figgs & Phantoms 4/74	9/1/74 (− 153)	2/75 (− 306)	10/74 (− 183)		5/15/74 (− 44)
Elephant & His Secret 4/15/74	4/15/74 (0)	11/74 (− 200)	8/74 (− 108)	5/5/74 (− 20)	
Two Good Friends 4/18/74	5/1/74 (− 13)	7/74 (− 74)			9/15/74 (− 149)
My Brother Sam . . . 9/23/74	10/15/74 (− 22)	3/75 (− 159)	4/75 (− 190)	11/3/74 (− 41)	12/15/74 (− 83)
House in Norham Gdns. 10/18/74	9/15/74 (+ 33)	2/75 (− 106)	2/75 (− 106)		12/15/74 (− 58)
Where the Sidewalk Ends 11/74	1/15/75 (− 75)	4/75 (− 151)	4/75 (− 151)	11/3/74 (− 2)	4/15/75 (− 165)

Communication and Education 221

This time lag ranged from just under two months (NYTBR, with reviews appearing on the average 54.6 days after publication) to Bulletin, with a 136-day lag. Booklist's lag was about two months (64.2 days), followed by SLJ at 80.7 days and Horn Book at 118.6. However, the uncertainty as to the actual publication date for both book and review suggests that this computed time lag is no more than a general indicator of promptness.

Characteristics of reviews

Unlike large academic and research libraries, which may aim for comprehensiveness, collections serving children and young adults tend to be fairly selective, for both philosophical and financial reasons. Therefore, the amount and type of information within reviews is of great concern, since in many libraries the review is the major source on which the selection decision is based.

Length. While longer reviews may merely reflect careless writing and editing, the assumption will be made that length of re-

TABLE 3
NUMBER OF WORDS IN REVIEWS OF THIRTY TITLES.
SELECTED FROM NOTABLE CHILDREN'S
BOOK LISTS, 1972–74

Titles of Books in Order of Publication Date	Booklist	Bulletin	Horn Book	NYTBR	SLJ
Wicked City		72	126		149
When Clay Sings	67	123	207	79	175
Only Names Remain	99	142	225	23	213
Freaky Friday	108	149	194	193	144
Count and See	84	89	115		113
William's Doll		166	228	114	176
Anansi	70	122		102	113
Beethoven Medal	123	175	167		146
Snow-White	72	53	193	1,536	182
Tales of Olga. . .	70	147	94		132
Taste of Blackberries	90	133	114		105
An Old Tale	139	168	389		98
Cathedral	114	121	200	299	142
Banjamin & Tulip	84	96	72		171
And Then What Happened . . . ?	124	74	120	101	107
Pocket Full of Seeds	101	148	239	322	186
Court of Stone Children	166	133	129	501	
Foundling	106	82	104	417	83
Mushroom in the Rain	112	168	93	64	108
My Grandson Lew	111	123			111
Firerose	131	133			175
Why the Sky . . .	122				97
Wrapped for Eternity	133	105		405	91
My Black Me	78	88		71	168
Figgs & Phantoms	128	120	272		237
Elephant & His Secret	143	219	227	97	
Two Good Friends	134	89			71
My Brother Sam . . .	215	232	233	256	121
House in Norham Gdns.	168	160	277		81
Where the Sidewalk Ends	84	74	91	611	81

view is an indicator of the amount of information contained. Therefore, the number of words per review was counted and the mean determined (see table 3). NYTBR reviews averaged 305.3 words, although the Book Review had both the longest and shortest reviews. Mean length for Horn Book reviews was 178.6 words and 134.8 for School Library Journal. Bulletin and Booklist reviews averaged 127.7 and 113.4 words, respectively.

Authorship. Who writes the reviews? Bulletin, Horn Book, and Booklist depend on reviews prepared by staff members. The first is primarily the work of the editor. Booklist children's review staff numbered between one and three during the 1972-to-1974 period. Six people were responsible for the Horn Book reviews of the sample titles, three of these having reviewed sixteen of the twenty-three titles.

Of twenty-eight SLJ reviews, only two people (both were staff members) were responsible for more than one title. Eight reviews were written by staff, sixteen by librarians, and three by library school faculty. One reviewer's background was unclear.

Four of the seventeen New York Times reviews were by Times staffers, one person being responsible for two reviews; a Louisville journalist also reviewed two titles. Seven authors (Jean Fritz, Barbara Wersba, Peter Spier, Johanna Reiss, John Gardner, Dee Brown, and Karla Kuskin) contributed reviews, Brown and Kuskin doing two each. The remaining review was written by a teacher/free-lancer.

Critical Themes. The content of each review was analyzed to determine the number of critical themes, which were defined as evaluative, subjective comments. A statement such as "a well-written, fast-moving story" would be counted as having two critical themes (see Table 4).

There were 137 critical comments made about the twenty-eight Notable Books reviewed by Booklist. The number of themes per title varied from one to fourteen with a mean of 4.89.

The Bulletin of the Center for Children's Books contained 152 critical comments about twenty-nine titles. The number of such themes ranged from two to eleven; the mean was 5.24.

The range of critical themes per Horn Book review ran from two to nine. One hundred forty-five critical comments described twenty-three titles, with a mean of 6.3.

The New York Times Book Review, with seventeen titles reviewed and 113 critical themes, had a mean of 6.64 critical themes per review. However, the presence of several very long reviews skewed the mean. No review had fewer than two critical themes; the longest had fourteen and twenty-eight, respectively.

TABLE 4

NUMBER OF CRITICAL THEMES IN REVIEWS OF THIRTY TITLES, SELECTED FROM NOTABLE CHILDREN'S BOOK LISTS, 1972–74

Titles of Books in Order of Publication Date	Booklist	Bulletin	Horn Book	NYTBR	SLJ
Wicked City		6	7		7
When Clay Sings	5	3	9	3	6
Only Names Remain	4	4	8	2	7
Freaky Friday	2	5	8	4	8
Count and See	4	4	8		7
William's Doll		8	8	5	4
Anansi	4	3		2	3
Beethoven Medal	5	7	2		6
Snow-White	8	11	7	28	18
Tales of Olga . . .	4	6	6		7
Taste of Blackberries	3	2	8		3
An Old Tale	4	6	8		2
Cathedral	6	8	9	5	5
Banjamin & Tulip	4	4	5		7
And Then What Happened . . . ?	7	3	7	10	11
Pocket Full of Seeds	5	7	4	3	5
Court of Stone Children	5	6	7	14	
Foundling	5	6	3	8	2
Mushroom in the Rain	3	5	3	2	6
My Grandson Lew	7	8			3
Firerose	9	4			3
Why the Sky . . .	1				3
Wrapped for Eternity	3	6		2	4
My Black Me	3	2		2	3
Figgs & Phantoms	7	5	5		7
Elephant & His Secret	4	4	5	5	
Two Good Friends	6	4			4
My Brother Sam . . .	3	6	9	9	5
House in Norham Gdns.	2	4	6		4
Where the Sidewalk Ends	14	5	3	9	8

The twenty-eight titles reviewed by School Library Journal received 158 critical comments. The mean thus was 5.64, with the actual number of themes ranging from two to eighteen.

When the total coverage was examined, the mean number of critical themes was found to be 5.63. Booklist had the smallest number of critical comments and the New York Times Book Review had the largest number. The greatest variety in extent of criticism was shown by the New York Times Book Review.

One type of critical theme examined separately was the attempt to predict usage or popularity of the book being reviewed. This was rarely found to be a feature of the New York Times or Horn Book. Bulletin included such information in three (10 percent) of its reviews of the sample titles, Booklist in seven (25 percent), and School Library Journal in nine (32 percent).

Another type of information that is more objective is the mention of similar titles or other works by the same author. Almost half (46 percent) of SLJ reviews cited other works, closely followed by Horn Book (43 percent) and New York Times Book Review (41 percent). Booklist (32 percent) and Bulletin (24 percent) were less likely to refer to other works.

Consistency. Strong consistency of critical opinion was shown in comparing the review titles. In only one case of 125 was a review fairly negative. Generally, reviews of a title were clearly positive to it, with enthusiasm varying in degree. There were differences in style and in what a given reviewer might comment on, but actual opinion was consistent. This is not a surprising finding in view of the use of a sample based on a positive consensus of critical opinion.

All periodicals studied suggested a range of reading or grade level for each title reviewed. While agreement was less than complete, the general ranges were similar. No periodical tended to give user levels that were consistently higher or lower than others. On occasion, Horn Book and NYTBR omitted indications of level.

Summary

All tools but NYTBR reviewed at least 75 percent of the sample titles. Booklist, School Library Journal, and Bulletin of the Center for Children's Books covered 93 percent or more. Thus, these tools are highlighting titles most likely to be considered for purchase. As for coverage of all juvenile titles published, only SLJ did very well (95 percent). Booklist (40 percent) and Bulletin (32 percent) were far less comprehensive in their total coverage, though still ahead of Horn Book (17 percent) and NYTBR (13 percent).

All sources published reviews some time after publication of the title. This lag averaged about eight weeks for the New York Times, nine weeks for Booklist, and eleven weeks for SLJ. Horn Book reviews appeared, on the average, seventeen weeks after publication, and nineteen weeks later in the case of the Bulletin.

Because of occasional in-depth coverage, the mean number of words per review was greatest in the New York Times Review. Brief mention was at least as typical. Booklist reviews were the shortest at 113 words. Bulletin and School Library Journal reviews were somewhat longer and Horn Book noticeably so (179 words).

The mean number of critical themes per review ranged from 4.89 (Booklist) to 6.64 (NYTBR). Horn Book reviews were relatively critical (6.3) while SLJ (5.64) and Bulletin (5.2) were in between.

General consistency of opinion among the five periodicals was apparent in terms of this sample.

Comments and conclusion

The need for increased coverage of juvenile publications and the need for more critical handling of individual titles are criticisms long leveled at the reviewing apparatus and supported by this study. Only School Library Journal makes any attempt to cover total publishing output, although Booklist seems to be doing more to include titles of possible library usage. The mean number of critical themes per review (four to six) suggests a lack of depth within reviews.

Of further concern is the lack of clearly stated, frequently published policy statements that help the user interpret what she/he is getting. Questions rarely dealt with are how titles are acquired for review, on what basis the decision to review is made, how titles are assigned for reviewing, and what criteria are used in evaluating books. More important than the statement, the user needs the assurance that all currently available publications are considered for review and that the final choice is not idiosyncratic or haphazard.

The need for subject access through internal indexing was underscored. Some library selection is retrospective, and it is extremely difficult to search a specific topic at the present without recourse to further library tools that are not always readily available.

Promptness has not been considered of particular importance in the reviewing of children's books. Nonetheless, there seems little reason for selectors to operate from unnecessarily limited information, particularly in the case of topical and seasonal books. Moves to speed up the process are to be applauded, especially since in some libraries ordering is done just once or twice a year.

This study bears out the fact that there is no single review tool adequate to the selector's needs. Because of the varying policies, points of view, and performance, use (although not necessarily ownership) of a number of selection tools is vital to collection building. All of the tools examined are basic to the selector, although some will be more useful in a given library than others. Nor are these the only sources that should be used. The selector, with limited time, must learn which review tools best serve him/her in a given situation and determine how to use each to maximum advantage.

Reference

1. This study was triggered by, and used some of the methodology of, one done by Charles Busha that dealt with adult book reviewing media. See Busha, "Book Selection in Public Libraries: An Evaluation of Four Commonly-Used Review Media," Southeastern Librarian 18:92-100 (Summer 1968).

Appendix A
Titles in Sample

Adoff, Arnold. My Black Me: A Beginning Book of Black Poetry. New York: Dutton, 1974.
Alexander, Lloyd. The Foundling and Other Tales of Prydain. New York: Holt, 1973.
Baylor, Byrd. When Clay Sings. New York: Scribner, 1972.
Bealer, Alex W. Only the Names Remain: The Cherokees and the Trail of Tears. Boston: Little, 1972.
Bond, Michael. The Tales of Olga da Polga. New York: Macmillan, 1973.
Cameron, Eleanor. The Court of the Stone Children. New York: Dutton, 1973.
Collier, James, and Collier, Christopher. My Brother Sam Is Dead. Englewood Cliffs, N.J.: Four Winds, 1974.
Dana, Doris. The Elephant and His Secret. New York: Atheneum, 1974.
Delton, Judy. Two Good Friends. New York: Crown, 1974.
Fritz, Jean. And Then What Happened, Paul Revere? New York: Coward, 1973.
Gerson, Mary-Joan. Why the Sky Is Far Away: A Folktale from Nigeria. New York: Harcourt, 1974.
Grimm Brothers. Snow-White and the Seven Dwarfs. New York: Farrar, 1972.
Hoban, Tana. Count and See. New York: Macmillan, 1972.
Jeschke, Susan. Firerose. New York: Holt, 1974.
Linevski, A. An Old Tale Carved out of Stone. New York: Crown, 1973.
Lively, Penelope. The House in Norham Gardens. New York: Dutton, 1974.
Macaulay, David. Cathedral: The Story of Its Construction. Boston: Houghton, 1973.
McDermott, Gerold. Anansi the Spider; A Tale from the Ashanti. New York: Holt, 1972.
Pace, Mildred Mastin. Wrapped for Eternity: The Story of the Egyptian Mummy. New York: McGraw, 1974.
Peyton, K. M. The Beethoven Medal. New York: Crowell, 1972.
Raskin, Ellen. Figgs & Phantoms. New York: Dutton, 1974.
Rodgers, Mary. Freaky Friday. New York: Harper, 1972.
Sachs, Marilyn. A Pocket Full of Seeds. New York: Doubleday, 1973.
Silverstein, Shel. Where the Sidewalk Ends. New York: Harper, 1972.
Singer, Isaac Bashevis. The Wicked City. New York: Farrar, 1972.
Smith, Doris Buchanan. A Taste of Blackberries. New York: Macmillan, 1974.
Suteyev, V. Mushroom in the Rain. New York: Macmillan, 1974.
Wells, Rosemary. Benjamin and Tulip. New York: Dial, 1973.
Zolotow, Charlotte. My Grandson Lew. New York: Harper, 1972.
──────. William's Doll. New York: Harper, 1972.

FIFTY YEARS OF "BOOKS FOR THE TEEN AGE"*

Lillian Morrison

A fiftieth anniversary is a time for taking stock, for looking back at beginnings, at purposes, at changes along the way. And in this case, it's also a good opportunity to express a few opinions on related matters such as book selection for the young in a world that continues to undergo shocks, explosions, and rapid change.

In February 1979, the New York Public Library published the 50th edition of Books for the Teen Age. This is an annually revised list of old and new books, arranged by subject, which covers a wide variety of interests, types of literature, and reading levels. The present list contains about 1250 titles and serves as a basic guide to young adults' reading interests. "Young adults," in the New York Public Library, means young people in the eighth grade through high school or approximately 13 to 18 years of age. Since adolescents are so contemporary in their interests, the list has become indicative of what's been happening in the world.

I have been closely involved in the preparation of this list for more than half of those 50 years and an editor for the last 12 years. And I was fortunate in my apprenticeship to have worked under three great librarians: Mabel Williams, a wise and delightful woman, who pioneered young adult work in the New York Public Library and edited the list from 1929 through 1951; and Amelia Munson, a maverick and poetry lover, who as Mabel Williams' assistant played a major role in all the lists during those early years. The author of An Ample Field; Books and Young People (American Library Association, 1950), she had wit, warmth, and a tremendous book knowledge. She was also a born teacher, as anyone who ever took her unique course in book selection for young people at Columbia can testify. And finally, Margaret Scoggin, whom I assisted, and who, as coordinator of Young Adult Services, edited the list from 1952 through 1967. She had great rapport with the young. Her brainpower and productivity were staggering, to say nothing of her gen-

---

*Reprinted by permission of the author and publisher from School Library Journal, 26:4 (December 1979) 44-50. Published by R. R. Bowker Co. (a Xerox company). Copyright © 1979 by Xerox Corporation.

erosity to those who worked under her. Her aim (and she made it seem possible) was to read all the books. The essential goal of all three women was the promotion of reading as a lifetime, pleasurable and practical, resource. This remains our goal today.

Why Prepare Booklists?

The mind likes lists. No matter what the subject or purpose, lists bring order to amorphousness. They point out saliencies--trivial or important. The Book of Lists by Wallechinsky and Wallace, appeared recently and became a best seller. And one of the books perennially asked for by teen-agers, The Guinness Book of World Records, is a list--popular, not so much because it is a list per se, but because it is a list of masteries, of standouts, of triumphs of human ingenuity, of foolish persistence, skill, and spirit. Almost everybody wants to be special in some way, at least in the Western world, and teen-agers especially, want and need to be special.

But we are concerned with booklists here. Making lists is a natural subdivision of what libraries do--finding out what exists in the realm of recorded ideas, selecting, classifying, and bringing it to the attention of others. Booklists are satisfying to do and are important. And when one makes a further culling from the larger collection to meet certain requirements and make access easier, it is similar to making an anthology. There is an element of pleasure in it--one's own, and the imagined pleasure of the reader.

As for making lists for the young such as Books for the Teen Age, here are a few truisms, or basic principles by which we have worked:

1. A list has value only as it represents a point of view-- some underlying philosophy or set of standards applied as consistently as possible.

2. No list is infallible. Lists are not to be taken as gospel, but as suggested guides.

3. Any list is an invitation to agree or disagree, to add to, or to subtract from, and especially to read for oneself.

4. All books listed should be reasonably available.

5. Everything is an influence, or a potential one--the people we know, the electronic media, the food we eat, the environment we live in, the books we read. Language has power--and books in particular have power not only to inform, to entertain and delight, but also to help share our understanding of life, or ourselves and each other, in one way or another.

This last statement is what makes being a librarian interesting and worthwhile. It implies a responsibility because we are deal-

Communication and Education

ing with people who are still formative. What makes providing books for them such a delicate and sometimes difficult matter, aside from limited budgets and the tremendously wide range of abilities and needs among adolescents, is that there is another responsibility (sometimes a conflicting one) in our democratic society. That is, peoples' right to read anything they wish, to learn to form their own opinions, to develop their own values (assuming, of course, the ability to read and to use one's mind to make necessary choices).

To make things more complex, there are the changing times, youth unemployment, the changing sexual mores, changing family relationships, beliefs in transition--all kinds of social upheavals and breakdowns--making it harder for young people to arrive at stable values. Add to this the proliferation of other media, pervasive and enormously influential, where ideas and images are recorded and sent forth, and then add the general lower reading levels and short attention spans among the youth of the nation, and you have quite a challenging situation.

Where does that leave us? For one thing, it leaves us with the great quality vs. popularity dilemma that each librarian has to resolve by asking: What is my purpose? What is my role with these young people and the society we live in?

If our standards are too high, we may fail to attract great segments of our public or not meet their needs, making libraries places for the elite.

If we accede to demand with little thought for anything else, telling ourselves anything young people read is okay as long as they read, we are copping out. We are leaving it (without a fight) to TV, comics, rock lyrics, and movies to shape our society. And we know these media, by and large, have much more interest in commercial profit than in the public good. All too often, we mindlessly repromote whatever they promote, thinking that makes us "in," contemporary, on teenagers' wavelengths. Either extreme is dangerous and most of us fall somewhere in between. It takes all the wisdom, judgment, knowledge of books and young people that we possess, as well as awareness of what's going on around us, to do a good job.

Distinctions & Decisions

In recent debates on the matter in the library literature, certain important, if subtle, distinctions are seldom mentioned, for example, the distinction between selecting for children and selecting for teen-agers.

Children have had little or no past experiences with books. So in selecting for them we're much concerned with the formation of taste. Since teen-agers are still impressionable, selection for them is concerned <u>somewhat</u> with the formation of taste and values.

But, because of adolescents' particular needs, changes, expanding interests and outlooks on life, selection in the public library is more concerned with teen-agers' present and potential interests--whether it's cartoons or computers, weight-lifting or witchcraft, Tolkien or tennis, romance or rock stars, disco-dancing or Dune, poetry or pregnancy. Also, since teen-agers are less willing than young children to accept someone else's opinion and must learn to make their own judgments, we tend to provide for them, not only the best books, but sometimes the second best and mediocre if it deals with what they really care about. But there are standards below which we should not go. And librarians still have to know what constitutes the best.

We still have the responsibility to distinguish between the specious and the genuine; between a trite formula and a good story, well told; between the TV tie-in a hack writer took 10 days to produce and the carefully crafted, deeply felt novel; between the cheap, the lurid, the sensational, and the serious work of merit which often contains sordid elements. The more discussion among librarians of specific titles, the more varied opinions expressed and book-selection principles elucidated, the better. But beyond this, and more important, we should be discussing with the teen-agers themselves what they read. We can't, and don't, want to protect them from books not meeting our approval. To quote Margaret Scoggin in her article, "Fables They Shall Not Read" (ALA Bulletin, November, 1952), "Young people will inevitably meet good and bad in books. Fortunately we cannot wrap them in cotton batting. We must help them judge books even as we ourselves have tried to learn. Young readers need an adult mind to challenge their ideas of books and authors. Let us be sure that the minds we provide as the challenge are both adult and functioning." (The italics are mine.)

Because we're asked for them as a result of recent TV series, we buy some formula books--a few Nancy Drew, a few Hardy boys, if they're not too racist or sexist--but that doesn't mean we should push them or fill our libraries with them. It's all a matter of proportion. Since funds for young adults services are limited, we let adult services buy the Donald Goines books, the Harlequins, and the Barbara Cartlands. Teen-agers find them on the adult shelves. Which brings us to other distinctions often overlooked in the great debates on censorship, popularity vs. quality, etc.--the distinctions between what is in the library as a whole (to which New York teen-agers have complete access), what is in a YA collection and is labeled YA, and what is put on a specially recommended list. Some examples:

- The Amityville Horror, The Omen, and books of that type are in our adult collections where any teenager is free to find them. We don't feel we are censoring them by leaving them off Books for the Teen Age. Those decisions are easy.

- Judy Blume's Forever was somewhat difficult. Although advertised as an adult novel, it is without the complexities

Communication and Education 231

of style, plot, or characterization one expects in an adult
novel, and without much real emotion for that matter.
And, it deals with a kind of explicit sex formerly taboo
in junior novels, and gives, in a simplified manner, information teen-agers are terrifically curious about. Forever
is in our YA collections, labeled YA, and is requested
much and much circulated, but it is not on Books for the
Teen Age, a listing which implies a special recommendation to teen-agers that they read titles cited. Many of our
librarians liked it and would have liked to have seen it on
the list. More of us considered it a shallow treatment of
a complex subject that requires much more skill and depth
to meet the list's standards of quality.

● What to do about Our Bodies, Ourselves was another
difficult decision. It is in our largest YA collections, but
it too is not on Books for the Teen Age because, after
careful committee consideration, we felt that in general it
was aimed at and more suitable for women 18 and over,
rather than the 13- to 18-year-old age group. SIECUS
(Sex Information and Education Council of the United States)
agrees with our judgment in their most recent booklist.
But it is always available for younger teen-agers who want
it.

And there are other decisions to make. How much astrology
do we buy for YAs? What about books like Van Daniken's Chariots
of the Gods and Velikovsky's astronomical theories. Which UFO
books do we buy? Do we put them on the list? Since 1969, we
have a "What Do You Think?" section where we have put some of
the better books of this controversial nature. Of course, we have
had and do have, on our list, books which have caused controversy
or been considered distasteful by some in the community: Slaughter-
House Five, Down These Mean Streets, Manchild in the Promised
Land, Catcher in the Rye, I Know Why the Caged Bird Sings, Soul
on Ice, Of Mice and Men, One Day in the Life of Ivan Denisovitch,
Autobiography of Malcolm X, and many others. These are books
we feel justified in recommending to teen-agers.

How simple life was for the librarian as materials selector
in those early days--pre-Hitler, pre-Hiroshima, pre-Vietnam, pre-
Watergate, and pre- the full flower of the communications explosion
and other technological advances. The librarian had only to choose
books, hardcover books at that. Now most teen-agers prefer to
read paperbacks. Now librarians must deal with lists of film and
videotape holdings in the New York Public Library that are starred
for YA suitability, and filmstrips, recordings, cassettes, and posters. Now every selector must, at some point, decide what proportion of the budget should be spent on nonprint materials and with
what justification. The different effects the various media have on
the individual, as compared to the effect of reading, still need
study. It's a whole, big, interesting open area.

They tell us that the average high-school graduate has spent
15,000 to 18,000 hours of his or her life watching television as
compared to 13,000 to 15,000 hours spent in school. This, combined with lowered educational standards, alienation, and a few other
social forces, has resulted in a dismaying literacy problem among
teen-agers. Now, in addition to Books for the Teen Age, we publish
a high-low listing, a separate Easy to Read Books for Teen-Agers
list that we revise every couple of years. There is more and more
tutoring going on in libraries and we hope to get a funded literacy
program for teen-agers in the branches. It is difficult to survive in
today's world without the ability to read.

Today there are a tremendous number of school dropouts and
runaways (who are victimized by porn purveyors and pimps), teenage unemployment, teen-age alcoholism and drug addiction, an increase in teen suicides, teen pregnancies, and VD epidemics. As a
result, there is a crying need for practical collections of information
and referral materials, learner's advisory collections for teen-agers,
and lists of available agencies providing information on health, sex,
jobs, and crisis centers. How much emphasis does one give to
what--with limited budgets?

With the influx into New York of so many non-English-speaking peoples, we now select books for teen-agers in Spanish, Chinese,
French, Vietnamese, and other languages. Books for the Teen Age
tries to reflect an awareness of all these changes in our social
fabric. It remains a strong root and trunk for all these branchings
in our work.

Preparation for the List

How is Books for the Teen Age prepared? It is very much a dynamic process that goes on throughout the year and gives our young
adult work a shape, in that it is easily integrated with every aspect
of YA service--the book order process, floor work with individual
teen-agers, talks in schools and other community agencies, and often
with programming, an important part of our work. The new books
help keep us knowledgable and up-to-date on contemporary problems,
new ideas, new technology, and interests or hobbies of young people,
thus feeding or supplementing our program activity. We also use
the list as a training tool with YA librarians who continually consult
it for background reading and read new books for it, thus increasing
their ability to serve teen-agers and to build up their booktalk repertoires.

At present, there are approximately 50 young adult librarians
in NYPL's branch library system, some of whom are in central offices. Most are working in branch libraries where they are responsible for knowing the neighborhood teen-agers through individual conversations and meeting them in groups, reading everything they can
of possible interest to them, listening to them, and finding out what
they honestly like and do not like in books.

Each librarian is a member of a book committee of his or her choice that meets once a month and discusses new books and reevaluates older ones within certain subject areas. This is because for every title we put on, one must come off, and we replace about one-third of the titles on the list each year. About 65 percent of the titles are chosen from adult publications and 35 percent are published as juveniles. It used to be more like 80 percent adult, 20 percent juvenile.

Selection of Titles

The actual selection for the list is based (in general terms because details vary for different genres) on:

1. The intrinsic merits of the book: style, plot, characterization, author's purpose and success in filling it, honesty, accuracy, integrity, etc.
2. Its value and appeal to teen-agers.
3. Teen-agers' own reactions to it.

In other words, is the book readable, accurate, and entertaining for teen-agers? And, in the course of time as the title is used, do teen-agers really read it and like it? No title has to be liked or used by all young adults, but every book on the list should appeal to some teenage readers. We make a special effort to put the odd book on, sometimes by a small publisher, to take care of special interests of which we are aware. Bruce Kurtz's Spots (Arts Communication) on the art of TV commercials on the 1978 list is one example; Outwater and Van Hamersveld's Guide to Practical Holography (Pentangle) is another.

It's not a definitive list. We make mistakes, but we try to find them and eliminate them the following year, or add titles we've missed the year before. All three of the criteria enumerated are in operation when we choose. It is the degree of emphasis given to each which makes for all the fun and argument.

The list is used by school and public librarians as a buying guide and information source, teachers use it as a guide to young adult interests but it is meant primarily for use by teen-agers themselves. The one-line annotations are addressed to them. We try to make these as precise and honest as we can. Sometimes we use subtitles.

We give the list to teen-agers on request, free of charge. We often use it with them to get them involved in finding books for themselves, especially those young people who are interested in a subject or type of book and don't know specific titles. A good librarian will know when to hand a teen-ager a list and to suggest checking off books he or she might like to read. Then they go and search the shelves together. It's a good way to get acquainted.

Past & Present Lists

The first printed list, entitled Books for Young People, appeared in October 1929, as an issue of the Bulletin of the New York Public Library. Its cover was a black and white drawing of a cowboy on a bucking bronco by Will James from his book Cowboys North and South. The list was an outgrowth of work begun some 10 years before by Mabel Williams. She was recruited in 1918 by Anne Carroll Moore, the head of children's work, who had seen the need for better service to this neglected age group whose interests were not being catered to in either the children's or adult departments of the library. I quote from the preface of that first edition:

> This list is primarily for use in the adult sections of the Library, to suggest books to boys and girls when they are first transferred from the Children's Rooms. It is not expected to replace any of the lists now used by the Schools. High School lists are naturally affected by the curriculum and the desire to give pupils an opportunity of knowing all forms of literature before leaving school. Furthermore, their use is dependent not only on inclination but also on compulsion, because of the various checking-up methods used in the schools. This list, on the other hand, includes only those books which boys and girls are known to have enjoyed either through their own discovery or the suggestion of a friend, a teacher, a librarian, or through the impetus received from book talks or reading clubs.

It is hard to realize in these days of free reading, what school was like in 1929. Often one textbook was used. Classics were heavily emphasized for outside reading, and recreational reading related to personal interest was pretty much ignored. So a list of this kind filled a great need.

The 1929 list was 20 pages long and contained just over 300 titles. There were 16 subject headings, actually 29 if we count subdivisions within sections (e. g., "Historical Tales," arranged by country). The 1979 list has 64 pages and some 1250 titles. It's arranged under five broad groupings: Here/Now; Mind's Eye: The Arts and Fiction; Science; Action, Adventure, and Other Things to Do; and The Global Village; there are 74 subject headings, counting subdivisions.

Headings have always been added as we see fit. A section gets too long so we try to put some of the titles under a new heading, or we find little new under a topic and consolidate, or we discover a new topic of teen-age interest. We don't want to be too exact in this regard, or too formal, since this isn't a required reading list, just something to surprise or nudge a reader. Still it is interesting to look back through the lists at the evolution of new sections that reflect, not only growth and change in teen reading interests, but also social change and how publishing keeps up with it.

Communication and Education   235

"Love and Sex" did not appear as a separate section until 1970. In 1929, there was a heading "Novels and Love Stories"--sex did not exist. In 1938 there was a "Manners" section which became "Personality Plus" in the 40s and 50s and included such books as Fedder's A Girl Grows Up and McKown's A Boy Grows Up, along with books on grooming and etiquette. From 1963 to 1968, it became the broader "Personality and Perspectives." The Art of Dating and other Evelyn Millis Duval titles were staples on it. It was changed to "Personal Development" in 1969 with more psychology added, including the landmark Love and Sex in Plain Language by Eric Johnson.

The lists reflected the struggle for human rights and the growth of ethnic and racial pride. In 1966, the New York Public Library published for young adults an extended separate booklist Books by and about the American Negro, but in Books for the Teen Age such books were either under "U.S.A.--the Current Scene" or spread throughout the list under other subjects. In 1969, a new heading "The Negro in the U.S." was started. The following year, it became "Black America," and contained current materials. Also in that year, separate listings for "Indians of the Americas," and "Puerto Rico and the Puerto Ricans" were added. "Women" was added in 1971, "Popular Spanish Books" in 1973, and in 1977, an additional section, "U.S.A.--the Americans" was included to take care of books on many other ethnic and racial heritages. We are not always Johnnys-on-the-spot. Sometimes it takes us a year or two before a new section corresponds to a new interest. Also, we don't add a new section until there are at least 10 or 12 books we are willing to recommend.

The list was limited to "Explorations in Science" in pre-atomic 1929. DeKruif's Microbe Hunters was included along with Carl Akeley's In Brightest Africa. Now there are 12 science headings. "Medical Science" came about early on, then "Astronomy," "Atomic Energy" (in 1949), "Exploration of Space" (in 1953), and many others as Sputnik gave the teaching of science a great push in the late 50s. The discovery of DNA, later recombinant experiments and other recent exciting developments in biology, physics, and cosmology are all represented. "Ecology" was added in 1971. Parapsychology, always a strong teen-age interest, became respectable more than five years ago through acceptance by the American Association for the Advancement of Science at the urging of Margaret Mead. So, we established "Mind Sciences and ESP" in 1974.

Advances in technology, new interests and new social problems resulted in further heading changes. They speak for themselves:

● From "Applied Science" to "Technology" in 1969, to "Energy and Technology" in 1977.

● From "Photography," big enough in 1948 to have its own section out of "Hobbies," to "Photography and Film" in 1968, to "Film, Photography, and Video" in 1974. An earlier "Radio and Television" section was absorbed into this and other sections.

● In the mid-1940s, the interest in World War II was shown in five or six headings: "War Stories," "Army and Navy," "Air Forces," "Theatres of the War," "Women in Uniform," etc. There was no comparable reflection in publishing or in teen-age interest during the Vietnam War. After World War II, one heading remained, "Men in War," later renamed "This is War." In 1969 it became "War and Peace."

● In 1969, also a new section "Folk, Pop, and Rock" evolved out of "Music." The following year it was, "Folk, Pop, Rock and Soul."

● In 1970, we added "Communication" featuring Marshall McLuhan's Understanding Media. That year, too, "Drugs" required a separate section. Now, with less interest in psychedelic drugs, titles reflect the rise in teen-age alcoholism.

● In 1978, we added "Working" to respond to recent practical, vocational needs. "Work" was the first heading on the list in 1933, one of the worst years of the depression. This heading appeared again in 1934.

Then and Now

Of the 16 subject headings in the 1929 list, those that seem a bit archaic now are:

"Tales of Romance and Daring" which contained such books as Malory's The Boys King Arthur, Donn Byrne's Messer Marco Polo, Tarn's The Treasure of the Isle of Mist. Kipling's Kim was in this section too, and Wilder's The Bridge of San Luis Rey, and also Alain-Fournier's The Wanderer (still on the 1979 list under "France").

"Essays and Sketches" had authors Charles Lamb, Agnes Repplier, and Christopher Morley represented. Did teen-agers really read their books? Stephen Leacock was included with his Oxford As I see It. How times have changed! In 1941, "Essays and Sketches" became "Essays and Humor." In 1967, it became simply "Humor." Essays, with their leisurely style, do not seem to interest many teen-agers, although Thoreau's Walden, an extended essay, was much read in the 60s and is still read by some who find it relevant. And our science-minded young people may read Lewis Thomas' books. We'll probably put his The Medusa and the Snail; More Notes of a Biology Watcher on the 1980 list.

"School and College Stories" had four books by Owen Johnson listed, including Stover at Yale. Also included were: Joseph Gollomb's That Year at Lincoln High, Jean Webster's Daddy Long Legs, and Josephine Dodge Daskam's Smith College Stories. I do not see one school story in our latest "Junior Novel" section unless Lois Duncan's Killing Mr. Griffin, in which a group of students kill their English teacher, can be considered a school story. That should tell us something. "School and College Stories" was incorporated in 1935 into "Girls' Stories." In 1968, "Boys' Stories" was added to include novels with a boy protagonist and a psychological emphasis. In 1971, thanks to the women's movement, these books were all combined under "Junior Novels."

"Historical Tales," a broad heading subdivided by country with a separate section for Greece and Rome, was the beginning of our present "Global Village" listing. Bulwer-Lytton's The Last Days of Pompeii and William Stearns Davis' A Victor at Salamis are included. Latin was much taught in the high schools then. Robert Fitzgerald's translation of The Odyssey under "Poetry," and The Trojan Women under "Plays," plus a few books now under "Italy," are what remain on the present list of the glory that was Greece and the grandeur that was Rome.

"Sports" in 1929, was a small section, 18 titles, as compared to 46 today (after a lot of paring and not counting the eight titles listed under "Stories of Sports and Action"). There was very little published in sports in those days, nothing like today's avalanche of baseball, football, and tennis books, and it is obvious they were hard put for titles in that section because we find Harold Kellock's Houdini, Roping by Chester Byers, and Jerome K. Jerome's Three Men in a Boat which might be fun to reread.

The "Humorous Stories" section also looks odd today. One finds Winnie the Pooh (for teen-agers?); Alice Hegan Rice's Mrs. Wiggs of the Cabbage Patch; Uncle Remus; David Harum; and three novels of Cape Cod by Joseph Lincoln (which I remember reading in high school and enjoying because of the names of the characters). There are many Booth Tarkingtons and three Wodehouses. Dickens' Pickwick Papers had a long life on the list. Now we're down to one Dickens title to represent all the rest, but Pickwick Papers may make it again some day. Huckleberry Finn, formerly under "Humorous Stories," is still on our list, but is under the United States in the "New Nation" category which places it in its proper historical context for today's teen-agers. Tom Sawyer, also on that 1929 list, now seems too juvenile. The number of young children's titles in this section of the 1929 list makes one realize that teen-agers are much more sophisticated or cynical in their taste for humor--or more sensitive perhaps about being identified with children. Mad Magazine has done its work. Today, young adults are also more visually developed--they love cartoons.

The 1929 "Poetry" section was a very long one. A number of the poets (Edwin Arlington Robinson, William Blake, Lewis Carroll, W. S. Gilbert) still make good reading for some teen-agers, but only two poets are represented on the 1979 list--W. B. Yeats and a posthumous Louis Untermeyer anthology. Tennyson, Noyes, Masefield, Millay are still on some library shelves, but no longer on the list. Walt Whitman, Langston Hughes, May Swenson, Gwendolyn Brooks, bilingual collections and collections of Native American poetry are more appealing for present-day young people.

Long-Lived Titles

It is interesting to see some of the titles which have remained on our list for 50 years--not many, to be sure, but here they are:

Jules Verne's Twenty Thousand Leagues under the Sea and H. G. Wells' War of the Worlds, first under "Adventure and Sea Stories," now under "Science Fiction," a genre which has burgeoned since the 40s. This heading first appeared in 1941 as "Scientific Tales" and became "Science Fiction" in 1950.

From the 1929 "Mystery and Detective Stories," The Adventures of Sherlock Holmes is still on, and Agatha Christie is still with us, although this year, The Murder of Roger Ackroyd was replaced by Sleeping Murder, the last Miss Marple. Edgar Allen Poe's Tales also remains.

Novels from 1929 still remaining on the list are: Jane Austen's Pride and Prejudice, Charlotte Bronte's Jane Eyre (her Shirley was on in 1929), Emily Bronte's Wuthering Heights, Willa Cather (although not the same titles), Orczy's The Scarlet Pimpernel, Melville's Moby Dick, and Crane's The Red Badge of Courage.

Also Shaw remains represented under "Plays," and Cervantes with Don Quixote, but for some reason, Shakespeare, on the list now, was not on the 1929 list. Other classics (James Fenimore Cooper, Thackeray, George Eliot, Walter Scott) exist only in the literature courses. They have been banished from the list for the sin of being unread by teen-agers. And other nonclassic writers and books, popular in their time, are "gone with the wind"--Howard Pease, John Buchan, Jessie B. Rittenhouse's poetry anthologies, Amelia Barr's stories of old New York, and many books about Teddy Roosevelt.

In the 1930 to 1939 lists, La Farge's Laughing Boy, Saint-Exupery's Night Flight, authors such as Langston Hughes and Andre Norton appeared and still remain.

Others that had long runs are Lane's Let the Hurricane Roar, Gunther's Inside Europe (and all the others which followed), Bagnold's National Velvet, Rawlings' The Yearling, DuMaurier's Jamaica Inn, Ross's The Education of Hyman Kaplan, Marquis' Archy and Mehitabel, and Eve Curie's Madame Curie. Some junior novels on the lists have been Mabel Robinson's love story Bright Island, the Sue Barton series, the Florence Means books, and the Lorimers' Stag Line and Heart Specialist (forerunners of DuJardin).

During the next couple of decades, the 40s and 50s, we had Arthur Clarke, Ray Bradbury, Anne Frank's Diary of a Young Girl, Hemingway's The Old Man and the Sea, Wright's Black Boy, Laurents' West Side Story, and many others. Maureen Daly's Seventeenth Summer appeared in 1945 and was popular with teen-age girls for the next 20 to 25 years.

In junior novels, there were Benson's Junior Miss, popular in the 40s, the first Betty Cavanna books, the first Beany Malone stories, and Headley's Date for Diane. John Tunis' sport stories were a great improvement over the Ralph Henry Barbour series and other books of that type. Tunis was superseded by Duane Decker's more breezy, action-packed stories. Both these authors were eventually superseded by teen-age boys' increasingly exclusive interest in sports non-fiction. Outstanding in the 50s were the fine books by Mary Stolz and Rosemary DuJardin's popular titles.

Then came the turbulent and anguished 60s, requiring a reexamination of our basic institutions and our conventional values. Such books as Baldwin's The Fire Next Time, Griffin's Black Like Me, Golding's Lord of the Flies, Green's I Never Promised You a Rose Garden, Carson's Silent Spring, Lee's To Kill a Mockingbird, Smith's Joy in the Morning, Autobiography of Malcolm X, the Vonnegut books, and others previously mentioned were listed in this period. In junior novels, S. E. Hinton's first book, The Outsiders, and Paul Zindel's first, The Pigman, both appeared in the late 60s.

As for the 70s, one can just dip in. It is our decade and we don't yet have the perspective of distance. A few books which stand out are: Herriot's All Creatures Great and Small and the sequels, Gaines' The Autobiography of Miss Jane Pitman, Read's Alive, Haley's Roots, Guest's Ordinary People, Kingston's The Woman Warrior, Baldwin's If Beale Street Could Talk. In junior novels, the books of M. E. Kerr, Richard Peck, Robert Cormier, Rosa Guy, and Anne McCaffrey come to mind.

A few books now under strong consideration for the 1980 list are: Ellease Southerland's Let the Lion Eat Straw, Robert Cormier's <u>After the First Death</u>, Ella Leffland's <u>Rumors of Peace</u>, R. D. Lawrence's <u>The North Runner</u>, and Carl Sagan's <u>Broca's Brain</u>.

    This has all been very sketchy. In the limited confines of an article such as this, it is impossible to do justice to the fascinating progression of books which have meant something to young adults over the past century, and all the implications of the rise and fall of their relevance. It should make a good doctoral thesis for someone. Meanwhile, bright new books continue to appear, containing all the various adventures of mind and deed. And as we talk to young people, try to anticipate needs, and choose among the new books for the fun and fact and feeling that will most appeal and benefit, there is always the hope that each year there will be a "find" (or two or more)--books good enough to mean something to some teen-ager for the rest of his or her life.

RITES OF PASSAGE*

Lois Ruby

> "My dear, we live in a time of
> transition," said Adam as he
> led Eve out of Paradise.
> William Inge

The sexual revolution surely began with Adam and Eve and the apple and that all-time Freudian symbol, the serpent. It didn't begin with the Flower Children of the 60s, or with the Women's Movement, when pantyhose liberated women from the bondage of girdles. Nor will it end with our generation, for it isn't a revolution at all; it's an evolution.

I would like to describe the sexual evolution in books for young people. Let's skip over the parlor courtship period, with Grandma sitting inconspicuously in the loveseat crocheting doilies. Let's get right to the ancient modern era, the Forties.

Boy meets girl, 1940s

Boy meets girl. Girl bats eyelashes, boy succumbs to her charms. Girl swoons, and her parents rush her off to Aunt Martha in Idaho. Boy plays baseball alot, and takes cold showers and does push-ups, until he's old enough to join the Army. With some good fortune, he's lost in action, and we never have to worry about him again.

Boy meets girl, 1950s

With relief, we hit the Fifties. Now, boy meets girl, and the battle lines are clearly drawn. Girl bats eyelashes, boy interprets this as come-on. He comes on. She grimly guards her honor as if she were a Vestal Virgin, while he sees her as one of the Sabine Women. They reach an impasse. She breaks up with him because, as

---
*Reprinted by permission of the author and publisher from Voice of Youth Advocates, October 1979, p. 9-14.

we all know, boys are after one thing. He finds a girl with a revolting reputation, and she finds a boy who has sublimated his urges into the school year book, and we end sadder but wiser.

Boy meets girl, 1960s

Fortunately the Sixties come along just in time, and things change radically. No one has sex in these books, but there's a pregnant girl in every story, as though babies come by mail order. A lot of people get married young, like MR. AND MRS. BO JO JONES, because obviously if a girl sleeps with someone, he's bound to be her intended spouse. Unless, of course, he's a big shot football star who's ill-used the wallflower, got her with child, and runs off down the field to score the point after. The girls in these books consider abortion for about two paragraphs, and then move on to suffer in silence. Birth control? No one ever heard of it. If you had sex, you got pregnant, shame on you, and disgraced your family. V.D.? Unmentionable. Homosexuality? Bisexuality? Masturbation? Not subjects fit for a nice young readership.

Boy meets girl, 1970s

Now comes the early Seventies. Boy meets girl. Boy doesn't notice her chest first thing; he's drawn to her mind. He calls her Ms. She pays for her own Coke and hamburger. BUT, he still has raging adolescent hormones. He says, "You would if you loved me." She says, "Should I? Everyone else does. Why not? What have I got to lose?" But he doesn't respect her in the morning. He says, "If only this were 1979, we could have a casual affair, but it's only 1972, and even though I'm kind of attracted to the track coach, I can't talk about this openly for about six more years."

And so to the present

Which brings us to the present. Boy meets girl. Girl says, "I like you, let's get it on." Boy feels threatened, can't perform (because he's read in a magazine that sex equals performance, in quality and quantity). Girl says, "So what, I'll go elsewhere for my needs. This is the time I can have an affair with my teacher." And he says, "Actually I prefer guys," and she says, "That's cool. We each do our own thing." And nobody gets married, not even their parents.

What's happening here? What's happening is that books for young people are changing with our social mores, but much more slowly. If teenagers, with one ear to the ground and the other to the transistor radio wrote books for one another, the changes might be more in pace with societal changes. But adults are writing books for teenagers, and we've got our own hang-ups about sex, our own possibly outdated sense of morality, and our own vested interest in being older, wiser and definitely in control.

Communication and Education

Anyway, how can we convince young people that virginity is the great prize, the ultimate wedding gift we give our spouses, when we know that more than half of the 21 million 15-to-19 year olds in this country are sexually experienced? When we read that gonorrhea is second only to the common cold as the most prevalent disease among teenagers? Obviously they are having sex. Puberty is occurring earlier with each generation, and the time between the onset of puberty and the onset of sexual intercourse is rapidly narrowing.

The mixed message

Well, they've probably said this in every generation, and perhaps nothing has changed. Generations ago people were married off early, before they became too aware of their sexuality, before they were tempted. Today, sexual cues are everywhere--in toothpaste commercials, on massive billboards, movie marquees, tee-shirts. It's common today for one's parents to be divorced, dating, rediscovering sex, playing sexual cat and mouse games. The overt message all around our young people is, DO IT IF IT'S FUN, AND SPLIT AS SOON AS IT ISN'T FUN ANYMORE. SEX IS okay. But is it really okay? No. The hidden message remains IT'S NOT OKAY UNTIL YOU'RE SAFELY MARRIED. Do you see what this gripping ambiguity does to young people? It causes mistrust, anxiety, confusion. Worse, it causes babies. I believe this mixed message directly contributes to the rise in teenage pregnancies. Each year more than one million teens become pregnant; one in five U.S. births is to a teenager. While this is alarming, it is not too surprising, because look what they're picking up from our mixed message. On the one hand, they believe that sex is good if it's natural, if it's spontaneous. And on the other hand, they're scared to ask their parents and teachers and doctors about contraceptives, because we adults clearly make them believe that if a young woman goes on the Pill, she's surely opening herself to promiscuity and degradation.

INSIDE TODAY'S BOOKS

While today's books for teenagers are certainly much more liberal and open, they still reflect the confusion we adult writers and book reviewers and librarians feel about adolescent sexuality.

I'm grateful for the chance to speak here, because it has forced me to evaluate my feeling and beliefs about teenage sexuality, and in the last two months, I've read everything I could get my hands on that even alluded to sex in books for young adults. I haven't been too open in my own books, so far. Of course, I've acknowledged that young people have sexual feelings, that they don't remain celibate, that they slip-up, get pregnant, even that they have sex that doesn't result in some sort of punishment (pregnancy being the standard literary punishment for the girl who's given in to the "You would if you loved me" syndrome). Incidentally, there's actu-

ally a book called You Would If You Loved Me, by Nora Stirling.
It's ten years old, and quite worn around the edges, aside from not
being too well written. It's been praised by clergymen, which is
probably the kiss of death. Of course, it turns out that the boy in
the story doesn't REALLY love her, because if he did, he surely
wouldn't ask her to give up her most precious possession, which is
--we all know what.

In Ursula LeGuin's book Very Far Away From Anywhere
Else, the girl also says no, but for much better reasons; not because her virginity is a sacred relic, but because she is unable to
commit herself to a sexual relationship since so much of her total
energy is spent in her music. Perhaps both writers are saying, "I
believe teenagers shouldn't copulate on the pages of a book," but
LeGuin says it so much better, without painting the boy as a hopelessly horny adolescent, or the girl as a high-collared tease whose
eyes say yes, but whose knees stay locked.

The tale of wisp and castrator

I'd like to compare two other books that openly handle sexual relationships. Neither could be classified as great literature, but one
treats the subject effectively, and one fails abysmally. It's much
more fun to talk about the failure. Norma Klein's Love Is One of
the Choices is my choice for the worst book of the decade for young
adults. I wasn't wild about Mom, the Wolfman and Me because it
bent over backwards to be hip and really into sex role reversal.
But that was the trend in 1972. Now Klein gives us the following:
a totally liberated, anti-feminine, wooden female, scared to death
of being dominated by a male, but who nevertheless slips out of her
shapeless denim overalls and into bed with some guy, while her
father's downstairs thinking it's marvelous that she's such a free
spirit. To me, the father seems irresponsible, and the girl comes
across as a totally castrating female. Then there's her insufferably
wispy friend--one wonders what on earth the two have in common.
Friend falls hopelessly in love with the science teacher. He seduces
her. They have a very hot affair, but of course he doesn't acknowledge her in the hallways of the high school. And what if her mother
finds out she's sleeping with the teacher? Not to worry. You see,
it turns out the mother is having her own affair, so everything's
cool. The teacher's wife conveniently cracks up and commits sui-
cide. Wisp and Teacher get married and pregnant, and live not too
happily ever after. Meanwhile, the one in the denim overalls has
an abortion--no second thoughts, of course--and her boyfriend paints
all sorts of people, including pregnant women, in the nude. And
everyone is so entirely liberal and up-to-date that it's almost like a
photo-realism painting, you know, like the larger-than-life Camp-
bell's Soup canvas.

The book doesn't work. It's humorless and dull, and worse,
it's a device with people plugged into all the modern sockets, but
shock-proof.

And then there is Ralph

Contrast this with Judy Blume's Forever. Here we also have two girls, one conventional and one a little off the wall. The off the wall one deals with her boy friend's impotency, while the conventional girl falls in love, wants to have sex, does, and eventually falls out of love. The difference between the two books is that Judy Blume covers the same material with tenderness, with dialogue like conversation overheard on a bus, and above all with humor. Anyone who has read Forever can't forget Ralph. At the same time, the book is quite informative. Sex in the book isn't always perfect; there's alot of bumbling about. The chapter where Katherine visits the Family Planning Clinic reveals how the examination is conducted, the interview, and the varieties of contraception. The girl's parents aren't saying, "Oh, we're just thrilled you're having a sexually satisfying relationship without marriage." Blume's book is realism on a deeper level than Klein's: this is how people ARE, not how sociologists say they SHOULD be.

Gay is here, too

Let me mention another medley of books, these dealing with homosexuality. Scoppetone's Trying Hard to Hear You handles most effectively, I think, a situation where two young men fall in love with each other. There's no limp wrist stuff here; both of them are sensitive, attractive to girls, quite masculine. It reminds me of something David Kopay said. He was the first nationally known football player to acknowledge publically his homosexuality. He compares himself to the black athletes who came out of the ghettos and into the forefront of professional sports. They were out to prove "that they were not inferior because of their race; I was out to prove that I was in no way less masculine because I was a homosexual."

Anyway, Trying Hard to Hear You handles the subject very openly and convincingly. The other young people in the conservative summer crowd on Long Island are incensed (perhaps read threatened?) by the male lovers. The kids are cruel, treat the boys shamefully at first, and ultimately come to a tenuous toleration of this homosexual relationship. Some grow more than others from it. On the whole, it's skillfully done.

Compare these relative innocents to Rita Mae Brown's outrageous Molly Bolt. Rubyfruit Jungle is not a YA book. Teenagers read it, of course; they read everything. But it's not a YA book because it has no moral point of view. I'm not concerned that Molly Bolt is a lesbian. I AM concerned that she is totally hedonistic. Brown allows Molly to act on all her impulses, everything from mixing rabbit droppings with raisins, to having wild affairs with other women. To act out all your fantasies, overcome all your inhibitions, shrug your shoulders at all those who try to overwhelm or control or limit you--this may be sanctioned adult FREE behavior. But teenagers cannot act on all their whims. If they do, they're

considered delinquents, incorrigibles, rotten kids. Nor would they
even want to. They seek reasonable limits from adults. They
thrive on the tension of unfulfilled fantasies. The best part of
Rubyfruit Jungle, I think, is the unbelievably moving scene between
Molly and her mother at the end of the book. This is the only part
of the book that rings true to me, the only tension in the story.

In the best books tension is the energy, the impetus, and the
most taut and skillfully written books are about tension, with no
excesses of sentimentality. I Am the Cheese, for example, is a
book in which the tension is sustained throughout. There was a
book a couple years ago by a fine Canadian writer, Margaret At-
wood. It's called Surfacing, and it is a most painful book to read
because the tension is never relieved, not even when the book ends.

The third book I want to mention in this medley dealing with
homosexuality is Isabelle Holland's The Man Without a Face. This
is easily the finest of the three books, because Holland handles some
very emotional and tender material with remarkable control. In
this story we have 14-year-old Charles Norstedt, a nice, normal
boy, bright, an underachiever, a little lonely. He has standard
family problems, including a thoroughly hateable older sister. But
on the whole, Charles is pretty well together--until he begins to
study with a seemingly heartless man whose face has been horribly
scarred in an accident. A fragile friendship grows between the two
of them, and Charles begins to feel something like love for Justin,
the man without a face. After a horrible night in which Charles
finds his sister and her boyfriend making love on Charles' bed, and
his cat at the bottom of the stairs, mangled and dead, he rushes
out of the house, terribly distraught. He runs to Justin, who
soothes him paternally. Charles has an ejaculation lying beside
Justin, and he is filled with shame and haunting doubts. Justin
comforts Charles, assures him that what has happened is perfectly
normal, that it does not mean that Charles, at 14, is a committed
homosexual. The pathos of the story, of course, is that Justin is
himself homosexual, but because he cares so very much for
Charles, he has carefully kept their intimacy non-physical.

I love this book for young teens because it's not at all unusual for adolescents to worry about being homosexual. They are
in a period of heightened sexuality, experiencing a welling up of
physical feeling for others of both sexes. This book points out that
what's normal behavior for one person does not have to be normal
behavior for another. Both are okay. And it does this with honesty
and immense emotional impact, making The Man Without a Face
one of the most memorable books I've read.

ABOUT MY WRITING GOALS

So far I've talked about books other people have written. That's
much safer than facing the fact, with you, that I've hedged away
from explicit sex scenes in my own stories, because I've never been

quite sure how to handle these scenes. I will continue to hedge away from meaningless pornography, but I am learning about how sex can be handled in fiction for young people. I am learning more about kids, about the craft of writing, about the convolutions of my own mind and the far borders of my limits. I won't go so far as to say that, like Lord Byron, "to my extreme mortification I grow wiser everyday," but I AM learning.

And these are some of the goals I am aiming toward in my stories for young people:

A foundation of morality

(1) To establish a foundation of morality--not based on virginity, or the loss of, but on a caring responsibility toward others. Sex used for exploitation, for domination, for humiliation, for one-sided pleasure; sex forcibly taken or deceptively given--all this, to me, is immorality. It is not immoral for a teenage couple to have sex without marriage, even without love. It IS immoral if one of the two pretends to love the other just for the sex. This honesty and mutual respect regarding sex are what I see as the moral issues.

Life as it is

(2) I want to show life as it is, as I understand it, but not a reality so bleak and merciless that there is no hope. I heard Hilma Wolitzer (Introducing Shirley Braverman and Out of Love) say recently that hope is the one thing that differentiates adult literature from children's literature. I read The Chocolate War the same week I heard Hilma Wolitzer, and while I think it is beautifully written, I was horribly depressed by its fatalistic outlook. I'm inclined to want to shelter young people from such brutal reality. I choose to write for young people, not adults; I choose to offer hope.

Books as education

(3) I would like to educate. All books for children and adolescents are, on some subtle level, didactic. That's because THEY'RE kids and we're adults. We're all teachers of youth, and why would we write for them if not to share some of what we've picked up on our journeys to middle age. Everything they read, like everything they hear, touch, smell, dream, expands their universe. In books for young adults we can teach about family planning, contraception, abortion, homosexuality, V.D., through fictional characters, in a non-threatening way. We can teach young people our own biases, which isn't necessarily bad to do. For example, we can show that sex without affection or respect is empty and not much more enjoyable than getting one's kicks going up and down on a merry-go-round pony.

The most important information other writers and I can impart to our young readers is that sexual feelings, thoughts, fantasies, and doubts are normal: that it's not unusual for adolescents to be attracted to people of their own sex; and that if they ultimately choose same-sex partners, and they're content and the partners are content, then they're going to have a tough time of it, but they're still okay.

I'll tell you something else we can teach young people: that maintaining the privacy of one's own body--virginity, if you wish to call it that--is a viable choice young men and women can make, because they want to, and not because adults tell them this is the right thing to do. Dr. Richard Lee, of Yale University School of Medicine, says that youth advocates overlook the most reliable and specific, least expensive and least toxic prevention of both V.D. and pregnancy, what he calls "the ancient, honorable, and even healthy state of virginity." My favorite recent passage on this subject is from Barbara Wersba's Tunes for a Small Harmonica. The girl in the story says:

> To say at this point in the story, that I was a virgin would be an understatement. I was not just a virgin. I was a monk. A nun. A contemplative. One of those angels in religious paintings who never have parts. I was, as a matter of fact, so sexually awakened as to be almost a neuter. Dutifully, and with great patience, I had read all the sex manuals of the day--books that described 204 basic lovemaking positions, books that recommended having sex in bathtubs and closets, books that told suburban housewives how to get jobs in massage parlors. I had attended pornographic movies ... and had sat there in a state of remote shock as though I were witnessing openheart surgery. Nevertheless, I was still as innocent as a kitten.

I think we can show in fiction that innocence can be by choice, not by default, and not merely a preventive technique or a negative, but a respectable, positive, rational option that may be right for some. Even though Anatole France said that of all sexual aberrations, chastity is the strangest, I suspect he wasn't referring to 16-year-olds parked in a car on Mulholland Drive.

But this brings up a vital point: young people today seem to feel a great pressure to, in the words of one teenager, "devirginize" with almost any willing partner. After all, we have no other puberty rite, no rite of passage from child to adult, and all the other cues are ambiguous. How do young people know when they actually reach adulthood?

Jeannie Melchione is a fictitious name given to a 16-year-old Boston girl quoted in the February 1979 issue of Psychology Today. Jeannie says:

> I don't even know what people mean by adolescent. It seems to me people nowadays jump from being a child to being an adult. You may not know that's what's happening,

but it does. It's like going on an airplane. You can't tell anything is happening. You certainly don't know how fast you're going. You just sit there. Then they open the door and you're in a whole new place--or anyway, you're supposed to be. It doesn't seem like time's even moving, but you're not where you started out. That doesn't mean I FEEL like an adult; I don't know what that feels like. I just mean I'm not where I was anymore.

Where are they, then, on this continuum of life? How do they know when they've magically become adults? Crossing the barrier from childhood innocence to sexual experience is seen by many teenagers as an assertion of adulthood, even though, as a number of recent studies point out, it's not uncommon for a teenager to cross this barrier, once, for the statement, and then return to a more childlike role that does not include active sexual behavior. In fact, a 1976 Johns Hopkins study concluded that teenagers are beginning their sexual experience at an earlier age, but are having intercourse much less frequently after the initial experience than was the case five years before.

However, this rush to "devirginize" is shocking to adults, who have been socialized to believe that sex is only healthy with marriage, with permanent commitment. But I submit that this getting rid of the burden of virginity while you're young and carefree isn't necessarily bad. It surely prevents anxious and disappointing wedding nights! More important, young people are delaying marriage until they are ready to settle down, make a commitment, rather than unraveling what Eric Toffler describes in Future Shock as "the long string of temporary marriages."

Characters to believe in

(4) The fourth thing I would like to do in my books is give young readers characters they can believe in--multidimensional people who can serve as behavior models or even rotten examples. I want to give readers in each story at least one character with a whole palate of emotional shades, with a sense of humor, of reality, of morality. And then anything that character does or says, as honestly as I can portray him, will be believable to the reader; not necessarily believed, but believable. This type of character is an excellent device for imparting information, values, and a myriad of acceptable feelings.

Unclogging communication channels

Yes, there are many things the writer can do for young readers, things all of us who are teachers, librarians, advisors, advocates of youth, can do. We can share information non-judgmentally. The library can be an open forum, a true information center where young people can get facts, where they can freely explore their own concepts and come to their own conclusions, within the limits of our culture. The library can sponsor adult/teen panels, helping to unclog the channels of communication between youth and parent, parent and school. What I'm advocating is that the YA librarian provide accurate, up-to-date information for reality testing. Murray Kappelman, in his book Sex and the American Teenager, describes the need for reality testing in this way:

> The neighborhood children begin relating feats of sexual expertise that simultaneously dazzle and frighten the young person. Here sexual success is equated with sexual prowess to suggest an athletic event rather than a mutual coming together of two human beings to express their feelings of love and affection. What the teenager gradually perceives as sexual adequacy then, is a totally distorted vision of normal sexual performance.

A teenager ought to have the opportunity to check this street information against the facts and values he or she finds in library materials.

The intimacy gap

Something else the library can do is provide an arena for non-sexual interaction of teenagers--things like rock concerts, book discussions, film festivals, community resource fairs, poster contests--all sorts of media related activities where young people can get together.

In other words, the library can begin to fill the widest gap which is swallowing up our young people, along with older people, that being the horrifying lack of intimacy in our lives. It seems likely to me that teenagers are embarking on early sexual relationships because they are starved for intimacy, and they perceive the joining of two bodies as the one and only means of intimate communication. Kappelman says we must teach teens that the "body is not the single force for communicating love and affection to the other person."

Look, they see adults afraid to touch, afraid of their own non-sexual sensuality. They hear us say that two guys hugging at the airport have GOT to be queers, and while we're more open now than we used to be, prejudices die hard.

Kappelman says we must help teenagers see that not all physical contact is sexual. They must see men and men, women and women, men and women, touch, hold, hug, without sexual overtones, at times, to test the reality of touching relationships they may have with their friends which need not toboggan into overt sexual activity.

Intimacy is what's missing in their lives. I came to this conclusion measuring my reading on adolescent sexuality against my experience with the people in a youth group I advise. The two didn't correlate at all well, and I wondered--almost worried--about how my Midwestern kids were hopelessly out of the mainstream of young adult life. After all, they're 15, 16, 17, healthy, developed; they've got hormones like everybody else, and they talk sex endlessly. But I've been on overnights with them, and nobody tries to climb into anyone else's sleeping bag. What's WRONG with my kids?

It's not what's wrong with them of course; it's what's RIGHT with them. They've grown up together in a small community. They are incredibly close, boys and girls together. They love one another, even the ones they don't like much. They cry together, laugh a whole lot, play physically, touch, kiss, hug, but non-sexually. They are a most intimate group. Now, I don't say that outside of the group each is as pure as the driven snow. I say only that these young people are fortunate to have intimate, relaxed, non-threatening relationships with people of their own and the other sex, and with an adult, so that they don't seem to be running headlong into casual sexual pairings to satisfy the human hunger for intimacy.

That word again, intimacy. What I want to give young people in my books, finally, is characters like themselves in all sorts of intimate situations--with parents, teachers, lovers and friends, clergy, with older people, with small children, with everyone. I want them to feel connected: connected to the Earth, to God as they perceive holiness, to other people, especially connected to themselves. And if the connection involves sex, there will be sex in my stories--not pornography, but honesty--and not always terrific, great-feeling sex. But the one compromise I will never make is in my belief that young people are entitled to a strong moral base in books designed for them. In my books it will be this: I will not condone my characters being users of people, sexually or any other way. And if my characters trifle with the feelings, bodies, or hopes of other people, the pain they've inflicted on others will surely return to them. Call it simplistic, Garden of Eden variety good and evil.

Christopher Morley once said, "The real purpose of books is to trap the mind into doing its own thinking." I'd like to do this to my young readers, trap them into doing their own thinking. But of course, writing is a two-way communication; I want something in exchange from them. I'd love for them to think of my stories the way a San Quentin inmate once described books: "Somebody's imagination stroking your mind."

Stroking--there's a loaded word today, and it brings us full circle back to sex. I'll leave you with the definitive word on the subject, Arthur Guiterman's pithy verse that goes like this:

> Amoebas at the start
> Were not complex:

> They tore themselves apart
> And started sex.

We are all so glad they did, of course, and who more-so than a young adult newly awakened to a symphony of sensations.

HOW WE CAN WIN:

A PLAN TO REACH AND TEACH

TWENTY-FIVE MILLION ILLITERATE ADULTS*

Jonathan Kozol

The problem is vast. The resolution is known and clearly within reach. The price of our refusal to confront the problem is unspeakable catastrophe.

Already, the dimensions of the problem dwarf the reaches of our comfortable imaginations.

Twenty-five million American adults can neither read nor write nor handle basic mathematical computations. An additional thirty to forty million American adults cannot read or write enough to understand a complicated danger warning on a bottle of medication, fire warnings in a factory, or instructions for operation of a piece of expensive and complex machinery in a warehouse. In few words, these people cannot hold even entry-level jobs.

The dimensions of the problem

A racial/ethnic breakdown renders these figures even more disturbing: Sixteen percent of white adults, 44 percent of blacks, 56 percent of those of Spanish surname, cannot read well enough to understand a want ad--or write well enough to fill out a relatively simple application for a job.

The personal price is repetitive humiliation, constant anguish, and the fear of being "caught." The social and economic price can be reduced to hard and measurable numbers. According to one source, the total cost to American taxpayers, solely in the funding of welfare programs and in loss of productivity, is at least six billion dollars yearly. Another six billion dollars are spent

---

*Reprinted by permission of the author and publisher from Wilson Library Bulletin, June 1980, p. 640-44; copyright © 1980 by The H. W. Wilson Company.

each year to maintain seven hundred thousand illiterate men and
women in Federal or state prisons. The loss of billions more dollars is attributable to needless accidents that lead to the destruction
of sophisticated technological equipment.

A simple example of the latter cost is documented by Senator
George McGovern in his speech of September 1978: "An astounding
thirty percent of Navy recruits ... are a danger to themselves and
to costly naval equipment because they lack basic educational skills.
One illiterate recruit recently caused two hundred fifty thousand dollars in damage because he could not read a repair manual."

The tragedy of the situation of the worker is underscored in
these words: "He tried [but] failed to follow the instructions."

A number of earnest efforts have been made to meet this
problem at the highest governmental level. Congress first addressed
the challenge of adult illiteracy in the Economic Opportunity Act of
1964--and again in the Adult Education Act of 1966. In spite of
these two major pieces of legislation, the current Federal allocation
amounts to only one dollar for each illiterate adult. The funds
available reach only two to four percent of those in need.

In 1972, Congress gave evidence of renewed commitment to
end illiteracy with the Right to Read program. The program was
downgraded six years later, in 1978, after being labeled a failure
by its own director.

The picture is not as bleak as it may seem from the statistics. There is no question that many men and women learned to
read and write as a direct result of excellent programs and painstaking efforts carried out by various government-sponsored programs, as well as by independent efforts carried out by earnest and
hardworking volunteers trained and organized by Literacy Volunteers
of America, Laubach Literacy International, and several other groups
that have been working at the grass roots throughout the past two
decades.

Hard work has been done. It has been done by good and
dedicated people. As we have seen, however, it has reached no
more than two to four percent of those in need.

Our task, in these first years of a new decade, is to reach
--and teach--those twenty to twenty-five million who have not been
reached before. It seems apparent that additional funding of ongoing
programs will not significantly alter the numbers of those who learn
to read and write. For those who have not yet been reached, it
seems apparent that something new is needed. That "something
new" is an approach that has never been ventured in this country:
an all-out effort, a total mobilization, a national campaign.

"Those who know, teach ..."

Up to this point in United States history, when we spoke of literacy efforts we were speaking of programs that involved at most two or three hundred thousand volunteers. In a nation of 25 million totally illiterate adults, it is obvious that a "literacy army" of at least five million volunteers will be essential if we are to train as many as five volunteers for every 25 illiterate adults.

How can we find so many potential literacy teachers? What methods will they use? Where will they carry out their work?

We will find them, if we dare to look and to transcend some of our age-old preconceptions, among the student populations of the high schools, colleges, and universities of the United States. Certainly we cannot hope to find five million volunteers among the teachers in the public schools. Those teachers who are already there, in largest numbers, will be obliged to stay. Many, moreover, will not be prepared to join a grass-roots struggle of this kind. Others may wish to join and help, but only in a supervisory role, or may be held back by permanent family obligations from the total, personal commitment to a struggle so consuming and so vast. It is not extravagant to suggest, then, that we might begin to look to students who are now in universities and high schools.

According to one scenario I have seen, students would first be formed into effective, tightly organized teams of twenty-five to thirty members each. Team leaders might be found among some of those highly motivated teachers who would otherwise be teaching the same students in schools or universities. In such a case, it would seem to make sense for college instructors to receive their customary salary from the college in which they would ordinarily be teaching. (Whether the colleges will agree to this or not is an entirely different matter; but it would not hurt to ask.)

Apart from all else, it seems to me that there is a high degree of practical and political logic in any plan that can liberate young people, for one full semester of their lives, from traditional courses such as "Problems of Democracy" in order to enable them, instead, to go out into the world and start to solve one of those problems.

In speaking of methods and of motivation, it seems to me that at least two issues are immediately at stake. One of them is the attitude of our youthful literacy workers as the energetic, but no longer patronizing, partners of their own illiterate pupils. The effort to transcend a long American tradition of benevolent, but too often condescending, generosity in earlier ventures of this kind may very well prove to be the most ambitious aspect of the struggle. There is a deep well of essential human kindliness and compassion in our nation; but there is at the same time--and in almost the same breath--a disturbing inclination to attempt to remake those who we help in our own image.

The consequence is cultural and psychological invasion of the least defended people in the land. It is, in my belief, for this reason above all others that literacy programs of the past have shown so little progress. The recipients of largesse from an outside party are seldom so eager, or able, to learn as those who work, with a sense of common cause, to win the power of the written word in order to possess and to transform some little portion of the world in which they dwell.

This leads, then, to the question of the methods we shall use. In every nation in which successful literacy campaigns have been carried out, the key to success has been a combination of the choice of teachers and the choice of words. In our own case I am convinced that we must not allow ourselves to choose a word, or a body of words, that come out of a preselected list of "appropriate vocabulary" chosen by others (experts, bureaucrats, or far-distant teachers), but rather to elicit--and then to give back again--the words that live already in the rich oral vocabularies of our pupils.

The words I suggest are called by some scholars, "active words," by others, "generative words." I call them "dangerous words"--strong and volatile syllables of passion and elucidation--the clarification, for example, of a complex system of oppressions that may or may not, before that moment, have been visible or vivid in the learner's mind.

What are examples of the kinds of words that we in the United States might logically attempt to use? I would not start with "Dick" and "Jane," but rather with words like "grief" and "pain" and "love" and "lust" and "longing," "lease" and "license," "fever," "fear," "infection," "nation," "doctor," "danger," "fire" and "desire," "prison," "power," "protest," "progress," or "police."

My purpose in suggesting these words is not to encourage a radical's version of cultural invasion by arrogant prescription. The goal is not to try to "plant" these words and concepts in the minds of those who wish to learn to read and write. The purpose, rather, is--first through the process of prior dialogue, later in the day-to-day relationship of teacher and learner--to dig down into the deep soil of those incipient concepts, dreams, longings, and ideals that exist already in the consciousness of even the most broken and seemingly most silent of the poor.

Where, in the most specific physical respect, would literacy instruction logically take place?

My suggestion would be to hold classes in the neighborhood, in the area where the people live. Prospective learners and teachers together might work at renovating an old discarded building in order to create a new literacy center for the client population. The center might offer a place of rest and sleep for literacy workers or a quiet place of study for the workers and their pupils during daytime hours. Being a joint venture, the product of the sweat and toil of both, the literacy workers might properly, and symbolically, hand over the building to the neighborhood people once the literacy work has been achieved.

It would remain--a symbol of decency, reminder of struggle --long years after the literacy workers have returned to their own families, to their studies and their homes.

Librarians: At the grass roots

What is the role of libraries and of librarians in all of the above?

From the very first, librarians have a natural, perhaps inevitable, stake in something so close to their own work and their professional concern. In the search for appropriate community members to represent the skeletal structure of a literacy drive, the local librarian is often the person best-suited to pinpoint those who have been articulate in enunciating the human needs of their community. In the more difficult search for the illiterates themselves, the local librarian ought to be in the forefront of those who know, locate, and encourage those in greatest need as part of a grassroots effort at recruitment. Humiliation of the most inhibiting kind will often render silent and withdrawn even the most intelligent man or woman. A neighborhood friend who has known that man or woman for long years--one, for example, who has seen that person timidly and tentatively explore the pages of a book, only to push it away in fear and anguish just at the moment when another man or woman would begin to read--that neighborhood friend, the person who directs a small branch library right on the block, for instance, is not only the one best-suited but potentially the most sensitive and subtle man or woman to sit down, disarm with honesty, and recruit with charm and decency the otherwise recalcitrant illiterate in our midst.

The library worker is in an even better situation to recognize and to identify potential literacy teachers, knowing so well those in the neighborhood who come back, day after day, week after week, in search of books to satisfy their curiosities and needs. When the campaign itself begins, the small branch library offers in many ways the ideal setting for the literacy lessons--at least before the literacy center is ready to move into operation.

From start to finish, there is every reason why the neighborhood librarians, school librarians--all, indeed, who work within the realm of libraries of any kind at all--should be in the forefront of the struggle to eradicate adult illiteracy in the United States.

In the vanguard

If much of the above is speculative and wistful, there is a certain amount of valuable collaboration between literacy and libraries that is already part of recent history.

In January of 1979, the National Commission on Libraries and Information Science--under the direction of Charles Benton and Jean-Anne South--initiated a series of conferences in Washington to raise the general consciousness of those in attendance about the dimensions of adult illiteracy and to bring together those who might, with most effectiveness, be able to work together to attack the serious nature of the problem. Among those present at the earliest session were Jean Coleman, Roger Farr, Tom Stitcht, Bettina Rubicam, Shirley Jackson, and Nancy Simpfle (representing George McGovern). Discussion was intense, constructive, and free-wheeling.

Three months later, after a second preparatory meeting, a major conference was held in Reston, Virginia. As the consequence of a lot of hard work by the staff of the White House Conference on Library and Information Services, a broad array of American educators, book publishers, and public-interest organizations came together for a valuable three-day meeting. Present and vocal among those who came together at this final conference of the spring were not only representatives of the sponsors, but also representatives of nearly every literacy group or coalition in the country. Leaders of Literacy Action, Laubach Literacy, Literacy Volunteers, and the Reading Reform Foundation mixed with members of the National Literacy Coalition--Yvonne Golden of San Francisco, Jack Wuest of Chicago, Tisha Graham of Boston. Government representatives were present too, as was the brilliant and articulate literacy scholar, Carman Hunter.

No miracles were wrought, and the multitude of differences between assembled parties could not possibly be resolved in such a short time. But a dialogue was begun among a number of determined and committed men and women who never before had the chance to meet each other. And a spark was struck, among those several hundred people who were present, that is still alive today.

Librarians do not have to prove themselves as vanguard workers in the cause of literacy struggle in this nation. They were there--and they were the leaders--when it all began.

Part IV

THE SOCIAL PREROGATIVE

Photo by Wayne Sides

WHITEWASHING WHITE RACISTS:

JUNIOR SCHOLASTIC AND THE KKK*

News media are reporting more and more incidents of Ku Klux Klan terrorism and murder, rising Klan membership, frequent Klan rallies and demonstrations, increasing verbal, written and physical attacks on Blacks, other Third World peoples, Jews, gays and union activists. Despite all this, a Klan member recently won the Democratic Congressional primary in the most populous district in California. Equally ominous are reports of increasing Klan recruitment in high schools around the country.

Given these developments and the Klan's history of bloodshed and terror, educators and parents should expect a recent article about the Klan in Junior Scholastic, the magazine for sixth to eighth graders (published by Scholastic Magazines), to be a well-documented exposé.

The article, entitled "Kids in the KKK," offers a few brief and distorted general comments about the Klan, information about (and the views of) two young Klan leaders, the views of a few students who appear to have little knowledge of the activities and history of the Klan, plus some speculation on "why" some young people join the Klan. By ignoring certain facts and misrepresenting others, the article gives a deceptive picture of the KKK.

The kindest interpretation of the article is that JS's editorial board wanted to present a "balanced" picture of the Klan, though why they would want to be balanced about the Klan is hard to imagine. (An unkinder but perhaps more realistic thought is that the editors did not want to offend readers sympathetic to the Klan.) Whatever the motives, many readers (see "Reactions" on the following page) find the article a decidedly unbalanced apologia for the Klan, biased in its presentation, naive--to put it mildly--in its lack of historical perspective.

What could children learn from the article? Given that most of the sixth to eight graders at whom JS is aimed probably don't

---

*Reprinted by permission of the publisher from Interracial Books for Children Bulletin, 11:5 (1980) 3-6, 21; copyright © 1980 by the Council on Interracial Books for Children, Inc.

know much about the Klan, they could easily take the article's description of that organization at face value:

> The KKK is a secretive organization that preaches the superiority of white people over all other races. The burning cross is part of their secret ritual. In the past [emphasis added], such crosses have been burned on the law [sic] of black families to warn them that the Klan could strike their homes. For years, the Klan used [emphasis added] its robes and ritual to terrorize people.

The paragraph quoted above--like the rest of the article--is insidious; it omits or misrepresents historical facts. The article fails to tell the whole story. Young readers who don't know about the Klan are told nothing of the Klan's terrorist attacks, its racist demagoguery or its virulent hatred of Blacks, Jews, Catholics, gays, labor organizations and others it deems unacceptable. Nor will they learn that the Klan's ideology of white supremacy has been--and continues to be--a direct threat for those who do not meet the Klan's "standards." Note, too, how the Klan's activities are described in the past tense--as if crosses are not still being burned in attempts to intimidate Black people (hasn't the author of the piece been reading the newspaper lately?). And why does the text say only that the Klan wanted to "warn" Black families--bad enough in itself, certainly, but again far from the whole story. Children need to learn that in its 100-plus years of existence the Klan has been responsible for the death, torture, mutilation and lynching of countless Black people, not to mention the desecration of Jewish houses of worship, violent attacks on labor organizations and the terrorization of numerous other groups.

The article's attitude toward the Klan becomes clearer in its description of a recent KKK rally. As if to emphasize that the Klan's rather intemperate behavior is a thing of the past, it paints a bucolic picture of current practices:

> This demonstration is peaceful. The Klansmen have gathered to hold a ceremony and make speeches. Solemnly, they raise one outstretched arm toward the burning cross. This is the Klan salute.

Considering the Klan's violent history and its use of the cross to terrorize, it is criminal to describe any such scene as "peaceful." (The Klan's use of Christian symbols and its version of Christian doctrine are nowhere discussed.)

The article continuously misrepresents the Klan's role, making it seem as wholesome as apple pie. It presents an interview with Aaron Morrison, an eighteen-year-old "Grand Dragon" and Klan Youth Corps leader. Such a nice boy, Aaron joined the Klan "because he saw too many of his fellow students taking drugs and wasting their lives." As if that weren't inducement enough, the Klan, says Aaron: "talks about the threat of communism. They

Photo by Wayne Sides

also talk about the need for tightly-knit families--that's what keeps
kids from going astray." Here's the Klan as defenders of the moral
life. Are readers to assume that to be anti-Klan is to be pro-drugs,
pro-loosely knit--or, even worse, pro-unraveled--families?

Only in the last paragraph of the interview with Aaron does
the issue of violence come up, and even there it's not clearly dealt
with:

> Aaron denies that the Klan would use violence. But as
> JS went to press, Aaron was being sought by police for
> questioning. Two shots had been fired into the home of
> a black family across the street. A police search of
> Aaron's home uncovered unlicensed rifles, pistols, brass
> knuckles, and bayonets hidden in the attic.

What does this mean? Are the weapons Aaron's--or perhaps his
family's? Should Aaron be considered innocent until proven guilty?
Is there any connection between Aaron's Klan membership and the
armory? The acts of violence that the Klan has always directed
at Black people--and others--are not discussed. The possibility
that Aaron's arsenal is a direct result of Klan policy is not even
considered. Why doesn't the author quote someone like Imperial
Wizard Bill Wilkinson, a Klan leader who says of the guns carried
by his men, "They're not for hunting rabbits. They are for wasting
people." Or what about Wilkinson's statement, "We're drumming
into the Youth Corps that there are other uses for baseball
bats than hitting home-runs."

An interview with Roy, another leader of the Klan's Youth
Corps, also presents a biased viewpoint without comment. Roy reports
that members of his Youth Corps get together once a month
to "exchange views and have fun." (Golly gee, do they go on picnics
and outings?) To make matters worse, Roy states,

> I joined the Klan because I had a lot of trouble with black
> kids when I was younger.... A person has to look at
> what's happening around the world. Take Africa....
> More and more countries there are turning to black-majority
> rule. Here in this country, we have affirmative action
> programs that give jobs to black people before more
> qualified white people are hired. What we need in this
> country is white-majority rule.

There is nothing to counter Roy's perspective. Nothing
about the history of colonialism or liberation struggles in Africa,
nothing about the long history of discrimination in this country that
affirmative action programs are designed in part to redress, nothing
that indicates that this country is under white-majority rule, much
to the detriment of minority peoples. Without such information,
how can young readers refute Roy's statement? How much more
likely it is that white children who have "trouble" with Black children
may think that the Klan does have "the answer." (The article,

The Social Prerogative 265

needless to say, does not deal with the "trouble" that Blacks have with white children.)

To "get some other views," the JS author interviewed some seventh and eighth graders who do not share the Klan's perspective. Unfortunately, none of those interviewed have much knowledge of the Klan (nor do any of them seem to be Black, Jewish, Catholic, Asian American or any other group threatened by the Klan). Says one,

> The problem with the Klan is that they want to force the things they believe in on other people. Only their way is right, according to them. They try to tell other people how they should feel and what they should think.

Says another youngster, "The Klan is against everyone except themselves." Again, an accurate but limited view of the Klan. How much more young readers would have learned if the author had interviewed adults better informed about the threat posed by the Klan.

Because the children interviewed don't know much about the Klan--or understand the threat it poses--they see the organization as irrelevent. One student reports that at her school, "No one here is singled out because of their color or race." Others echo her perception. "Racial problems don't really touch us here," reports a seventh grader. "Maybe that's because there aren't that many minorities here." Nobody talks about the realities of racism in our society. (The "racial problems" that one child mentions are, after all, usually taken to be open conflict between Blacks and whites-- and there is usually an implication that Blacks instigated the "problem.") The closest that anyone comes to condemning the Klan is a student who says that the Klan thinks what they are doing is right "in the same way that Adolph Hitler thought he was right." Since most children know very little about Adolph Hitler--or the consequences of his racist policies--this statement hardly counters the pro-Klan statements. To counter the pro-Klan arguments that author should have interviewed anti-Klan activisits; surely members of the Anti-Defamation League, the Southern Christian Leadership Conference or any member of the National Anti Klan Network would have been happy to say a few words. The children quoted simply are not knowledgeable enough to be effective spokespeople for the anti-Klan perspective.

Given children's ignorance of the Klan, it's not surprising that Klan membership is increasing among young people. The JS article glosses over the Klan's recruitment program, although a little alarm-raising would not have been amiss. As Time magazine noted:

> Today's KKK units are also trying to recruit children. In more than a dozen cities throughout the country, Klan sympathizers have distributed leaflets to high school students asking: "Are you 'fed up to here' with black, chicano and Yang [Asian] criminals who break into lockers

and steal your clothes and wallets?" The solution, according to the leaflet, is to join the Klan Youth Corps. At a KKK summer camp in Jefferson County, Ala., robed counselors teach girls and boys ages ten to eighteen the fundamentals of race supremacy and how to use guns. Time, (November 19, 1979).

It couldn't have been easy to discuss the Klan without mentioning racism, but the JS article does it--and that's undoubtedly its worst flaw. Nowhere does the article discuss the Klan within the context of a racist society. It ignores the pervasive racism that led to the formation of the Klan, that kept the Klan going and that feeds the recent resurgence of Klan activity. (An excellent article in Freedomways, Vol. 20, No. 1, entitled "The Ku Klux Klan Mentality--A Threat in the 1980's," provides the perspective the JS article lacks.) The fact that the Klan has been a constant presence in U.S. history for over 100 years--and not an aberration or the refuge of a few extremists as it is usually presented--is never discussed in the JS article. What has spurred Klan activities in the past and why the Klan is reviving now are also ignored. Surely these concepts would be valid and valuable topics for classroom discussion.

Instead of an historical perspective, the JS article gives young readers a psychiatric approach--with Dr. Joyce Brothers' comments on why some young people join the Klan. Dr. Brothers notes some of the factors that may motivate such children--a need for structure, a desire to feel important, lack of parental guidance, etc. Again, an explanation that's partially true. However, it's irresponsible--and totally inaccurate--to suggest that such factors are the only or even the main reasons that children join the Klan. (It also ignores the fact that many parents "guide" their children right into the KKK.) To focus on psychological factors obscures the role that institutional racism plays in our society, that the Klan enjoys considerable power and support in many areas, that racism is part and parcel of our U.S. heritage. (It should be noted that the material accompanying the JS article--a brief history of the Klan, a teacher's guide and questions for students--also ignores the realities of the Klan's history as well as racism. The strongly political nature of the Klan's activities--beginning with its successful efforts to disenfranchise Black voters during Reconstruction--is also ignored.)

The Klan has the last word in the JS article. The piece concludes with a statement from Klan Youth Corps leader Aaron Morrison:

> What the Klan is trying to do ... is to get the kids off the streets and give them something to do. We in the Klan believe that it's the Klan Youth Corps that holds the key to the future of the Klan. We have a saying, you know. It goes:
> "Whoever has the youth has the future."

Aaron is right--whoever has the youth does have the future. And that is why we should all be alarmed at an article such as the one that JS offers. We need to help children learn more about--and become motivated to change--an unjust social system, not present them with a whitewashed version of a racist terror organization that threatens the very survival of so many people in this society.

Reactions to "Kids in the KKK"

The Ku Klux Klan and its program for the American people have become of increasing interest to the national and local press. Unfortunately, the majority of articles written about the Klan have failed to examine the central part of the Klan program: genocide and terror against vast sections of the people.

Junior Scholastic's article "Kids in the KKK" continues this trend. Surely a magazine read so widely by U.S. school children should present an accurate and factual account of Klan activity. Conspicuously missing from the article is any mention of 1979/1980 Klan actions; just a short summary would include the following:

● A much needed health clinic in rural Alabama is attacked by the KKK because it is staffed by a Black physician.

● Migrant farmworkers, Black and white, are beaten viciously by the Klan in Southern Alabama because they share a common house.

● Demonstrators in Greensboro, North Carolina, are murdered by KKK and Nazi sharpshooters.

● Five elderly Black women from Chattanooga, Tennessee, are shot in the legs by the leader of the KKK in Chattanooga.

● Civil Rights demonstrators are fired on in Decatur, Alabama, by the KKK.

● Union activists are intimidated in Laurel, Mississippi, by a former member of the KKK who was indicted for the murder of a local NAACP leader.

● A cross is burned in July, 1979, in front of the New Haven, Connecticut, mayoral campaign office of the State Treasurer, the state's highest ranking Black official.

● A Klansman is charged with murder and arson in the death of a white woman in a fire in her home in Clinton, Tennessee in 1979. The fire was lit because the woman's sister had a Black husband and the woman had Black friends.

The list of incidents investigated by the Justice Department in 1979 and 1980 is twice as long as the list above. It includes activity in 24 states and more than 60 cities that involve allegations of violence.

The children of this country must be given a full picture of the sordid history of the Klan as well as its "companion in arms," the Nazi party.

We ask that Junior Scholastic print another article which reflects and exposes the real program of these racist, anti-democratic organizations. --Mary Joyce Carlson, National Anti Klan Network

•

"The Junior Scholastic article masks the fact that the Klan is training young people for racial hatred and thuggery. On subjects like this kids need real information--meat, not pablum. The Klan is no fun-loving secret club. The Klan kills. JS should know better."-- Holly Knox, Director, Project on Equal Education Rights, NOW Legal Defense and Education Fund

•

We have received several complaints about the article titled "Kids in the KKK." We find we must agree with these complainants, who feel that some parts of the article portray the Klan in such a benign way that some young readers may be moved to see the Klan as exciting, even attractive, and worth experimenting with.

It goes without saying that we do not infer any sympathy for the Klan or its obnoxious views on the part of the author or Junior Scholastic. Yet, in an apparent effort to present a balanced, objective picture, the article fails to convey the true, vicious qualities of the Klan and its long and all-too-clear record of racial violence and terrorism. --Irwin Suall, Director, Fact Finding Department, Anti-Defamation League

•

We are shocked by the Junior Scholastic article. It ignores and therefore reinforces institutional racism (a) by sympathetically presenting the young people who join the Klan; (b) by the use of the past tense to describe the Klan's acts of violence; and (c) by ignoring the continuation of terrorist activities in the present, as witnessed recently in North Carolina.

As librarians, we depend on accurate media reporting to provide information to our users. The JS article is destructively inadequate in this respect.

As library workers, we commend the coverage of the same topic in Southern Exposure magazine's summer 1980 issue in "Just

Like the Scouts: The Klan Youth Corps" (the issue, which contains a special section on the Klan, is available for $3. from P.O. Box 531, Durham, N.C.). --Social Responsibility Round Table, American Library Association

•

"Kids in the KKK" is an irresponsible article.

1. It is irresponsible at any time (but especially now when civil rights are so threatened) to print an article that distorts the history and purpose of a group such as the Ku Klux Klan. After reading this article, one could assume that any terrorist tactics (not to mention out and out murder) are part of the Klan's past, and that it is now a "club" with some strange but harmless rituals.

2. It is irresponsible to give the only answer to "Why do they join?" the fact that "many young people join the Klan because they lack parental guidance." WHAT HAPPENED TO RACISM? Certainly, racism is a far more pertinent and important motivation to discuss than the lack of "love and concern of a parent."

The thought that this article is being read by so many young people, giving them false information about institutions as deadly and as insidious as racism and the KKK, is truly frightening. The fact that it appears in an "educationally approved" journal is unforgivable. --Merle Froschl, Director, Non-Sexist Child Development Project, The Woman's Action Alliance

•

Racist oppression must be identified for what it is, and this the JS article fails to do. If the magazine editors had sought out current Klan literature, they would have discovered that hate-mongering and intimidation in that organization are alive and thriving. It is ironic that a magazine having the word "scholastic" in its title failed to research KKK literature or to interview the victims of the Klan's activities. Not only does the article not fully reveal current Klan oppression, but it also fails to portray the Klan in its full historical context of murder and violence. To say, "For years, the Klan used its robes and rituals to terrorize people" is woefully incomplete.

Unfortunately, times are right for the current resurgence of the Klan. People are overwhelmed by global crises and serious economic problems. Some find the scapegoat they need through organizations like the Klan. Others are so burdened that they ignore this threat to their own liberty. Charles Morgan, Jr. said it quite well: "Justice and liberty die quietly because men first learn to ignore injustice and then no longer recognize it." Action Against Apathy fears this is what happened at <u>Junior Scholastic</u>. --Action Against Apathy of St. Louis

•

Thank God for Junior Scholastic! It lets us know what our real problems are and who is helping to accelerate them.

The pretty picture of the Klan which JS painted has done more to shake us teachers out of our apathy than all of the recent shootings and killings in North Carolina, Georgia, Alabama, and other places combined.

If JS had been interested in showing the Klan for what it is, it could have chosen a gory picture for the cover; bodies lying in the street; a house unceremoniously burning while its new owners looked on; four innocent women being shot down like bottles in a shooting gallery.

I require of JS only what I require of myself and of those leaders I try to influence: "Become part of the solution, or remain part of the problem." It seems clear to most people who talk to me that JS is not intentionally a part of the solution, so.... -- Samuel B. Ethridge, Special Assistant to the Executive Director, National Education Association

●

After reading the article "Kids in the KKK," I got the uneasy feeling that I was reading an American rationale for the coming of fascism. The literature in Nazi Germany that preceded the rise of fascism differed only in degree. In the resurgence of the Klan, we now see an attempt to give the organization a respectability it never had before. This is most dangerous because the Klan's target is the American white youth who, 20 years from now or less, will be running for public office. The rash of articles about the KKK in other publications such as The New York Times and the magazine Esquire shows how far this dangerous trend has already gone. This new and most sophisticated Klan will test all of us to show where we stand in our commitment to racial democracy. Let no one say they did not know. --Professor John Henrik Clarke

●

Write for a free catalog listing the anti-racist, anti-sexist print and audio-visual materials developed by the Council on Interracial Books for Children, 1841 Broadway, New York, New York 10023.

CENSORSHIP VS. SELECTION

A ROUND TABLE DISCUSSION*

Deirdre Boyle

"The censor may attack anything. You can't avoid censorship."--John Robotham
"When we stop getting complaints is when we have to worry."
--Robert Allen

"Is it necessary to have a written film selection policy?" "When does 'selection' become a form of censorship, or self-censorship?" "How does one deal with censorship pressures or attacks on specific titles?" These and other searching questions engaged a distinguished panel of librarians and media center directors at a discussion held during the American Film Festival last May. The panelists were well-qualified for the task, since most had firsthand experience countering film censorship attempts in their libraries.

Connie McCarthy, film consultant for the Connecticut State Library, was "facilitator" for the session designed to cover selection in all types of libraries. School media centers were represented by Frances Dean, director of the division of instructional materials for the Montgomery County Public Schools in Rockville, MD, and current chair of the American Library Association's Intellectual Freedom Committee. She was joined by Dr. Clifford J. Ehlinger, director of the media division for the Grant Wood Area Education Agency in Cedar Rapids, IA. Speaking for public libraries were B. Penny Northern, head of the film department for the Kansas City (MO) Public Library; and John Robotham, a New York Public Library branch librarian and former chairman of the New York Library Association's Intellectual Freedom Committee. Robert Allen from Pennsylvania State University's AV Services discussed censorship in university libraries. Library schools were represented by Mary K. Chelton, assistant professor at Rutgers University Graduate School of Library and Information Studies, and a specialist in materials for young adults; and Dr. Ronald F. Sigler, assistant professor

---

*Reprinted by permission of the author and publisher from Sightlines, Fall 1979, p. 8-11, 13-14; copyright © 1979 by the Educational Film Library Association.

at the University of Wisconsin-Milwaukee School of Library Science, and editor of Sightlines' "Freedom to View" column. Angeline Suhr, AV librarian of the North Carolina State Library, joined Connie McCarthy in representing state libraries. EFLA librarian Maryann Chach provided background comments and questions.

The rambling, yet spirited four-hour discussion touched upon a number of controversial issues: labelling, community input, the "myth of objectivity," among others.

A Separate Written Policy?

Questioning the very premise for the meeting, the panel's first debate centered on whether there should be a separate selection policy for film. John Robotham opined that all media should be treated alike, because singling out a particular medium sets it apart. But Mary K. Chelton disagreed: "Inherent in a selection policy is some degree of 'taxpayer accountability', " she said. "Films are by definition extremely expensive. It is not unprecedented for libraries to make specific handling procedures for expensive print items. Constraints in purchase price as well as other industry constraints--distribution and leasing rights--call for a specific policy for films."

Also opting for a separate policy was Cliff Ehlinger, who countered with another argument: "I am concerned over what I'm hearing. Is it because of the cost of film that we need a separate policy? I don't quite agree with that. We're looking at film as a medium. It's the impact, how it's used, that really determines a separate policy for film, not because it may cost $300. The same statement can be said for video. Even if a disc is $15, it's the impact that affects your decision, especially if you are showing it to large groups. It's how the group process works with a medium."

Chelton agreed with Ehlinger, but added, "I have seen some very peculiar collection development because people couldn't afford the price. For example, a small film collection looking for a film on rape. I've seen [a film] glossed over for two reasons; there wasn't enough money to buy another film (they look for one film that will do everything); and the other reason was that the film demanded a discussion, it didn't 'stand on its own.' And librarians are notoriously terrified of anything that doesn't 'stand on its own,' whatever that means.

"I've seen a lot of people go for ... the lowest common denominator of filmmaking in that sensitive area. That's what worries me. Because if you don't spell out some of the cost considerations ... that kind of decision-making is going to go on."

Ron Sigler suggested that "a specific film selection policy directly related to the unique attributes of film as a medium of expression, which notes the unique contributions film makes as well as some of the problems film incites, might prevent some of the censorship problems that have occurred." Sigler was speaking from his own experience in the well-known film censorship case at the Los Angeles County Library, where he had been discouraged from developing such a specific policy, and had to rely on the library's general selection policy.

Angeline Suhr told how the North Carolina State Library was currently engaged in a censorship case of the film About Sex. Since the state library had no selection policy, the case is still pending; they can't defend the film until a selection policy is developed. She urged libraries to have a written film policy that clearly outlines the scope of the collection.

The panel expressed unanimous approval for a written selection policy for film, then went on to consider whether there should be one model policy for all libraries or individual models geared to the very different missions of some libraries.

The One and the Many

Connie McCarthy urged that there be one policy for every institution: "I'd like library people as a whole to acknowledge that the visual media have a power distinct from the printed word. I think that's a step toward integrating all audiovisual materials into the library."

There was discussion of the divergent needs schools and public libraries have for film selection policies, focusing on the range of materials considered and whether use was the determining factor. Schools have limited budgets tied to curriculum-based materials; they are generally restricted in the range of media choices. Schools must defend their media selections on the basis of their instructional use, often requiring board of education approval for materials shown to a "captive" audience.

In the instance of censorship of The Lottery, Frances Dean explained that schools do not defend the merits of the story or the film but its instructional use. Ron Sigler pointed out that one has a stronger case in court if policy is properly developed and the material in question is in your own collection, not borrowed from a public library or rented from a distributor. And Dean added that her library even has an approval plan for rental films.

In public libraries, on the contrary, there is the whole spectrum of film to choose from and a total population to serve. Owning or showing a film is not "tantamount to endorsement of its content" in a public library where free access to information, barring stated restrictions, e.g., to schools, is the case.

The panel, in the wake of this discussion, resolved to work on a model selection policy with broad recommendations that could then be adapted by institutions for their own purpose. Once agreed that there should be a written policy with broad application, the next consideration was: What should this policy contain?

"I think the principles should be the first thing, " Chelton said. "I don't think it hurts to reprint the First Amendment, given the ignorance of the Bill of Rights in this country. Then, an affirmation that libraries exist in general to make information available to an informed electorate, or something of that sort ... I wouldn't get into any procedural aspects until there was a very strong philosophical statement."

"I also agree, " she continued, "that the affective response to the visual media is almost limitless compared to print. If we could articulate that in some way, I think we'd be better off."

During discussion of the impact of visual media, debate arose over whether the panel was discussing film, visual media, moving visual media, or audiovisuals. There was some difference of opinion over the relative impact of the various media forms, which the discussion never clearly resolved, so films, visual media, and audiovisuals were used interchangeably throughout the rest of the session.

Maryann Chach suggested that, instead of using the expression "the power of visual media, " it might be better to emphasize that they appeal to a greater audience, in order to steer clear of the negative implications of "power." "There are more people who respond to audiovisual media than the printed word, " Chach said. "Since we are living in the age of TV and film, the visual media would have a greater impact on people than the written word. We can't cut out audiovisual media for that very reason. It's a necessary access to information."

Connie McCarthy commented on her recent censorship involvement with the controversial film About Sex. The local opposition had wanted an anti-abortion film shown, but the library board responded that there was sufficient print material in the library to adequately cover both sides of the question. McCarthy concluded that, "It's not necessary to match film with film, record with record, or book with book." But in light of consideration of the affective power and impact of visual media compared to that of print, McCarthy's assertion was challenged.

She agreed that providing an anti-abortion book is not the same as counterbalancing About Sex with another film. "But, in realistic terms, it's not something that you promise when you set up a film collection, " she said. "A balanced film collection doesn't necessarily mean it will show everything on all sides of all questions."

Frances Dean commented, "I would like to see librarians stop talking about 'balanced collections' (because none of us know what we're talking about), and go to a statement of needs assessment, because what's balanced for one library would change for another."

"In preview procedures, " noted Chelton, "if you've done a proper needs assessment (which I'm beginning to wonder if libraries of any type are capable of doing) so that you understand what you're attempting, it's almost mandatory politically to have community people sit in on the previewing and give their opinions. "

Community Input--In or Out?

Robotham registered worry that community input into selection was dangerous, "a tricky business. " "But because it's tricky, everybody's opted to avoid it, " replied Chelton. "The problem is, we can't judge the community per se by the loud mouths who make trouble for us. I remember how much it added to discussion to have Planned Parenthood people, people from the Association for the Retarded, representatives for whatever the topic of interest was. We would let people know what was being previewed to get their opinion. The level of discussion altered the level of ignorance of the librarians by 100%. "

McCarthy added, "It's extremely valuable, but it's awfully cumbersome. In every library in Connecticut, we have forms for groups to suggest films. It's been helpful; groups that have been quiet will send in surprising suggestions. "

"When I went to the Westchester County (NY) Library System, " Chelton noted, "I discovered that as far as the film collection was concerned, the women's movement had never occurred. So we ordered the standard films. The film librarian kept saying, 'No one will use these. We have no call for them. ' So we stacked the preview committee to get them bought. And then we sent some judiciously well-placed press releases to community groups we had identified that had never used film before. Now the films are worn out. That's why I come back to needs assessment. Friends and enemies hopefully cancel each other out. "

Robert Allen explained the situation in universities: "Faculty are involved, but when it comes down to the decision of buying, they are not involved since the funding is controlled centrally. We can't buy everything that has been evaluated. "

"We've gone with the term 'recommendation committees', " Ehlinger said. "This avoids the term 'selection. ' It's outlined for the committee that I have final authority on what is purchased, based on input from many sources. "

Getting community input was seen by the panel not only as helpful in making the initial selection of films, but also as insurance in fending off censorship trouble before it arises.

"Watching the court fight over the book **Our Bodies, Ourselves** in Prince George's County, " Chelton told, "showed how the local groups the YA services people had worked with came out with letters of support and lined up at hearings to get a local obscenity bill defeated. ... "

"This all goes back to the recommendation committees, " Ehlinger said. "If I can say I am getting input from someone on the committee, rather than say I talked with a film rep who dumped it in my collection, or if I give a teacher's name--that's the kind of accountability I need. "

Allen agreed with Ehlinger, but added, "I will say that we had seven faculty members evaluate a film. I won't identify them, because I don't think it's fair to put someone in the hot seat. "

Taste--A Can of Worms?

Chelton reluctantly raised the question of taste--"A major can of worms in all book selection policies, " she noted, "because taste is based on a myth of objectivity ... I think there should be some broad aesthetic criteria, saying that there are a variety of formats and taste levels in the country. Insofar as it is financially possible, film librarians will attempt to accommodate them, so that people who like the television mode of cinema can see it, and people who like the most avant-garde, independent film can see it. "

John Robotham capped the policy discussion by reading the New York Public Library's selection policy, which included a description of the community served and the goals and objectives of the library; indicated who had authority for selection and responsibility for maintaining the collection; provided a statement on withdrawals, discards, and gifts and a statement on Freedom to Read. Under this last item were subtopics on controversial materials--outlining that they were to be acquired, a section on age, plus others on closed shelves, labelling, and complaint procedures.

The panel agreed to recommend that libraries make needs assessment a first priority. As for a selection policy, the panel decided to begin with a broad philosophical statement that quoted the First amendment in its entirety plus inclusion of EFLA's Freedom to View statement, followed by an acknowledgment of the power of audiovisual media and their capacity for affective experience. Next, came a statement of the unique characteristics of audiovisuals and the necessity for providing access to audiovisual information, thus recognizing all the information needs of the population.

Complaints and Appeals

The subject of complaints and appeals procedures engaged the panel at length. To McCarthy's question--"What should be in a complaint form?"--Robotham urged serious consideration of the title of the form, recommending a positive tone. The New York Public Library uses a form titled Patron's Comments on Library Materials. Chelton said, "I don't think it should be called a 'reconsideration form. ' The form is promoted to keep the censor at bay, but this implies you will reconsider and throw out the item if everyone agrees. No one uses a form with that in mind. The title should be positive."

Sigler thought the form should ask, "Have you seen the work in its entirety?" since many censors have only heard or read about the film they object to. Robotham suggested including, "What item would you put in its place?" But Chelton objected, saying, "I'd rather see something like, 'If you find problems with this or feel it doesn't adequately represent your point of view, what would you like us to consider for purchase that did respond to your point of view?' Always leave the person with the feeling that we do consider other points of view, but we'll add, not substitute."

McCarthy suggested, "What are your comments? How do you feel about it?" But here Dean objected, saying, "There's a danger in getting it too simple. Some committee will be using the form for reevaluation. The more information that is given, the more helpful it is if you're going to do an honest job of reevaluating."

"There's a fine line between someone legitimately offended who, once acknowledged, may feel she's been heard. Giving someone a stuffy form makes him mad as hell, and then you've got a vendetta," said Chelton.

"I think you have to regularize it," McCarthy said. "You have to ask what the problem is, and you have to have an action resolution, whether it be reconsideration or whatever. That's the rough part. You can't just ask for comments."

"It's also important to tell them what will happen," Dean noted. "And possibly a deadline for response," added Chelton.

Dean explained her procedures. "When I get a complaint, the first thing I do is acknowledge receipt, say what I'm going to do with it, and give the projected date the person will be getting a letter from the Superintendent." (For schools, the Superintendent and the Board of Education are typically the ultimate authority; in public libraries, the chain of command ends with the Board of Trustees, the County Commissioners, or perhaps the County Board of Supervisors.)

Chelton returned to the format. "I just want the tone of the form not to escalate an emotional complaint. I don't want to promise something I can't deliver. I'd rather leave the action open-ended.... And you also need internal procedures to back you up with an appeal. These procedures should also include what to do when someone bypasses you." She explained a case at Prince George's County Library where the complainants went directly to the president of the library Board of Trustees and from there to the County Board.

McCarthy contributed her experience in Waterbury, CT, where a Right to Life group, protesting <u>About Sex</u>, went straight to the mayor, who promised, "I'll get that film out of the collection."

"When you go to court, if you have a complaint procedure, that is your first line of defense," Dean advised. "You should formally have your policy adopted by whatever the governing board is-- the board of directors in a public library or the elected school board. You also need to have an appeal process. Parents complained about The Learning Tree, and the Superintendent decided our system would continue to use it as a book, and it was all right for kids to use the film, bring it in, whatever. A parent appealed that decision to the Board of Education, and the Board held to the Superintendent's decision. Now it's going to the State Board of Education. You do need a structure to handle complaints.

"About Sex" and the Library

"We didn't have adequate structures," Penny Northern began, "so we were a prime example of what happens in many places. When we put ABOUT SEX in our collection, my intuition prompted me to have several groups look at it, including my boss, so that he was aware that we were considering it. Later, the decision was made to buy it, and that decision was mine. The film circulated in the collection for two years. And then out of the clear blue we were contacted by an irate patron who said, 'Heads will roll because this is in the collection.' I think we said things we mightn't have, had we not been caught off guard.

"This was why Mr. Jenkins, my boss, decided to stop circulation on the film to the extent that we didn't take additional bookings. We did honor the bookings in the file, but he wanted the film on the premises so that anyone, board member or patron, who wished to see the film could come in, and it would be available. (We only had one print.) That was why we kept the film for three weeks, without taking additional bookings.

"There was some comment about this. Some people interpreted that to mean we were pulling it out of the collection. That wasn't our purpose. I think it is a credit to the community that it didn't create more of a hassle. We had a few letters to the editor of the newspaper, pro and con, and no more than a few phone calls. A radio program director looked at the film and devoted an entire evening talk show to it.

"The radio station went to the trouble of inviting Mr. Martinez, the man who was in the film, to come, but he was in Hawaii at the time. So they arranged a telephone hookup. Martinez was able to talk, particularly to the woman who was the most vocal complainant. She was out to sink Planned Parenthood, not the public library. We were simply tools for her."

Dean asked Northern if she had had a complaint procedures process to follow. "No," said Northern. Then, McCarthy asked if the film were reviewed by a committee again.

The Social Prerogative

"No, " Northern answered, "Mr. Jenkins thought perhaps it should be, but I said, 'How many more seals of approval do we need? We've had the film two years; it's been out almost 100 times, and out of that number, one person has made a vocal complaint.' 'You're right,' he said. 'The greatest committee of all has already spoken, the community that uses the film.' That was the very day he lifted the ban on additional bookings. From then on, no more problems.

"One year later, the same woman sent another letter to the editor. I felt one of her hangups was that she had never understood the difference between the role of the public library and the role of the school. Her letter said, 'If the schools rejected that film as being unsuitable in the Kansas City School District, why is it still in the public library?'"

"I think, " Northern continued, "the teacher has some accountability. There should be some policy or procedure that the schools have for materials which they use. There's indiscriminate use of films from public libraries in schools."

Angeline Suhr explained how one copy of About Sex had been removed from the North Carolina state film collection, and another print had been "edited" by a borrower who cut out several scenes.

McCarthy commented that librarians should be aware that some national organizations send out newsletters alerting their members to check their libraries for "explosive, dangerous material." She attributed such a campaign to the widespread attack on About Sex.

Ehlinger explained that most of his film reconsiderations are on nonsexist or multicultural grounds, especially for older films. His reconsideration committee is appointed for a year and meets four times. These meetings are scheduled in advance and cancelled if there are no complaints. This way, sessions occur routinely, so that "it doesn't seem like fire fighting."

Any items, print or nonprint, that are challenged are brought to the regular meeting, and resource people from the schools--teachers and curriculum specialists from the district, other districts, and the university--serve as experts on that material.

Labelling

If a film is full of four-letter words or graphic nudity, does one say that in the catalog? Are you imposing a value system on the film by doing so?

Dean submitted that this wasn't labelling. "I think that's just telling it like it is. The more information you give people about the film, the better."

Robotham noted that "labelling speaks to the fact that some libraries set aside sections of books with Xs on them, branding them as questionable materials. And then there are separate catalogs, for YA materials, for example, and that in a sense is labelling."

McCarthy suggested that "what we're talking about is total access to the collection without characterizing certain films." And Ehlinger furthered that comment by saying, "Total access is making every film available and providing some type of information for individuals relative to content."

"Perhaps since we're always saying that procedures will have to be locally adapted, we should say that political and negative labelling should be proscribed," Chelton concluded.

Self-Censorship or Poor Management?

Deirdre Boyle outlined a situation where librarians will hesitate to buy a film from a filmmaker or small, unknown distributor because they are not sure they will be able to secure replacement footage or duplicate prints five years later. When such concerns enter into a selection decision, she believes it constitutes self-censorship.

Boyle presented a second form of self-censorship--inadequate cataloging--because of the potential cataloging has to limit access to a collection. Last, Boyle suggested that internal censorship occurs when the proper environment for viewing and hearing audiovisuals is not provided. While these may not be as dramatic as someone threatening to remove a film from a collection, such practices constitute ways the public can be barred from access to audiovisual materials.

Ehlinger countered that the latter point was not really censorship but poor management. He said that if his viewing facilities are inadequate, then he is not discriminating against any specific film. And Dean said she would hate to be accused of censorship every time anything goes wrong.

But Boyle stressed the chronic state of inadequate conditions, noting that this reflects a lack of understanding of the unique characteristics of audiovisual media or a lack of concern that playback must be adequate.

Dean maintained she had problems considering censorship restricting use as the kind of censorship you go to court over, and she insisted this was poor management. Boyle replied that it is not the same _kind_ of censorship, but that it is potentially more dangerous because it is so subtle and insidious within libraries.

Chelton said, "If you don't take practical access matters into account, and you take a purist view of censorship, then people pat themselves on the back. They're not going to court, and they're buying everything that's wonderful, but they're impeding access in a variety of ways."

Chelton addressed another self-censorship issue. "I'm constantly seeing in preview committees absolute terror about buying a film that is very provocative and needs a discussion. Too many librarians prefer the blandest pseudo-objective film where all you have to do is start a projector and scuttle out of the limelight as soon as possible. I go around looking for films that will be provocative discussion starters, and I have a terrible time when I suggest that they be purchased for collections. I don't know what we can do about this. Part of it is a staff development problem; we have to tell the preview and film librarians that they don't necessarily have to be the person to lead the discussion, but discussions are valuable."

Maryann Chach asked the panelists to name other films they knew of that had provoked censorship battles. She began with California Reich. Others added How to Say No to a Rapist, and on Public TV, Blacks Britannica (WGBH) and Black Perspective on the News (WNET). Chelton mentioned the New York Library Association's Intellectual Freedom Committee's tilt with Time-Life over its decision to withdraw or limit distribution of several BBC-TV films on nuclear power, among them Go Play in a Nuclear Power Park, films for which Time-Life has sole U.S. distribution rights.

The Good Fight

The panelists ended their debates, still arguing pure censorship versus functional censorship, with some minds changed about the necessity of a separate film selection policy, and better informed about the censorship concerns of school, university, state and public libraries. As survivors of censorship attempts, the panelists remained undaunted, and better aware of what it takes to fight another day.

FREEDOM OF INFORMATION ACT EXCEPTIONAL OPPORTUNITY FOR THE SPECIAL LIBRARIAN*

Robert V. Cuddihy

In 1966, Congress enacted the Freedom of Information Act (FOIA). Its purpose was to solve a particular problem: the tendency of federal officials and agencies to restrict public access to government information and documents. The concept of "freedom of information" had not previously been recognized in federal law. Until 1967, public access to documents held by the executive branch of the federal government was controlled by a "need to know" policy, derived from a 1789 housekeeping statute authorizing agency directors to prescribe regulations regarding the custody, preservation and use of records and papers. A provision of the 1946 Administrative Procedure Act indicated that matters of official record should be made available to the public on a "need to know" basis; but also stated that an agency could restrict access to its documents "for good cause found" or "in the public interest."

The federal bureaucracy had become conditioned to a policy of official secrecy by the experiences of World War II and the subsequent Cold War period. The selective and sometimes destructive use of internal government information for witch hunts by Senator Joseph McCarthy--one of the most vociferous critics of government secrecy--and the efforts by the Eisenhower and Kennedy administrations to reduce the Executive workforce, encouraged the federal bureaucracy to resist having its activities and operations disclosed to the public, the press, or to other government entities. The prevailing law tolerated this state of affairs, offering no clear procedure for gaining access to government information. Then, in 1966, the "need to know" policy was reversed.

The passage of the Freedom of Information Act established the rights of private citizens to obtain information from the govern-

---

*Reprinted by permission of the author and publisher from Special Libraries, 71:3 (March 1980) 163-68; copyright © 1980 by Special Libraries Association.

ment and the duty of the government, in many cases, to provide it. As stated in the Attorney General's 1967 memorandum, the act is based upon the theory that "a democracy works best when the people have all the information that the security of the nation permits" (1). However, a careful and thorough reading of this memorandum suggests that the senior officials of the Justice Department entertained a less-than-enthusiastic and rather restrictive view of the new law. Subsequent practices in many agencies mirrored this feeling, leading Congress to amend the Freedom of Information Act in 1975 to compel more frequent and rapid disclosure.

Since that time, a significant number of papers have been issued describing legal challenges to non-disclosure (2-5); the administrative practices surrounding the law (6-8); avenues open to prevent disclosure of government-held information (9-11); and proposed amendments to prevent allegedly unintended applications of the law that have become customary practices (12, 15). To the author's knowledge, there have been no papers published guiding the information specialist through the vast array of available government data and the means to access it for the benefit of individual organizations.

The FOIA regulations have generated tens of thousands of requests each year for information from various agencies of the executive branch (16). Used skillfully, FOIA offers management a potential tool to gain strategic competitive advantages.

Types of Information Generally Made Available

Under the Freedom of Information Act the following information must be published in the Federal Register by each federal agency:

1) Central and field office locations, staff organization, and methods whereby the public can secure information;
2) The general methods by which its functions are channeled and determined;
3) Rules of procedure and forms involved for requests;
4) Policy statements and substantive rulings of general applicability.

In addition, each agency must make the following information available to the public:

1) All final opinions (concurring and dissenting) and all orders made in adjudication of cases;
2) Those statements of policy and opinion informally adopted by the agency and not published in the Federal Register;
3) Administrative staff manuals and instructions to staff members that affect any member of the public. Here identifying details may be deleted to protect individual privacy;

4) All other records, except those expressly exempted by the law, upon request and within published rules for time, place, and fee;
5) Agency proceedings.

Exemptions from Disclosure

Specifically exempted from disclosure are nine categories of information:

1) Agency personnel and medical records;
2) Trade secrets;
3) Inter- and intra-agency memoranda;
4) Investigatory files for law enforcement purposes;
5) Classified national defense and foreign relations secrets;
6) Records specifically forbidden from disclosure by some other law;
7) Exclusively internal management matters;
8) Bank examination records;
9) Certain mineral geology information.

Attempts by corporations to obtain union registration data in certification of bargaining agent actions before the National Labor Relations Board have been denied (13). This data has been held as "confidential commercial" information in three federal court districts and upheld on appeal in the New York district (14).

Congress' original intent in designing the Freedom of Information Act was to encourage and permit the general public to monitor governmental decision-making. The legislative history of FOIA indicates that its authors did not want it to be a vehicle for competitors or members of the public to delve into sensitive company files (15). The drafters of this legislation particularly envisioned the frequent application of its principles by members of the news media. However, agencies report only rare utilization of FOIA by these individuals (17, 18). Far more commonly, FOIA has been employed by private industry to require the federal government to facilitate competitive snooping. This is to be expected considering that agencies of the federal government have functioned for several decades as ubiquitous collectors of data on virtually all facets of American life, including corporate life, and since FOIA administrative procedures are intended to create an inherent agency bias in favor of disclosure. As one prominent Washington, D.C. attorney remarked: "The opportunities for gaining information about your competitor and his products are limited only by your initiative" (19).

Creative Uses of FOIC

With a little creativity, special libraries can also access information and documents that might be of benefit to their organizations. The following are prime examples of information that have been suc-

The Social Prerogative   285

cessfully extracted from the government under the Freedom of Information Act:

1) Company facility inspections conducted by any one of hundreds of individual agencies (sought either by the company itself or its competitors) (18);
2) Affirmative action plans, equal employment opportunity forms and compliance review reports (13);
3) Audit reports pertaining to allowability of costs incurred by a government contractor (15);
4) Operational manuals and compliance policy documents prepared in any agency (13);
5) Administrative enforcement records compiled by any agency (13);
6) Internal Revenue Service (IRS) instructions to its staff, all final opinions and orders made in adjudication of cases, and IRS policy interpretations employed within the agency (20, 21);
7) Scientific and technical grant applications made to federal agencies, whether they have been approved, rejected or remain pending (21, 22);
8) Federal Trade Commission investigational data in such areas as restraint of trade, impact of advertising on specific markets, and so on (18);
9) Virtually all scientific research data developed by the federal government directly or under grants, subject to national security considerations (24), plus a considerable body of data submitted by private industry to various agencies, subject to "trade secret" interpretations (25, 26);
10) A potential alternative to conventional criminal discovery procedures (27);
11) Personal files on individuals, held by virtually every federal agency (4).

Through its inspection and decision-making activities, the government plays a judgmental and regulatory role in the business world. Most business organizations, therefore, are vitally interested in data relevant to this activity, eg., site inspection reports, orders and final decisions in individual cases (whether made public or not), data upon which agency decisions were made, and operational manuals for various agency functions. One can readily visualize the gold mine of information, both governmental and privately submitted, that rests in this area.

Before FOIA became effective, the government functioned like a restrictive library, revealing only a small volume of its total data, usually through the mechanism of published documents and reports. FOIA has now transformed our government into a more open library with few "closed stacks." In the light of these developments, it is worthwhile to examine procedures for applying the Freedom of Information Act to specific problems special librarians may encounter.

Procedural Access to Federal Documents

The first step is to develop an approach for establishing awareness and identification characteristics of potentially relevant federal documents. Systematic review of the Federal Register, trade publications, the Congressional Record, and various government reports is essential. Although some corporations have established offices in Washington with explicit FOIA monitoring responsibilities, most organizations presently appear to be availing themselves of the services of one or more members of the vast FOIA "cottage industry" that has sprung up in the Capitol. These groups scan, on a daily basis, all publically available new information, reporting those items of potential interest to their clients. Items identified through this process or which come to attention through any other mechanism, may be requested under FOIA.

The general procedure for filing a FOIA request is as follows. In the Code of Federal Regulations (CFR), usually at the beginning of the regulations for every agency or department, there is a section devoted to public access to the documents of the agency. This prescribes the procedures to obtain information from that agency. The person making the inquiry is required to file a request that "reasonably describes" the desired information.

Usually, the envelope containing the request should be labeled "Freedom of Information Request." The reason for this is that there is a statutory time limit placed upon FOIA requests. The agency has ten days to inform the applicant whether or not it will comply with the request. In exceptional circumstances, the agency may be given an additional ten days to answer. The label clearly expedites transferral of the request to the proper office.

If the request will be met, access to the records is not to be obstructed by cost. Although agency fees will vary, ten cents per page has been the average charge for copying, while FOIA search fees start at under five dollars per hour. Congress expressly insisted that agencies recover only the direct costs of search and duplication, not including examination or review of records. Congress also specifically required each agency to make available for public inspection and copying a current index identifying information to facilitate public requests.

Making an Appeal

The speed of reply in providing the actual information requested varies with the agency and the complexity of the request that has been made. Generally, an FOI inquiry will be handled in a timely manner, ranging from a matter of days to a few weeks. If a request is denied, it may be appealed to the agency head who, in turn, has 20 days to reply.

The enforcement provisions of the Act are focused upon the time frame for reply. If an agency does not reply within the statutory length of time, or if the request has been denied, administrative remedies may be considered exhausted. The next recourse is to appeal to the district court. Filing complaints under FOI can be expensive, although the court has the latitude to assess attorney's fees and court costs if the suit succeeds. Initially, it may be preferable to restate the request, indicating an intention to pursue the matter in court, if necessary. The Justice Department is less likely to defend an agency in an FOIA suit with each passing year as its backlog grows. Sometimes a more assertive approach will succeed after a first failure.

Value of Information Obtained Under FOIA

The primary value of information obtained under FOIA tends to be strategic rather than tactical. In the first place, the time requirement for actually obtaining the information may be several weeks (or even several months). Secondly, most governmental information gathering tends to be retrospective, focusing upon the past. Thus the time lags in the system tend to restrict the use of FOIA-derived information primarily to long-range strategic planning and actions. Examples of this type of material might be agency operations manuals or tabulations of administrative decisions. These might lead to significant insights into current agency philosophy or modus operandi. Similarly, data obtained from a competitor's data submission to the government may offer valuable information on his capacity, employee training, or even design specification from a federal contract.

A great deal of valuable information can be derived from the government, particularly if one's needs can be anticipated months in advance. In these situations, the opportunity for intelligence gathering is vast. Every information professional could do well to become acquainted with the provisions of FOIA and the means to use it for competitive advantage.

References

1. Attorney General's Memorandum on the Public Information Section of the Administrative Procedure Act (II), 1967.
2. Lacher, M. D. /The Freedom of Information Act Amendments of 1974: An Analysis. Syracuse Law Review 26:951-993 (1975).
3. Developments Under the Freedom of Information Act--1975. Duke Law Journal 1976 (no. 2):336-408 (1976).
4. Developments Under the Freedom of Information Act--1976. Duke Law Journal 1977 (no. 2):532-564 (1977).
5. Furby, T. E. /The Freedom of Information Act: A Survey of Litigation Under the Exemptions. Mississippi Law Journal 48:784-817 (1977).
6. Relyea, H. C. /The Freedom of Information Act: Its Evolution and Operational Status. Journalism Quarterly 54:538-544 (1977).
7. Relyea, H. C. /The Provision of Governmental Information: The Federal Freedom of Information Act Experience. Canadian Publications Administration 20:317-341 (1977).

8. Cox, M. P. /A Walk Through Section 552 of the Administrative Procedure Act: The Freedom of Information Act; The Privacy Act; and the Government in the Sunshine Act. University of Cincinnati Law Review 46:969-987 (1978).
9. Reverse-Freedom of Information Act Suits: Confidential Information in Search of Protection. Northwestern University Law Review 70:995-1019 (1976).
10. Sher, I. /Openness in Government: Protecting the Informant's Confidential Information Against Discretionary Release. Federal Bar Journal 34:348-351 (1975).
11. Wallace, Jr., J. H. /Proper Disclosure and Indecent Exposure: Protection of Trade Secrets and Confidential Commercial Information Supplied to the Government. Federal Bar Journal 34:295-300 (1975).
12. Gilson, Jr., R. P. /Administrative Disclosure of Private Business Records Under the Freedom of Information Act: An Analysis of Alternative Methods of Review. Syracuse Law Review 28:923-980 (1977).
13. Connolly, W. B., and J. C. Fox. /Employer Rights and Access to Documents under the Freedom of Information Act. Fordham Law Review 46:203-240 (1977).
14. Labor Letter. Wall Street Journal 182:1 (Dec 12, 1978).
15. Patten, T. L., and K. W. Weinstein. /Disclosure of Business Secrets Under the Freedom of Information Act: Suggested Limitations. Administrative Law Review 29:193-208 (1977).
16. Montgomery, D. B., et al. / The Freedom of Information Act: Strategic Opportunities and Threats. Sloan Management Review 19:1-13 (1978).
17. ASNE Problems of Journalism. Proceedings of the Convention of American Society of Newspaper Editors, Wash., D.C., 1973, p. 256.
18. Duscha, J. /Business Peeks into U.S. Files. The New York Times. Business Section (Nov 30, 1975). p. 8.
19. Pendergast, W. /Food and Drug Law Institute Seminar on Freedom of Information, Washington, D.C., Apr 1975.
20. Gibson, C. H. /What the Freedom of Information Act Means to Tax Practice and Practitioners. Taxation for Accountants 10:204-206 (1973).
21. Korn, E. D. /Availability of Grant Applications. Science 190:736 (Nov 21, 1975).
22. Moore, J. A., et al. /Freedom of Information. Science 191:136-137 (Jan 16, 1976).
23. Rosenbloom, H. D. /More IRS Information May Become Public Due to Amended Freedom of Information Act. Journal of Taxation 45:258-265 (Nov 1976).
24. Prying Out the UGDP Data: An Eight-Year Battle with HEW. Medical Tribune (Aug 23, 1978). p. 1, 8.
25. Young, A. L. /Recent Developments under FOIA and FACA Directly Affecting the Pharmaceutical Industry. Food, Drug & Cosmetics Law Journal 31:507-520 (1976).
26. Montgomery, D. B., et al. /The Freedom of Information Act: Strategic Opportunities and Threats. Sloan Management Review 19:1-13 (1978).

27. Jordan, W. L., et al. /The Freedom of Information Act: A Potential Alternative to Conventional Criminal Discovery. American Criminal Law 14: 73-161 (1976).

AFTER FIVE YEARS:

AN ASSESSMENT OF THE AMENDED

U. S. FREEDOM OF INFORMATION ACT*

Trudy Huskamp Peterson

The Congress of the United States in 1974 passed tough amendments to the 1966 Freedom of Information Act. These amendments required that "any reasonably segregable portion of a record" be released, set tight time limits for responses, amended two exemption categories, and established penalties for non-compliance. Critics of the Act argued that the impact of the amendments would be to invade the privacy of citizens, impair decision making, hamper investigatory and regulatory agencies, and cost untold sums. President Ford vetoed the bill; but Congress, acting in the torment of the Watergate year, passed it over his veto.[1] Most archivists applauded the measure; archivists are, after all, generally committed to opening records to public view. Now, after more than five years of experience with the amended Act, it is time to look at its impact on records creation, records disposition, and records availability.

Availability is the easiest of these three to measure. The amended Act requires that the departments and agencies make an annual report to Congress on their administration of the Act, and these reports give the general statistical picture of the research use of the Act. Here, however, it is important to remember several things. First, there is no legislative definition and no consensus of what constitutes an FOI request. Some agencies count any request from the public for records as an FOI request, whether the request is for a press release or for a top secret document; others count only those requests that specifically mention the Freedom of Information Act. Consequently, it is not reasonable to argue that without the amended Act all or most of the information released in response to FOI requests would not have been released, for some portion of it surely would have been. Second, the typical researcher using the Act is not the typical archival researcher. The Justice Department,

---

*Reprinted by permission of the author and publisher from The American Archivist, 43:2 (Spring 1980) 161-68; copyright © 1980 by The Society of American Archivists.

for instance, has a high number of FOI requests from convicts seeking records about themselves; some regulatory agencies report a large number of requests from businesses and corporations for information on competitors or on the decision-making process. These are not the archivist's usual clientele. Third, a denial may be made not only on the basis of substantive information in the requested record, but also because the record does not exist, the record is not in the possession of the agency, or the researcher's identification of the document is inadequate ("please give me everything you have on me"). Consequently, the number of denials at the initial request stage must be sorted into substantive and nonsubstantive categories. But even after the substantive denials are isolated, it remains a quirk of the reporting process that the denial of one word in a document is reported as a denial, just as if the entire document, volume, file, or series had been denied.

Perhaps the best statistics to use in measuring increased access due to the Act are the statistics on releases in response to appeals and to litigation. Here the agency would have denied the information to the researcher and, without the Act, the researcher would have been unable to obtain it. Here, too, most appeals and lawsuits are for records that are known to exist in the possession of the agency; few researchers will appeal or sue based on an agency's reply that the records do not exist in the agency's files. And at the appeals and litigation stages the statistics indicate whether the information was denied in full or in part, enabling us to see the release of information with greater precision. In 1976 there were 4,179 appeals, and 440 (12 percent) were granted in full, 1,535 (42 percent) granted in part. This means that more than half of the appeals resulted in the release of information and more than 2,000 requesters got information that would not have been obtained without the Act. In 1977 there were 5,190 appeals, of which 12.5 percent were granted in full and 34 percent were granted in part. Again, about 2,000 requesters gained additional information.[2] The General Accounting Office studied FOI litigation during the period 1975-77, and found that over half of the litigants received the documents they requested, received them in whole or in part.[3]

But what kind of information is being released? Here statistics are silent. The FBI argues that the Act has made information on informants and techniques available to criminals and organized crime, jeopardizing informants and agents and compromising certain investigative methods. Corporations have gone to court to prevent the release of business information supplied to the government. These suits are known as "reverse FOI cases" because they seek to prevent release rather than to obtain it. It is probably a safe guess that most information released at the initial request level is either information that is already public or information about the individual or organization making the request. Requests for information about third parties (i.e., information about persons other than the individual making the request or the officials of the federal agency) probably make up a higher percentage of appeals and lawsuits than do initial requests; but the preponderance of information released at those later stages is probably still information about the individual or organization making the request. And the release of personal information to an individual, about that individual, does not necessarily open those records to general research; an individual has more rights to access to records about himself than does a third party. Release of information about third parties, however, generally opens the information to all. Consequently, we may theorize that the FOI is an effective means for gaining access to information about yourself, your organization, or your business; but it releases less information for general research than the statistics would suggest.

A second major concern, the impact of the amended Act on records creation, has generated considerable fear and controversy. While the 1974 amendments were being debated, many government officials argued that a tough Act would have a "chilling effect" on records creation. They believed that the likelihood of disclosure would inhibit some officials from documenting decision-making, that it would make officials reluctant to provide candid advice in writing, and that outsiders would be reluctant to furnish information to the government. And to some extent, this has all occurred. Shortly after the amendments went into effect, government officials could be heard to say, "Don't write that down--it could be released under FOI." And in at least one instance, I personally was very conscious of the Act as I compiled information, knowing that the records in the file would be nearly impossible to deny if requested under the Act.

However, for several reasons, much of the civil servant's initial fear of the Act has diminished. First, it is impossible to manage large federal agencies without issuing written instructions and documenting decisions and reporting on programs and problems. Also, experience with the law has shown officials which exemptions are and which are not likely to be upheld, either by the Department of Justice or by the courts. Experience, in other words, has shown officials how to live with the Act. Then, too, the law requires federal agencies to document their activities, and agencies generally do so, although surely more to meet their own administrative, legal, and fiscal needs than to comply with the requirement that functions be documented.

It is incontrovertible that private individuals and organizations are increasingly reluctant to furnish information to the federal government because of the possibility that the information could be released under the FOI. Over time, this could pose a serious problem to the government; however, there are a number of steps that could be taken to ensure that truly confidential information is not released. [4] First, agencies must define more clearly for their employees the type of information that is covered by an exemption, and then the agencies must be consistent in the application of that definition. Certainly the Justice Department and the courts are the final arbiters, and definition will become easier as a body of legal precedent on FOI cases develops; but agencies can contribute to better definition through good guidelines, handbooks, and repeated training sessions. Similarly, agencies can take more care in the actual process of making deletions from the documents. If a name is excised on one page, only to appear on another, it will often undermine the entire effort to protect the identity of the source. Given the thousands of pages handled by the agencies each year in fulfilling FOI requests, it is inevitable that some accidental disclosures will occur; but the public must be made confident that agencies are taking all reasonable precautions to prevent such disclosures. The key problem here is trust: the private sector's trust that the government will assert the appropriate exemption, that the agency personnel will do a good job of identifying and sanitizing the records, and that the courts will uphold appropriate use of the exemptions. [5]

The most serious impact of the amended Freedom of Information Act on the archivist may be in the area of records disposition. There are four emerging problems here, all of them little predicted when the amendments were passed: (1) growing demands by the private sector that certain files be destroyed to prevent disclosure; (2) a developing tactic in litigation of using the Act to prevent the destruction of records; (3) an increasing confusion about the definition of federal records; and (4) a growing tendency to assert that the records received by an agency are not subject to FOI, thereby undermining the principle that the records of an agency are both those made and those received. These are ominous signs.

When the amendments were passed, observers predicted that agencies would try to schedule and quickly destroy those records that would pose difficult FOI problems for the agency. And in some cases this probably happened. Unexpected were pleas from the private sector for destruction of records. Two cases will serve as examples. In one, the Southern Christian Leadership Conference and a number of individuals sought the destruction of the FBI's records of the telephone taps on Martin Luther King, Jr. In that case, the judge ordered the materials held at the National Archives under seal for fifty years. In the second case, an individual who had discovered, through the Privacy Act, that the FBI maintained a file on him, obtained a court order instructing the FBI to destroy the file and the portion of the index referring to it. The FBI did so. These experiences have alerted archivists to the external as well as the internal demands for destruction. We have certainly not seen the last of this type of litigation. [6]

Conversely, just as the Act has been used to impel destruction, so has it been used also as an argument to prevent destruction. In 1979 a number of organizations and individuals filed suit to prevent the disposal of the field office case files of the Federal Bureau of Investigation. A NARS-approved records schedule covered these files, which were to be destroyed after their administrative value had ceased. The plaintiffs said that in the past they had requested FBI documents under the Freedom of Information Act, that such documents were being destroyed, that they intended to make similar requests in the future, and that the court should prevent the disposal of the records. After a lengthy hearing, the judge issued a preliminary injunction against disposal of any FBI files and ordered the development of a new retention plan to be approved by the court. While the new plan has not been completed as of this writing, it seems likely that for FOI purposes some FBI case files may have to be retained for time periods beyond their actual administrative value. [7]

As soon as the amendments to the Act were effective, the question of what records were covered by the Act assumed a new urgency. It was clear that the Act covered records of federal agencies and not the records of the courts, the Congress, or the White House Office; but the Act offered no specific definition of a record of a federal agency. In the absence of such a definition, most federal officials assumed that the definition of records in the Federal Records Act was controlling. [8] However, in the spring of 1978, the United States Court of Appeals for the District of Columbia Circuit surprised most FOI cognoscenti by declaring, in the case of Goland and Skidmore v. Central Intelligence Agency, et al., that the definition in the Federal Records Act was not controlling in FOI cases, pointing out that Congress "had ample opportunities" to refer to that definition in the FOI Act or its amendments, but had not done so. Just because the Federal Records Act contains the only definition of a federal record, the court seemed to say, that does not make it the FOI definition. The problem is that the court did not provide any alternative definition of records, and since the decision was handed down there has been essentially no definition, for the court suggested that the question of whether a document was an agency record would have to be decided on the basis of individual facts of each case. [9]

Another development pertaining to the definition of records under the Freedom of Information Act came in the August 1979 hearing on the proposed FBI charter. Attorney General Benjamin Civiletti was asked about the charter provisions on destruction of FBI records, and he reportedly said that unsolicited information that does not pertain to any of the FBI's lawful responsibilities would be retained only until its administrative value expired, adding that this information "would in the long range not be subject to the FOIA because it is unnecessary and would not be retained."[10] As the Justice Department is responsible for the government's position on FOI litigation, one wonders whether the "necessity" test will become part of the criteria for defining a record covered by the Act. If so, this is yet another step away from the definition in the Federal Records Act.

The greatest threat to archives from the rapidly developing body of law and practice on the FOIA is the tendency to distinguish between records made by the agency and records received by the agency, and to declare the latter outside the reach of the Act. One of the first clear indications of this direction was in the Goland case mentioned above. In that case, the plaintiffs asked (in part) for the release of the CIA's copy of a transcript of a House of Representatives hearing. CIA argued that the transcript was not an agency record but was, rather, a "legislative document under the control of the House of Representatives" and therefore, since the Congress was not subject to the FOIA, was not reachable under the provisions of the Act. The plaintiffs lost in the lower court and appealed, basing their appeal, in part on the Federal Records Act definition of records, arguing that records include all materials "made or received by an agency of the United States Government, " and that no one denied that the CIA had received the transcript. They lost. The courts at both levels held that the transcript was "released to the CIA for limited purposes as a reference document only" and that it remained "within the control of Congress" and was, therefore, a congressional document outside the reach of the FOIA.[11] The next cases to follow this reasoning were two attempts to obtain access to questionnaires completed by U. S. Senators about nominees for federal judgeships, and then sent to the Justice Department. Although the questionnaires are filed in that department and the Attorney General's staff sends out, receives, and analyzes the completed forms, the judge ruled that they were "the collective product and property of the President, the Attorney General, the Senators, and the state [nominating] commissions, none of which are agencies for FOIA purposes. " Thus, he said, the forms were not under the control of the Department of Justice, for the Attorney General was merely acting as counsel and adviser to the President to help him exercise his constitutional powers to nominate new judges.[12] The most recent case (at this writing) to use this argument is the denial of a request for pre-sentence reports on convicts. Despite the fact that these reports are filed at the U. S. Parole Commission, a federal agency, the judge ruled that the reports remain in the control of the courts and thus are court records not subject to the Freedom of Information Act.[13] As is quickly apparent, the courts have now used this argument to protect the three clear exclusions from the Act: the Congress, the White House Office, and the courts.[14]

The next step would appear to be that a corporation would claim that the information it supplied to the government is still its property and, as it is not a federal agency, the information is outside the reach of the Act. In the case of Government Sales Consultants, Inc. v. General Services Administration, Honeywell and Burroughs, two computer companies that had intervened in the lawsuit, argued that the records requested by the plaintiff were not federal records for purposes of the FOIA and the companies could demand the return of the records at any time. They lost, but have appealed.[15] Such challenges by other companies are likely to occur in the future.

What does all this mean? It means that the Freedom of Information Act is working, releasing some information that the agencies would like to withhold and withholding some information that requesters would like released, probably striking a balance. Appeals and lawsuits are both successful means to further release. The initial negative impact on records creation by federal employees has been mitigated, at least in part, but there remains a negative impact on the willingness of the public to supply certain kinds of information. While agencies cane take some steps to reassure the public, the fear that the information provided will subsequently be released to the detriment of the provider will probably continue. Probably, too, there will be continuing efforts to modify the exemptions to afford more protection to the members of the public who provide the information. The attempts to exclude categories of information from the reach of the Act will continue, with unclear results for the current definition of federal records. Archivists must be alert to this trend, for the result may be filing practices that segregate records that are and are not covered by the Act; and in turn it may be more difficult to persuade agencies that all records are part of the federal records system. And, as we know all too well, federal practices are often reflected in state and local government. It is up to archivists to state the concept of records so clearly that everyone--agencies, researchers, lawyers, and even judges--will understand it. This will be a continuing challenge in the 1980s.

The opinions expressed in this article are solely those of the author and in no way reflect the official position of the National Archives and Records Service.

References

1. 5 U.S.C. 552. Some agencies, including the National Archives and Records Service, were implementing the FOIA properly long before the 1974 amendments. However, the Act was implemented unevenly in Executive Branch agencies, and in several agencies implemented hardly at all. The procedural amendments to the Act, including a mandatory annual report to Congress from each agency on its administration of the Act, were intended to bring all agencies into compliance. The Ford veto was based in part upon the opinion that the amendment to the first exemption on classified information was unconstitutional.
 The best handbook on the Freedom of Information Act is A Citizen's Guide on How to Use the Freedom of Information Act and the Privacy Act in Requesting Government Documents (Washington, D.C.: Government Printing Office, 1977). Current information on FOIA developments is found in Access Reports/FOI, a biweekly newsletter published by Plus Publications, Inc. A more expanded discussion of the 1974 amendments and the National Archives can be found in my article, "Using the Freedom of Information Act to Acquire Archival Materials," Law Library Journal (Fall 1979).
2. Harold C. Relyea, The Administration of the Freedom of Information Act: A Brief Overview of the Executive Branch Annual Reports for 1976; ibid., ... for 1977 (Washington, D.C.: Congressional Research Service, Library of Congress, 17 October 1977 and 15 November 1978).
3. "Filing Suit under FOIA Effective in Getting Information, GAO Report Finds," Access Reports, vol. 5, no. 22, 13 November 1979, pp. 1-2.

4. One proposed solution is that persons or organizations named in the records be notified before records relating to them are released. As archivists are quick to realize, this would mean not only a great slowing of response time, and increased cost, but it would also mean dozens of letters a week for George Washington, Thomas Jefferson, and others long dead. In March 1978 the Office of Management and Budget requested agencies to notify contractors and potential contractors when their names appear in procurement records sought under the Freedom of Information Act. No time limits were suggested, so, potentially, this covers information submitted by contractors for the Union Army during the Civil War!
5. If necessary, the government can obtain some types of information from private citizens and organizations by passing specific legislation requiring the submission of such information, or by using subpoena powers. This, however, is complex and certainly not as desirable as voluntary cooperation.
6. Bernard S. Lee v. Clarence M. Kelley, et al. (Civil Action no. 76-1185) and Southern Christian Leadership Conference v. Clarence M. Kelley, et al. (Civil Action no. 76-1186), United States District Court for the District of Columbia, 31 January 1977. At the time of this writing there have been about eighty, NARS-approved destructions of individual FBI cases as a result of the pertinent individual's Privacy Act demand.
7. American Friends Service Committee, et al. v. William H. Webster, et al. (Civil Action no. 79-1655), United States District Court for the District of Columbia, 10 January 1980.
8. 44 U.S.C. 3301.
9. Susan D. Goland and Patricia B. Skidmore v. Central Intelligence Agency, et al. (Civil Action no. 76-1800), United States Court of Appeals for the District of Columbia, 23 May 1978.
10. "Proposed Charter for FBI Would Limit Information Available Under FOIA," Access Reports, vol. 5, no. 16, 7 August 1979, pp. 1-2.
11. Goland and Skidmore v. CIA, et al.
12. Tom W. Ryan, et al. v. Department of Justice (Civil Action no. 79-1042) and Charles R. Halpern, et al. v. Department of Justice (Civil Action no. 79-1043), United States District Court for the District of Columbia, 11 July 1979.
13. Burchel L. Carson v. Department of Justice, et al. (Civil Action no. 79-0140), United States District Court for the District of Columbia, 25 July 1979.
14. The problem of explaining that documents received by an entity are part of the records of that entity has also arisen in the legal tangles over Richard Nixon's materials. Courts have found it difficult to grasp that a memorandum from the Secretary of the Interior to the President, written on Interior Department letterhead stationery, is a part of the

President's materials and not a record of Interior. The fact that the carbon copy that remains in Interior might be treated differently from the copy in the President's files seems to them to confuse the issue still further. And when you add the fact that if the memorandum bore a national security marking, the access to the copy in the President's files would be controlled by Interior so long as that marking remained in effect, the courts figuratively throw up their hands.

15. Government Sales Consultants, Inc. v. General Services Administration (Civil Action no. 77-1294), United States District Court for the District of Columbia, 31 January 1979.

A PROGRESS REPORT ON INFORMATION PRIVACY AND DATA SECURITY*

Gerard Salton

Introduction

Most information scientists are by now well aware of the role and importance of information banks in modern society. There now exist hundreds of different data banks involving hundreds of millions of records, and a large proportion of these data banks carry personal information about the employees or customers of a given organization, the patients in a hospital, the staff and students of educational institutions, the drivers of automobiles, the applicants for certain jobs, the prisoners in penal institutions, and so on. Furthermore, the (completely legal) use of such information banks has been increasing rapidly over the last few years, spurred on in part by the availability of on-line technology which makes it possible to interrogate the files using console entry devices and to obtain answers to the search requests more or less instantaneously. Tens of millions of searches of mechanized information banks are currently conducted each year, a large proportion involving private information about individual persons or groups.

Over the years computer and information scientists have learned to cope with many technical problems affecting the collection, storage, retrieval, and dissemination of information. Thus procedures are available for generating information identifiers attached to individual information items either manually or automatically, for organizing information items in storage in such a way that searches for individual items can be conducted efficiently, for comparing query statements with the stored records, and for rapidly retrieving a large proportion of the items which actually prove pertinent to the search requests under consideration. Additional technical progress may be expected in the foreseeable future in the areas of information classification, the determination and identification of relationships among information items, the initial formulation and

---

*Reprinted by permission of the author and publisher from the Journal of the American Society for Information Science, 31:2 (March 1980) 75-83; copyright © 1980 by John Wiley & Sons, Inc.

subsequent improvement of query statements, the rapid searching of large information files, and the dissemination of output products.

In addition to the previously mentioned technical problems, the existence of information banks also raises a host of nontechnical questions of a social, legal, and ethical nature. These have to do with the propriety of collecting and storing information of various kinds in automatically searchable files, with criminal activities resulting from the misuse of stored information, and with the general role assigned to technology in various human endeavors.

In considering these nontechnical questions, it is found more often than not that their treatment is far more complex than expected and that many of the issues are a good deal more slippery to deal with than the more familiar technical problems. Even the critical formulation of many of the social and ethical information problems may be controversial, and methods of attack leading to reasonable solutions are often not at hand.

The present study deals with a particularly difficult problem: information privacy. As will be seen the privacy issue is not mainly technological, but rather social, legal, and political in nature. However, in modern society, social and technological issues are often difficult to separate. For this reason certain technological issues dealing with the confidentiality and security of stored information are treated in this report, following a description of the principal nontechnical privacy issues and an examination of the existing legal framework dealing with the privacy problem.

2. The Privacy Problem

Privacy problems arise in three kinds of areas: in relation to property, in relation to person, and in relation to information [1, 2]. Concerning first the question of property, most societies recognize privacy rights of ownership to house and land, and the United States Constitution specifically forbids unlawful entry, as well as the quartering of soldiers in private homes without the owner's consent. Concerning privacy of person, it is well known that most people wish to preserve a degree of physical and psychic distance from their fellow human beings. This becomes obvious especially in situations where human beings are jammed together in tight spaces against their will. Finally, in connection with information, the privacy issue deals with the right of the individual to control the processing and use of information about his personal attributes and activities. It is this latter kind of privacy which is of concern in the present context.

Why is the issue of information privacy such a difficult one in modern society? Because there exists an obvious and fundamental conflict between society's need for information of many kinds and the individual's right to privacy protection. Most governmental systems require information in order to operate efficiently, but a democracy

The Social Prerogative 301

in particular flourishes on information, and that information needs to be reliable, accurate, and timely if the system is to be effective. In a democratic society, information is needed for many worthwhile purposes such as the provision of services, the collection of taxes, protection against crime, and the maintenance of a free press. The attitude of most citizens is therefore divided between a desire to preserve one's own private sphere of action and the wish to partake in the many benefits derivable from an open society: freedom of speech and press, essential government operations, effective planning for future contingencies, and so on. These dual aims are unfortunately difficult to reconcile.

Assuming that individual privacy protection is legitimate, a question arises about how much protection should in fact be afforded to each citizen. The answer to this question depends principally on one's own view of the proper governmental role in society. If one assigns to the existing authority a minimal role by asserting, as did John Stuart Mill in the last century, that "the sole reason for exerting power over individuals is the protection of others, " then each individual may claim maximal protection for his own personal sphere. If, on the other hand, one takes an activist view and assigns to the government a maximal role ("the proper role of government is to secure public good"), then inevitably minimal protection results for the individual.

It is fair to assume that, under current conditions, the second alternative is preferred by the vast majority of the citizens. Most people have become far too dependent on a variety of government services to be willing to relegate the authorities to a minimal role. In these circumstances, privacy considerations must necessarily take second place. Furthermore, a great many additional personal factors work against the protection of individual privacy:

(a) Many people are delighted to relinquish what privacy may be available; they answer surveys and exhibit themselves on radio or television; certain classes of individuals such as public figures, politicians, and film stars may also directly profit from a lack of privacy.

(b) Most people enjoy conveniences and creature comforts, for example, in the form of credit privileges, and to obtain these they relinquish privacy rights by filling out forms and supplying personal information.

(c) In the end, most people tend to feel that the democratic institutions under which they live are sufficiently robust to handle serious privacy threats should they arise; hence it is argued that special protection measures are not required for the protection of individual privacy.

Before turning to a description of current practices as they relate to information privacy, it may be useful briefly to recall why the privacy issue has suddenly come to the fore with such insistence.

Until recently private information was easy to protect: the information was superficial and scattered across many information files; access to the files was difficult to obtain; and the information itself was hard to interpret. In earlier times, the main privacy threats did not in fact pertain to information but consisted of actual forced entry onto property, eavesdropping by ear, and extraction of information by force. The United States Constitution addresses these threats by rendering illegal the search and seizure of property without court warrant (fourth amendment) and by protecting the citizens against self-incrimination (fifth amendment).

Most of the earlier conditions no longer apply at the present time: the stored information is now largely centralized, but the access is decentralized in the sense that a given file can be interrogated from many remote points; a certain amount of standardization has been introduced so that access protocols are easy to follow; furthermore, much of the record-keeping activity enjoys low visibility, even though multiple copies of many files may exist and the number of file search and retrieval operations is steadily increasing.

An additional factor is the availability and use of new technologies which render privacy protection much more difficult and onerous: these include the telephone, the microphone, the polygraph and other psychological surveillance devices, the so-called truth drugs, the microminiaturized "bugging" devices, television operations, and many other kinds of listening and broadcasting systems.

The overall conclusion seems to be that the balance of success has shifted from the individual seeking protection to the potential infringer wanting access to private information. Furthermore, since information and data are essential ingredients in the modern world, and determine to some extent the conditions in which we live, privacy protection is considered by some to constitute the most modern form of the human rights issue whose importance increases as the amount of computer usage becomes more widespread. The privacy issue has thus attracted more and more attention in recent years, and has begun to preoccupy the legislators in many countries as well as a substantial portion of the public at large.

3. Current Interpretations of Privacy Protection

Instead of supplying additional comments about the current state of privacy protection, it may be more instructive to review a number of recent legal decisions dealing with the interrelations between data banks and privacy. The circumstances surrounding each case are reviewed and excerpts are used from the actual court opinions to illustrate the controlling arguments.

A. Menard vs. Saxbe

Dale Menard was a 19-year-old college student working in Los Angeles during the summer of 1965 [3]. On August 9, he visited with

The Social Prerogative 303

friends in the evening, and late that night he went to Sunland Park
to await pick-up by a colleague who was to drive him back to his
home in the suburbs. The friend failed to arrive and Menard fell
asleep on a park bench. During the night he woke up and walked
across the street to peek through the windows of a rest home in an
attempt to determine what time it was. The residents of the building called the police to complain about a prowler. Menard was
picked up around 3:00 a.m.; the police found a wallet containing ten
dollars lying on the ground near the park bench on which Menard had
slept.

Menard was arrested, booked, fingerprinted, and held in custody for two days. No criminal complaint was filed. No evidence
was submitted that the wallet had been stolen--in fact Menard
claimed not to have known anything about the wallet. Menard's
friend corroborated the story about the missed appointment in Sunland Park. Menard was released after two days, no charges having
been brought against him. However, the Los Angeles police followed
routine procedure in forwarding Menard's fingerprints to the print
file maintained by the Federal Bureau of Investigation (FBI) as part
of the National Crime Information Center. A notation attached to
Menard's prints read "released--unable to connect with any felony
or misdemeanor at this time."

Menard's mother, worried about her son's "criminal" record,
wrote to the FBI a few weeks later but, again in accordance with
normal procedure, she was unable to obtain any information concerning her son's file. It is impossible in the present context to describe in detail the operations of the FBI's criminal record system;
suffice it to say that several hundreds of millions of fingerprint sets
are stored (not all of them in the criminal section of the file), plus
a large variety of other records, including lists of stolen cars,
driver's licenses, and so on. The FBI retains all stored records
and will not normally amend or alter a record or reveal its existence to private individuals, taking the point of view that each record
actually belongs to the local law enforcement agency that submitted
the particular information in the first place. The local police and
other law enforcement agencies, on the other hand, normally refer
any inquiries about a stored criminal record to the FBI.

Mrs. Menard, having been given the runaround by the FBI,
the Los Angeles police department, and the California Department
of Justice for some two and a half years, filed a legal complaint in
January of 1968 seeking removal of her son's record from the FBI
criminal files. Following the filing of the complaint, an FBI agent
was asked to review the file, and in April of 1968, Menard's record
was changed to read: "released--unable to connect with any felony
or misdemeanor ... not deemed an arrest but a detention only."

Unable to obtain relief expunging the arrest record through
administrative processes, Menard turned to the U.S. District Court
and eventually to the Circuit Court of Appeals, where the case was
argued in January of 1973 and decided in April of 1974.

The following excerpts from the court's opinion are self-explanatory:

> ...there is an undoubted social stigma involved in an arrest record. It is common knowledge that a man with an arrest record is much more apt to be subject to police scrutiny--the first to be questioned and the last to be released....
>
> The arrest record is used outside the field of criminal justice. Most significant is its use in connection with subsequent inquiries, or applications for employment, and licenses to engage in certain fields of work.
>
> ...what began modestly in 1924 (the FBI Identification Division) is now ... out of effective control. Due to the Bureau's limited resources, there is no follow-up to assure that records of arrest are frequently amended to show an ultimate noncriminal disposition. There are no controls on the accuracy of the information submitted by contributing agencies.
>
> ...having been informed that Menard's encounter with the Los Angeles police was purely fortuitous, the FBI had no authority to retain this record in its criminal files along with the mass of arrest records ... the continued inclusion (of Menard's prints) in those (criminal) files is, in our view, inconsistent with the intent of Congress.

The time required to effect a relatively simple alteration in a stored personal record ran from August 9, 1965 until April 23, 1974 and the cost involved in obtaining relief must have run into hundreds of thousands of dollars. One can conclude that only an exceptionally tenacious individual possessing substantial means and outside support can in fact follow Menard's example in a similar situation.

B. Anderson vs. Sills

This case had its origins in the civil disorders that occurred in various parts of the United States during the summer of 1967 [4]. Several states, including the State of New Jersey, experienced riots at that time, stemming in part from protests against the Vietnam war. In response to the disorders and in the hope of preventing further disturbances, the Attorney General of the State of New Jersey prepared a memorandum in April 1968 entitled "Civil Disorders --The Role of Local, County, and State Government." The memorandum was sent to all local law enforcement agencies in New Jersey and outlined various guidelines that could be followed by local agencies in preventing and/or controlling disturbances.

Among the recommendations made by the Attorney General was the establishment of data banks containing records of incidents such as civil disturbances, riots, rallies, protests, demonstrations, marches, confrontations, and so on. Included in the incident records were to be names and identities of the individuals involved, as well as information about sponsoring organizations and other participating groups. The memorandum specified details about the manner in which the records were to be prepared. Thus, under "type of organization, " the memorandum listed entries such as "left wing, right wing, civil rights, militant, nationalistic, pacifist, Ku Klux Klan, extremist, " and so on.

Upon learning of the existence of the memorandum by the Attorney General, Denise Anderson and a number of other persons, apparently associated with the New Jersey branch of the National Association for the Advancement of Colored People (NAACP), filed suit for judgment declaring that the use of a reporting system by local and county officials to gather and compile information relating to potential and actual civil disorders violated the constitution; in Anderson's words: "as an organizer of rallies, marches, protests, and demonstrations, I feel that I must warn potential participants that they are subject to being investigated and classified by the police despite the lawfulness of our activity. "

The Superior Court of Hudson County sided with the plaintiffs and issued an injunction forbidding the Attorney General to proceed with his plans, thereby effectively preventing the maintenance of the proposed data bank of civil disorders. The Attorney General (Arthur Sills) thereupon appealed to the Supreme Court of New Jersey. The excerpts that follow are from the opinion rendered by that court on June 1, 1970:

> It is a serious matter for the judiciary to interfere with the preventive measures devised by the executive branch of government in response to its constitutional obligation to protect all citizens; surely such interference must not rest upon a hypothetical exposition of what could happen ... rather the premise must be accepted, absent proof the other way ... that a lawful exercise of the judgment and discretion vested in the local police is involved.
>
> ...the basic approach must be that the executive branch may gather whatever information it reasonably believes to be necessary to enable it to perform the police roles, directional or preventive; a court should not interfere in the absence of proof of bad faith or arbitrariness.
>
> ...the issue as projected by plaintiffs ... is a mere abstraction; ... plaintiffs envision that a mere rally, protest, demonstration, or march of a pacifist group will precipitate a police dossier of everyone who attends, including therein his butcher's and banker's opinion of his credit, ... plaintiffs enlarge upon their hypothetical horribles and see each such citizen harried amid his family, friends, and business associates; there is not an iota of

evidence that anything of this kind has occurred, or will,
or that any person has been deterred by that prospect, ...
the prospect of wrongful conduct (by the authorities) must
be real and not fanciful.

In other words, in overruling the opinion of the lower court
and siding with the Attorney General, the Supreme Court of New Jersey declared that the prospect of injury caused by the existence of
a personal data bank must be a real and immediate threat before
suit can be brought. The mere existence of the data bank and the
possibly "chilling effect" that such a file may produce on various individuals is not sufficient to warrant its destruction.

C. Laird vs. Tatum

The background for this case is similar to that of Anderson vs.
Sills, the principal difference being that the intelligence-gathering
system in question here was one maintained by the United States
Army rather than by police agencies in the State of New Jersey [5].
To understand this case, it is necessary to go back to the summer
of 1967 when President Johnson had ordered federal troops to assist
local authorities at the time of the civil disorders in Detroit and
during the disturbances following the assassination of Martin Luther
King.

The Secretary of the Army argued that since it was the President's duty "to quell insurrection and other domestic violence," no
logical case could be made for compelling the military to use blind
force; in such circumstances, the same tools and the same information was required by the military as that to which local police forces
had routine access. A data bank was therefore created by the Army
during 1967 and 1968, including information about public activities
with potential for disorder. As in the previously described case of
Anderson vs. Sills, the Army data bank was to contain information
about persons and organizations, sponsors, identity of speakers,
number of persons attending, ideology of group, and so on.

Tatum and others filed suit against the Secretary of the Army
claiming that it was not the Army's business to engage in "surveillance of lawful political activity." The United States District Court
for the District of Columbia initially denied relief. Tatum appealed
to the U.S. District Court of Appeals which reversed the original
opinion and directed the Army to terminate its data-gathering activity. The Secretary of the Army (Melvin Laird) then appealed to the
Supreme Court of the United States which decided on June 26, 1972
by a vote of seven to two to reverse the opinion of the Appeals Court.

Consider first the majority opinion of the Court:

...to entitle a private individual to invoke the judicial power to determine the validity of executive or legislative action he must show that he has sustained, or is immediate-

> ly in danger of sustaining, a direct injury as the result of that action....
>
> ...the respondents do not meet this test; their claim, simply stated, is that they disagree with the judgments made by the Executive Branch with respect to the amount and type of information the Army needs ... allegations of a subjective "chill" are not an adequate substitute for a claim of specific present subjective harm, or of a threat of such harm.
>
> ...There is a traditional and strong resistance of Americans to any military intrusion into civilian affairs; that tradition has deep roots in our history and found early expression, for example, in the Third Amendment's explicit prohibition against quartering soldiers in private homes without consent....
>
> ...there is nothing in our history, including our holding today, that can properly be seen as giving any indication that actual or threatened injury by reason of unlawful activities of the military would go unnoticed or unremedied....

In summary, the majority of the Supreme Court argued, as did the State Court in the previous case, that in order to have a standing to sue one must be able to show direct harm or a substantial threat of harm. The Court also suggests that the institutions will prove sufficiently robust to take care of real troubles (caused by misuse of information banks) whenever they should arise.

To show that the case can be argued from a different viewpoint, consider now some excerpts from the dissenting opinion written by Mr. Justice Douglas:

> The action of turning the "armies" loose on surveillance of civilians was a gross repudiation of our traditions; the military, though important to us, is subservient and restricted to purely military missions....
>
> ...the Army's surveillance was ... staking out teams of agents, infiltrating undercover agents, creating command posts inside meetings, posing as press photographers and newsmen, posing as students, shadowing public figures. Surveillance of civilians is none of the Army's constitutional business, and Congress has not undertaken to entrust it with such a function.
>
> ...this case involves a cancer in our body politic; it is a measure of the disease which afflicts us; Army surveillance, like Army regimentation, is at war with the principles of the First Amendment ... when an intelligence officer looks over every nonconformist's shoulder ... the America once extolled as the voice of liberty heard around

the world no longer is cast in the image which Jefferson
and Madison designed, but more in the Russian image....

D. Zurcher vs. Stanford Daily

This case [6] involves not only the information privacy issue and the
Fourth Amendment injunction against unreasonable searches and seizures but the additional variable of freedom of the press, because
the files being "searched and seized" in this instance were those of
the Stanford Daily, the student newspaper at Stanford University.

The case stems from an antiwar demonstration at the Stanford
University Hospital in early April 1971. The demonstrators had
seized the administrative offices of the hospital, and at the request
of the Stanford University authorities, the police were called in to
evict the intruders from the hospital. As the police officers forced
their way into the hospital, they were attacked by demonstrators with
clubs and sticks, and all nine police officers were injured; one of
them suffered a broken shoulder and three received head injuries.

There were no police photographers in attendance during the
eviction attempt, and the officers themselves were able to identify
only two of the assailants. However, a photographer, later identified as working for the Stanford Daily, was seen to take photographs
during the assault. The District Attorney of Santa Clara County
therefore secured a warrant from the municipal court for a search
of the Daily's offices for negatives, film, and pictures showing the
events and occurrences at the hospital on the evening of April 9.
A search of the Stanford Daily's files was accordingly conducted
soon afterward; the search revealed only the photographs published
by the Daily on April 11, and no materials were removed from the
Daily's office. The Stanford Daily, however, brought suit, claiming
that the search of the newspaper files had deprived them of their
constitutional rights.

Before examining the opinions of the courts, it is necessary
to describe briefly the difference between a search warrant and a
subpoena requesting surrender of documents. A search warrant effectively gives permission to conduct an unannounced search and to
seize whatever documents appear useful for a particular investigation. A "subpoena duces tecum, " on the other hand, is an order to
a person possessing specific information and documents to appear
with specifically named documents before some legal authority for
further examination. A subpoena thus involves no search at all, but
represents a request for the production of documents; a search warrant covers unnamed items and is normally executed without prior
announcement.

The U. S. District Court for the Northern District of California granted relief, holding that the Fourth and Fourteenth Amendments forbade the issuance of a warrant to search for materials in
possession of one not suspected of a crime, unless there is probable

cause to believe, based on facts presented in a sworn affidavit, that a subpoena would be impracticable. The District Court held further that where the innocent object of a search is a newspaper, First Amendment interests are involved, rendering such a search permissible only in the rare circumstance where there is "clear showing" that important materials will be destroyed, and a restraining order would be futile.

The District Attorney first appealed the ruling to the Circuit Court of Appeals which upheld the lower court ruling, and eventually to the Supreme Court of the United States. By a five to three vote the Supreme Court overturned the opinions of the lower courts using the following arguments in support:

> ...the critical element in a reasonable search is not that the owner of the property is suspected of crime but that there is reasonable cause to believe that the "things" to be searched for and seized are located on the property to which entry is sought.
>
> ...the Fourth Amendment (forbidding unreasonable searches and seizures) has itself struck the balance between privacy and public need, and there is no occasion or justification for a court to revise the Amendment and strike a new balance by denying a search warrant in the circumstances present here.
>
> ...the District Court held that ... where the innocent party (whose premises are being searched) is a newspaper, there are additional factors derived from the First Amendment (dealing with freedom of the press) that justify ... a rule forbidding a search warrant. The claim is that
>
> a) searches will be physically disruptive and ... timely publication (of the newspaper) will be impeded;
> b) confidential sources of information will dry up and the press will lose opportunities to cover various events because of fears of the participants;
> c) reporters will be deterred from recording and preserving their recollections for future use if such information is subject to seizure;
> d) the processing of news ... will be chilled by the prospects that searches will disclose internal editorial deliberations;
> e) the press will resort to self-censorship.
>
> There is no reason to believe that magistrates cannot guard against searches of the type, scope and intrusiveness that would actually interfere with ... a newspaper.
>
> ...aware of the long struggle between Crown and press ... the Framers (of the Constitution) took the enormously important step of subjecting searches to the test of reason-

ableness and to the general rule requiring search warrants issued by neutral magistrates; they nevertheless did not forbid warrants where the press was involved ... and did not insist that the owner of the place to be searched be implicated in the offense.

...if the Framers had believed that the press was entitled to a special procedure, not available to others, ... one would have expected the terms of the Fourth Amendment to reflect that belief.

The dissenting opinions, written by Justices Stewart and Stevens, raised questions about two main points: the possible damage to the freedom of the press and the propriety of subjecting innocent parties to unannounced searches. Consider first the dissent by Mr. Justice Stewart concerning the freedom of the press.

...it seems to me self-evident that police searches of newspaper offices burden the freedom of the press....

...today the Court ... says that "it is not convinced that confidential sources will disappear and that the press will suppress the news because of fear of warranted searches"; this facile conclusion seems to me to ignore common experience; it requires no blind leap of faith to understand that a person who gives information ... on condition that his identity will not be revealed will be less likely to give that information if he knows that despite assurances his identity may in fact be disclosed.... Since the undisputable effect of such searches will thus be to prevent a newsman from being able to promise confidentiality ..., it seems obvious to me that a journalist's access to information, and thus the public's will thereby be impaired.

...the end result, wholly inimical to the First Amendment, will be a diminishing flow of potentially important information to the public.

The other dissenting opinion by Justice Stevens deals mostly with the "third party" search question, where the party whose privacy is being invaded is not implicated in any wrongful action:

Just as the witnesses who participate in an investigation or a trial far outnumber the defendants, the persons who possess evidence that may help to identify an offender, or explain an aspect of a criminal transaction, far outnumber those who have custody of weapons or plunder; countless law abiding citizens--doctors, lawyers, merchants, customers, bystanders--may have documents in their possession that relate to an ongoing criminal investigation; the consequences of subjecting this large category of persons to unannounced police searches are extremely serious ... and may create an entirely unjustified injury to the reputation of the person searched.

... of greatest importance, however, is the question whether the offensive intrusion on the privacy of the ordinary citizen is justified by the law enforcement interest it is intended to vindicate. Possession of contraband ... gives rise to the inference that the custodian is involved in criminal activity ... mere possession of documentary evidence, however, is much less likely to demonstrate that the custodian is guilty of any wrongdoing.

... the only conceivable justification for an unannounced search of an innocent citizen is the fear that, if notice were given, he would conceal or destroy the object of the search ... probable cause that the custodian is a criminal.

E. Conclusion

The foregoing legal interpretations permit only one unequivocal conclusion: at the present time, the climate for the protection of information privacy in the United States is not favorable for three principal reasons:

(a) There does not exist in the United States a clear definition of what constitutes personal information, and there are no institutional procedures to protect against improper collection of information.

(b) Most categories of information do not enjoy any statutory protection; disclosure of such information may be compelled by legal process as is illustrated in Zurcher vs. Stanford Daily.

(c) No institutional procedures exist for guaranteeing the accuracy and integrity of stored information, and in most cases no provisions exist for the correction of erroneous information and for the deletion of improperly collected information (see Menard vs. Saxbe for a case in point).

What is needed for the immediate future is first a consensus that privacy aims are legitimate and second procedures that insure the confidentiality of the information deserving to be protected. Some ideas in this connection are examined in the remaining sections of this study.

5. Some Thoughts on Data Confidentiality and Privacy Legislation

In contrast to privacy which refers to the rights of the individual, confidentiality implies that the data themselves and the information they represent must be protected and that their use be confined to authorized purposes by authorized persons. In the United States, certain types of information, such as the data collected by the Census Bureau, are exceptionally given confidential status; but on the whole the policies and procedures which control collection and disclosure of personal information are either nonexistent or in any case exceedingly lax.

Certain of the European countries appear to have given substantially more thought to the problem of personal privacy and data confidentiality [7]. In a number of countries all data banks containing personal information must be licensed by a privacy protection authority. Extensive regulations often exist specifying the manner in which information is to be collected and used; these regulations generally apply to all personal records. Several countries also restrict the transmission of data to other countries, in the sense that a sender must obtain prior approval from his authorities before transmission is permissible.

Several reasons may account for the tougher attitude of the Europeans in the privacy area. First, the degree of mistrust exhibited by many Europeans toward their government may be greater than in the United States; hence there may be greater willingness to legislate instead of relying on custom or precedent. Second, many European countries feel a need to underline their national integrity and independence; hence the rules restricting transborder data flow. Finally there may be a genuine, strong interest in the preservation of individual freedom and human rights, and this translates itself into appropriate privacy legislation.

In the United States the only important privacy legislation currently in effect is the Privacy Act of 1974, which permits access by individuals to the personal information contained in certain government files, prevents agency-to-agency transfer of certain stored information, and permits individuals to seek injunctive relief to correct certain errors present in the stored information. The act is, however, much weaker than it should be in that it applies only to government files, while additionally exempting all files managed by law enforcement agencies (such as, in particular, the previously mentioned FBI National Crime Information Center). Furthermore, no Data Board exists in the United States with any kind of regulatory authority.

A number of proposals for future legislation have been prepared such as the so-called Code of Fair Information Practices conceived by the Special Advisory Committee on Automated Personal Data Systems [8, 9]. The following main provisions are included in this proposal:

(a) no personal data record system should be secret as to its existence;
(b) an individual must be able to determine what information is on record about him, and how the information is actually used;
(c) an individual must be afforded the opportunity to correct or amend a personal record that proves to be in error;
(d) an individual must be able to prevent the transfer of

information obtained for some particular purpose to be used for some other, previously unannounced, purpose;
(e) an individual must be told whether he has the legal right to refuse to give certain kinds of personal information;
(f) each organization in charge of a personal data file must guarantee the reliability of the data and take precautions to prevent misuse.

The difference between this proposal and the existing privacy legislation is striking in that the proposal affects all personal data records, whether government owned or not, and does offer guarantees of reliability and assurances against transfer and misuse. It is not likely that really effective privacy rules will be created in the United States until such time as a popular consensus emerges concerning the fundamental importance of information privacy, on a par with the role currently attributed to the freedom of speech, the freedom of the press, and the freedom of assembly. That day is not yet at hand.

6. A Postscript on Data Security

Unlike personal privacy and data confidentiality, data security is a technological and operational issue: security denotes the technical and operational methods used to carry out effectively the confidentiality policies that may be enacted [10, 11].

Security issues related to automated record systems are normally separated into three distinct components:

(a) physical security which protects the physical access to the computer and controls the computer environment including building access, air conditioning, data communications, and so on;
(b) operational and procedural security which imposes constraints on the employees of data-processing organizations to counteract potential embezzlement, record falsification, larceny, and so on [12].
(c) internal computer security which concerns the use of controls and protection mechanisms within the hardware, software, and data communications equipment, thereby insuring the accuracy and integrity of the files and preventing misuse.

It is the third kind of security which is of principal interest for the present study, although it is obvious that secure computer hardware and software methods are of no avail in the absence of other safeguards against physical damage and dishonest personnel.

The computer security problem is rendered vastly more difficult by the fact that so many information retrieval and data management systems currently operate in a time-sharing mode where a multiplicity of users can effectively share the resources of the computer system and simultaneously access and process the same data files. In such a situation multiple programs may be in operation, all of them sharing the same files and memory space; at the same time, each individual user is given the impression that the entire computer system is devoted to his exclusive ends.

In a multiuser environment, it is necessary to isolate individual processes and to protect the corresponding memory space and data files, while at the same time insuring that the rightful owner of a given process or file is not denied access and use. A large variety of different methodologies and devices are currently in use which offer service to the rightful users while protecting the system against deliberate or accidental damage. However, the conventional wisdom has it that no resource-sharing computer system is currently in operation that will not yield to sustained penetration attempts by sufficiently persistent unauthorized individuals. Furthermore, fully personalized data base management systems are not currently operational.

In principle, it is desirable to implement user identification systems that securely identify all rightful users and at the same time prove impervious to misuse by unauthorized persons. Furthermore, the memory access system should be able to prevent all accesses by unauthorized users and confine rightful users to certain declared memory portions only. Each user could in principle also be restricted to certain pieces of equipment, certain data structures, and certain operations.

In practice, such totally secure and foolproof systems are simply not available. A battery of different security devices is used instead in the hope that collectively the various methodologies will discourage most unauthorized operations. The following security components are of interest in this connection:

(a) The physical safeguards may include secure locks for the computer room, fire protection, redundant circuitry, and special memory protect mechanisms.

(b) Personnel safeguards consist of background checks, controls on persons authorized to make system changes, and verification of prospective user identities.

(c) Communication safeguards may include the enciphering of information stored in computer systems or sent over computer networks, as well as the protection of individual access devices.

(d) Software procedures include the compartmentalization of individual processes; the isolation of particularly sensitive functions; user identification by means of passwords, plastic encoded cards, and eventually voice or fingerprint identification; threat-monitoring methods that detect unusual access patterns by potential unauthorized users; access control information specifying all authorized operations for each system user; data integrity systems to verify that the stored data conform to previously stated constraints; and restart and recovery procedures which make it possible to "roll-back" the system to a safe point from where operations can be resumed in case of system failure.

A number of important recent advances must be registered, for example, in the use of password strategies needed to distinguish rightful from unauthorized users [13], and especially also in the generation of data encryption techniques [14, 15]. In the latter area, so-called public key systems have been developed which appear to be unbreakable in practice. Two different keys are used, one of which (the public key) services to convert a clear text to an enciphered version, and another (the private key) to convert cipher to clear text. The two keys are mathematically related in the sense that given a private key it is easy to compute the corresponding public key, but not vice versa. Each person's public key is published in a widely available directory, and can thus be used to encipher communications destined to that particular individual. To decode a given enciphered text the recipient's private key is necessary, and as stated earlier, the private key is not easily derivable from the public counterpart. *

If these enciphering systems should prove to be implementable inexpensively in practice, there is hope that authenticated communication may become possible between large user groups; such systems will then also solve the secure user identification problem in multiuser environments.

Whether the technical data security problems will prove easier to solve than the political and ethical questions relating to information privacy remains to be seen. The former are eventually likely to yield to the ingenuity and knowhow of trained experts. Whether the latter will ever be tackled seriously depends on a consensus among large portions of the population concerning the fundamental importance of information privacy in the modern world.

References

1. Westin, A. F., Ed., Information Technology in a Democracy. Cambridge, MA: Harvard University Press; 1971.
2. Westin, A. F.; Baker, M. A. Databanks in a Free Society. New York: Quadrangle/New York Times Book Co.; 1972.
3. Menard vs. Saxbe, 498 F. 2d. 1017, decided by the U.S. Court of Appeals for the District of Columbia on April 23, 1974.

─────────────

*Corresponding public and private key pairs are related mathematically by inverse operations with widely differing degrees of computational complexity: for example, it is easy to multiply two numbers (used to obtain a public key from the private key), but hard to compute the factors of a product (used to obtain a private key from the public version); alternatively, it is easy to raise a given number to a power, but hard to invert the process and compute a logarithm.

4. Anderson vs. Sills, 56 N.J. 210, decided by the Supreme Court of the State of New Jersey on June 1, 1970.
5. Laird vs. Tatum, 92 S. Ct. 2318 (1972), decided by the Supreme Court of the United States on June 26, 1972.
6. Zurcher vs. Stanford Daily, 98 S. Ct. 1970 (1978), decided by the Supreme Court of the United States on May 31, 1978.
7. Hirsch, P. "Europe's Privacy Laws--Fear of Inconsistency." Datamation. 85-88; February 1979.
8. Turn, R.; Ware, W. H. "Privacy and Security in Computer Systems." American Scientist. 63:196-203; 1975.
9. Turn, R.; Ware, W. H. "Privacy and Security, Issues in Information Systems." IEEE Transactions on Computers. C-25(12):1353-1361; 1976.
10. Saltzer, J. H.; Schroeder, M. D. "The Protection of Information in Computer Systems." Proceedings of the IEEE. 63(9):1278-1308; 1975.
11. Martin, J. Security Accuracy and Privacy in Computer Systems. Englewood Cliffs, NJ: Prentice Hall; 1973.
12. Parker, D. B. Crime by Computers. New York: Charles Scribner's Sons; 1976.
13. Morris, R.; Thompson, K. Password Security: A Case History. Computing Science Technical Report. Murray Hill, NJ: Bell Laboratories; April 1978.
14. Rivest, R. L.; Shamir, A.; Adleman, L. "A Method for Obtaining Digital Signatures and Public Key Cryptosystems." Communications of the ACM. 21(2):120-126; 1978.
15. Needham, R. M.; Schroeder, M. D. "Using Encryption for Authentication in Large Networks of Computers." Communications of the ACM. 21(12):993-999; 1978.

LIBRARIES AND ALTERNATIVES:

AN ESSAY*

Patricia Glass Schuman

The library is the only social institution whose main ethical underpinning is the collection, preservation, and dissemination of all manner of information. This, at any rate, is the library's avowed goal. It rarely becomes a reality, and for good and sundry reasons: budget constraints, space limitations, personnel shortages. The danger is not so much that the library often falls short of its heady and laudable goal, but that librarians are sometimes seized by an almost pathological smugness. In short, they come to believe that the goal is actually being realized.

Professionals are always limited by their cultural and educational biases. Most librarians, for example, think of information in fairly narrow terms: the written word, usually contained in the pages of books, magazines, and newspapers. Similarly, the publishing industry tends to be perceived as several thousand corporations whose works and authors are listed or indexed in the standard reference works, whose publications are reviewed and advertised in the major media and displayed and distributed nationwide. These are the visible publishers. It is simple to deal with them, to learn about their products, to purchase and handle their output. There is a good reason for this ease and simplicity: some 3.3 per cent of 6,000-plus companies control about 70 per cent of the publishing industry's volume, and they make it their business to put their books on library shelves. [1]

Of course librarians' professional training and experience have taught them to deal with other types of publishers as well: government agencies, research centers, university presses, trade or labor associations, and organizations which are not publishers per se but rather producers of information as a by-product of another major purpose. They are often noncommercial or nonprofit; they produce not only books and periodicals, but also pamphlets, flyers, films, microfiche, videotapes, phonograph records, data bases, and other nonprint formats.

---

*Reprinted by permission of the author and publisher from Collection Building, 2:2 (March 1980) 7-11.

The larger of these information producers are sometimes encompassed in bibliographic and reference works; in some cases, special tools have been developed to access their products. Many libraries have designed procedures to deal with them, and wholesalers will stock their publications if there is sufficient demand.

But there is another category of publisher with which few librarians are prepared to deal, either by training, experience, or orientation. This mixed bag of publishers is variously referred to as alternative, small, or independent. While none of these labels is entirely satisfactory, alternative probably fits best, because such publishers do indeed provide alternatives to the more traditional publishing and information networks.

By definition, all are small and independently owned, though of course not all small publishers can be considered alternative. Alternative publishers purposely present information with a particular point of view: political, cultural or literary. By choice, as well as definition, their publications fall outside the mainstream of commercial publishing. This may also put alternative publishers outside the mainstream of traditional bibliographic tools, review media, and distribution channels. Further, it means that they are often outside the peripheral vision of librarians who buy 25,000 copies of Books in Print but less than 4,000 of Alternatives in Print.

Most alternative presses, limited by size and capital resources, can not afford to give away masses of review copies, hire sales people, utilize staff to fill out bibliographic forms, mail promotional materials to libraries, bill in triplicate, wait ninety days for payment, etc. Moreover, alternative publishers are sometimes unaware of the potential for selling to libraries and the special kinds of library requirements. Frequently, they are one-or-two-person operations that never find time to develop this expertise. This is unfortunate, because alternative publishers are on the cutting edge of important issues.

Twentieth century pamphleteers

The role of the pamphleteer in America has been well established at least since the days of Thomas Paine. In the realm of political and social concerns, the alternative press--in whatever format--is our modern pamphleteer. Much of its publishing output arises from the need for activists to communicate with each other--rapidly. Standard information sources cannot cope with emerging issues: abortion, feminism, rape, alternative energy, nuclear dangers, gay rights, senior citizen power, alternative lifestyles, vitamins and organic foods, the excesses of government and its intelligence agencies; the list is nearly endless. None of these issues is new, though many are relatively unfamiliar to libraries because they were not dealt with earlier by the major publishing houses. The alternative press has been publishing material on such topics for almost two decades.

The Social Prerogative

An excellent example is the development of information concerning rape as a social issue. The first rape crisis center, established in 1971 in Washington, D. C., was inundated with requests for information, and published a pamphlet "How to Start a Rape Crisis Center." The first feminist article on rape, "Rape: The American Crime," by Susan Griffin, was published in Ramparts in September, 1971. Few libraries then subscribed to Ramparts, and even fewer had ever heard of the original pamphlet, How to Start a Rape Crisis Center. At the same time, groups like the New York Radical Feminists were publishing statements on the politics of rape.

Not for several years did the standard periodical literature begin to catch up with the issue of rape as a social, rather than an individual, issue. Newsweek and The New York Times carried articles in 1972; Time in 1973. The New York Times Index still only accesses the subject under "sex crimes." The peak year for the topic in standard periodical literature was 1975. Thus it was not until almost half a decade after materials from alternative press services were available that books treating rape as a socio-political issue were available from major publishing houses--for example Susan Brownmiller's Against Our Will: Men, Women and Rape (Simon & Schuster, 1975).

In a similar vein, how many libraries bought Rubyfruit Jungle when it was published by the small feminist press Daughters instead of Bantam? How many subscribed to the Whole Earth Catalog from Portola Institute before buying the Last Whole Earth Catalog from Random House? Our Bodies, Ourselves was available for years for 35¢ from the New England Press before it was taken over by Simon & Schuster and reissued at $4.95.

Remarkably parallel histories can be traced for many other issues. Energy is probably the most current example. While part of this problem results from the structure of the publishing industry, the phenomenon also stems from the ways in which knowledge is communicated. Activists tend to communicate with other activists, researchers with other researchers, and so forth, until an issue is brought to the public's attention. Then there is a concomitant time lag until material can be synthesized, written, and published in a popular format. If libraries are to collect and access information on issues which have the potential to change the fabric of our society, they must get it directly from those who are creating it. The information produced by alternative publishers is not always neatly packaged, reflective, or even necessarily scholarly. But it is timely, and it is the raw material from which societal transformations are forged.

The alternative media do more than play a vital socio-political role. They also make an important cultural and literary contribution. The publishing outlets for fiction, essays, and poetry have shrunk dramatically in the last twenty years. The alternative press, particularly through its literary magazines, chapbooks, and pamphlets, is one of the only outlets for these genres open to new, and sometimes, even more published writers. As librarians, we should take seriously our responsibility to develop, as well as preserve, the written word. Libraries play a significant role in what gets published, as well as in what information gets distributed to whom. Our plain duty is to make sure that all voices have an opportunity to be heard.

The marketplace

We live in a society in which access to information is fast becoming essential to survival. Libraries are central institutions in the information arena. Certainly they are key in the marketplace of information, part of the underpinnings of the communications industry. Libraries are key collectors, indexers, and distributors of information. Their role becomes even more important as a small group of powerful interlocking conglomerates takes over more and more publishing houses and bookstore chains. An excellent discussion of this phenomenon is found in Celeste West's Booklegger's Guide to: the Passionate Perils of Publishing, Booklegger, 1978.

The terms of the marketplace may seem commercial, but they represent reality. Libraries are a market, and an important one. The latest Publishers Weekly statistics, compiled basically from the traditional publishing industry's sales, show that in 1977 libraries spent close to $500 million on books alone. Libraries are the major buyers of nonfiction hardcover books, and of children's books. A good review in Library Journal can account for 2,000 sales, while an average nonfiction hardcover sale is about 5,000 copies and novels are often less.

Libraries are quiet and steady customers. Library sales are a base, but they do not generate the volume from which bestsellers are made. Since most libraries order books through wholesalers, they are not particularly visible to the larger publishers. They are even less visible to the smaller publishers, who are frequently unfamiliar with library ordering and selection procedures. This, coupled with some very real procedural problems, makes it difficult for libraries to collect the alternative press. But the bureaucratic arrogance which underlies many selection criteria and acquisitions procedures should not prevent librarians from collecting and making available material that represents different points of view. The economic power of libraries is large enough as a total market that libraries can keep the alternative press alive and healthy.

Ways must be developed to overcome the sometimes almost obsessive methodologies by which librarians handle new or different materials--as experimental appendages, or so-called extra services. Some academic and research libraries collect the alternative press, but the majority of these treat it as a special collection. This sort of labeling can create barriers that an integrated approach will avoid. The alternative press is not an artifact; it is vital and important. The problem is not simply to acquire alternative information, but to make it known, and accessible, to the library's users. Procedural difficulties can be eliminated; librarians are limited only by their failure to recognize their own power. We are the major buyers of indexes, reference books, and bibliographic tools; the major customers of several wholesalers; and if we buy alternative publications in sufficient numbers, alternative publishers will eventually be stocked by these wholesalers. Librarians can help by initiating and maintaining meaningful contact with a broad spectrum of alternative publishers.

Reference

1. Celeste West and Valerie Wheat, The Passionate Perils of Publishing (San Francisco: Booklegger, 1978), p. 1.

THE MAN WHO WAS CONVICTED

OF READING A BOOK*

Nat Hentoff

In its December 4 "Supreme Court Roundup," the New York Times gave the case only three skimming paragraphs. The New York Law Journal could spare only one paragraph for Giese v. U.S., and the Washington Post's Supreme Court coverage that day did not mention it at all. After all, the High Court had simply refused to review someone's conviction. Happens all the time. Besides, this case--although six years old--had been almost entirely ignored by the press all along the way.

So why focus on it now? To warn you--if you occasionally read "dangerous" books. Because the teaching of Giese v. U.S. is that reading a book can put you in prison.

A report of the frightening odyssey of ex-professor Frank Stearns Giese will also reveal something of the judicial philsophy--and capacity for fury at injustice--of the likely first woman Supreme Court Justice, if Carter is still President when the next opening occurs. Shirley Hufstedler, now the nation's first Secretary of Education, provided the lone dissent against Giese's conviction in the record of these proceedings. Long considered a cool moderate in her judicial views, Hufstedler tried mightily to sound a very loud alarm about this case while she was on the Ninth Circuit Court of Appeals: "Freedom of speech would be totally destroyed if the shadow of the prosecutor fell across the pages of the books we read."

That shadow has so fallen, and unless the trial court judge decides to be merciful and give Giese extended probation, the man who read the wrong book will now be sent to the slammer for five years.

It all began, not in Czechoslovakia but in Portland, Oregon, when Navy and Army recruiting stations in that city were bombed in January 1973, presumably in protest against American participation

---

*Reprinted by permission of the author and publisher from The Village Voice, December 31, 1979, p. 22-23.

The Social Prerogative   323

in the Vietnam War. Giese was one of five people indicted for various directly criminal acts and also for conspiracy to commit those acts. Before trial, one of the five pleaded guilty and agreed to testify as a government witness. Of the remaining defendants, only Giese was acquitted of all the charges concerning the actual commission of the crimes. He was, however, convicted of conspiracy for having participated in the planning and financing of the bombings.

At the time of the 1974 trial, Giese was 58, a professor of French at Portland State University and proprietor of the Radical Education Project bookstore. He had also been a volunteer worker in prisons, leading group discussions, for example, at the Oregon State Correctional Institution. It was there and at the bookstore that Giese had come to know his codefendants in the trial. But is knowing someone sufficient proof that you later entered into a conspiracy with him to, let us say, bomb recruiting stations?

Of course not, under our system of justice. The prosecution had to provide substantive evidence that Giese was indeed part of the conspiracy. Try as it might, the government could find no physical evidence linking Giese in any way to the bombings. Except for his fingerprints--on a single book far from the scene. (More of which clever sleuthing anon.) There were two main witnesses against him, however. One was the codefendant who had turned state's evidence. The other had a bountiful criminal record as well as a long history of mental illness. As Court of Appeals Judge Hufstedler was to point out later, "The Government's case against Giese rested almost entirely upon the credibility of the testimony" of these two men who "had unsavory records and ... were seriously impeached during the trial."

Well, the government's case also rested on those fingerprints. In searching the homes of the various defendants, the prosecutor's minions had picked up a number of books. A few revealed that their owners might have been on an earnest self-improvement kick: <u>The Blaster's Handbook</u>, <u>The Underground Bombing Manual</u>, <u>Firearms and Self-Defense</u>, <u>Department of Army Manual: Electronic Blasting Equipment</u>. But none of these treatises had been found in <u>Giese</u>'s home or, for that matter, in his bookstore. Indeed, he had never stocked a single one of them, and the government was unable to show that he had had any connection with them.

Ah, but another book had been apprehended, <u>From the Movement Toward Revolution</u>, edited by Bruce Franklin and published by Van Nostrand Reinhold Company. It is an anthology of political rhetoric, from liberal to revolutionary. Giese had written nothing for it; the writers were all strangers to him. However, Dr. Giese's fingerprints were found on pages 146, 166, 167, and 168 of the book. The government's expert witness testified, by the way, that he couldn't be sure when Giese's prints got onto the pages, but it could have happened any time within the past seven years. <u>This was the only physical evidence the government had against Frank Giese.</u>

From the Movement Toward Revolution had not been found by the police in Giese's apartment but at a pad shared by some of the codefendants. Giese said, however, that he had once bought a copy at Portland's largest commercial bookstore. (Passing moral: be careful whom you lend books to.)

At the trial, Giese further admitted he had read "snatches" of the book at one time or another. At that point, the prosecutor, to more firmly link the defendant with this baleful book, told Giese to read aloud to the jury sections of the pages on which his fingerprints had been found. One of the passages declaimed by Giese had been written by unidentified members of the Black Panther Party:

> "Racism, colonialism, sexism and all the other pigisms ... can only be ended by revolution, and revolution is violence, revolution is war, revolution is bloodshed."

In his final argument to the jury, the prosecutor used From the Movement Toward Revolution as the central element of his case against Giese (for the only other "case" he had was the testimony of the self-discredited witnesses).

"This is basically a conspiracy action," the prosecutor sternly informed the jury, "and I would like just briefly to take excerpts from pages which contain Mr. Giese's fingerprints."

These were the excerpts:

A revolutionist sees death as a national phenomenon, must be ready to kill to change conditions. Revolution is armed struggle, violence, war, bloodshed, and the duty of a revolutionary is to make revolution.

Let's all try to pick targets with more care and planning. The object is to destroy the economy, like bombing sites which will effect the economy the most, rip off weapons and money, sniping attacks. Remember, in a revolution, one wins or dies. The stakes are very high.

Do you recall the old words, 'Ask what you can do for your country?' Destroy it, mentally, morally, psychologically and physically destroy it. And whatever you do, do it good.

Triumphantly, the prosecutor looked straight at the jury: "Did we make up the Frank Giese fingerprints on the book, From the Movement Toward Revolution?... You read those pages. It talks about bombing, sniper attacks. You read that book. You read other pages throughout there. Look at page 51, for instance; look at the preface. Throughout that book are references to the very thing that these people did."

Verdict: Guilt. Sentence: Frank Giese to serve five years in prison because his fingerprints were on four pages of a book.

On May 2, 1979, a panel of the Court of Appeals for the Ninth Circuit affirmed Giese's conviction by a vote of 2 to 1. The

The Social Prerogative

majority, in utter contempt of the First Amendment, found nothing wrong with the prosecution tying a man's having read a book to his participation in a criminal conspiracy. The book, the majority said complacently, was used to show "the intent, purpose, aim and motives of participants in the conspiracy." It was also helpful in proving that Giese had associated with the other defendants since the fingerprints of three of them had also been found on the pages of this very book touched by Giese.

Do you know the previous readers of volumes you've bought at second-hand bookstores or borrowed from friends? The opportunities opened by this case will come as a boundless delight to prosecutorial weavers of nets of conspiracy. Am I being hyperbolic? Remember Guy Goodwin, John Mitchell, A. Mitchell Palmer, and, for that matter, Ted Kennedy and his theories of criminal justice as embodied in his Grandson of S.1 now before Congress.

In withering dissent, Judge Shirley Hufstedler got to the core of the government's conspiracy against Giese: "The prosecutor's transparent purpose in requiring Giese to read the inflammatory passages of the book was to convey to the jury that the words of the author were the words of Giese ... and that he acted on those ideas to form a conspiracy to blow up recruiting centers. Giese was thus convicted of conspiracy by book association in egregious violation of the guarantees of the First Amendment." (Emphasis added).

She went on to make what until now would have been an unassailable interpretation of constitution law--let alone plain common sense: "The contents of the books that a person reads cannot be used as evidence of his peaceable or nonpeaceable character. No inference of any kind can be drawn about a person's character from the kinds of books that he reads. We have no basis in human experience to assume that persons of 'good' character confine their reading matter to 'good' books, or that persons who read peaceful books are peaceful people, or that persons who read books involving violence are violent people."

But since the Supreme Court has refused to review Giese's conviction, books now can be used as evidence of a defendant's character.

However, if Hufstedler does get appointed to the Supreme Court, we'll know where she stands on these matters: "The author's writing of the book and Giese's reading of the book are constitutionally protected. The freedom to write books and to read books, to advocate ideas and to listen to ideas are fundamental constitutional rights that may neither be denied or abridged.... Even during the evil thralldom of McCarthyism, we did not embrace the concept of guilt by book association.... Giese had not been indicted for his politics or his literary tastes, and he should not have been put on trial for either."

As for the notion by the majority of her brethren that Giese's fingerprints on the pages of the books established that he had "associated" with felonious others of its readers, Judge Hufstedler said caustically:

> "The fingerprint evidence did not prove that the persons whose prints appeared had been associated with each other. The evidence only proved that the persons who handled the book had been associated with the book.... The proof of book association was not relevant to any issue in the case."

When Giese appealed to the Supreme Court, the American Civil Liberties Union filed a friend-of-the-court brief because of the "dangerous precedent" set by the lower courts in this case. Also coming in as <u>amicus</u> was the Freedom to Write Committee of PEN. The latter, relying on what every schoolchild is supposed to know about the First Amendment, pointed out that the government cannot "use judicial inquiries into reading habits to chill the freedom to write, read and discuss ideas."

But the High Court's December 3 refusal to review Giese's conviction now frees prosecutors to do just that. Although every constitutional lawyer I'd talked to about the case was convinced the Court <u>would</u> hear it, not a single Justice was listed as desirous of granting review. Not even the First Amendment's most passionate remaining supporter on that bench, William Brennan. Was there any debate in conference? Were any trades made for votes in future cases? Alas, because Bob Woodward and Scott Armstrong are not exploring the current term, we are not likely to ever know. I asked several experienced Court-watchers, and they were at a total loss. All, however, were gloomy as to what may happen when the next cycle of political conspiracy cases comes along--unless they involve functional illiterates.

As for Frank Stearns Giese, he lost his teaching job when he was indicted in 1974 and has continued to run his bookstore. Since his conviction, Giese's record has been clean, as it always was before (except for the fingerprints on that book); and now he's hoping the Federal trial judge in Portland won't send a 63-year-old reader to jail. But Giese is ready for that too, though he still can't quite adjust to the fact that all this has happened to him under the Constitution of Madison, Jefferson, and all those other fearless readers of books.

NOTES ON CONTRIBUTORS

PATRICIA BATTIN is Vice President and University Librarian at Columbia University in New York.

SANFORD BERMAN is the Head Cataloger at Hennepin County Library in Edina, Minnesota.

DANIEL J. BOORSTIN is the Librarian of Congress.

CASIMIR BORKOWSKI is a member of the faculty at the University of Pittsburgh's Department of Computer Science.

DEIRDRE BOYLE teaches media courses at Rutgers University Graduate School of Library and Information Studies, Fordham University, and the New School for Social Research in New York City.

SUSAN SPAETH CHERRY works for American Libraries as a staff writer.

THOMAS CHILDERS is a professor at the School of Library and Information Science at Drexel University in Philadelphia.

ANDREE CONRAD, a historian of ancient art, is also a writer and translator. She lives in Miami.

ROBERT V. CUDDIHY is the associate director for Research Data Processing at Sandoz, Inc. in East Hanover, New Jersey.

RUTH FRALEY is the head librarian at Hawley Library of the State University of New York at Albany.

MAURICE J. FREEDMAN is an associate professor at the School of Library Service at Columbia University, New York.

NAT HENTOFF is an author whose latest publication, The First Freedom: The Tumultuous History of Free Speech in America, will be published later this year.

KEN KISTER is a free lance reference book critic based in Tampa, Florida and is the author of the widely cited, Encyclopedia Buying Guide and Dictionary Buying Guide.

JONATHAN KOZOL is a scholar of public education and author of
  *Prisoners of Silence: Breaking the Bonds of Adult Illiteracy
  in the United States.*

MURDO J. MacLEOD is a professor of history at the University of
  Arizona at Tucson.

S. MICHAEL MALINCONICO is the Associate Director for Technical
  and Computer Services at the New York Public Library (the
  Branch Libraries).

LILLIAN MORRISON coordinates the Young Adult Services for the
  New York Public Library.

JUDITH K. MOWERY is the Assistant Librarian for Research Services at Breice Library of the University of Akron at Ohio.

BONNIE R. NELSON works as a reference librarian and Assistant
  Professor at the John Jay College of Criminal Justice of the
  City University of New York.

TRUDY HUSKAMP PETERSON is based at the National Archives in
  Washington, D. C.

PHYLLIS A. RICHMOND is a Professor of Library Science at Case
  Western Reserve University, Cleveland, Ohio.

FRANK ROMANO is the President of the Association of Graphic
  Arts Consultants and independent consultant in the field of
  automated typographic composition devices and systems.

LOIS RUBY is a freelance writer who lives in Wichita, Kansas.

GERARD SALTON is a faculty member of the Department of Computer Science at Cornell University in Ithaca, New York.

PATRICIA GLASS SCHUMAN is the president of Neal-Schuman Publishers, Inc.

MARY ROBINSON SIVE published *Media Monitor*, a newsletter that
  alerts educators to timely resources, and is the author of
  Selecting Instructional Media.

HUGH A. TAYLOR works at the Public Archives of Nova Scotia in
  Halifax, Nova Scotia.

VIRGINIA WITUCKE is an Associate Professor at the Graduate Library School at the University of Arizona, Tucson.

BETTINA H. WOLFF, formerly administrative officer at the New
  York State Library, is currently a doctoral student in the
  Graduate School of Public Affairs, SUNY Albany.

ARTHUR P. YOUNG is an Associate Professor at the Graduate School of Library Service, University of Alabama in University, Alabama.